Transnationalism and Translation in Modern Chinese, English, French, and Japanese Literatures

Transnationalism and Translation in Modern Chinese, English, French, and Japanese Literatures

Ryan Johnson

Anthem Press
An imprint of Wimbledon Publishing Company
www.anthempress.com

This edition first published in UK and USA 2022
by ANTHEM PRESS
75–76 Blackfriars Road, London SE1 8HA, UK
or PO Box 9779, London SW19 7ZG, UK
and
244 Madison Ave #116, New York, NY 10016, USA

First published in the UK and USA by Anthem Press in 2021

Copyright © Ryan Johnson 2022

The author asserts the moral right to be identified as the author of this work.

All rights reserved. Without limiting the rights under copyright reserved above,
no part of this publication may be reproduced, stored or introduced into
a retrieval system, or transmitted, in any form or by any means
(electronic, mechanical, photocopying, recording or otherwise),
without the prior written permission of both the copyright
owner and the above publisher of this book.

British Library Cataloguing-in-Publication Data
A catalogue record for this book is available from the British Library.

Library of Congress Control Number: 2020950326

ISBN-13: 978-1-83998-565-2 (Pbk)
ISBN-10: 1-83998-565-8 (Pbk)

Cover image: *Tokyo Station*, Onchi Kōshirō, 1945;
purchased with the support of the F. G. Waller-Fonds

This title is also available as an e-book.

CONTENTS

Acknowledgments	vii
Introduction	1

PART 1 World Literature, Literary Worlds

Chapter One	Literary Worlds and Degrees of Distance	21

PART 2 Dramatic Worlds

Chapter Two	The Chou-Hughes *Bardo Thödol* and the Problem of Classification	51
Chapter Three	What We Disagree about When We Disagree about Nō	83

PART 3 Poetic Worlds

Chapter Four	Paul Claudel and Kuki Shūzō in the 1920s: France, Japan, and the World	125
Chapter Five	Tradition East and West, English and Chinese: The Cross-Cultural Poetry of Bei Dao and Ted Hughes	155
	Conclusion	191

Works Cited	199
Index	209

ACKNOWLEDGMENTS

I have accrued many debts of kindness in the creation of this work, and it is with pleasure that I acknowledge them here. To my supervisor in the French Department at Keio, Ayako Nishino, I extend my sincere gratitude. Her insight into French and Japanese literature, especially the work of Paul Claudel, and into the process of comparing literature across languages and cultures, has taught me more than I could hope to express. My approach to comparing French and Japanese literature would be impoverished without her guidance. My greatest thanks go, meanwhile, to my supervisor at Sydney University, Mark Byron. His innumerable insights and steadfast guidance in conversations throughout the past years, along with his inspiring personality and work, have led to a piece of work far better than I would have been able to achieve without him. What I owe him is incalculable. The current manuscript has profited in untold ways from his encouragement and suggestions.

The work in revising this manuscript, reshaping it at a book, could not have been carried out without the aid of numerous people. Anthem Press has been unfailingly helpful from the beginning of this process. The editor of Anthem's Global English Literatures series, Paul Giles, offered unflinching patience and perspicacious insight, and without his help it is no overstatement to say that the work would not have arrived in its present form. It is a privilege to have learned so much from his guidance. My thoughts have also benefited from numerous conversations and helpful suggestions from colleagues in Australia, Europe, and Japan. Among them I list Ryland Engels, Ryoichi Imai, Tomoe Terashima, and Kazuko Nagamori. Stephane Cordier gave perceptive tips on translation. The comments I received on my doctoral thesis fortified my work immensely, and I thank Yunte Huang, Josephine Park, and Christopher Bush for their perceptive comments. Lastly, I have accrued a debt to Jessica Sun the extent of which I cannot hope to repay. Her tireless proofreading and wealth of suggestions were indispensable for the completion of this monograph. I offer my utmost thanks to her.

Material from Ted Hughes' original manuscripts housed at Emory University is reproduced here with the permission of the Ted Hughes Estate. My special thanks to the Estate, as well as to Emma Cheshire at Faber and Kathleen Shoemaker at Emory for their aid in securing the permissions.

Part of Chapter One was published as "A Critique of Literary Worlds in World Literature Theory: Multidimensionality as a Basis of Comparison" in the *Journal of World Literature* vol. 3, no. 3 (2018): 354–72, and Chapter Four was founded on an article in

French published as "La Poésie de Paul Claudel et de Kuki Shūzō durant les années 1920: le Japon, la France, et le monde" in *Cahiers d'études françaises* vol. 23 (2018): 31–46. I am grateful to all who helped refine my thoughts during the publication processes of both, and for both journals' permission to use elements of those articles here.

A final word goes to my family, and to Gabriela, to whom I dedicate this work.

INTRODUCTION

The focus of this book is how translation between East Asian and Western literatures in the twentieth century challenges contemporary theories of world literature. Through detailed analyses of the attempts of East Asian and Western writers—including Kuki Shūzō, Bei Dao, Ted Hughes, Yukio Mishima, and Paul Claudel—to translate or adapt the same premodern East Asian texts into their own languages and cultures, I show that the "world" of world literature is not unified, but made up of many smaller literary worlds. But each world is not a clear, easily understandable object that can move with ease across the constellations of East Asian and European literatures. Nor are the elements of a literary world easily transferable from one tradition to another, such that, to give one example, we can see a desire in a literary work to destroy the present social and aesthetic order as "Romantic," regardless of whether it occurs in a text from Europe or East Asia, and regardless of when.[1] On the contrary, each literary world, as this book will show, is made up of several dimensions—religious, historical, formal, stylistic. When a literary world, say the world of the *Genji Monogatari* or of the poetry of Paul Verlaine, is translated into a new language and a new time period, some dimensions are preserved while others are discarded. The result is that the translated piece of literature is not so much a version of the original, but a new literary work whose relation to the original is vague.

Though David Damrosch has characterized world literature as writing that achieves another life in a new language, "circulating out into a broader world beyond its linguistic and cultural point of origin," and appearing "differently abroad than it does at home," the vague identity of literary texts in translation means that we keep returning to a question Damrosch himself asked at the start of *What Is World Literature*: "Which Literature, whose world?"[2] Though it is true, as Damrosch says, that a piece of world literature is a compromise between the host and target culture, we need to stress that the original is, in its entirety, unknowable to us; and the compromise of translation does not lead the original text to be a hybrid sitting easily between two cultures, but a new entity, itself of vague composition, that has been captured for the host culture as part of a scheme of dealing

---

[1] Such is the position of Eric Hayot, whose work we will meet in more detail in the next chapter. Though Hayot's work on literary worlds is considered and illuminating, its tendency to generalize across different cultures, and the markedly little attention paid to East Asian literature and religion in his consideration of literary worlds, makes his theory too universalizing. For his remarks on realism, romanticism, and modernism as transcendent modes embedded in a universal human attitude toward the world, see *On Literary Worlds*, Oxford: Oxford UP, 2012, 118–35.

[2] David Damrosch, *What Is World Literature?* Princeton: Princeton UP, 2003, 1, 4, 6.

with the ontological vagueness of the original. When dealing with translations between East Asian and European languages and cultures, with their many historical, linguistic, and religious or ontological differences, the full weight of this changeover, and the way it alters our understanding of the world literary system, becomes palpable. "Boundaries are relative," as Haun Saussy says in his most recent book, *Translation as Citation: Zhuangzi Inside Out*, "'Languages' are composed of dialects until a national pedagogical norm elevates one of them to the status of a rule in its particular jurisdiction, and languages are more or less porous, full of traces of contact."[3] What we need is an understanding of literature that indicates how not only languages but texts themselves are of vague identity, and recoil before our attempts to fix them in a universalized field.

"Vagueness," or better still "ontological vagueness," is the key phrase of this book. Vagueness is a term borrowed from metaphysics and modal logic. It refers to the state of having words or terms that hover on the borderline of applicability, as when an object seems both "red" and "not red." For literary scholars, the most immediate example of vagueness is perhaps the "impossible heap" in Samuel Beckett's *Endgame*:

> CLOV (fixed gaze, tonelessly): Finished, it's finished, nearly finished, it must be nearly finished. (Pause.) Grain upon grain, one by one, and one day, suddenly, there's a heap, a little heap, the impossible heap. (Pause.) I can't be punished any more. (Pause.) I'll go now to my kitchen, ten feet by ten feet by ten feet, and wait for him to whistle me. (Pause.) Nice dimensions, nice proportions, I'll lean on the table, and look at the wall, and wait for him to whistle me.[4]

Clov is reflecting here upon the Sorites paradox. If we start with one piece of grain and add another to it, we do not have a heap. So it seems reasonable that the addition of a single grain does not make enough of a difference to make a pile that was not a heap into one. Yet if we keep adding grains, we certainly do wind up with a heap; but where we draw the line is unclear. Is it the 400th grain? The 450th? The 401st? Anywhere we draw the line seems arbitrary, so the concept of "heap" is vague. We are never entirely sure what counts as a heap and what does not. The vagueness of the heap contrasts with the "Nice dimensions, nice proportions" of Clov's room, and ultimately signals the arbitrariness of those dimensions and proportions as well.

The argument of this book is that vagueness characterizes world literature and the literary worlds within it. This is not due to a lack of our knowledge but a fact of the texts of world literature themselves. When something is vague, and remains vague no matter how much knowledge we gain of it, we call that thing "ontologically vague." When a reader or translator encounters a text in a different language, she is unlikely to know all of the dimensions of the text. She cannot know, for instance, all of the significances of all of the words found in the *Genji Monogatari* as they might have been known to the members of the Heian Court in which that text was produced. She cannot know all of the ideas and intentions of *Genji*'s author, Murasaki Shikibu. She cannot know for certain how

---

[3] Haun Saussy, *Translation as Citation: Zhuangzi Inside Out*, Oxford: Oxford UP, 2017, 10.
[4] Samuel Beckett, *Endgame*, London: Faber, 1958, 12.

the various religious and philosophical beliefs circulating in Heian Japan—Shintoism, Buddhism, Confucianism—would have affected the contemporary reader's reception of *Genji*. Hence, the composition of the world of *Genji* is already vague for the contemporary reader. To translate the text, the translator has to deal with this ontological vagueness by highlighting certain dimensions and making them comprehensible by drawing an analogy with ideas, works, or belief systems current in her own time and place. This means reducing the elements of the original text to a simplified set, and crossing that set with elements from the language into which the text is being translated, so that, for example, *Genji* draws on the language of medieval chivalry to make the story of nobility and romance intelligible to a Western audience, even though European chivalric culture was utterly unknown to Murasaki and her readers. As such, not only is the original work vague, but the connections between the original and the translated version are vague as well.[5] As with our heap, how do we determine whether a work in translation is significantly "like" the original? What dimensions weigh the most in this judgment? Where do we draw the line?

In the 1978 publication "On Difficulty," George Steiner diagnosed similar issues in our comprehension of literature. For Steiner, there are four difficulties we encounter: "contingent" (not understanding a word or phrase), "modal" (finding a poem too foreign or strange to grasp), "tactical" (a text deliberately defying our usual modes of comprehension), and "ontological" (being estranged from the basic world view of the text).[6] Though I agree with Steiner's ingenious schema, I would like to push beyond his short essay, in which he is more concerned with readers contemplating authors from afar and not with the actual work authors undertake to build their literary worlds, and in which he sees ontological difficulty as emerging in the nineteenth and twentieth centuries with European and American writers rebelling against the Greeks and Romans. The modal and ontological difficulty of comprehension across Eurasian literatures, with their often invisible logical inconsistencies, is not a point Steiner was able to address.

---

[5] My hypothetical translation of *Genji* might seem far-fetched, but consider how Ian Buruma has described Arthur Waley's translation of the same: "The two most famous English translations of 'Genji'—Arthur Waley's, in the nineteen-twenties and thirties, and Edward Seidensticker's, in 1976—could hardly be more different. Waley regarded gorgeous prose as more important than accuracy. When he found a passage, or even a whole chapter, too boring or obscure, he just skipped it. He compensated for the *vagueness* of the original Japanese by making up something equally lyrical in Bloomsbury-period English" (emphasis mine). See Ian Buruma, "The Sensualist: What Makes *The Tale of Genji* so Seductive?" *New Yorker* (July 13, 2015), web. https://www.newyorker.com/magazine/2015/07/20/the-sensualist-books-buruma. As we will see in the next chapter, Waley's translations, immensely readable but often unfaithful to the original, have spurred many debates about the proper practice of translation. As I will show, "vagueness" is not a property of *Genji* alone but is dispersed throughout world literature, and comes to the fore when we try to get to the heart of East Asian texts from a transnational point of departure.

[6] George Steiner, "On Difficulty," *Journal of Aesthetics and Art Criticism* vol. 36, no. 3 (Spring 1978): 263–76.

The emergence of world literature on the critical scene over the past few years has been associated with universalizing impulses, a trend remarked and deplored by Gayatri Spivak and Emily Apter.[7] Importantly for this study, recent pushback has come from scholars of East Asian literatures. Karen Thornber and Satoru Hashimoto note that "scholarship on world literature has tended to be limited to studies of texts that have circulated in, and at times only in, Western languages."[8] Such bias toward the circulation of texts in the West encourages critics to miss how the "cultural, economic, environmental, legal, medical, political, religious, social, and other phenomena in Asia were transcending boundaries of all types long before the emergence of the West as a self-proclaimed agent of world history."[9] I would add that ignoring East Asian views on earlier East Asian texts also encourages us to ignore how Chinese and Japanese writers have made sense of earlier texts from the region, and this in turn makes us blind to the continuing legacy and utility of *alternate* modes of belief in contemporary world literature. Far from passing into obsolescence with modernity, classical and medieval forms of East Asian culture and religion continued to affect how texts were interpreted and adapted among Chinese and Japanese writers in the twentieth century. Agreeing with Hashimoto and Thornber that "rich histories of transregional cultural interactions [...] put into question the notion of the 'world' as a process to which nations, as defined by their cultural particularities, contribute, and call for re-interrogations of the normativity of that process,"[10] I have structured this book to ensure that equal voice is given to translation not just East–West, but East–East, not just across languages, but across time periods as well. The effect is intended to weaken the universalizing tendencies of world literature.

But these problems are not new. Damrosch's *What Is World Literature?* reignited interest in the discipline, but world literature has roots stretching back to German Romanticism. In "Conversations on World Literature," J. W. von Goethe is reported to have said, "'I am more and more convinced [...] that poetry is the universal possession of mankind, revealing itself everywhere and at all times in hundreds and hundreds of men.'"[11] Convinced that "poetry" is present in every culture, Goethe advocates a transnational understanding of literature, one that can appreciate the work of Serbian and Chinese writers as much as that of German ones. He suggests that an enlarged understanding of literature will lead to greater art. It is worth quoting him at length:

> But, really, we Germans are very likely to fall too easily into this pedantic conceit, when we do not look beyond the narrow circle that surrounds us. I therefore like to look about me

---

[7] See Gayatri Chakravorty Spivak, *Death of a Discipline*, New York: Columbia UP, 2003; Emily Apter, *Against World Literature: On the Politics of Untranslatability*, London: Verso, 2013.

[8] Satoru Hashimoto and Karen Thornber, "Trans-Regional Asia and Futures of World Literature," *Journal of World Literature* vol. 4, no. 4 (December 2019): 460.

[9] Ibid.

[10] Ibid., 460.

[11] J. W. von Goethe and J. P. Eckermann, "Conversations on World Literature," *The Princeton Sourcebook in Comparative Literature*, ed. David Damrosch, Natalie Melas, and Mbongiseni Buthelezi, Princeton: Princeton UP, 2009, 22.

in foreign nations, and advise everyone to do the same. National literature is now rather an unmeaning term; the epoch of world literature is at hand, and everyone must strive to hasten its approach. But, while we thus value what is foreign, we must not bind ourselves to some particular thing, and regard it as a model. We must not give this value to the Chinese, or the Serbian, or Calderon, or the *Nibelungen*; but, if we really want a pattern, we must always return to the ancient Greeks, in whose works the beauty of mankind is constantly represented. All the rest we must look at only historically, appropriating to ourselves what is good, so far as it goes.[12]

We note that "world literature" is both forward-looking—it logically comes after the period of national development has exhausted itself—and backward-looking—it is a "return to the ancient Greeks," who, despite their antiquity, possessed a worldliness beyond that of Goethe's contemporaries.

Numano Mitsuyoshi notes that Goethe's desire to "usher in the age of world literature" was not part of a desire to form a logical system of world literature in theory but a more contradictory impulse to both keep and go beyond national literature.[13] The utopian impulse streamed into brief but famous pronouncements on world literature by Karl Marx and Friedrich Engels, according to which, thanks to the international flow of capital, the "intellectual creations of individual nations become common property. National one-sidedness and narrow-mindedness become more and more impossible, and from the numerous national and local literatures, there arises a world literature."[14] For Marx and Engels, this is both a deplorable event (it results from the capitalist destruction of local cultures) and yet a positive development (internationalism will finally unite workers across petty borders against the bourgeoisie). These contradictory and idealist streams join in David Damrosch's, Pascale Casanova's, and Franco Moretti's modern foundational work on the topic.[15] Neither "utopian" nor "contradictory" carries a negative charge here, but are simply used to point out that world literature began and persisted with an abstract vision the logical foundations of which scholars have tended to neglect. The most salient contradiction of all remains as to how local literatures exist within a larger, ostensibly unified literary system of which they are uneasy members. Though critics such as the Warwick Research Collective have done important work in this domain by attempting to extend the world systems theory on which Casanova relied,[16] my focus in this book will be

---

[12] Ibid., 23.
[13] Numano Mitsuyoshi, "Sekai (bungaku) to ha nanika," *Shisō* no. 1147 (November 2019): 10. Unless otherwise noted, all translations in this book from Chinese, French, and Japanese are my own.
[14] Karl Marx and Friedrich Engels, "The Communist Manifesto," in *World Literature: A Reader*, ed. Cesar Dominguez, Theo d'Haen, and Mads Rosendahl Thomsen, London: Routledge, 2012, 17.
[15] Numano, "Sekai," 10–15. The three foundational texts in the contemporary study of world literature are: Damrosch, *What Is World Literature?* 2004; Pascale Casanova, *La république mondiale des lettres*, Paris: Éditions de Seuil, col. Points, 2004; Franco Moretti, "Conjectures on World Literature," *New Left Review* vol. 1 (January–February 2000): 54–68.
[16] See the Warwick Research Collective, *Combined and Uneven Development: Towards a New Theory of World Literature*, Liverpool: Liverpool UP, 2015, especially 49–56.

on a different school of thought, what I will call "literary worlds theory." With its origins in modal logical, literary worlds theory, conceiving of literary works as generating possible worlds, appears primely placed to solve the contradictory foundations of world literature. But, as I will show, the theory as it currently stands runs into a host of problems when trying to extend beyond Western and postcolonial literature, and beyond the modern.

First, however, I want to step back a bit and switch focus from world literature in theory to world literature in practice. Let us look at one Chinese poem and two translations. The poem is Du Fu's 杜甫 "Dawn Landscape"曉望:

曉望

白帝更聲盡,
陽臺曙色分。

高峰寒上日,
疊嶺宿霾雲。

地坼江帆隱,
天清木葉聞。

塞扉對麋鹿,
應共爾為群。

Written in regulated verse, the poem is rich in allusions and appears steeped in Daoist cosmology. Particularly striking are the antitheses: mountains and rivers, clouds and cracked earth, the human and nonhuman. Each couplet shifts from one extreme to another, from the heights to the depths, before meeting somewhere in the middle, on firm land where the speaker, presumably a mountain hermit in the Daoist tradition, comes to meet ambassadors from the natural world, deer, themselves symbolic of Daoism. The hermit and the deer see each other's "kind" (群) in one another, and the dualities appear to be transcended, permeating one another like the yin and yang (note the apparent pun on "yin" in the first couplet, here designating the shadow of the mountain, but hardly failing to recall, in this context, the yin of yin/yang of which the character is the same: 陰). Some scholars have gone so far as to argue that regulated verse or *lüshi* (律詩), with its stress on tonal and semantic antithesis, parallel and nonparallel couplets, that gradually leads, in the closing couplet, to a new synthesis, is itself a product of Daoist thinking.[17] Whatever the case, the evidence for interpreting Du Fu's poem through a Daoist lens is strong.

The first translation comes from David Hinton's seminal 1989 *The Selected Poems of Tu Fu*:

---

[17] For example, Zong-qi Cai, *Configurations of Comparative Poetics: Three Perspectives on Chinese and Western Literary Criticism*, Honolulu: U of Hawaii P, 2002, 173. Zong-qi points to the yin and yang, complimentary opposites that are always morphing into one another and back again.

Dawn Landscape

The last watch has sounded in K'uei-chou.
Color spreading above Solar-Terrace Mountain,

a cold sun clears high peaks. Clouds linger,
blotting out canyons below tangled ridges,

and deep Yangtze banks keep sails hidden.
Beneath clear skies: clatter of falling leaves.

And these deer at my bramble gate: so close
here, we touch our own kind in each other.

The second translation is again Hinton's. Convinced that Du Fu's poetry required comprehensive knowledge of Chan Buddhism and philosophical Daoism, Hinton retranslated the 1989 volume, and published with it a commentary-cum-philosophical treatise, *Awakened Cosmos: The Mind of Classical Chinese Poetry*, in which he gives an extended exposition of some of the new translations:

Dawn Landscape

The last watch has sounded in Amble-Awe.
Radiant color spreads above Solar-Terrace

Mountain, then cold sun clears high peaks.
Mist and cloud linger across layered ridges,

and earth split-open hides river sails deep.
Leaves clatter at heaven's clarity. I listen,

and face deer at my bramble gate: so close
here, we touch our own kind in each other.

Hinton's original hews closely to an imagistic archetype of "Chinese" translation. The lines develop logically, with a clear indication of cause and effect: clouds hide the mountains, the deep Yangtze conceals the sails, leaves sound as they fall. These images are not obviously tied to one another—there is no immediate logical connection between the clouds over the mountains and the leaves falling under the "clear skies." But if we take them together, we get a collage, with the repeated alternation between perspectives high (clouds, mountain ridges, skies) and low (river depths, earth, falling leaves) economically painting a tranquil autumn landscape. The sudden emergence of the first person in the final line ("my bramble gate") surprises the reader as it indicates that this seemingly objective scene is being filtered through a nameless narrator. The abrupt transition paves the way for the communion between nature and human, with the two "kinds," human and animal, coming into contact just as the speaker has bumped up against the natural world, sublime and dwarfing traces of humanity suggested by the sound of the watch and the boat sails, with the synecdoche reducing these human activities and items further. The poem, then, can be read as a vaguely "Chinese" meditation on the superiority of the natural over the human world, which leads to a point of exchange between the two, with hints of Daoist and Chan Buddhist ideas about impermanence and the interdependence of the self and world.

The retranslation aims to make these hints central to the poem. If the 1989 version derived its imagistic quality in part from end-stopped lines and straightforward syntax, the new translation, heavily enjambed and full of anastrophe ("earth split-open," "sails deep"), presents a fuzzier image. What, for instance, does "deep" modify? Naturally, the river should be hiding the sails in its depths, but deep could also be modifying the sails themselves. "Depth" itself does not appear in the original; 地坼江帆隱 means most evidently, to me, that the earth cracks open, the river hides the sail or sails. Hinton chose to ignore this first part in the 1989 translation, but capitalizes on it here as a further addition to the depths that contrast with the tranquil heights described in the previous couplet. Whereas the "clatter" of the leaves in the first translation clearly owed to their falling, here the action is left unsaid, and rather than passively falling, the leaves almost seem to be actively resonating with the heavens. The antithesis between a clear heaven and an earth full of noise, violent imagery, and mystery is bridged by the "mist and clouds" that "linger" around the mountains and conceal the extent of the change between the two poles, allowing both to look as if they are entirely distinct yet always in danger of spilling over into one another, much like the yin and yang themselves.

Such is Hinton's explanation of the new version. "The poetics of Ch'an-imagism, empty-mind mirroring the world perfectly," he writes, "shapes the poem's first three couplets [...] At the same time, the poem animates that edge where form and formless blur together, allowing consciousness to witness or inhabit the formless generative tissue of the Tao."[18] Striking is Hinton's reference to imagism. The remark is not accidental. In *Awakened Cosmos*, Hinton states:

> as Ch'an's influence became pervasive across the arts in the centuries preceding Tu Fu, this empty-minded mirroring led to a poetry made of clear and concise images [...] This is the imagism that migrated via Japanese haiku into Ezra Pound's poetics, from which it shaped much of modern American poetry.[19]

Contending that something authentically Chinese passed into Ezra Pound's poetry, and hence into modern American poetry itself, is, as Eric Hayot has demonstrated, an older move in scholarship, one perhaps best exemplified by the work of Zhaoming Qian.[20]

---

[18] David Hinton, *Awakened Cosmos: The Mind of Classical Chinese Poetry*, Boulder: Shambhala, 2019, 107–8.

[19] Ibid., 17.

[20] See Eric Hayot, *Chinese Dreams: Pound, Brecht, Tel Quel*, Ann Arbor: U of Michigan P, 2004. For Zhaoming Qian's takes, see *Orientalism and Modernism: The Legacy of China in Pound and Williams*, Durham: Duke UP, 1995. I should also mention Rupert Arrowsmith, who shows the incalculable influence of East Asia on English modernism. See Arrowsmith, *Modernism and the Museum: Asian, African, and Pacific Art and the London Avant-Garde*, Oxford: Oxford UP, 2010.

But Hinton is here making a different move: rather than using medieval Chinese poetry to help us understand modern American poetry, he is, however briefly, referencing modern American poetry to help us understand medieval poetry. The familiar terrain of Pound's imagism serves as a pathway to the strange and mysterious world of Du Fu's poetry, filled, in Hinton's estimation, with Buddhist and Daoist ideas, even if those ideas are rarely mentioned explicitly. Perhaps that is why the new version reads less like a "Chinese" poem in the imagist vein than the 1989 one. The familiar imagist method is no longer a way of translating the foreign into English, of making it intelligible in English, but a way of translating the reader's perspective into that of an eighth-century poet.

Hinton's implicit claim is that Du Fu's poetry cannot be grasped by focusing on the literal meaning of the poem, attending to the intertextual references Du Fu makes to older Chinese poets, or by scrutinizing Du Fu's intentions or circumstances. Instead, we must enter into the mind of a poet living in the intellectual climate of the Tang, and become immersed in the cosmology that underpinned Tang thought. John Butler puts it thus in his review:

> As a translator he puts a different emphasis on what he believed Tu Fu was doing and had a different agenda. As Hinton writes, "A typical classical Chinese poem appears to be a plain-spoken utterance about a poet's immediate experience" […] Hinton, however, moves beyond the literal meaning of the poems, their "apparent content", and opens up a universe far beyond their emotional appeal, and that's why anyone now reading Tu Fu should definitely keep a copy of *Awakened Cosmos* handy.[21]

Hinton's new translations of Du Fu present two ways of thinking about transnationalism and translation. Against an implicit model that pays more attention to the movement of a text across cultural and linguistic borders, Hinton's theory of Du Fu's poetry insists that readers delve, per Butler, into the "universe" of belief in which the piece of literature first emerged. To put it differently, if one model looks at the movement of literature throughout the world, and at the changes a text overcomes as it passes into new lands, the other insists on the supremacy of the lost "world" of the original text, and the cosmological framework that first fixed it.

Now let us shift our focus back to the more theoretical side of this debate. In recent years, critics of Franco Moretti and Pascale Casanova's application of Immanuel Wallerstein's world literary systems theory to literary theory have argued that not one world but many possible worlds make up world literature. Following in the footsteps of the work of Thomas Pavel and Lubomír Doležel,[22] these critics have described

---

[21] John Butler, "Review of 'Awakened Cosmos: The Mind of Classical Chinese Poetry' by David Hinton & 'The Selected Poems of Tu Fu', translated by David Hinton," *Asian Review of Books*, November 14, 2019, web, https://asianreviewofbooks.com/content/awakened-cosmos-the-mind-of-classical-chinese-poetry-by-david-hinton-the-selected-poems-of-tu-fu-translated-by-david-hinton/.

[22] See Thomas Pavel, *Fictional Worlds*, Cambridge, MA: Harvard UP, 1986, and Lubomír Doležel, *Heterocosmica: Fiction and Possible Worlds*, Baltimore: Johns Hopkins UP, 1998.

world literary systems as Eurocentric, and accused them of ignoring the peripheral and semi-peripheral centers from which literature emerges. Possible worlds attempt to break free from this perceived imbalance in world literary theory. A possible world is a world that is not identifiable with a place or a time in the actual world, or the physical world that all humans, presumably, share. The notion of possible worlds is most familiar from modal logic, which talks about how things might be or might have been in terms of necessity and possibility.[23] Alexander Beecroft, Eric Hayot, and Haun Saussy are prominent among those who have attempted to ground literary theory in something akin to modal logic, and it is their work that I will focus on in the next chapter of this book.[24] The contingency of the concept of "world" as, in Pheng Cheah's words, "a temporal category, from which its normative dimension derives," is a larger issue in world literature with ties to postcolonial theory.[25] Though this book is sympathetic to these approaches as well, and though its findings affect this more politically inclined, and Heideggerian, concept of "world" and "worldliness," my intention in this work will be to explore further the fascinating territory adjoining logic and analytic philosophy opened by Pavel, Doležel, Hayot, Saussy, and others. I will push the analogy with modal logic further to uncover problems with how literary worlds place the critic in relation to texts and texts in relation to one another. Namely, I will be concerned with how literary worlds run into trouble regarding symmetry between worlds, the distinction between possible and impossible worlds, and trans-world identity of characters.

All the same, the invocation of literary worlds chimes with recent work in modern literature at large. Weak theory has emerged in the past decade as a way to adapt literary theory to a scholarly field cautious after the sweeping claims of literary trends of the past 30 or 40 years, including post-structuralism and indeed the early "world systems" mania of world literature itself. The term was initially applied to genre theory, though it does resonate with interest in "weak connections" in other parts of the humanities.[26] It is, in

---

[23] For two famous contributions to our conception of necessity and possibility, see Saul Kripke, *Naming and Necessity*, Oxford: Blackwell, 1980, and David Lewis, *On the Plurality of Worlds*, Oxford: Blackwell, 1986, 165.

[24] We might also include here, again, Apter, who has argued against world literature and for the notion of "untranslatability" between different languages and literary cultures. Apter's denial of mutual intelligibility puts her outside of the modal version of world literature that this chapter considers, but it is worth keeping her *Against World Literature* in mind as the denial of a single world of world literature taken to its logical end.

[25] Pheng Cheah and David Damrosch, "What Is a World (Literature)?" *Journal of World Literature* vol. 4, no. 3 (August 2019): 307.

[26] See Alexandre Geffen and Sandra Laugier, *Le pouvoir des liens faibles*, Paris: Éditions CNRS, 2020. The authors declare that some people want to consider weak links as a tool for success in life, as something practical to be used to achieve something else, while, in fact, weak links are things that we cannot seek out but that wait for us and challenge us to make sense of them. Hence, according to Geffen and Laugier, the need to place facts before theories. The exigency of having a theory that places a fact before a totalizing theory recalls Wai Chee Dimock and Paul Saint-Amour.

Wai Chee Dimock's words, a "lower-level kind of theorizing" that does not try to prioritize any genre or system above any other and makes "no prediction about being the last word."[27] It "highlights non communicability as something we can almost count on," and acknowledges that when looking at encounters between different literary systems we can derive significance "as much from missed connections as from consequential contact."[28] Putting weak theory into contact with literary worlds theory is fructive. Just as weak theory seeks, as Paul Saint-Amour puts it, to avoid reducing modern literature to literature as seen from a unilateral or "strongman" perspective and to theorize modernism in "specific, non-totalizing ways,"[29] so also literary worlds theory as I am advancing it retains the idea of world literature without the totalization of world systems. Naturally, "weak theory" also goes with "weak modernism," which allows for the term "modernism" to have a generous semantic stretch and encompass, à la Hayot and Susan Stanford Friedman, literary worlds and periods outside of the modern.[30] Yet there is another way of understanding "weakness." "Weakness" could focus not only on how we classify literary works and define literary genres and periods, or, as Stephen Ross fears, weaken such classifications and definitions to the point of meaninglessness.[31] Rather, "weakness" could also be valued as a property inherent in all literature, a natural vagueness that focuses on "sets," "networks," and "constellations" of rhetoric, language, and, indeed, ontological assumptions. Saint-Amour and some of his interlocutors already point out the utility of these former aspects of literature.[32] What I want to contribute here is an understanding of the importance of this last, of ontological clashes and reorganizations, the very meat of translation and transnationalism. This would open world literature to many diverse ways of conceiving of the world, with attention to the worlds of "East" and "West" that arise as different smaller worlds come into contact. In the context of world literature, needed is a way of weakening literary worlds theory itself better to account

---

[27] Wai Chee Dimock, "Weak Theory: Henry James, Colm Toibin, and W. B. Yeats," *Critical Inquiry* vol. 39, no. 4 (June 1, 2013): 733.

[28] Ibid., 752.

[29] Paul Saint-Amour, "Weak Theory, Weak Modernism," *Modernism/Modernity* vol. 25, no. 3 (September 1, 2018): 455.

[30] Susan Stanford Friedman, *Planetary Modernisms: Provocations on Modernity Across Time*, New York: Columbia UP, 2015. The approach that Friedman "asks for is a fundamental rethinking of modernity that posits it as a geohistorical condition that is multiple, contradictory, interconnected, polycentric, and recurrent for millennia across the globe" (4). The tactic rhymes with Hayot's assertion that "Modernism" is not a period in literature but describes any work that tries to overturn "the normative world-view of its era." See Hayot, *On Literary Worlds*, 131–33. My contention is that these are "strong" theories because they assume mutual intelligibility between different literatures and periods in advance.

[31] Stephen Ross, "Provocations on the Philosophy of Weakness," *Modernism/modernity Print Plus* vol. 4, cycle 2 (May 2019), https://modernismmodernity.org/forums/posts/responses-special-issue-weak-theory-part-iv.

[32] Saint-Amour, "Weak Theory," 444, 452; Polly Hember, Suzanne Hobson, Gareth Mills, and Jeff Wallace, "Weak Theory and Digital Modernism: a BAMS Workshop," *Modernism/modernity Print Plus* vol. 4, cycle 2 (May 2019), https://modernismmodernity.org/forums/posts/responses-special-issue-weak-theory-part-iv.

for the contradictions and vague boundaries that emerge between the worlds of different texts, traditions, and languages.

Chapter One narrows the focus to the history of "world literature" as a conceptual tool. Though this is the only chapter in the theoretical Part 1, its breadth, touching on issues proper to the four languages and different literary media that compose the rest of the book, makes it in some ways the most expansive chapter of this work. The chapter is most interested in a particular model of understanding world literature: literary worlds. Beginning with the work of Thomas Pavel and Lubomir Doležel in the 1980s, literary worlds have become influential again as a way of allowing, within the framework of a single "world" of world literature, for disconnections between different literary traditions founded on contrasting ways of carving up and interpreting the world. Some of the scholars most prone to use the metaphor of literary worlds are, interestingly, scholars of Chinese literature or its reception in the West: Eric Hayot, Alexander Beecroft, and Haun Saussy. But the theory falters when dealing with the trans-world identity of characters, or the identity of characters across multiple texts or worlds, and when explaining how logically inconsistent worlds access one another. By referencing recent work in modal logic, philosophical approaches to vagueness, and G. E. R. Lloyd's notion of the multidimensionality of literature I offer a more flexible model that helps to explain literary interactions between East and West.

Chapter Two is the first of four in-depth analyses of literary works that attempt to fuse East and West. It is also the start of Part 2, in which drama and the peculiar problems that staging poses for literary world formation are the prime issues. In each of these four chapters I triangulate three texts: an East Asian text, with "text" understood in a wide sense, and two responses to it, one by a French or English writer and one by a Chinese or Japanese writer. Each triangulation will cover a broader area. The first triangulation is the unfinished collaboration between Chou Wen-chung and Ted Hughes on an operatic adaptation of the *Bardo Thödol*, more commonly known as *The Tibetan Book of the Dead*. Though Chou and Hughes were dealing with a Tibetan text, or rather Walter Yeeling Evans-Wentz's eccentric translation of a Tibetan text, both Chou and Hughes saw the *Bardo* project as a way to bring East and West together in a new sort of literature, one that transcended older national classifications and embraced the mixing of cultures that was already well underway as Chou and Hughes worked in the late 1950s.

Chapter Three turns to the Japanese dramatic form of Nō. It considers two adaptations to the classical nō *Kantan* 邯鄲, Mishima Yukio's *shinsaku nō* or "new nō" *Kantan*邯鄲 and Scène VII, Journée III of Paul Claudel's *Le Soulier de Satin*. Although this chapter deals with three separate texts, the focus on ways of blending Eastern and Western ideas remains. Only at this point does the difficulty of making separate ontologies cohere in a single text become starker, as the Buddhist-influenced classical Nō is made to fit with Claudel's Catholic conception of the world or Mishima's postwar Japanese vision. My aim here will be to see whether we can think of these three texts as being separated from one another by degrees, or whether there is another, more sensitive way of understanding the identity relations between them.

Part 3 moves to poetry, a medium with its own issues in the process of literary world formation. In Chapter Four, Paul Claudel again figures, but his partner is now the poet and philosopher Kuki Shūzō. As Claudel worked as ambassador to Japan in the 1920s, during which time he crafted a series of poems and essays on and influenced by Japan and its arts, Kuki studied in Europe. In Germany and Paris he wrote *tanka* on his experiences living in a foreign land and a book, *Iki no kōzō*, outlining the essential differences between Japan and the West. Kuki and Claudel are not responding to a single text, but to one another's home cities: Tokyo and Paris. The chapter looks at what happens to "Japan" and "France" and the arts associated with them as they enter Claudel's and Kuki's constellations of belief. The role of *impossible worlds* comes into view as a means by which to understand the process of assimilating foreign ideas into a different constellation of belief.

Chapter Five compares the exile poetry of Bei Dao with Ted Hughes's vision of China in the final years of his life. It examines how both Bei Dao and Hughes attempt to situate their poetry in a clearly defined national, and occasionally ethnic, tradition and how their poetic treatments of China modify their understanding of their literary inheritance. The chapter looks at Hughes's substantial revision of his poem "The Trance of Light," which originally takes a stand against the industrialization of the Calder Valley in his native Yorkshire, but then is transformed into "Chinese History of Colden Water." My attention fixes on how Hughes's decision to rewrite the poem correlates with his changing attitudes toward English literature. It also treats, with an eye on Stephen Owen's famous critique of Bei Dao's work, the poetry Bei Dao wrote reflecting on China and the Chinese tradition during his time in exile. Because the triangulation here involves not a response to a single text or even city or nation but to the idea of tradition in the late twentieth century, it is the most complex piece of this work. Yet it also shows most clearly the ontological vagueness of literature, and the ways in which understandings of East and West shift depending on the terms brought to the comparison.

The concluding chapter reconsiders the methodological framework introduced in Chapter One. It evaluates how well multidimensionality and ontological vagueness help to explain the many texts analyzed earlier in the book. It suggests how the model developed in this book might be applied to East–West literature and comparative literature more broadly. Conceiving of East–West literature as multidimensional and ontologically vague, accepting, that is, that the terms and entities we deal with are often necessarily imprecise, can help us, intriguingly, more firmly to grasp our often puzzling materials. We can have vagueness without giving way to total ignorance; it is the task of this book to show how such knowledge of the imprecise can be not only possible but beneficial.

The structure I have given this study relies not primarily on author or country as much as on how each writer addresses the different ways in which literary worlds and world literature are created. I have, of course, divided the case studies into two parts: two chapters on drama followed by two chapters on poetry, with my choice of forms being part of an effort to expand world literature still further from its favorite form, the novel.[33] Yet the concept that I have been referring to as "triangulation," comparing an East Asian

---

[33] See David Damrosch, *Comparing the Literatures: Literary Studies in a Global Age*, Princeton: Princeton UP, 2020, 277, for more on Damrosch's own attempts to broaden the study of world literature

and a Western writer's views on the same work or set of works fixes the structure of this book. The first triangulation is between two people responding to the same text, *The Tibetan Book of the Dead*, to create one new work, *Bardo Thödol*. The second is between two people responding to one medieval text, *Kantan*, to create two discrete plays, *Le Soulier de satin* and the "new" *Kantan*. The third involves two people reflecting on great works in one another's languages to create new poetry collections in the 1920s *à la franco-japonaise*. The last treats people using one another's traditions to reconceptualize what tradition itself might mean in the era of "world literature." The structure is meant to reveal the various meanings that "world literature" can carry. It also shows the heterogenous interventions that world literature can make, both on individual works, collections, and the very framework through which authors interpret their own writings. That Hughes appears at the start of this study and at its conclusion breaks up how we would usually interpret him; but it also indicates how "world literature" is not a stable, unified concept but something that can manifest differently depending on how we view a writer—with whom we contrast the writer, and with which conceptual questions we address the writer's work.

This book could be divided in several ways. The two chapters dealing with Ted Hughes might be consecutive, as could the two concerning Paul Claudel. This would have the added benefit of keeping two chapters geared mostly toward Chinese literature together, and doing the same for two chapters touching mostly on Japanese literature. Here, however, a chapter on Hughes and Chou Wen-Chung flows on to one on Claudel and Mishima Yukio and another on Claudel and Kuki Shūzō before returning to Hughes at the end. I have selected this structure seriously ro engage with "weak theory" and putting aside strongman interpretations of literary works. When we read literature, we are used to accepting standard modes of reading: one author's corpus is only intelligible in terms of his or her own private universe, and one literary tradition is essentially closed, a world unto itself. Though such assumptions are valid to an extent, they do not provide us with a complete map of world literature. The world of world literature is rather more open and complex, composed, and our reading process, as Damrosch has suggested, takes us from "basic history to expand via hyperlinks into nested levels of greater depth and specificity."[34] As this book shows, these different hyperlinks often lead to different definitions of the same works, authors, traditions, and worlds. Hughes's world, like the world of all of the authors studied here, is not a static totality that sits outside of world literature, but a vague, a dynamic entity the borders and contents of which change depending not only on Hughes's activities and interests, but those of other writers, wherever they may be, approaching the same texts and asking the same questions. Hence we begin with Hughes and return to him at the end, and the effect is that we more readily can discern how the Hughes we encounter changes depending on both Hughes's own comprehension of East Asian literature, as well as on, in that larger world of world literature, East Asian writers'

---

from its fixation on the novel most recently encouraged by Moretti's championing of the form in his theory of distant reading.

[34] David Damrosch, "Toward a History of World Literature," *New Literary History* vol. XXXIX, no. 3 (Summer 2008): 489.

comprehension of East Asian materials, and of Western writers like Hughes. Thinking not merely of individual authors or texts but of grander questions of theory and literary medium, or world literature and literary worlds, of dramatic worlds, of poetic worlds, we notice how each case study fits into and diverges from ideal transnational categories.

"Triangulation" will allow us better to see just what *can* happen to a literary work as it is adapted across time,[35] space, language, and ontology. Call the literary work itself a world. This world exists as part of a *set of worlds*, which are the totality of the author's works and beliefs along with the social and philosophical (ontological) principles that might have fed into his or her texts and thoughts. This set is itself placed within a *constellation of belief*.[36] The constellation of belief is the author's wider historical and social context, including what we might call the dominant modes of thought or ontologies that correspond roughly to the time at which the author was writing. Obviously, we cannot know the totality of beliefs of any given time, including our own. Thus, the literary world, set of worlds, and constellation must remain epistemically vague to us: we simply do not have the necessary knowledge to fix the boundaries or flesh out *in full* the interior of any of these things. But we can have a more precise idea of how they correspond, if we adopt a model or a frame of mind analogous to philosophical approaches to vagueness. Ontological vagueness comes in once we consider that there are a large variety of constellations within the *universe* that comprises the totality of literary works. Since a world is necessarily coherent (it operates according to some logic, even if that logic is nonclassical or non-Western), borrowing from it may cause parts of it to become deformed as they are moved into new constellations and sets of belief. There is quite simply no fact of the matter according to which interpretation is correct, for an interpretation that is valid relative to one constellation may not be valid relative to another. After establishing the methodology, the scope of this book will therefore expand: starting with a collaboration; moving to a reaction to a single text; going through responses to parts of French and Japanese literary traditions; and concluding with the concept of tradition writ large. Using the framework I set in Chapter One, I will be considering how a single text coheres in translation, how multiple texts belonging to different literary constellations relate to one another, and how worlds, sets, and constellations are conceived in relation to the entire universe of literature.

Now, it is important to address what we mean by the "constellation of belief" of a given world, or the society in which it was created. Naturally, no culture at any given time is unified. There are contradictions and disagreements among contemporaries, or between authors and groups across time. Hinton, in his new translations of Du Fu, surely does not mean that Du Fu's thought is necessarily Buddhist simply by virtue of being Tang. The Tang itself was composed of competing schools of thought; Confucianism

---

[35] David Lewis mentions that the problems of trans-world identity are analogous to the problems of identity over time. See Lewis, *On the Plurality of Worlds*, 202–10.

[36] See Phillipe Monneret, « Fiction et Croyance », in *La Théorie littéraire des mondes possible*, ed. Françoise Lavocat, Paris: Editions du CNRS, 2010, 259–91. I differ from Monneret in that I do not say that literary works range across several worlds but that each world coheres to fit into its constellation, which accounts for deformations as aspects of other literary works are translated into new constellations of belief.

jostled with Daoism, originally thought a strain of witchcraft proper to Southern Barbarians such as the ones Confucius's near contemporary Qu Yuan drew inspiration from for his now canonical *Li Sao*.[37] Early Chinese Buddhists might have drawn analogies with Daoism to understand the Buddhist texts flowing through the Silk Road from India. But Buddhism itself fractured into different schools, Sanlun, Huayan, and Chan, none identical to the other and none identical with earlier schools of Buddhism or constant themselves over time. I could adduce more examples. The point, though, is clear: culture is too complex to be encapsulated in a single school of thought. My claims about the world of a text are limited just to that world, and are not meant to be generalizable to large swaths of people.

The various pieces of literature examined across this book will show East–West literature emerges from shocks that occur from an encounter with the unfamiliar. The utility of the non-actual, or of those things which transcend human existence, has become an increasingly important part of literary studies in recent years thanks to the work of, among others, Spivak and Wai Chee Dimock. While Spivak focuses on "planetarity" and the necessity of engaging with the "other," Dimock stresses "deep time," or geographic time that arose before humans existed and will persist after humans pass away. As Takayuki Tatsumi notes, both of these theories function in part due to an encounter between humans and something that seems inscrutable from common human sense: the emergence of dinosaurs in fiction for Spivak, for instance, entities which seem entirely unbeholden to modern rationality, or rock formations and geological strata for Dimock.[38] But in either case we are dealing with the non-actual, dinosaurs that no longer exist, or periods in the earth's history that are deep in the past or far in the future. Tatsumi points out that confrontations with evolutionary theory were similarly destabilizing for nineteenth century American writers, whose conceptual systems were jolted by the extension of history and the relative brevity of the dominance of humankind on the earth to the point where the common frog could signify a lost world of ferocious dinosaurs.[39]

Though I will not be concerned with planetarity and deep time in quite the same way, I will try to show how the shock of the non-actual leads to literary creativity. The non-actual here could mean glimpses of older literary worlds, suffused with religions or practices not believed in by the reader or translator. I want to take seriously the challenges afforded by East Asia. Though many critics such as Zhang Longxi and

---

[37] For the links between Daoism and "barbarism" in the context of *Li Sao*, see David Hawkes, *The Songs of the South: An Ancient Chinese Anthology of Poems by Qu Yuan and Other Poets*, Harmondsworth, UK: Penguin Books, 1985, especially p. 22. For a more recent appraisal of the philosophy underpinning Qu Yuan's verse, see Paul W. Kroll, "Daoist Verse and the Quest of the Divine," in *Early Chinese Religion, Part Two: The Period of Division (220–589 AD)* (2 vols.), ed. John Lagerwey and Pengzhi Lü, Leiden: Brill, 2009, 953–85.

[38] Takayuki Tatsumi, *Modanizumu no wakusei*, Tokyo: Iwanami Shoten, 2013, 236–41. For Wai Chee Dimock, see *Through Other Continents: American Literature Across Deep Time*, Princeton: Princeton UP, 2009.

[39] Ibid., 242–43.

Rudolf Wanger have spoken against dividing the world literature into "East and West" or "distinct Eastern and Western Ways of knowing,"[40] I will demonstrate that not taking seriously the disconnects between East Asian and European thought can lead to the erasure of non-Western forms of knowledge in the world literary sphere. Being forced to grapple with ideas from radically different traditions, or things that are aloof from our typical modes of thought, does, as Spivak and Dimock say, lead to important breakthroughs in our understanding of the world and of literature. Yet we seldom pay enough attention to these moments of conflict between different modes of thought or ontologies because we privilege Western ways of reading, the circulation of East Asian texts in the modern West, or East Asian reception of Western texts. We too seldom consider East Asian responses to premodern East Asian literatures. No wonder, then, that we often fail to see vagueness inherent in world literature, how the pieces of literature within it seem ontologically vague and difficult to make sense of without translating them out not only of their native languages but their native belief systems.

Hence the call for proper attention to the reception of premodern Chinese and Japanese literary worlds among modern Chinese, English, French, and Japanese writers. These worlds force the reader to make sense of them, and to incorporate them somehow into her constellation of belief. Naturally, she cannot accommodate everything in the world, nor know everything about the actual world of the text, the social sphere in which the text was produced. Consequently, in translation, or in adaptation, the writer will reduce the known information about the original literary world a simplified set, the data of which will either be accommodated in the constellation of belief or banished to an impossible world. Hence, translations are not merely a compromise between the original text and the language into which it is translated—what we could call the source and the target language. When we deal with languages we are dealing not only with words as such but with entire networks of belief and context.

By taking seriously the challenges that East Asian literatures and ontologies offer world literature and comparative literature, we can arrive at a richer, more multifaceted understanding of world literature. Accepting that the literary worlds we deal with are ontologically vague does not scupper the entire project. Instead, it encourages to adopt a "weak" approach that accounts for the limits of our knowledge and our literary categories, that, to cite Dimock again, "no prediction about being the last word." Then we can arrive at glimpses of distant worlds like Du Fu's as described in Hinton's *Awakened Cosmos*, worlds that function thanks to the blurring of categories and our recognition of the limits of our thought. The result will be a theory that is rewardingly vague and suitably "weak."

---

[40] Rudolf Wagner, "Can We Speak of East/West Ways of Knowing?" *KNOW: A Journal on the Formation of Knowledge* vol. 2, no. 1 (2018): 31–46; Zhang Longxi, *The Tao and the Logos: Literary Hermeneutics, East and West*, Durham: Duke UP, 1992.

Part 1
WORLD LITERATURE, LITERARY WORLDS

Chapter One

LITERARY WORLDS AND DEGREES OF DISTANCE

> Les choses ne sont pas seulement des objets de connaissance,
> mais des motifs de co-naissance. Elles provoquent, elles déterminent dans le
> sujet toutes les attitudes impliquées par sa construction.
> Elles suscitent en lui une image animée, leur symbole commun.
> Elles lui fournissent le moyen de co-naître,
> de se connaître par rapport à elles, de produire et
> de diriger la force nécessaire pour assurer
> entre les deux termes contact.[1]

When Paul Claudel began to compose *l'Art Poétique*, he was taking his first look at the "grand livre de l'Orient" as a young consul in China. Fed up with the "l'ancienne [logique qui] avait le syllogism pour organe" (the old logic with the syllogism as its motor), Claudel constructed "une nouvelle logique" that could explain the correspondences he found in the "East":

> Jadis au Japon, comme je montais de Nikkô à Chuzenji, je vis, quoique grandement distants, juxtaposés par l'alignement de mon œil, la verdure d'un érable combler l'accord proposé par un pin. Les présentes pages commentent ce texte forestier, l'énonciation arborescent, par Juin, d'un nouvel Art poétique de l'Univers, d'une nouvelle Logique. (*Po.* 143)[2]

This new logic accounts for the co-naissance of self and other, the way in which two things fill one another's gaps and bring one another into being, just as the greenery of the maple rises to accord with the pine at Chuzenji. It might be more just to say that the

---

[1] "Things are not merely the objects of knowledge [*connaissance*], but the motifs of *co-naissance* (being born together). They provoke, they determine in the subject all of the attitudes implicated by their construction. They elicit in him an animated image, their common symbol. They provide him with the means to *co-naître*, to know himself in relation to them, to produce and to direct the force needed to assure contact between the two terms." Paul Claudel, *Œuvre Poétique*, ed. Jacques Petit, Paris: Gallimard, 1967, 187. Subsequent references to this work will be made in-text and use the abbreviation *Po.*

[2] "Once in Japan, as I went up from Nikkō to Chuzenji, I saw, however greatly distant, juxtaposed by the alignment of my eye, the green of a maple tree fill the harmony [*accord*] proposed by a pine tree. The present pages comment upon this forest text, the arborescent enunciation, by June of a new Poetic Art of the Universe, of a new Logic." Ibid., 143.

two things bring a new aspect of one another into existence. The pine and the maple complement one another and create a third image that arises from their fusion.[3] When we compare in order to carry out world literature in theory, and when the writers we study compare to carry out world literature in practice, we carry out a similar process. We create a new simplified set of the two things we are comparing. This set includes properties we believe are held by each thing, be it the "East," "China," "France," or "Britain." But, like Claudel's maple and pine, this image needs the image of the comparand, the thing to which it is compared, in order to be complete: there are gaps in both that to be filled require a complement. The obscure boundaries of literary categories, of "East" and "West" themselves, suggest their *ontological vagueness*. They are indeterminate, not because we do not know enough about them, but because their boundaries are fixed in comparison and fluctuate depending on the comparand that is used to fix them.

The purpose of this chapter is to expand on and test the various theories of world literature, literary worlds, and vagueness upon which the introduction to this book touched. I will, that is, refine the theory of literary worlds, the theory that works of literature generate imaginative worlds that stand apart from the actual world, in order to make the theory accommodate the materials given to use from the literary and religious traditions of East Asia better. In order to do so, I will perform some close readings of premodern Chinese and Japanese texts and consider how well the theory of literary worlds handles them. My aim will be to show that literary worlds theory, relying as it often does on the idea of a neutral "actual world" that we all inhabit, and the ontology of which we all more or less agree on, stands precariously when we try to make East Asian and Western materials sit together in a single, noncontradictory world. That is not to say that all East Asian pieces of literature disagree with all Western pieces of literature, or that the boundaries between "East Asia" and the "West" are fixed and easy to highlight. But it is to take seriously the challenge of making world literature not just a collection of works that flatter a single ideology or easy-to-grasp vision of the world, a sort of "greatest hits" that reaffirm our current worldview, but as a conglomerate of materials that might sometimes sit uneasily with our current, Western- and particularly American-centric visions of world literature. When we answer this challenge, we see why the theory of literary worlds hits a wall when dealing with symmetry between worlds, the distinction between possible and impossible worlds, and trans-world identity of characters, and why we must take the presence of ontological vagueness and contradictory worlds more seriously. Can we find a way to understand these interactions; can we find a "new logic" that is not too strong, but weak and open to the kinds of unexpected arrangements and new creations that comparison calls forth?

---

[3] The mention of "fusion" in this context of a meeting between "East and West" naturally directs our attention to Ernest Fenollosa's "The Coming Fusion of East and West" and his work more generally. Though Fenollosa is slightly out of the scope of this book, his importance for East–West literature cannot be ignored. For a discussion, see Josephine Nock-Hee Park, *Apparitions of Asia: Modernist Form and Asian American Poetics*, Oxford: Oxford UP, 2008, 4–22.

I will begin this theoretical survey with an overview of Thomas Kuhn, W. V. O. Quine, and Donald Davidson on translation across ontologies.[4] This will allow us to understand where critics are coming from when they speak of literary worlds and incommensurable paradigms. I will then look at Alexander Beecroft, Eric Hayot, and Haun Saussy and connect their work to Asian Analytic Philosophy (AAP) and G. E. R. Lloyd's notion of multidimensionality. AAP and Lloyd also deal with the problem of translation across literary and conceptual spaces, but they arrive at slightly different solutions. Saussy is an intermediary between the more famous literary worlds model and the conception of multidimensionality that I will advance, and he will be instrumental in my attempt to reconcile the two.[5] I will weigh the pros and cons of each approach, and gradually move toward a different model of transnational or world literature.

Two names have become synonymous with the problem of mutual intelligibility, Thomas Kuhn and W. V. O. Quine. Kuhn's *The Structure of Scientific Revolutions* argues that science is not progressively getting closer to absolute truths about nature; rather, science operates within paradigms that are mutually unintelligible. For instance, the change from classical mechanics to relativistic mechanics was not a refinement of a worldview. The relativistic paradigm dethroned the classical; a scientist, according to Kuhn, could not subscribe to both paradigms at once. The reason is that the terms used by both paradigms appear the same but have different extensions. In classical mechanics mass is discrete, but in relativistic mechanics mass is integral with energy. A scientist could not use the term "mass" in both the classical and relativistic senses at once because it refers to two different things. A scientist working within the classical paradigm and one within the relativistic paradigm live, Kuhn says, in "different worlds."[6]

Quine argues for the indeterminacy of translation and the inscrutability of reference. His well-known thought experiment, to which Saussy devotes much time, imagines being with a member of a tribe whose language we do not know. A rabbit jumps forth and the tribesman utters *"gavagai."* Quine argues that we cannot know whether *gavagai* means "rabbit" or whether it has an extension unknown in our language such as "undetached rabbit parts" or "time slices of rabbit."[7] There is no fact of the matter that determines

---

[4] From this point, the core of this chapter was published as "A Critique of Literary Worlds in World Literature Theory: Multidimensionality as a Basis of Comparison," *Journal of World Literature* vol. 3, no. 3 (2018): 354–72.

[5] Given Saussy's long and rich career, pinning him down to a single viewpoint is difficult if not impossible, but note that his first monograph begins by arguing, cautiously, against those who would make too much of incommensurable ontologies, before showing the importance of what does not translate in the formation of comparative literature. The role of ontological difference that I am highlighting throughout this book is different and read in the light of different approaches to comparative literature, but it is worth revisiting Haun Saussy, *The Problem of a Chinese Aesthetic*, Redwood, CA: Stanford UP, 1993, 1–12.

[6] Thomas Kuhn, *The Structure of Scientific Revolutions*, Chicago: U of Chicago P, 1962, 116–17. Both supporters and critics have regretted Kuhn's metaphor. See, for example, Richard Rorty and John Searle, "Rorty v. Searle, at Last: A Debate," *Logos: A Journal of Catholic Thought and Culture* vol. 2, no. 3 (1999): 48–50.

[7] W. V. O. Quine, *Word and Object*, Cambridge, MA: MIT Press, 2013, 27.

what *gavagai* means. Any translation we attempt will always refer to the conceptual scheme upon which our language is based, which Quine calls the "background language."[8] Therefore, we have no absolute reference to determine what a word in another language means. Since all reference is relative to a specific background, all reference is contingent. Given this contingency, Quine's argument may seem adequate for world literature, but the idea of indeterminacy throws the entire enterprise of literary comparison into doubt, and each of the critics to whom I will shortly turn attempts to balance their relativism with an absolute ground that ensures mutual intelligibility between languages and literatures.

In an essay that would go on to influence Lloyd's and Saussy's approaches, Donald Davison criticizes Kuhn. In "On the Very Idea of a Conceptual Scheme," Davidson argues that Kuhn and Quine have a mistaken idea of communication. While agreeing that experience is relative to a conceptual scheme, he notes that incommensurability presupposes the comparison of the supposedly incomparable. "The dominant metaphor of conceptual relativism, that of differing points of view, seems to betray an underlying paradox," writes Davidson, since we need "a common coordinate system" to notice difference.[9] There must be a common ground to make the very concept of failed translation intelligible; otherwise, we would be unable to measure the success of translation at all. Davidson notes that for Kuhn the shared ground is "nature," while for Quine it is "experience."[10] Where Kuhn and Quine go wrong, according to Davidson, is in presupposing the "dualism of scheme and reality," since our sense of reality always grounds our conceptual schemes.[11] And language mediates our understanding of schemes. Yet, we cannot know the totality of truth conditions of the propositions of our own language, let alone the language of another person. Working within this ignorance, we are bound by the principle of charity in interpretation: "whether we like it or not, if we want to understand others, we must count them right in most matters [...] Nothing more is possible, and nothing more is needed."[12]

In sum, Kuhn's incommensurable paradigms and Quine's indeterminacy of translation and inscrutability of reference cause us to doubt the grounds on which the circulation and comparison of literature takes place. Davidson encourages us to doubt in turn Kuhn and Quine as he draws attention to the necessity of some shared ground for even the charge of incommensurability and indeterminacy to make sense.

---

[8] Ibid., 2.

[9] Donald Davidson, "On the Very Idea of a Conceptual Scheme," *Proceedings and Addresses of the American Philosophical Association* vol. 47 (1973): 6.

[10] Ibid., 12.

[11] Ibid., 20.

[12] Ibid., 19. Cian Dorr gives a persuasive critique of the principle of charity. Arguing that the language of ontology is not the language of ordinary English, or of any ordinary language, the language best suited to communicating across ontologies is one based on nihilism, the view that nothing exists. Dorr, "What We Disagree about When We Disagree about Ontology," in *Fictionalism in Metaphysics*, ed. Mark E Kalderon, Oxford: Clarendon Press, 2005, 234–86.

Literary Worlds

That takes us to literary worlds theory itself. I will focus in this section on Beecroft, Hayot, and Saussy's theories. I will order them in terms of how discrete they believe literary worlds are and, concomitantly, how much overlap their ideas have with world literary systems. I will then criticize literary worlds theory by referencing modal logic and AAP. Most of my attention will be on Hayot and Saussy, but it is worth looking at Beecroft because his work is a bridge between totalizing world systems and discrete literary worlds.

But first I will look at a core text of the theory of literary worlds, Thomas Pavel's *Fictional Worlds*. Pavel distinguishes between "segregationist" and "integrationist" attitudes toward fictional discourse.[13] Segregationist attitudes are strongly associated with the work of logical atomists such as Bertrand Russell and more recent analytic philosophers including P. F. Strawson and John Searle. Segregationists keep fictional and nonfictional discourse strictly separate. In general, they rely upon the correspondence theory of truth and the truth-making principle to divide fictional claims from nonfictional ones. The theory and the principle both assume that sentences have meaning in relation to the real or actual world: a proposition is true if and only if there is an entity or state of affairs in the world that makes that proposition true. Since fictional entities have no correspondents in the actual world, propositions relating to them can be construed as meaningless. There is no one way of keeping the two distinct: "While in a Russellian framework segregation rests on ontological and logical grounds, the speech-act theory [associated with Searle and J. L. Austin] derives fictionality from the linguistic attitude of the speaker."[14]

Integrationists, on the other hand, "claim that no genuine ontological difference can be found between fictional and nonfictional descriptions of the world."[15] Alexius Meinong and his followers belong to this camp. For Meinong, anything that possesses a property is real, whether or not it exists. Among such objects are the golden mountain and the square circle.[16] In fact, it is Meinong's tolerance of impossible objects that prompted Russell's segregationist approach. Pavel gravitates toward Meinong's theories. He adds the stipulation that we consider that there are degrees of being, a notion that "may serve in the internal ontological models describing mythical and religious thought, and more generally symbolic activities of the mind."[17] He does not develop this notion of degrees but leaves it as a heuristic tool.

Pavel also looks at how we gain epistemic access to literary worlds. Epistemic access is not constant over time. He writes, "The actual world as well as the relation of accessibility are different for the authors of medieval miracle plays compared to the author of a modern mystery novel."[18] Every person, when presented with a proposition or a

---

[13] Thomas G. Pavel, *Fictional Worlds*, Cambridge, MA: Harvard UP, 1986, 11.
[14] Ibid., 20.
[15] Ibid., 11.
[16] Ibid., 28.
[17] Ibid., 30.
[18] Ibid., 47.

fictional sentence, must determine whether the new information belongs to the realm of possibility.[19] What is this realm of possibility? Pavel takes his lead from the work of Saul Kripke: there is an actual world that we inhabit that exists among a universe of possible worlds. Propositions describing impossible things are out of this universe. Those propositions may be mapped onto impossible worlds, though Pavel does not resolve the issue of what those impossible worlds consist of and how we gain epistemic access to them if they are outside of our "universe."[20] No more does he ever quite resolve the problem of having multiple actual worlds, or of having different multiple actual worlds between East and West. This is not an indictment of Pavel's insightful and influential work: he is not a specialist in East Asian literature, and his work, being the first to bring to bear advances in modal logic on literary theory, remains immensely valuable. Later I will return to the problem of degrees and impossible worlds. For now, let me turn to more contemporary critics writing in response to the development of the discipline of world literature.

Beecroft does not use the term "worlds." In "World Literature without a Hyphen: Towards a Typology of Literary Systems," he takes world literature as the mereological sum of all literary texts, with each place in which a text emerges operating under a specific mode of textual production.[21] Elsewhere, criticizing the economic models underpinning world systems, he speaks of modes as "ecologies" of literature. As do all literary worlds theorists, Beecroft opposes Franco Moretti and Pascale Casanova's core-periphery schema. Looking at ancient and modern literature, Beecroft distinguishes between "cosmopolitan" or "panchoric" literature and "vernacular" or "epichoric" literature. Often empires, bringing with them the mass circulation of literary works and ideas, usually in print, produce the panchoric. The epichoric stems from oral tradition and small-scale circulation. It precedes the panchoric and persists at the margins of empire.[22] Beecroft is more concerned with the transmission of literature than with its ontological status. His ecologies, though resembling worlds, obey transcendent laws. The relation of ancient Japanese literature to Tang Chinese literature is of the same type as the relation of Norse literature to Latin literature in the Middle Ages, even if, as he stresses, they are qualitatively different. With modernity the relationships change, but the generality of Beecroft's theory remains the same. Each ecosystem has its own climate, flora, fauna, and other peculiarities, but each is, as a literary ecosystem of the world a totality, subject to the same rules and so mutually intelligible. Beecroft's approach attempts to modify world systems to allow for relativism between literary worlds and strives for more focus on peripheral literatures without sacrificing the common ground that Moretti and Casanova establish for comparison across even the most disparate

---

[19] Ibid., 47–48.
[20] Ibid., 49.
[21] Alexander Beecroft, "World Literature without a Hyphen." *New Left Review* vol. 54 (November–December 2008): 87–100.
[22] Alexander Beecroft, *An Ecology of World Literature: From Antiquity to the Present Day*, London: Verso, 2015, 30.

literary works.²³ Helpfully, Beecroft notices that "some existing texts cannot survive in the new environment, others survive in a marginal or altered role, while others still flourish in their new and unexpected surroundings."²⁴ The comment provides a fine starting point from which to drill down further and see the logical processes and ontological barriers at play in reforming texts, and parts of texts, in translation.

Hayot opposes the "'world' of 'world literature'" to the "'world' of 'world systems.'"²⁵ The world of world systems is total. More precisely, it is a unified market that emanates from the West. Moretti traces the novel as it emerges in Europe and spreads across the globe, with a "compromise between a western formal influence (usually French or English) and local materials."²⁶ Casanova speaks of literary capital. Certain capitals of culture—Paris, New York—determine the criteria for what is high art and artists from around the world adopt these criteria to further their careers.²⁷ In both Casanova and Moretti, Hayot notes, the center, usually Europe, is in tension with the periphery, usually the so-called third world. He writes that by generalizing European aesthetic criteria the world systems model can not only distort our appreciation of non-European literature but also blind us to what goes on in the "peripheral" areas of literary production.²⁸ Thus comes his notion of literary worlds, in which the "world" in world literature does not mean the whole world but the world of a particular group, place, or time. Drawing upon the Heideggerian concept of "worlding," he writes that worlding in

---

[23] Beecroft tends toward unity of literary systems, most notably in his "Eurafraisiachronologies: Between the Eurocentric and the Planetary." *Journal of World Literature*, vol. 1, no. 1 (2016): 17–28, in which he tries to eschew "Eurocentric" periodization. Rather than relying on European periodization, Beecroft seeks "a more inclusive narrative one which identifies elements of change and of continuity in all regions, and which seeks to understand the development of late premodern cultures on their own terms, and not from the end-point of European modernity they were foredoomed not to reach" (22).

[24] Beecroft, *An Ecology*, 198.

[25] Eric Hayot, *On Literary Worlds*, Oxford: Oxford UP, 2012, 33.

[26] Franco Moretti, "Conjectures on World Literature." *New Left Review* vol. 1 (January–February 2000): 58.

[27] Pascale Casanova, "Literature as a World," *New Left Review* 31 (January–February 2005): 71–90.

[28] Hayot, *On Literary Worlds*, 35. Hayot takes the Chinese word for literature, 文 (wen), as an example: "There is no guarantee that this latter term is not the universalizing vision of a European concept inappropriate to the analysis of texts and stories operating under radically different conceptions of the meaning of writing or storytelling—as in the Chinese context, where the word *wen*文 includes forms of textual production and culture that do not belong to 'literature' in its modern European uses. That is why Damrosch and others are willing to risk making both 'literature' and 'world' more expansive categories, and to insist that any literary history worth its salt will have to take account of a far broader list of works and movements than has so far been necessary under the largely unconsciously Europe-centered regimes of literary study" (35). This problem has long beset comparative literature. See also, Earl Miner, *Comparative Poetics. An Intercultural Essay on Theories of Literature*, Princeton: Princeton UP, 1990, and Françoise Lavocat, "Le comparatisme comme herméneutique de la défamiliarasation," *Vox-Poetica* 5 (April 2012), http://www.vox-poetica.org/t/articles/lavocat2012.html#_ftnref45.

literature draws attention to the act of making a social world, for to "world is to enclose, but also to exclude."[29] Each world has many undetermined parts. We do not know the price of apples in Charles Dickens's London or what time of day Jean Racine's Phèdre prefers. There is no right answer; the original or subsequent writer or audience may supply answers and fill in the missing details of the literary world. Rather than being a closed totality, the world of world literature is a multiplicity of possible worlds that can expand and change over time.[30]

Though Saussy is more critical of Moretti and Casanova, his approach strongly resembles Hayot's. In his opinion, world systems risk "flattening" literary study, identifying literature with its place of production as a dot on the map, and missing the underlying dimensions of literary texts. What are these dimensions? They are akin to Hayot's worlds. "There may be only one physical world," writes Saussy, "but there are a great many imaginative projections of possible and conceivable worlds; and people spend most of their lives in those latter worlds."[31] Literary works are the result of a writer coming into contact with the social and physical reality of her time and place. But the literary work does not describe that world; it is its own world. How can a literary work be a world unto itself? Simply because it is rooted in a particular way of viewing the world—a particular ontology. A literary work is a world determined by each writer's engagements with reality, and reality is already determined by the concept and norms of each writer's society. The literary world is not generalizable because the society in which it was produced constrains it. In other words, not all concepts found in a literary world are transferable. This has implications for how the critic of world literature approaches the literary text. Saussy stresses that world literature contends with the "uncertainty of reference" occasioned by encounter with different ontologies that structure different literary texts.[32]

Hayot and Saussy vary in how they connect literary worlds to one another. Hayot, we have seen, is more concerned with connections between worlds, Saussy with disconnections. While Hayot is aware of "the dangers or the uniformity of the actual world's single-worldedness,"[33] he proposes that every literary text is itself a product of and contributor to "world."[34] Here the lines blur between "world" as a totality and the "world" of a particular group of people. But what Hayot seems to mean is that by contributing to the structure and understanding of a particular world, literary texts contribute to the structure and understanding of the world in which every person lives. The world of Murasaki Shikibu's *Genji Monogatari* is distinct from the world of Charles Dickens's *Bleak House*, yet both of these particular worlds are part of the world of world literature. Hayot can say that there are certain transcendent modes—romanticism, realism, and modernism—that characterize all literary texts' relation to the larger world because, however differently imagined, the world of world literature is ultimately *one*.

---

[29] Hayot, *On Literary Worlds*, 40.
[30] Ibid., 61.
[31] Haun Saussy, "The Dimensionality of World Literature," *Neohelicon* vol. 38, no. 2 (2011): 293.
[32] Ibid., 291.
[33] Hayot, *On Literary Worlds*, 37.
[34] Ibid., 85.

Saussy also argues that there is a common ground for all literary works. Like Kuhn, he calls this "reality," or more precisely "the reality effect." Every ontology, he says, stems from the encounter between a group of people and one and the same reality, so mutual intelligibility between even the most radically different ontologies is possible.[35] However, without the transcendent modes that Hayot proposes, Saussy's approach is more contingent. For Saussy, the comparatist is always unsure of "what to expect" when approaching the world of a foreign literature.[36] There are no familiar modes indicating the author's worldview. Hayot and Saussy agree that all literary works have a common ground, but they disagree about how connections between worlds affect the critic.

There are three problems with Hayot and Saussy's literary worlds. I will begin with the problem of symmetry. Simply put, the relationship between the critic's world and the literary world is not symmetrical. There are many different ideas on this in hermeneutics, but I will argue here that a literary world is necessarily closed in so far as it belongs to a prior time. Whenever the critic approaches a text, the text is complete. This is true even if the text is a work in progress, for there is always a latest stage at which the text has arrived before the critic begins analyzing it. Take again the world of the *Genji*. Everything that happens in the text has been written, even if there are lost manuscripts and other details of which we are unaware, and everything that happened in the society in which *Genji* was set, Heian Japan, has already happened. Theoretically, we could know everything that occurred in Heian Japan down to the most banal details of what each member of that society thought at a given moment. And there is a possible world at which a member of the court had a flash of insight and developed quantum mechanics. Because the same writer or other writers can expand the world of the original text, then these sorts of possible events allow the literary world to expand indefinitely. This is not true, though, from the standpoint of the critic. The society in which a work arises is finite: there is a limit to what could have happened and what did happen. In contrast, the critic works in the present in a society unknown to the writer and audience of the original literary world. Naturally, there is a limit to what the critic can know and what can happen in her society. But that limit is, at the time at which the critic works, necessarily unknown simply because the future is unknown. It follows that the literary world cannot access the world of the critic. This is the asymmetry between the literary world and the critic's world.[37] That is not to say that criticism of which the author or original audience of a text may not have thought, say a feminist reading of *Genji*, is unfounded, only that the boundaries of the

---

[35] Saussy approvingly cites Davidson here. For a similar argument that builds upon Davidson without speaking of possible worlds, see Zhang Longxi, *Unexpected Affinities: Reading Across Cultures*, Toronto: U of Toronto P, 2016, 1–26.

[36] Haun Saussy, "Interplanetary Literature," *Comparative Literature* vol. 63, no. 4 (2011): 447.

[37] Asymmetry violates the second constraint on accessibility relations in modal logic: σ : for all w1, w2, if w1Rw2, then w2Rw1 (for any two worlds, if world1 accesses world2 then world2 accesses world1) (Graham Priest, *An Introduction to Non-Classical Logic*, Cambridge: Cambridge UP, 2001, 36). The critic's world goes beyond the critic's knowledge and any alteration to the texts that make up the literary world still leaves the world anterior to developments in the actual world.

literary world are fixed in a way the borders of the critic's world are not. Although we can find new readings, those readings are constrained by what has already been written.

From the problem of symmetry follows the problem of accessibility. In modal logic, worlds are connected by accessibility relations. If there is no accessibility relation between our world, the actual[38] world @, and another world w, then w is considered an impossible world.[39] There are metaphysically impossible worlds and logically impossible worlds. Here, I will focus on logically impossible worlds. A logically impossible world somehow violates the logic that obtains at @. We might say that at @ the law of noncontradiction holds absolutely: nothing can both be and not be. It cannot be the case that I am currently in Sydney and Tokyo. At a logically impossible world w, contradiction is true: I can be in both places at once. Between @ and such an impossible world, there is no accessibility relation.[40]

Does accessibility impact our critical approach? I will argue yes, but first will look at a counterargument from a modal logician. In AAP, a debate has been taking place over the ontological status of some Buddhist logic. Some Buddhist logic uses the tetralemma, which has four truth values: True, False, Neither True nor False, Both True and False. It is obvious that this makes a world at which fourfold logic holds inaccessible from most academics' understanding of @. Some philosophers, such as Takashi Yagisawa, do not see this as a problem for mutual intelligibility between worlds at which this type of logic obtains and @. These worlds are impossible worlds, but they are no more difficult to understand than other impossible worlds, such as a fictional world in which Pegasus, the winged horse of Greek myth, exists.[41]

Yasuo Deguchi, Jay Garfield, and Graham Priest (henceforth DGP) object to the way Yagisawa defuses the problem. In criticism, we are used to encountering fantastic or paradoxical situations, hence the utility of the willing suspension of disbelief. DGP contend

---

[38] I define the actual world as existing in a physical space that we all share, though which we can perceive differently, and at the vague moment "now." I understand a text as having an existence prior to any criticism of or reflection upon it. How we understand "now," and time in general, is also an artifact of our culture: for example, in Greek and Buddhist thought we can find examples of circular time at odds with our conception of linear time. Whatever conception of time the critic has, the problem of accessibility between @ and a literary world would hold.

[39] For an argument that the determination of @ in logic is a metaphysical claim, and that asserting a metalogic (like a world system?) that governs all relations between the actual world and possible world risks closing down other ways of thinking in favor of our own, see Timothy Williamson, "Logic, Metalogic and Neutrality," *Erkenntnis* vol. 79, no. S2 (2014): 211–31. Françoise Lavocat attempts to defuse this metaphysical bias in literary worlds by saying that a single real world generates many actual worlds, which in turn generate literary worlds. I am not certain this solves the problem, rather than just deferring it. See Françoise Lavocat, "Les genres de la fiction: État des lieux et propositions," in *La Théorie littéraire des mondes possibles*, ed. Françoise Lavocat, Paris: CNRS Éditions, 2010, 15–53.

[40] Takashi Yagisawa, *Worlds and Individuals, Possible and Otherwise*, Oxford: Oxford UP, 2010, 177.

[41] Note that Yagisawa diverges from David Lewis. Lewis argues that all possible worlds, or all worlds other than the actual world @, are real, so there can be no room for impossible worlds (165).

that suspending disbelief and confining certain literary worlds to impossible worlds prejudices our critical view and has implications for how we interpret and classify literary texts from ancient and foreign literary traditions.[42] They reason that Buddhism seeks to eliminate suffering in this world, so when a Buddhist text speaks of true contradictions[43] it is speaking of contradictions that are about this and not a possible or impossible world. Full understanding, not simply a disinterested evaluation of truth and falsity, comes when the actual world of the critic coincides with the world of the text. Saussy admits this when he says that to fully understand Hebrew poetry, the reader must live as if she were one of the ancient Hebrews and "forget that there is a wider world of poetry out there."[44] DGP write,

> How could the Madhyamaka project be to know that at *other* worlds, but not at this one, everything is empty? It is not like the analogous temporal case, where knowing things about the future and the past can tell us something about the present. This is so because there are causal connections between situations at different times. There are no causal connections between situations at different worlds.[45]

It follows that relegating tetralemmic worlds to impossible worlds distorts our appreciation of Buddhist philosophy. More strictly, DGP reject the compromise of making tetralemmic worlds possible worlds. They argue that this world is itself paraconsistent, that is, it has true contradictions. This acceptance of true contradictions seems a prerequisite to understanding strains of Buddhist philosophy. Now, this is an extreme stance. Though Priest has been advocating dialetheism, the view that, contra classical logic, contradictions are true, for 30 years, his view remains contentious. Surely a critic does not need to subscribe wholly to the views of the text she reads, in order to evaluate it; surely, contra Kuhn, we do not actually live in different, irreconcilable worlds if we have different conceptual schemes. At the same time, DGP make an intuitive argument: if we treat a text as belonging to another world, possible or impossible, our approach to that text does, as I have been arguing, change. DGP often liken Buddhist logic to quantum physics, where, in famous cases such as the wave-particle theory of light and the problem of Schrodinger's cat, the actual world itself appears contradictory. We do not necessarily

---

[42] This resembles Hans-Georg Gadamer's argument for the necessity of prejudice. See Gadamer, "Le Problème Herméneutique," trans. J. -M. Fataud, *Archives De Philosophie* vol. 33, no. 1 (1970): 3–27.

[43] DGP are not saying that all Buddhist texts assert true contradictions, only some texts descended from the Madhyamaka school. Whether these texts do assert true contradictions is itself a matter of debate. See also, Koji Tanaka, "On Nagarjuna's Ontological and Semantic Paradox," *Philosophy East and West: A Quarterly of Comparative Philosophy* vol. 66, no. 4 (2016): 1294–98.

[44] Jacob Edmond, Haun Saussy, and David Damrosch, "Trying to Make It Real: An Exchange between Haun Saussy and David Damrosch," *Comparative Literature Studies* vol. 53, no. 4 (2016): 671.

[45] Yasuo Deguchi, Jay Garfield, and Graham Priest, "The Contradictions Are True—And It's Not Out of This World! A Response to Takashi Yagisawa," *Philosophy East and West* 63, no. 3 (July 1, 2013): 371.

need to be versed in quantum mechanics to understand, say, the poetry of medieval Sōtō Zen poet Dōgen, but it does seem, as DGP claim, to help us grasp the logic of Dōgen's work. This is another way of thinking of the problematic accessibility relations between @ and literary worlds.[46] Even if we reject their prescriptions, we should look more closely at the conceptual difficulty DGP have uncovered.

I have noted that all versions of literary worlds theory assume a common ground that allows for mutual intelligibility. Here, I will look at that ground more closely. For each critic, the ground is shared physical space. Neither Beecroft nor Hayot criticizes Moretti and Casanova too much; both simply wish to supplement the world systems model with literary ecologies or worlds that allow for more pluralism. Saussy, on the other hand, sharply rebukes Moretti and Casanova. He writes:

> Moretti commends "distant reading": not reading actual literary works but reading descriptions of literary works, compiled by experts in the different languages and traditions, and making possible a kind of universal overview. Such encyclopedism really only takes to a caricatural proportion a certain relation often found between comparative work and the work in "national languages," as we call them, that comparison relies on for its material.[47]

In Saussy's opinion, world systems "flatten" literary works, robbing them of their depth, reducing them to points on a map. He advocates comparison that is constantly "reaching over into other people's areas of knowledge" and mapping "new frontiers."[48] Yet Saussy's literary worlds still exist in a single dimension. This is evident when he takes the metaphor of literary worlds literally, speaking of comparison as akin to communicating with unknown planets[49] or different attempts to chart the universe in the eighteenth century.[50] Although Saussy rejects the world systems model, he relies upon spatial metaphors to understand how communication between literary worlds is possible. For Beecroft, Hayot, and Saussy, literary worlds may be out of this world, but they are never out of this universe.

Practically, what does a constellation of belief do for a literary work? We saw in the introduction the importance of the Chan Buddhist and Daoist constellation of belief in which Hinton puts the literary world of Du Fu. Let us take another example from a different tradition: the poetry of the *Kokin Wakashū* 古今和歌集. The oldest imperial poetic anthology, the *Kokin Wakashū*, or *Kokinshū* 古今集 for short, bathes in the Buddhist atmosphere of early Heian 平安時代 Japan. The collection is divided into 20 books spread across different parts: the seasons (1–6), the most important topic; various events

---

[46] As Friedrich Schleiermacher writes, inhabiting the world of the writer is impossible. The literary critic forms an approximate idea of the meaning of a text by reference to the unknowable totality of meanings of the writer's language. See Schleiermacher, *Hermeneutics: The Handwritten Manuscripts*, trans. James Duke and Jack Forstman, ed. Heinz Kimmerle, Atlanta: Scholars Press, 1977, 78–84.
[47] Edmond, Saussy, and Damrosch, "Trying to Make it Real," 667.
[48] Ibid., 673–74.
[49] Saussy, "Interplanetary," 446.
[50] Edmond, Saussy, and Damrosch, "Trying to Make it Real," 668.

including partings 離別 and travel 羈旅 (7–10); love (11–15); and miscellany including laments哀傷 (16–20). The seasons are the key to the world of the *Kokinshū*. The structure, starting in spring in ending in winter, endows all aspects of the collection with the sense of an inevitable trajectory—the freshness of spring leads to the austerity of winter, the joy of meeting leads to the sorrow of parting. Yet while nature renews itself each year, the loss experienced in human life cannot be redeemed. All of this fits within a Buddhist world focusing on the impermanence of earthly life and the insignificance of humanity within the cosmos.[51] Naturally, nothing in this description makes such poetry mutually unintelligible to European poetry to, giving just one example, the elegies of John Donne. When we think about the legacy of the *Kokinshū* in later poetry, however, we can see how the willingness or not to enter into this constellation of belief affects later poets' interpretations of the collection, and the analogies used to make the *Kokinshū* fit into the ontology of a modern poet.

When critics like Hinton, Saussy, or Hayot talk about the world of a poem, the implication is that the world is coherent, and remains so when accessed by different readers. However, when we think about the relations between parts of the texts and the whole, or between individual poems and a collection, we find, unremarkably, that elements of a world might become salient to one reader while other elements are ignored. For instance, imagine we encounter a reader who believes that the *Kokinshū* is crystalized by this sentiment:

花の色はかすみにこめて見せずともかをだにぬすめ春の山かぜ[52]

(If you cannot reveal the colors of the flowers that lie concealed in the mist, at least send bursting forth their scent, Spring Mountain Breeze.)

Rather than this one:

わがまたぬ年はきぬれど冬草のかれにし人はおとづれもせず[53]

(The new year I do not await comes tomorrow. The winter grass has withered, and from that distant person there have been no tidings.)

Both of these poems touch on the intangible (the unseen weighs most heavily here, be it the lost friend or the unobservable scent), but the spring poem suggests that the unseen could be transported back (on the clothing of a friend or lover returned back home?) as an adequate token of the actual object. There is no such replacement for the departed friend in the winter poem. Taken together, these poems affirm the cosmology outlined earlier, the supremacy of nature, the impermanence of human ties, the linking

---

[51] Cf. Haruo Shirane, *Japan and the Culture of the Four Seasons: Nature, Literature, and the Arts*, New York: Columbia UP, 2012, 21–22.
[52] Tsurayuki Ki. *Kokin wakashū*, ed. Tsuneya Okumura, Tōkyō: Shinchōsha, 1978, 55.
[53] Ibid., 130.

of the four seasons to the decline of a human life. If, however, a reader, or, better still, a modern poet, drawing inspiration from the *Kokinshū*, were to base her work on the sentiment in the first poem while ignoring the pessimistic attitude of the second, what would our response be? Likely, we would say that she has not quite understood the work, or that she has an eccentric vision of it. But we would not say that she has entered fully into the world of the imperial poetry collection. From this obvious point we reach a more important one: our evaluations of understandings of literary worlds do indeed assume that the deep-level ontology, the entire constellation of belief, is necessary. And much of modern transnational literature, as later chapters of this work will show, owes to the efforts of writers who could only partly enter into the world of older works to approach these older literary worlds by degrees.

A common ground is indispensable for world literature, but does that entail a metalanguage, or something like Beecroft and Hayot's modes? In the next section, 'Ontological Vagueness' we will see that Lloyd explicitly rejects a metalanguage. Here, let us look at what Priest has to say. The limits of expression and thought, Priest says, always lead to contradiction. We noted earlier Davidson's claim that the totality of truth conditions is beyond the knowledge of any one speaker. For Davidson, as Priest notes, the truth conditions of every language form a Tarskian theory of truth: A theory of truth for a language allows us to give truth conditions for any sentence in that language. Any statement in language L can be described through a metalanguage M, allowing us to analyze L without the circularity that analyzing one sentence in L with another sentence in L would entail. Priest says that a theory of truth will give an analysis of a sentence s such that "s is true IFF s is not true," that is, the theory will generate the Liar Paradox.[54] The same is true for the ineffable: "To say what cannot be expressed, one has to express the very thing."[55] What this means is that meaning of all the sentences of a language always goes beyond what that language can express. What about Quine, who declares that all reference is relative to a language and conceptual scheme? According to Priest:

> Quine says that we can make the sense of a query determinate by translating into a background language. But it cannot do this if the statements of the background language do not themselves have determinate sense. And of course, they do not, according to Quine.[56]

Since the background language must, following Quine's logic, be itself indeterminate, there is no way to understand "how we manage to refer to one thing rather than another."[57] Priest says that this too is a contradiction, because if reference is not absolute it would be relative, which would take us down a regression where truth "is relative to an idiolect, and so to a person," which Quine himself rejected elsewhere.[58] In order for his theory of indeterminacy to work, Quine ends up needing the absolute reference that he

---

[54] Graham Priest, *Beyond the Limits of Thought*, Oxford: Oxford UP, 2002, 206.
[55] Ibid., 207.
[56] Ibid., 202.
[57] Ibid.
[58] Ibid., 203.

disavows. Priest shows that Quine and Davidson alike wind up with self-contradictory notions of translation.

What about trans-world identity, when one character appears across worlds? A change in a text could create a new literary world or change a possible world to an impossible world. Let us imagine changes in character. Take the character Sherlock Holmes. Arthur Conan Doyle explained that after being defeated by Professor Moriarty, Holmes spent two years posing as a Norwegian in Tibet. Recently, Jamyang Norbu picked up on this idea and wrote *Sherlock Holmes: The Missing Years*, which develops the story of Holmes's time in the Himalayas. Intuitively, we understand Norbu's Holmes to be the same as Doyle's, and the world of *The Missing Years* to be the same as the world of *A Study in Scarlet*. Still, we understand that Norbu, writing from a postcolonial perspective, has described neither Holmes nor Tibet as Doyle would have done. Upon reflection, it seems that Holmes has multiple identities given to him by writers responding to his original creator, Doyle. We might say that one is Norbu's Holmes and the other Doyle's Holmes. There is, naturally, the distinction between world types and world tokens: every instance of Sherlock Holmes in fiction is part of a token world of the type "Sherlock Holmes." Different representations of Holmes lead, as Priest notes, to "bifurcating worlds."[59] Yet, if this leads to worlds where not only has Holmes drastically changed from his typical characterization but also where the very ontology of the world has become one that is inaccessible from @, then the problem of critical understanding reemerges. Here the difference between modal logic (which is concerned with truth) and literary worlds (about the truth of which we usually do not care) becomes important. The criteria of identity for a literary work and for literary characters can lead to contradiction when we adopt literary worlds theory, and our own sociohistorical grounding can cause us to behave differently toward characters of the same type across different worlds. Literary worlds can reproduce the problems that Beecroft, Hayot, and Saussy, by invoking modality, strive earnestly to avoid.

On this point, it is important to note the "classical" texts, to which the writers we meet across this book respond, are themselves the products of an analogy between something familiar and something foreign. This is most obvious in the "ancient" text we meet in the next chapter, the *Tibetan Book of the Dead*. In 1919, Walter Evans-Wentz, the book's "translator," "chanced upon a Tibetan text and asked the English teacher of the Maharaja's Boarding School for boys in Gangtok, Sikkim to translate it for him. What is known in the West as the *Tibetan Book of the Dead* is the result of their collaboration."[60] The *Tibetan Book* is not the only text known as the *Bardo Tödöl* in Tibetan, nor is the Evans-Wentz text, with its mass of commentaries and prefaces, nearly equivalent to any one of these *Bardos*. Evans-Wentz and his collaborator worked with an eighth-century text attributed to "the great Indian tantric master Padmasambhava, who visited Tibet in the eighth century," a

---

[59] Graham Priest, *Towards Non-being*, Oxford: Oxford UP, 2016, 121.
[60] Donald S. Lopez, *The Tibetan Book of the Dead: A Biography*, Princeton: Princeton UP, 2011, 2. Lopez mentions that Evans-Wentz never visited Tibet, and argues that the popularity of the *Tibetan Book* owes in part to Tibet never having been colonized by European powers and remaining a mysterious and "largely inaccessible" place (5–6).

text which was subsequently lost before being rediscovered in in the fourteenth century.[61] Not only is the *Tibetan Book* not well-known in Tibet, but it has been translated, commented upon, and received worldwide in such a way that it is less a Tibetan than an American book. As Donald Lopez puts it,

> Removing the *Bardo* from the moorings of language and culture, from time and space, Evans-Wentz transformed it into *The Tibetan Book of the Dead* and set it afloat in space, touching down at various moments in various cultures over the course of the past century, providing in each case an occasion to imagine what it might mean to be dead.[62]

The *Tibetan Book* is a modern amalgam masquerading as a classical piece. All the same, the process Lopez sketches can be found in "authentic" texts as well. Lucas Klein has forcefully argued that both modern and Classical Chinese texts are the product of a compromise between "foreignization" and "nativization." In Klein's words, "poetic Chineseness itself is a product of translation, nativizing and foreignizing from sources abroad and in the past."[63] Du Fu participates in a dialogue across different cultures in the present (what Klein calls "horizontal") as well as within his culture over time (what Klein calls "vertical") as much as does a twentieth-century poet like Bian Zhilin. Du Fu's canonization hides the ways in which his work was a compromise between the foreign and the native, or the vertical and the horizontal. But the process, as Klein describes it, is a constant in the history of Chinese literature, and, as I will show, in many more literatures besides. Klein's "horizontal" and "vertical" axes recall Moretti's "waves" (the international spread of literature and literary genres) and "trees" (national traditions),[64] but the crucial difference is that Klein's eschewing of Moretti's "distant reading" allows his approach to be adapted to serious consideration of the ontological restricting that occurs in translation.

For a simple example, we can return to the Tang dynasty. In 枕中記 (zhěnzhōng jì), known in English as "The World inside a Pillow," we find a Daoist and Chinese Buddhist image of the world.[65] A *chuanqi* 傳奇 ("strange tale," but usually designating any piece of fiction or *xiaoshuo* 小説 written during the Tang) by historian and writer Shen Jiji 沈既濟, the *Zhenzhong ji* recounts the encounter between a young man, Lu Sheng (盧生), and an old Daoist monk, Lü Weng (呂翁), at an inn in the city of Handan 邯鄲 in modern Hebei 河北. Lu Sheng complains of his failures and general unhappiness in life. Lü Weng gives the young man a porcelain pillow on which to sleep, and as the two men wait for the innkeeper to prepare millet Lu Sheng dreams that he achieves great power and happiness in life. He passes the imperial examinations, and obtains a beautiful wife and

---

[61] Ibid., 2–3.
[62] Ibid., 10–11.
[63] Lucas Klein, *The Organization of Distance: Poetry, Translation, Chineseness*, Leiden: Brill, 2018, 22.
[64] See Moretti, "Conjectures," 54–68.
[65] Nonreligious interpretations of the story are, of course, available. Ming Dong Gu gives a Freudian reading according to which *chuanqi* like Shen Jiji's are expressions of the repressed desires of Tang literati. See Gu, *Chinese Theories of Fiction: A Non-Western Narrative System*, Albany: U of New York P, 2006, 58.

family. Yet his success causes his colleagues to become envious, and, becoming the victim of vicious rumors, Lu Sheng is captured and imprisoned. Lu Sheng comes to realize that his desires caused his downfall and concludes that his life was pointless, before he dies in the dream. Awaking, he finds the Daoist monk eating, and realizes that all had passed in the time it takes to cook a bowl of millet. The monk tells him that "all human happiness is such" (人生之適、亦如是矣).[66] And thus Lu Sheng achieves enlightenment.

A detailed analysis of this *chuanqi* is beyond the scope of this chapter. We can, however, look at how this story and the characters in it have appeared across Japanese literary worlds since Shen Jiji's time. One, Mishima Yukio's *Kantan*, will be discussed in Chapter Three. Here, I will look briefly at the Nō *Kantan* 邯鄲, and Akutagawa Ryūnosuke's short story "Millet Dream" 黄粱夢.[67] In the Nō, which takes its title from the location in which the *Zhenzhong ji* takes place, Rosei 盧生 sets out to meet a Buddhist monk on Mount Yōhi 羊飛山 in the kingdom of Chu. Along the way, Rosei stops at an inn in Handan, where he tells the mistress of the inn—Lü Weng is not found in the Nō—about his despair at not having devoted his life to Buddhism, and his hopes that the monk will help him to find the purpose of his existence. The mistress offers to let Rosei sleep on a pillow she received long before from a Daoist monk, a pillow which, she says, makes the sleeper achieve enlightenment. Rosei agrees to sleep on it while the mistress cooks millet. Rosei dreams that he rises to become emperor of Chu. At a lavish court ceremony, Rosei receives chrysanthemum wine that will ensure the prosperity of Chu in perpetuity. But time begins to blur for Rosei, the seasons rapidly pass, and quickly he finds himself in the depths of winter as the chorus chants of the merging of all seasons into one. The rapid unfolding and sudden blurring of time ceases with the mistress waking Rosei to eat his millet. Seeing that 50 years have passed in such a short time, Rosei achieves enlightenment, and begins the Buddhist chant of admiration for the Three Treasures of Buddhism, *namu sanbō, namu sanbō* 南無三宝、南無三宝.[68]

Akutagawa's "Millet Dream" complicates the picture further. Here, we have only a glimpse of the original *chuanqi*. The story picks begins with Rosei's awakening: "Rosei thought he was dead" (盧生は死ぬのだと思った).[69] The wailing of his dream children and grandchildren fades as he wakes to Lü Weng, called Ro'ō in Japanese, and the innkeeper's millet "even now seemingly not ready" (未だに熟さないらしい).[70] Rosei

---

[66] Shen jiji, "Lü Weng," in *Taiping guangji*, ed. Fang Li, Dai er ban, Beijing: Zhonghua shu ju, 1961, 528. Though the story is most commonly known as *Zhenzhong ji*, the version recorded in *Taiping Guangji*, the Song-era collection of short stories with which I am working, takes its name from the character of the monk.

[67] Foxtail millet 黄粱 is part of the phrase 黄粱一炊, "to lose riches and honor," but literally "the time it takes to cook millet." Hence, Akutagawa's title in Japanese already alludes to the Tang story, and highlights a temporal aspect (the brevity of fortune, or the fleetingness of human vanity) while the title of the Nō highlights a spatial one (the fact of the story taking place in "Kantan," in China and not in Japan).

[68] "Kantan," in *Utaibon Collection*, Tokyo: National Library of Japan Digital Collection (c. 1600), 10–11.

[69] Ryūnosuke Akutagawa, *Akutagawa Ryūnosuke zenshū*, Dai ni maki, ed. Shin'ichirō Nakamura, Tōkyō: Iwanami shoten, 1964, 39.

[70] Ibid.

tells Ro'ō of his dream of having passed the imperial examinations and having risen in the court, acquired a beautiful and modest wife, producing five children and numerous grandchildren, been slandered and sent away yet recalled to court, and finally having died past the age of 80. Ro'ō tells Rosei that all life is like that, and asks Rosei whether, having experienced joy and sorrow, fortune and loss, in the dreamworld, the real world has not become by comparison boring and hollow. Rosei's reply is that he now desires to live even more, to live to the fullest, "truly" (真に).[71] Rosei asks whether the monk does not agree, to which "Ro'ō, with a wry face, gave neither an affirmative or a negative reply" (呂翁は顔をしかめたまま、然りとも否とも答えなかった).[72]

How do we think of the relations between these different 盧生 (Lu Shengs/Roseis)? The changes from the Tang *chuanqi* to the medieval Japanese Nō are numerous. But among them we note that Daoism has been sidelined for Buddhism, and the span of Rosei's life has been brought in line with the cult of the seasons we noted in our discussion of the *Kokinshū*. More subtly, the medieval Japanese fascination for the mountain hermit, here in the guise of the Buddhist monk Rosei seeks, has been inserted into the tale. The shift from Daoism to Buddhism is not a massive shift; as Priest reminds us, early Chinese Buddhism emerged through a synthesis of Buddhist texts with existent Daoist ideas.[73] More interesting is the fact that Japanese Buddhism, developed out of this synthesis between Daoism and Buddhism from India, is then transmitted back in the Japanese imagination to China. Satoru Hashimoto has argued that world literature is an attempt to return back to the origins of a culture or language, to use a foreign text to imagine a different starting point for the native.[74] The implication, in the Nō play, is that the Japanese strain of Buddhism has its origins in a semimythical Chinese source, exemplified by this story taking place in the city of Kantan that would have been, for the medieval Japanese audience, a purely imagined city, distant and mysterious. Consequently, the literary world of the Nō wishes to overwrite the world of the original, to place contemporaneous Japanese ideas at the source, and to act not as if Buddhism came out of Daoism, but as if contemporary Buddhist ideas coexisted with Daoist ones in the remote past.

If we say that this is the same character across two different worlds, we are confronted with the fact that the Japanese text wants to erase the original Lu Sheng. To allow Lu Sheng and Rosei to be the same entity appearing in two different possible worlds is, for the literary critic, perfectly acceptable; but it means that the critic cannot quite enter into the world of the medieval Japanese text, the structure of which intends to negate Lu Sheng in order to create Rosei. And the world of the *Zhenzhong ji* had no inkling of the rival Rosei that would spring up hundreds of years later in a different country. If the world of the *Zhenzhong ji* is unable to access the world of *Kantan*, then symmetry is again

---

[71] Ibid., 40–41.

[72] Ibid., 41.

[73] Graham Priest, *The Fifth Corner of Four: An Essay on Buddhist Metaphysics and the Catuskoti*, Oxford: Oxford UP, 2018, 96.

[74] Satoru Hashimoto, "World of Letters: Lu Xun, Benjamin, and *Daodejing*," *Journal of World Literature* vol. 1, no. 1 (2016): 39–51.

violated. Yet this is perhaps the most accurate way of understanding the world of the original text.

Akutagawa's story is not so much a rival to the Tang story. "Millet Dream," written in 1917, throws us into the world of the *Zhenzhong ji* just at the climax. Akutagawa gives us what we would expect: the Daoist priest, the dialogue between Rosei and Ro'ō about life and enlightenment. Unexpectedly, however, Rosei does not seem to achieve enlightenment and liberation from attachment to this world, but becomes even more committed to life. In itself, this move does not estrange Rosei from Lu Sheng. It is certainly possible that Lu Sheng could have reacted to his dream in such a way. The estrangement comes rather through the final enigmatic line, Ro'ō's refusal to answer. There are, I think, two ways of understanding this silence. On the one hand, we might take it as a "modernist" ending, open-ended and hermetic.[75] The ending would remind us of other abrupt Akutagawa conclusions such as that to "Rashōmon" 羅生門, in which we are given no closure as to the protagonist's whereabouts. This moral relativism, or this failure to choose between different possibilities, with all its shades of Paul Valery's *La Crise de l'esprit*, released two years later in 1919, takes us far from the clear moral message of the Tang text. On the other hand, we could read this refusal to answer as itself a Daoist or Buddhist attempt to transcend dualities, or to answer through silence. This would appear to bring Akutagawa's world in line with Shen Jiji's, yet its focus on the ineffable also removes the modern story from the Tang literati's, with his preference for Confucian didacticism. Though Akutagawa's can be read as expressing a similar Daoist idea to the original, it runs closer to Daoist ideas about transcendence than the original itself does, or outstrips the original and approximates Chan or Zen practices that were solidified centuries after the *chuanqi*.[76] Accordingly, the "modernist" reading can encompass the Tang Daoist-Confucian one, but the "Daoist" reading of Akutagawa cannot accommodate the original, which does not transcend truth and falsity because it has Lü Weng give a yes/no proposition about the meaning of life. We might say that Akutagawa's story is also attempting to rewrite the original world even as it requires the reader to understand the Tang story. If *Kantan* wants to replace the *chuanqi*, "Millet Dream" structures its world by making its relation to the original vague.

The point here, to which we will return in more detail in Chapter Three, is that asserting the identity between characters and links between literary worlds can mask deep-level dissimilarities between worlds and characters. More than that, it can encourage us to overlook what the certain worlds are trying to do: if we assert that the literary world of *Kantan* emerges from that of *Zhenzhong ji*, and that its Rosei is the same as Lu Sheng, we miss that *Kantan* wants to usurp *Zhengzhong ji*, and replace Lu Sheng with Rosei. It makes us miss as well, perhaps, that "Millet Dream" plays upon the vagueness of the link

---

[75] Whether any Japanese literature could be classified as "modernist" is a debate in its own right. See Christopher Bush, "Modernism, Orientalism, and East Asia," in *A Handbook of Modernism Studies*, ed. Jean-Michel Rabaté, Chichester, UK: John Wiley & Sons, 2013, 193–208.

[76] Robert Sharf, "Mindfulness and Mindlessness in Early Chan," *Philosophy East and West* vol. 64, no. 4 (October 1, 2014): 933–64.

between Lu Sheng and Rosei, Lü Weng and Ro'ō, and the worldview of the *chuanqi* and that of its own.

The discussion here reminds us of Nan Da's *Intransitive Encounter: Sino-U.S. Literature and the Limits of Exchange*. Da proposes that we think of transpacific and East–West encounters as "intransitive," intransitivity being characterized by literature's "own awareness of the relational scheme into which it has been drawn and the social task to which it has been assigned."[77] That is, when literature moves abroad, it is forced to cohere into a social, or ontological scheme, that is not its own, and the resultant piece of literature, bearing new meanings and a new cultural valency, is not transferred back to where the original piece originated. The argument is quite astute, and my objective is not to argue against Da but to show how this coherence works, and how it is a constitutive part of transnational and world literature generally. We can see this in the relations between *Zhenzhong ji* and its two adaptations. Because accessibility relations are asymmetrical, *Zhenzhong ji* gives rise to two Japanese works that modify the original to fit within their own cultural matrix, but the world of the original is left intact. Identity here is intransitive. The point is important for the understanding of literary worlds, and shows their utility in world literature. When new literary worlds emerge from older ones, they create a set, a selection of salient elements from the original, that serve as a point of contact between old and new. This process is essentially a way of dealing with the problem of intransitivity, as it makes the old and the new seem as if they are in mutual dialogue. But in fact, the original world remains out of reach. Though we as literary critics seem to have access to all three worlds, as DGP submit in their analysis of Dōgen and possible worlds, intuitively there is an important distinction between what we can entertain as possible *within the world of fiction* and what is possible within *this world*. By saying that one or all of the worlds of *Zhenzhong ji* or *Kantan* are possible as fictional worlds, we are performing a similar ontological rearrangement as the one undertaken by the Nō and Akutagawa's short story to make the Tang original intelligible in a different context.

I have no desire to claim that we cannot make comparisons across different cultures and ontologies. It would be disingenuous to do so in a book on comparative literature. My argument is that there is reason to doubt whether the principle of charity itself is enough to sustain such comparison, and that the cogent work of Lloyd and Saussy would benefit from being put in dialogue with recent work in philosophical approaches to vagueness. The very fact that I have been comparing pieces of literature founded on different ontological schemes suggests that mutual intelligibility is possible. Otherwise, as G. E. R. Lloyd rightly points out, comparison itself would be off limits. The question remains, however, of just how all of these different visions of the world can cohere such that readers can understand them.

We return yet again to Saussy. In *Great Walls of Discourse and Other Adventures in Cultural China*, he draws attention to the ambiguities that make translation possible. Translators, of course, do not reproduce in the target language that which they found in the source

---

[77] Nan Da, *Intransitive Encounter: Sino-U.S. Literature and the Limits of Exchange*, New York: Columbia UP, 2018, 29.

language. Instead, they make words make sense *for* a select group of people, into whose network of language and social practices the translated word comes to fit. In Saussy's words, "the job of the translator is not reproductive, representing a pre-existing meaning in a new milieu, but rather expository and applicational—the task of making something mean something to somebody."[78] He suggests that a translated text amounts to an allegory, since an allegory "is unstable, suspenseful, loosely related to facts, latently contradictory—and so, as I see it, it furnishes a model for a global media culture that addresses everybody all the time but does not stop to integrate all the responses."[79] The translated work transcends the particular boundaries of its place of origin and enters into the world. But it does so by entering into an uneasy compact between its original meaning and the meaning given to it by its translator and the group of people for whom she is translating. Or, rather, the meaning is just that negotiation between the original language and its social situation and the language and social situation, the language game, we might say, of each society.

I think Saussy is correct, but I would like to modify his theory by considering not only translations but adaptations as well. In an adaptation, the translated word, and by extension the translated text, is not a correspondence between two stable entities (the word in the source and the target language) or collections of entities. Rather, words and texts on both sides become ontologically vague through the act of translation. As it is translated from one culture to another, or what I have been calling one constellation of belief to another, the text undergoes a deformation of meaning. In exchange for some of those which they possessed before, texts and the words of which they are composed accrue new senses in virtue of the approximate equivalences that they are given in the new language and constellation. Yet the original constellation itself changes through this act. In the act of making new equivalences when writing across East and West, our understanding of the original constellation of belief changes—those new senses become a part of our understanding of the original constellation. We will see this in Chapter Three: both Claudel's and Mishima's adaptations of the original took those elements which they thought could fit with their own beliefs. In doing so, their understanding of *Kantan* becomes bound up with the adaptation, and this occurs for our understanding as well. We can think here of T. S. Eliot's formulation of tradition: the space that the texts of a given tradition occupy changes as new texts enter into the space and alter the relations and, at the same time, the significances of all other texts contained therein.[80] The same is true of our understanding of *Kantan*. Once these adaptations, these "equivalences," between original and adaptation are established, they become part of our corpus of knowledge surrounding the original text; yet the world of the original text is not itself

---

[78] Haun Saussy, *Great Walls of Discourse and Other Adventures in Cultural China*, Cambridge, MA: Harvard University Asia Center, 2001, 31.
[79] Ibid.
[80] T. S. Eliot, "Tradition and the Individual Talent," *Perspecta* vol. 19 (January 1982): 37–38, doi:10.2307/1567048.

changed. Our understanding of tradition changes with our constellation of belief; the worlds of earlier texts, contra Eliot, stay as they were.

If this is the case, then something peculiar has happened to our understanding of the original text. I proposed earlier that the actual world @ of any text is inaccessible to the critic. Does this commit us to an odd understanding of @? It seems that, if the actual world of any text is inaccessible to us after its completion and publication, the reason must either be that we have imperfect knowledge of @ as such, or @ changes from moment to moment. The latter interpretation appears absurd: if @ changes from moment to moment, the "actual world" is akin to an indexical expression. Just as that to which "I" refers changes depends on the speaker, and changes even given the "same" speaker, depending on the spatiotemporal point occupied by and the physiological composition of the speaker, so too the actual world refers at every moment to something different. This, of course, is thinly veiled idealism, precisely the sort that I have rejected. The only other possibility is that we simply have imprecise knowledge of the @ of any given text, which sounds like a more workable proposition. Yet we run into similar problems. If our understanding of @ is always imperfect, and this makes the @ of a given text inaccessible, then surely each of us possesses an understanding of this @ that is subtly different from everyone else's knowledge. Idealism too rears its head here. Worse, this means that none of us ever inhabits the same @ as any other. And, moreover, it *invites* the problem of the first alternative: our usage of @ becomes indexical, shifting depending on time and place of use. If this is how we understand @, our notion of an "actual world" is too loose to tell us anything useful.

Are we able to save this understanding of @ that I advanced? It is intuitive. Few scholars would contest that our knowledge of all of the conditions that went into the production of any given text is incomplete, and so also our knowledge of what makes up the @ of the text is imperfect. Could we retain this conception without giving in to idealism? I think the answer is yes, but we first need to find out what happens to things that move from being real *and* actual to being apparently inaccessible from our actual world. And we need to find out how community consciousness fixes the boundaries of the actual world.

Ontological Vagueness

We have seen that models of world systems, literary worlds, and pragmatic compromises between one and many worlds all feature some flaws in their efforts to model that which happens in the communication and comprehension of literature between languages and literatures. My concern now will be to supplement the concept of literary worlds and multidimensionality with current work in the philosophy of vagueness. For the rest of this chapter, and the rest of this work, I am going to argue that *ontological vagueness* characterizes the space of literary interaction. By *ontological vagueness* I mean that the boundaries between ideas are indistinct; there are no sharp cut-off points. The boundaries are not fuzzy because we are unaware of where the boundaries lie—that would be epistemic vagueness, and the fault would be our own ignorance. On the contrary, the borders between ideas are necessarily fuzzy, and, regardless of how much we know, fuzzy they will remain. I will present a "weak" model that, building upon recent work in philosophical logic and world literature, allows us to map relations between different literary works. But first I need to justify my claim of ontological vagueness.

The "very otherness of the Other," Lloyd contends, "when we can get a hold of it, is a precious resource for us to broaden our intellectual and imaginative horizons."[81] Focusing on difference can allow critics to imagine alternatives to their concepts. Do we need one origin to explain everything? That is, do we need all cultures and literatures to have a common origin in order to compare? The question is not particular to Lloyd, but has also been raised in the study of world literature itself. Numano Mitsuyoshi, using similar language, asserts that the term "'world literature' has many 'dimensions' (側面), and unifying them all in a single definition is impossible" (「世界文学」といっても様々な側面があり、一元的な定義は不可能である).[82] A common origin or ground may be asserted but comparatists, Lloyd argues, do not need to prove that different concepts need to be compared before comparing. The fact that concepts can be put in some sort of opposition entails mutual intelligibility. No "meta-language" is needed. "Cosmologies are not generally encapsulated in well-formed formulae and normally allow a good deal of room" for interpretation.[83] This is a Davidsonian approach, of course. The point is that the ground on which comparison takes place is primitive, unable to be grounded without circularity, as, for instance, in the assertion that all human propositions are mutually intelligible because all human propositions are human.[84]

Nonetheless, Lloyd does envision a *tertium comparationis*: reality. Unlike Saussy's formulation, reality here is not synonymous with nature, but does remind us of Quine and Davidson's emphasis on intersubjectivity as the basis of communication. Lloyd believes that nature is an artifact of human culture. Different cultures carve up nature in different ways. Lloyd's favorite example is that of color. One culture may classify color according to hue, others according to luminosity, but there is no one correct classification.[85] These different ontologies suggest that our experience of nature is not a given but varies according to how we experience reality. It is difficult to say what "reality" itself is, but presumably it is the brute physical world, or the world of sense data, that each human being encounters. This is the multidimensionality of reality. Rather than having a single actual world @, or an actual world that is a mereological sum of its parts, we can speak of an actual world with many dimensions. Multidimensionality draws attention to the ontological beliefs of the critic and the writer and the many contending ontologies that abound in the actual world. Reality is stripped down to the most basic level, that of a

---

[81] G. E. R. Lloyd, *Analogical Investigations: Historical and Cross-Cultural Perspectives on Human Reasoning*, Cambridge: Cambridge UP, 2015, 31. On the surface, this is similar to Francois Jullien's belief that the alterity of China is a valuable resource for French scholars. However, Lloyd is concerned with degrees of difference between separate languages and literary traditions, not irreconcilable otherness. For a critique of Jullien, see Zhang, *Unexpected Affinities*, 11–14.

[82] Mitsuyoshi Numano, "Sekai (bungaku) to ha nanika." *Shisō* no. 1147 (November 2019): 9–23, 9.

[83] Lloyd, *Analogical Investigations*, 38.

[84] Ibid., 121.

[85] Ibid., 24.

shared space, and all of our presumptions of what reality entails are called into question. These are aspects that, as DGP have shown, may not even be present.

It is best, then, to think of two literary worlds, not as possible worlds that access (or do not access) one another, but as composed of different dimensions that have different correspondences with different worlds. Each "dimension" of a literary space is made up of multiple domains: stylistic, formal, historical, ontological.[86] This multiplicity with porous yet imprecise borders that bleed into one another captures the vexing problem that Numano himself flags in relation to the current study of world literature: to study world literature, with all the desired breadth, it is not enough to know a few languages, it seems, nor even all the languages of Europe, impossible as the task may be, but all the languages and literatures of the world,[87] each with its own background; yet, because of globalization dividing up literatures into neat compartments is becoming all the more trying.[88] Obviously, we cannot rise to this impossible task, but we can better delimit our knowledge by stressing the many planes on which transnational and world literature exist, and the seemingly paradoxical fashions in which literary worlds appear to access and not access one another. The correspondences between Tang and modern *tanka* or French poetry are different in terms of what is shared and how much is shared from the correspondences between Tang and Heian poetry. I am taking my lead here from probabilistic approaches to vagueness. Nicholas J. J. Smith describes his probabilistic approach as "motivated by the basic idea that outside precise realms such as mathematics, objects may possess properties to intermediate degrees, in between complete possession and complete lack thereof."[89] This is in contrast to modal logic in which each proposition is mapped to a crisp (i.e., non-fuzzy) domain as a subset of a possible world.[90] Instead of the all-or-nothing problem that underlies literary worlds, when we apply this line of thinking to world literature we allow for the unexpected overreaches into other people's

---

[86] Without considering ontological differences, Hoyt Long and Richard Jean So have recently tried to map stylistic proximity between literatures. I believe their approach is congenial to multidimensionality. See Long and So, "Turbulent Flow," *Modern Language Quarterly* vol. 77, no. 3 (2016): 345–67. My argument also recalls recent work by Harsha Ram on a "scalar" account of global modernism, an account that tries to deal with "the collision of nation and empire and the persistence of shifting older legacies, local and transregional." Ram, "The Scale of Global Modernisms: Imperial, National, Regional, Local," *PMLA Publications of the Modern Language Association of America* vol. 131, no. 5, (October 2016): 1375, doi:10.1632/pmla.2016.131.5.1372. The difference of my approach in relation to Ram's is that my interest is not only in how different literary traditions interact in the modern era but also in how foreign and older ideas are brought into the realm of intelligibility.

[87] We might think here of Erich Auerbach's early-twentieth-century assertion of a like idea: the materials and languages of comparative literature are too vast, and we cannot aspire to know them all. We can find a suitable "point of departure" (*Ausgangspunkt*) for our enquiry, and understand our comparisons as delimited by the reference frame of this point of departure. See Auerbach, "Philology and 'Weltliteratur,'" trans. Maire Said and Edward Said, *The Centennial Review* vol. 13, no. 1 (Winter 1969): 1–17.

[88] Numano, "Sekai," 14.

[89] Nicholas J. J. Smith, *Vagueness and Degrees of Truth*, Oxford: Oxford UP, 2008, 211.

[90] Ibid., 225.

areas of knowledge that Saussy calls for without relegating those areas to different worlds. We keep all the worlds here as dimensions of the same reality. This is possible because vagueness is built into our understanding of how world literature works.

The particular concept that I wish to take from Smith and add to multidimensionality is *relative closeness*. Closeness refers to the judgment a competent speaker of a language makes regarding the degree of similarity between a group of objects. Smith defines *relative closeness* as a ternary relation: "x is at least as close to y, in F-relevant aspects, as it is to z."[91] For multidimensionality, let us say that "F" is a predicate, such as "is Buddhist," "is Modern," "is Tang." Here, x, y, and z are texts or parts of texts. We automatically discern closeness relations between works and types of literature; this is what goes toward making up literary worlds, or, more generally, classification of movements like modernism or genres like theater. This notion of closeness reveals an underlying metrical structure, a mapping of items linearly according to their distance from a given predicate, that accords well with the spatial metaphors that underlie literary worlds theory and Lloyd's multidimensionality. It also highlights the role of contrast in forming literary worlds. To say that a work from an author other than Arthur Conan Doyle is part of the world or set of worlds of Sherlock Holmes, we ask whether the work in question presents a world that is at least as similar to a work already known to be in the world of Sherlock Holmes as it is to any other work. The notion here of what makes up a world, and so what properties we are comparing is vague, and any attempt make such a comparison would imply an effort beyond the scope of this work. The *F*-relevant predicate may focus on style, voice, character, depiction of background characters, or stances toward colonialism. For the time being, let me say that this approach is one of contrast or difference: classification depends on a text being at least as similar to another text as it is to any other text rather than being "sufficiently" similar to any text.[92]

Vagueness gives us a better sense of what happens in translation between East and West. This approach especially tries to retain the sense of difference that each of the critics I have discussed finds important to the study of literature. It does so by foregrounding the different ontologies upon which works of world literature are based. Though it is not possible to view Hebrew poetry as the Hebrews did, or for most critics to appreciate aspects of Dōgen with the immediacy of a dialetheist, bringing deep ontological differences to the fore can enhance our appreciation of foreign works. Discussing *Journey to the West*, whose Buddhist themes Arthur Waley downplayed in his translation, Anthony C. Yu states that "our understanding of the text demands our taking the allegorical elements seriously."[93] A translation or a critical appraisal that makes the foreign familiar and tries to ground the many works of world literature on a single plane helpfully reminds us of the common elements that all texts, if only as human productions, share. Yet we also need

---

[91] Ibid., 143.

[92] This is analogous to some recent work in cognitive science in the field of conceptual spaces. See Richard Dietz, "Comparative Concepts," *Synthese* vol. 190, no. 1 (2013): 139–70.

[93] Anthony C. Yu, *Comparative Journeys: Essays on Literature and Religion East and West*, New York: Columbia UP, 2008, 178.

"[e]xternal knowledge and references" to help "in our attempt to decipher intentionality and meaning" that a particular author or society had.[94] By focusing on ontologies, we foreground the deeply rooted elements that make up the texts of world literature, that nourish literary ecologies and create literary worlds. We get the sense of otherness, but we also get a sense of commonality because everything stems from contact with a single reality and exists as a dimension of this one world. The metaphor of multidimensionality ultimately balances the twin claims of identity and difference better than does that alone of literary worlds that are either too immanent or too remote. Speaking further about *Journey*, Yu writes, "I can conclude with the assertion that taking religion seriously in the case of this novel has the paradoxical effect of retrieving historicity by attentiveness to contemporaneity, of preserving foreignness in the very quest for readability."[95] This paradox of living in one world that seems to be several, of having one conceptual scheme yet being capable of understanding others, is the bedrock of multidimensionality.

Any formulation of the theory here would take into account two principles: asymmetry and ontological vagueness. Asymmetry says that the more x something becomes, the less y it becomes. Applying this to world literature, we say that the closer one gets to living in, to use our standard example, the world of the Hebrews, the less one lives in any other world, including @. Ontological vagueness says that there is no sharp cutoff between parts of literary dimensions. There is no precise moment at which we cross from, say, the stylistic domain of Tang poetry to that of early Japanese imperial collections like the *Kokinshū*. And differences between dimensions are not equal. Instead of all-or-nothing accessibility relations, we have degrees of proximity, so that Tang poetry may be closer to French symbolism than either is to Anglo-Saxon hagiography. Everything is connected, but those connections are manifested variously.

The problem with accessibility relations between possible worlds and @, then, is not that each individual person has an @ that changes moment to moment and cannot access any other (this would be absurdly solipsistic and render much, if not all, scholarly work useless). Rather, it is the problem of changing we-consciousness. *Who* makes up the *we* in this consciousness is itself vague. We could not pin down all of the members of a Nō community in medieval Japan, or fix all the points in the constellation of belief in which Akutagawa's vision of the world is contained. It is a non-crisp set, or set of such sets, that we are bound to use heuristically. We can neither be sure exactly which elements go into the set nor know when exactly the set ceased to be actual. No more can we precisely know when our own set came into existence and what boundaries it has. Yet, by paying attention to this concept of accessibility and vagueness we can guard against the overreaching confidence that, as I have shown, can go into the study of East–West literature.

If this is correct, then we need a revised understanding of the Davidsonian principle of charity. Since the principle makes a statement spoken in reference to one ontology coherent in another, it can actually make a statement less intelligible. Priest also touches

---

[94] Ibid.
[95] Ibid., 307.

on it, and does so more directly in relation to fiction. Should a critic encounter an inconsistent story (a story closed under a nonclassical logic), it would be incorrect to use the principle of charity to make the story intelligible to the critic and his or her audience. Priest wrote his own inconsistent short story, "Sylvan's Box" closed under a paraconsistent logic (a logic that allows for contradiction) to illustrate the point. Priest writes that

> it is quite possible to have a story that is inconsistent, and essentially so. *Sylvan's Box*, [...] is a story that is inconsistent. But the inconsistency is no accident; it is essential to the plot. In particular, anyone who misapplied the principle of charity to interpret the story in a consistent way would have entirely misunderstood it. And its essence is entirely lost in any (collection of) consistent parts of it. Yet it is a coherent story. There is a determinate plot: not everything happens in the story; and people act in intelligible ways, even when the inconsistent is involved.[96]

If Priest is correct, and I am inclined to think he is—the various examples of understanding across cultures and languages that make up the rest of this book will show my reasons for so agreeing—then there is not necessarily a danger, but a deformation that can occur when the principle of charity is applied. Why this deformation occurs and how we, as literary critics should approach it, is still to be addressed.

Here is the coincidence of weak theory, weak modernism, and literary worlds. We might well call it "weak world literature." Weakness, or the open-mindedness, the willingness to be surprised by one's own data, is a useful tool for world literature and transnational studies because literature in translation, be it across languages or across times, is fundamentally vague. This is at odds with approaches like those of Susan Stanford Friedman and Eric Hayot, insightful as they are, because it distinguishes between the pastness of the past and our attempts to make it present. When Friedman identifies Tang poetry as modern or Hayot sees Heian prose as realist, what they are doing is similar to the process of world formation we have seen across this book: making something strange make sense in a contemporary belief system. This is "strong" world literature because, though it weakens the boundaries of modern categories like "realism" and "modernism" and spies their presence in older, non-European contexts, it ultimately assumes that all literatures and times cohere seamlessly in a single world system. And even if we borrow our terms from non-European traditions to create a metalanguage of modernism by, say, calling "prose" not prose but 散文, *sanbun*, "scattered composition," we necessarily change the concept by wrenching it from its original ontology and placing it in a new one, just as the bits of *Kantan* metamorphosed in translation onto the medieval and modern Japanese stages. The process is a creative one. But we must distinguish between the (epistemological) act of understanding a text and the (ontological) act of making it fit into a single system.

"Weak" world literature pays attention, on the contrary, to the disconnections, the ruptures, the ways in which concepts from one literary world *don't* get ferried across to another world, or become something else entirely on the way. By taking seriously the ways

---

[96] Priest, *Towards Non-Being*, 121.

in which East Asian languages and literatures have traditionally had their own worlds, and their own ontologies, not all of which suddenly evaporated in the face of imperialism and modernity, we will see the utility of this weak world literature and the importance of ontological vagueness that it heeds.[97] Beginning with the Chou-Hughes *Bardo Thödol*, the following four case studies will help to work through the notion of vagueness and identity in literature, through how the literary world, the set of worlds, and the constellation of belief as I described them in the introduction interact in practice. The case studies will enable us better to see when "charitably" interpreting a foreign text furnishes a useful bridge over a cultural divide, and when, as Priest and Lloyd suggest, the "very otherness of the other," and the challenges of understanding the limits of our current theories, calls for us to weaken our approach and search, like Claudel, for "une nouvelle logique."

---

[97] On the persistence of East Asian literary worlds in the modern era, see Satoru Hashimoto, "Afterlives of the Culture: Engaging with the Trans-East Asian Cultural Tradition in Modern Chinese, Japanese, Korean, and Taiwanese Literatures, 1880s–1940s," Harvard University Dissertation, 2014.

Part 2
DRAMATIC WORLDS

Chapter Two

THE CHOU-HUGHES *BARDO THÖDOL* AND THE PROBLEM OF CLASSIFICATION

In 1958, Ted Hughes moved to America. At that time, Hughes was not the poetic institution that he was to become, nor the controversial figure that his relationship with his first wife, Sylvia Plath, was to make him. On the contrary, Hughes was a little-known poet who came to the United States in order for his new wife to take up a faculty position in English at Smith College. Hughes himself began teaching that year at the University of Massachusetts. During this time of change and uncertainty Hughes decided to spend time at the artist colony Yaddo in upstate New York. The move was to have far-reaching, if often subtle, influences on the rest of Hughes's career. It was also to generate an incomplete text the composition of which exemplifies the process of world formation in transnational and world literature: the libretto for a planned operatic adaptation of the *Bardo Thödol*, known best in the West as the *Tibetan Book of the Dead*.

Conceived in collaboration with the Chinese American composer Chou Wen-chung, whom Hughes had met at Yaddo, the *Bardo* is an operatic adaptation of Walter Evans-Wentz's 1927 *The Tibetan Book of the Dead* (hereafter, the *Tibetan Book*), a translation of texts related to Tibetan Buddhism. The opera was never staged, and we have very little direct knowledge of the *Bardo*, nor much knowledge of its intended audience, aside from the assumption that it would have likely been American or British. Neither Chou nor Hughes ever stated in detail what type of opera they envisioned the *Bardo* to be, nor did they explain but in passing the evident debt of the libretto script to East Asian and European theaters. To understand the *Bardo*, we need to examine both the unfinished *Bardo* text and the scraps Chou and Hughes left behind. Such a process reveals the *Bardo* as a fascinating, if failed, attempt to fuse East and West, an attempt that would preoccupy Chou and Hughes throughout their careers. The *Bardo* project takes us across disciplines, media, nations, and time periods, and, for good measure, includes attempts to define and transcend "Westerness" and "Chineseness." By looking at the *Bardo* in depth, I will make my first case for the utility of a weakened version of literary worlds theory for the study of translational literature. By looking at the project both as an important moment in the development of both Chou's and Hughes's aesthetics, and as a case of literary world formation, we grasp the multidimensionality of the work and the ways in which it uses the vagueness of world literature to create a unique product. To go back to Paul Saint-Amour and "weak theory," however, this entails that we treat the *Bardo* in "specific, non-totalizing ways," and attend also to the ways in which the work seems to split apart and reorganize the worlds of its source material. The fact that the *Bardo* is unfinished allows us more readily to see how it plays, or was meant to play, on the ontological vagueness of the original to become a new world in which "East" and "West" could flow together. Lucas Klein's division between "horizontal" and "vertical" transmission, where vertical refers to transmission within a literary tradition across time and horizontal across different literary traditions in the present, will be instrumental here. I will try to push this further to connect Klein's schema to recent work on the structure of analogy itself. The payoff will be a more lucid view of the process of creating literary worlds in transnational literature, with all of the ontological shuffling involved brought more fully to light.

Our first stop is the *Bardo* typescript itself. Before diving into this dense world, let us have a look at it from afar by way of a general sketch. The action goes thus. The Reader of the Bardo and a "Guide and Instructor," termed "A" and "B" in Hughes's draft, await the appearance of a dead soul, called "Solo." Throughout there is a chorus of mourners and karmic voices. A and B begin by invoking the names of the Buddha and various deities. They coax Solo into accepting his death. Should he do so, he will attain Buddhahood. Solo is not willing. He is confused by the sight of mourners around his dead body. He wishes to return to life, and misses the first opportunity at Buddhahood. A and B continue to coach him. Solo becomes fixated on a series of deities that slowly grow more threatening. Solo misses chance after chance to "break the cycle of death and rebirth." His "passions" bind him to his body. Eventually, Buddhahood passes him and he is doomed to be reborn. At the end A, B, and Solo invoke the Holy Dharma. Solo swears never again to be bound to the flesh and to succeed when next in the Bardo.

Hughes's libretto is, superficially, not terribly different from his early work:

A: Bound by evil Karma, bound by terror and longing,
Resisting Grace, the five great Lights, the five wisdoms, you linger.
These are illusory:
These are your own mind:
Had you recognised them
Long since you had been gathered into a glorious Buddhahood.
B: Now you remain in the miseries of the Bardo.[1]

I will return to Hughes's eccentric understanding of Buddhism and the other religious elements of this text later. For the moment, let us linger over the form of the text. With its irregular blank lines, its dialogue that reads more as narrative, and its rhetorical flair—the anaphora of "bound," "the five," and "these are"; the asyndeton that piles up clauses before and dwarfs the addressee as in the first three lines; the abrupt final line written in more straightforward syntax—all of these recall Hughes's technique in his first poetry collection, 1957's *The Hawk in the Rain*. To give but one example from that collection, take the conclusion of "Vampire":

You plead, limp, dangling in his mad voice, till
With a sudden blood-splitting cough, he chokes: he leaves
Trembling, soon after. You slump back down in a chair
Cold as a leaf, your heart scarcely moving […]

---

[1] Ted Hughes, *Selected Translations*, ed. Daniel Weissbort, New York: Farrar, Strauss, and Giroux, 2006, 6.

> Deep under the city's deepest stone,
> This grinning sack is bursting with your blood.[2]

Among the similarities, we might even chalk up the interest in exotic, the macabre, represented in the one by Tibetan ritual and in the other by the near-Eastern figure of the vampire. The rhetorical figures of the original are present: the anaphora of "you plead [...] you slump"; the anastrophe of the second line, though this introduces chiasmus not present in the *Bardo* extract; the use of the present tense and the second person, with the closing couplet again more syntactically regular than the preceding lines. Added to this are the heavy alliteration of this extract— "Deep under the city's deepest stone, / This grinning sack is bursting with your blood"—that resonates yet further with the *Bardo* extract—"gathered into glorious Buddhahood"—and pulls both poems toward a Yeatsian world in which rhetorically taut and rich lines are made to convey dark supernatural content. Finally, while "Vampire" is more visceral than the *Bardo* here, as later extracts in this chapter will show, the *Bardo* matches the older poem's taste for gory details. Looking at the *Bardo* from this angle, we see it merely as Hughes using a tried-and-true mold on new, but in many ways expected, material. Yet, a closer look at the history of the Chou-Hughes project uncovers a complicated process of world making.

In a letter in December 1960 to Sylvia Plath's mother and brother, Hughes expands on his work on the *Bardo* and Chou's plans:

> I wrote this oratorio for the Bardo Thodol, The Tibetan Book Of The Dead. I've just sent off a final version. That will be something for you to hear: it's quite awesome. It's the progress of the soul during the 49 days between death and rebirth, a sort of Buddhist Mass. I really enjoyed doing it, though I spent all the summer months just getting the material into shape and telling myself I ought to be working harder at it. However, if the musician, Chou Wen-chung is ready for it, in himself, it could easily be a terrific musical work as it provides wonderful opportunities. He wants to do it with an illuminated backcloth, showing the various deities as they rise before the soul, and the various lighting effects of the different regions through which the soul is driven by his furies, and with a dancer—to mime the events of which the chorus *and* solo sing. So, when this work is completed you shall both have tickets.[3]

Crucial is Hughes's reference to the *Bardo*, not as an opera but as an "oratorio." The distinction between the two may appear slight, but, historically, oratorio in European music has a greater association with high culture and with religious works than does opera. *The Oxford Companion to Music*, for instance, defines oratorio as "an extended setting

---

[2] Ted Hughes, *Ted Hughes: Collected Poems*, ed. Paul Keegan, London: Faber & Faber, [2005] 2012, 39.

[3] Ted Hughes and Christopher Reid, *Letters of Ted Hughes*, ed. Christopher Reid, London: Faber and Faber, 2007, 174. Subsequent references to this work will use the abbreviation *Letters* and be made in-text.

of a religious libretto for chorus, orchestra, and vocal soloists, and for either concert or church performance, i.e. without scenery, dresses or action."[4] By referring to the *Bardo* as an oratorio, Hughes is, I believe, attempting to underline the religious and deeply cultural aspects of the source material of the *Tibetan Book* as central to the project in a way that goes beyond mere entertainment or superficial exoticism. Both Hughes's and Chou's efforts to translate the religious content of the *Tibetan Book* into the language and medium of the *Bardo* eventually strained both artists' time and attention to the point where the *Bardo* project could not be finished. Yet, the Quixotic effort helped both to produce elaborate theories of how to blend older Western and Eastern art and thought in a new literary world.

Reflecting the interests of its author and his collaborator, the *Bardo* libretto is a heterogeneous text. It borrows elements from genres East and West, from texts including *King Lear* and Yeats's *Wanderings of Oisin*, and from a variety of theatrical modes. As such, the *Bardo* has a significant amount in common not only with Elizabethan drama and Irish and modernist literature, but also with Nō as interpreted by Yeats and Chinese Yuan Drama (雜劇; *zaju*) and the later *kunqu* or *kunju* (昆曲; 昆劇), a more sophisticated and recondite form of musical theater that arose during the Ming dynasty (1368–1644) as interpreted elsewhere by Chou himself.[5] On the surface, this is not terribly interesting. Hughes, like Yeats before him in his experiments with crafting Nō from Irish myth, tried to blend elements from multiple sources to make a new kind of theater. But what I will look at here is just what happens to these heterogeneous elements founded on different conceptual schemes as they are made to cohere in a single, overtly religious text; what happens, that is, when a Tibetan Buddhist text becomes a "Buddhist Mass."

For Hughes in the 1950s, the greatest source of inspiration was W. B. Yeats. Yeats's influence on the *Bardo* was substantial. Evans-Wentz himself was fascinated by Yeats, and dedicated his first book, *The Fairy-Faith in Celtic Countries*, to the Irish poet and his compatriot George William Russell.[6] The "fairy-faith" was Evans-Wentz's interpretation of Celtic myth, at the heart of which he puts "Fairyland," "a supernatural state of consciousness in to which men and women may enter temporarily in dreams, trances, and in various ecstatic states; or in an indefinite period at

---

[4] Percy A. Scholes, *The Oxford Companion to Music*, 10th edition. London: Oxford UP, 1970, p. 720. For more on the history and religious background of oratorio, see Howard E. Smither, *A History of the Oratorio*, Chapel Hill: U of North Carolina P, 1978, and "Oratorio and Sacred Opera, 1700–1825: Terminology and Genre Distinction," *Proceedings of the Royal Musical Association* vol. 106 (1979): 88–104.

[5] *Kunqu* is officially known as "Kun Qu Opera" by UNESCO, though *kunqu* was not inscribed as an intangible heritage property until 2008. Both *zaju* and *kunqu* are part of *xiqu* (戲曲), or traditional Chinese theater. Though *zaju* would have had musical accompaniment, its music, unlike *kunqu*'s, is no longer extant. For more on *kunqu*, see Josh Stenberg, "Three Relations Between History and Stage in the Kunju Scene Slaying the Tiger General," *Asian Theatre Journal* vol. 32, no. 1 (2015): 107–35.

[6] Donald S. Lopez, *The Tibetan Book of the Dead: A Biography*, Princeton UP, 2011, 23.

death."[7] A critic would be hard-pressed not to recognize the line connecting Evans-Wentz's first book to his most famous project.

It is unknown whether Hughes was aware of Evans-Wentz's admiration of Yeats, but it is fitting regardless that he chose for his collaboration with Chou a "Tibetan" text passed through the hands of a fellow admirer of his Irish forebear. Hughes told Ekbert Faas that "Yeats spellbound me for about six years. I got to him not so much through his verse as through his other interests, folklore, and magic in particular. Then that strange atmosphere laid hold of me."[8] These six years spanned the period from the middle to the end of the 1950s. In his collected letters, Hughes directly mentions Yeats 18 times throughout the decade, then only once in the 1960s. The last incidence occurs just under three months before Hughes and Plath would arrive at Yaddo in a letter of June 19, 1959, to Lucas Myers. Hughes derides Hart Crane and praises John Crowe Ransom for failing and succeeding to capture the "whole human being" (*Letters* 146). Invoking Eliot's "disassociation of sensibility," he writes that this "wholeness" died in English poetry with the Glorious Revolution of 1688, in which James II and VII was deposed and William III was installed as monarch of England, Scotland, and Ireland, thanks to "the inner-conflict of upper and lower classes in England, the development of the English gentleman with the stereotype English voice (and the mind, set of manners etc that goes with the voice) & the tabu on dialect as a language proper for literate men" (*Letters* 146). He asserts that "the best moments of Shakes, Donne, Yeats, even Eliot, are 'gestures' [a concept that Myers conceives of as related to the Poundian persona] in [Myers's] sense. But in all that I've written since my book this 'gesture' is just what I've been trying to avoid" (*Letters* 146). A month before that, in a letter dated May 19, 1959, Hughes writes to Myers: "Don't you really like the Yeats before Byzantium? There's something spoiling my taste for Yeats. Maybe I knew him too well. Something inflexible about him that disagrees with me at present" (*Letters* 145). On account of his desire for "wholeness," or sincerity, in poetry, Hughes's mania for Yeats ended just before meeting Chou at Yaddo. The *Bardo* project may have appeared as a new path for Hughes after he tired of the route he was traveling on.

I will use Chou and Hughes's *Bardo* in this chapter to explore what can happen when "East" and "West" are brought together in a cross-cultural collaboration. My attention will be on whether the multiple elements that make up the *Bardo* cohere into a recognizable unity. For all of its heterogeneous sources, the *Bardo* is yet a work that, rather than being given an amorphous label like "hybrid" or "globalized," does have a definite composition. As we will see, however, that composition is given its coherence thanks to an organizing principle that structures the literary world. The necessity of making the various elements that go into an "East–West" work like the *Bardo* changes the aspect of the various elements that are included in the libretto, as different senses

---

[7] Ibid., 26, quoting Walter Evans-Wentz, *The Fairy-Faith in Celtic Countries*, New Hyde Park, NY: University Books, Inc., 1966, 2.

[8] Ekbert Faas, *Ted Hughes: The Unaccommodated Universe, with Selected Critical Writings by Ted Hughes & Two Interviews*, Boston: Black Sparrow Press, 1980, 202.

accrue to terms borrowed from other literary constellations in different cultural and linguistic universes.

General Background

How the *Bardo*, and "Asian" aesthetics broadly, fits into Hughes's oeuvre is at first difficult to see. Hughes is after all known first for his poetry, second for his works for children. In comparison, his theatrical productions have not received much attention. His best-known work for theater is perhaps *Orghast* (1971). A collaboration with the British director Peter Brook, *Orghast* is an experimental drama written in a nonexistent language. A printed version of the play is not in circulation. Indeed, the only available manuscript and typeset copies are contained in Hughes's library at Emory.[9] The play draws freely from Ancient Greek and Near Eastern myths and was performed in Tehran by an international cast, including a Japanese actor, Katsuhiro Oida, and players from such disparate places as France, Iran, and Cameroon. The composition and performance of *Orghast* encapsulates Hughes's general approach to foreign art and literature: the desire to find beyond all appearance of difference an essential, primordial *spiritus mundi*.[10]

When approaching Hughes's *Bardo*, we should bear in mind that the text is incomplete. It is incomplete, first, because it was never performed or published. It never received a "final" version which would have taken into account that which Hughes and Chou would have learned as they transferred the libretto to the stage. It is also incomplete because it lacks Chou's music. The *Bardo* is, after all, a joint project. Chou's music is as important as Hughes's text in understanding this version of the *Bardo*. Aside from the scraps we get from Hughes's letters, we do not know how the words and actions of the performers were to function in relation to the music. Finally, the *Bardo* is incomplete because the text has few stage directions. As he wrote the libretto, Hughes would have imagined the actors' gestures, their placement on stage, and their costumes. He has nonetheless given us no indication of any of these things. In fact, we do not know in detail how the dancing and threatening deities whom Solo describes throughout the *Bardo* were to be represented. Given that the actions of the deities are the most dramatic elements of the *Bardo*—they are the only ones who are described as moving, not

---

[9] The play is described in detail in A. C. H. Smith, *Orghast at Persepolis: An Account of the Experiment in Theatre Directed by Peter Brook and Written by Ted Hughes*, London: Eyre Methuen, 1972.

[10] The preoccupation may stem from what Reid, in his edition of Hughes's *Letters*, calls "Hughes' unusual teenage reading, in which Shakespeare, Yeats, Jung, folklore and Robert Graves's *The White Goddess* dominated," thanks to which "Hughes appears to have set out on a journey" (10). I also draw attention to Hughes's fascination with Jung. Jung even wrote an introduction to Evans-Wentz's translation of the *Bardo* that Hughes owned. Studies of the similarity between Hughes's poetry and Jungian psychology include Ryan Hibbett, "Ted Hughes' 'Crow': An Alternative Theological Paradigm," *Literature and Theology* vol. 17, no. 1 (2003): 17–31, and Elizabeth Bergmann Loizeaux, "Reading Word, Image, and the Body of the Book: Ted Hughes and Leonard Baskin's 'Cave Birds,'" *Twentieth Century Literature* vol. 50, no. 1 (2004): 18–58.

simply speaking—their representation would have been crucial any performance of the opera. All of these uncertainties hinder an interpretation of the libretto that Hughes left.

What we do have is a text that foreshadows Hughes's later preoccupations with birth, death, and myth. Whereas those later texts mix various mythic ideas to form a new mythic substructure, here we have Hughes adapting an East Asian religious text. This means that the mythic substructure here is, oddly for Hughes, restricted to one region and religion. The text gives us a rare glimpse of Hughes working specifically with East Asia. As such, it gives us our best glimpse into how Hughes imagined the region. The *Bardo* allows us to see what Hughes felt he had to adapt in his habitual poetic practice to work with materials from East Asia.

I say "East Asia" here rather than "Tibet" because Hughes draws from Chinese and Japanese aesthetics to structure his text, and uses a complex method of analogy to assert fundamental similarities between all the traditions of "Asia." To put it differently, the content is Tibetan, or rather is Tibetan material, already deformed by Evans-Wentz's "translation." The form, however, is more amorphous. To give the *Bardo* a recognizable structure, Hughes, I will show, drew upon a wide range of possible sources, and crafted an eccentric analogy between "shamanism" and English literature in order to make the Tibetan original intelligible to him. Given Hughes's collaboration with Chou, the most obvious theatrical referent for the *Bardo* is Chinese opera. Chou drew upon the opera throughout his career. That Chou's composition of the *Bardo* would have evinced a strong debt to the Chinese opera seems likely, and we will see why in the final section of this chapter. While Hughes was at Yaddo, he was working on *The House of Taurus*. In a letter to T. S. Eliot in 1959, Hughes mentions working on a play that he initially conceived of as an opera, for which he had been awarded the Guggenheim Fellowship. Christopher Reid, the editor of Hughes's letters, conjectures that *The House of Taurus* is this initially operatic play (*Letters* 142–43). If so, then when Hughes met Chou at Yaddo he would have been more easily persuaded to take on Chou's project, the thought of the opera already on the Englishman's mind. Indeed, it is possible that this mutual interest in opera, albeit opera from two very different traditions, drew the two men to collaborate. Hughes would have had Chinese opera topmost in his mind when writing the *Bardo*. We assume that there are parallels between Hughes's text and knowledge of the Chinese opera that could have been reasonably available to him in 1960, aside from that which Chou could have communicated to him.

From the sketches provided of the action in this chapter thus far, we can see that little happens in the text. Solo is offered the chance of liberation, but does not take it. He is to be reborn and to return at some date to the Bardo. Indeed, he may have already passed through the Bardo and been reborn numerous times. We doubt even whether Solo has learned from his experience. Consequently, the plot is circular. The end of the play brings us back to the beginning. Nothing has been accomplished; nothing has changed. Michael Sayeau argues that an interest in the uneventful marks modernist narrative. The modern paradox, he writes, is that we live in a world of endless change and endless boredom.[11]

---

[11] Michael Douglas Sayeau, *Against the Event: The Everyday and the Evolution of Modernist Narrative*, Oxford: Oxford UP, 2013, 3.

Whereas much post–French Revolution literature deals with the possibility of an event by which an old order is destroyed and a new one built, modernism is defined by its distrust of novelty and its sense that the world is composed of the quotidian rather than of "revolutionary shocks."[12] Sayeau believes that our interest in modernism is as much in the movement's use of older forms as in any novelty it contains, though the use of old forms is much of modernism's novelty.[13] We glimpse in the *Bardo* this fascination with the nonevent.

Naturally, Hughes was born far too late to be a modernist *sensu stricto*. As Daniel O'Connor points out, though, "Hughes' work is not a wholesale rejection of Modernism but is in many ways late Modernist."[14] Hughes's work is late modernist because it retains the modernist preoccupation with myth. Just as James Joyce used, to paraphrase T. S. Eliot in "Ulysses, Order, and Myth," a mythic "method" to structure banal events occurring in Dublin on July 16, 1904, according to the events of Homer's *Odyssey*, thereby adding depth to modern mundanity,[15] in the background of rural life in twentieth-century England Hughes often places myths drawn from every corner of the globe. Yet, in much of Hughes's work, there is a crucial difference between his handling of myth and the modernist preoccupations that Sayeau highlights. As we will see in Chapter Five, the Calder Valley becomes in Hughes's hands the site of a mythic restoration of the primacy of nature, with the decaying industry of the region swept away first by northern European mythic forces, then, in a complex dream vision, by Chinese mythology, and the area returned to its natural state. The idea of the revolutionary moment that restores order, an idea that Sayeau says modernists rebelled against, is alive in Hughes's writing. Not only does this make it more difficult to classify Hughes as a late modernist, it makes us wonder why he should have produced such an uneventful libretto.

Part of the reason for this might owe to Hughes's eccentric vision of the ideal English text. In this regard, Neil Corcoran traces Hughes's attitude to Shakespeare. Corcoran reminds us that Hughes thought Shakespeare adopted a "pincer" movement,[16] drawing close the common tongue and the aristocratic tongue.[17] This, Corcoran says, fits in with Hughes's dialectical view of the history and language of England: the Celtic against the Saxon; the Saxon versus the Norman; the feminine (Catholicism) against the masculine (Protestantism); the various dialects of the country, Hughes's West Yorkshire dialect included, versus standard English; the Anglo versus the Latinate. According to Corcoran,

---

[12] Ibid., 3–5.
[13] Ibid., 39.
[14] Daniel O'Connor, *Ted Hughes and Trauma: Burning the Foxes*, London: Palgrave Macmillan, 2016, 2.
[15] T. S. Eliot, *Selected Prose*, ed. Frank Kermode, San Diego: Harvest Books, 1975, 177–78.
[16] The "pincer movement" is hendiadys, the use of two nouns rather than a noun and its qualifier, as in "storm and weather" rather than "stormy weather"; though, as Neil Corcoran notices, Hughes never uses the term 'hendiadys' (193). The "pincer" is a predicate with one Anglo-Saxon and one Latinate word. See Corcoran, "The Nation of Selves: Ted Hughes's Shakespeare," in *This England, that Shakespeare: New Angles on Englishness and the Bard*, ed. Margaret Tudeau-Clayton and Willy Maley, London: Ashgate, 2010, 185–200.
[17] Ibid., 190.

Hughes aims to bring all of these contradictions together and rescue peripheral dialects from the "smothering figure" of the "Queen's English."[18] Eventually Hughes became resigned to the necessity of "silence" in relation to Shakespearean language and English at large, silence necessitated by the antinomies of English. But what Corcoran does not point out is the contradiction in Hughes's own stance. Hughes certainly liked to think of himself as antiestablishment. He took pride in his accent and rural upbringing and stubbornly clung to them despite his life at Cambridge and later as the poet laureate. Yet Hughes was also, as Corcoran points out, resentful of the Glorious Revolution, which was a revolt against the aristocracy and Catholicism, and which sped up the process of parliamentary rule that had begun with the English Civil War. In this, I think, we see something of Yeats and Eliot, that opposition not to elitism but to the middle class. Hughes's identification with the rural was also an identification with a deposed elite; his antipathy was directed at the middle class even as he himself became a member of it. The stance explains Hughes's desire to produce an opera that, uneventful and foreign to a contemporary British audience, would not easily have achieved popular appeal.

The focus of the play is on speech. But we would be hard-pressed to say that this is dramatic dialogue. A, B, and Solo appear to hear one another but do not pick up on the threads of one another's statements. A small sample of the text will help to indicate this:

Solo: Others, others. Who are these others?
A&B: Recognise Vajra Heruka, the blood-drinker;
    Recognise Vajra Krotishaurima:
    Recognise Ratna Heruka, the blood[-]drinker;
    Recognise Ratna Krotishaurima;
    Recognise Padma Heruka, the blood-drinker;
    Recognise Padma Krotishaurima;
    Recognise Karma Heruka, the Blood-drinker;
    Recognise Karma Krotishaurima.
Solo: I am blown like a breath through the Bardo.
B: Evil Karma drags you further, further and deeper into the Bardo.
Solo: I am blown like ashes through the Bardo.
B: Evil Karma catches you from yourself and from Liberation
A&B: Recognise these forms for your own mind
Solo: Filling the skies they crowd me away
A[:] Evil Karma carries you away,
    Darkens your eyes, fills you with terror, bears you deeper into the Bardo.[19] (*Bardo* 16)

---

[18] Ibid., 195.
[19] Ted Hughes, *Bardo Thödol*, TS, Box 116, folder 2, Emory University, 16. Subsequent references to this will be made in-text and use the abbreviation *Bardo*.

Solo demands to know who the fearful gods before him are. When A and B tell him in detail, Solo seems to take no notice. Rather, he focuses once more on his own suffering and speaks monotonously. The difference between the lengthy and highly stylized expository speech of A and B and Solo's more direct lyricism separates the three characters. Because Solo's register diverges from A and B's, because Solo's concern is with his suffering while A and B's is with exposition of that which passes in the Bardo, the three characters cannot enter into conversation. They seem to be speaking past one another. No sense of drama or character development emerges from their dialogue.

Turning again to Hughes's letters, we glean a better idea of how the play was to capture the audience's interest. In a letter to Chou dated January 1, 1960, Hughes writes: "[After you left Yaddo] I got a great deal done—my play, among other things. The play is, I believe, unperformable save as a curiosity, but among its extravagances I did achieve here and there what I set out to do" (*Letters* 154). He then promises to send part of the play to Chou. As he wrote, Hughes appears to have been unaware of how Chou hoped to structure the play. He looked forward to receiving Chou's thoughts and revising the play following "a year or two at other things" (*Letters* 154–55). Hughes was aware of the dramatic limitations of his *Bardo* and knew that any performance of it would rely heavily on the nonverbal elements handled by Chou.

Chou's idea for an "illuminated backcloth," mentioned in Hughes's letter to Plath's mother and brother quoted earlier, solves the problem of representing the various fantastic supernatural beings that Solo and the chorus describe throughout the play. With the dearth of action and dramatic dialogue, the main interest in reading Hughes's typescript of the *Bardo* lies in its ornate poetry and in the descriptions of the deities. These figures are by turns seductive and horrifying.

> Solo: A figure out of the East
> White-hot, moon-white,
> Brandishing the blade
> Bearing the skull
> That brims blood,
> Body coiled
> By a white woman
> And furiously dancing, furiously dancing,
> Smiling upon me:
> Strengthen me, strengthen me
> B: Do not fear them, do not fear them:
> Supplicate them, supplicate them.
> Solo: Out of the South
> A figure of flame
> Flame-yellow, a figure
> Flourishing a blade, balancing a skull
> Brimming blood, and furiously dancing
> Wrapped in the flame of a yellow Dakini,
> Smiling upon me. Out of the West

> A figure crimson
> As the sun's core
> Wound by a woman
> Crimson as the sun's core
> Furiously dancing. (*Bardo* 11–12)

Hughes has written "furiously dancing" here and in other places in the typescript. We do not know how "furious" the dancing represented on the backdrop would have been. We can remark that this sense of movement and power stands in marked contrast to the motionlessness of Solo and A and B in the typescript. The three, at least in the typescript with minimal stage direction, only stand and speak. The discord between the motionless actors and the figures represented only by an abstraction of their movements on an illuminated backdrop adds a dramatic element that is difficult to quantify.

Parts of the vagueness of the work might owe to how Hughes modified much of Evans-Wentz's rendering of the *Bardo Thödol*. Rather than narrating the experience of the deceased in the Bardo, the *Tibetan Book* is read aloud to the dying. It specifies how much time should pass for the reading of a given part of the text, according to where the soul is in the Bardo. For example, we read:

> But if it be feared that the primary Clear Light hath not been recognized, then [it can certainly be assumed] there is dawning [upon the deceased] that called the secondary Clear Light, which dawneth in somewhat more than a mealtime period after that the expiration hath ceased.[20]

Hughes ignores this entirely. The text specifies different readings for people of "noble" or "common" birth.[21] Hughes does not. We can also see that Evans-Wentz, like Hughes, uses a slightly antiquated diction. There are poetic passages, "prayers," that closely resemble Hughes's text. However, the reader of the *Tibetan Book* instructs the deceased to repeat the prayer, a detail missing from Hughes's *Bardo*.

> Put thy whole thought earnestly upon Vairochana and repeat after me this prayer:
>
> "Alas! when wandering in the Sangsāra, because of intense stupidity,
> On the radiant light-path of the Dhartna-Dhātu Wisdom
> May [I] be led by the Bhagavān Vairochana,
> May the Divine Mother of Infinite Space be [my] rearguard;
> May [I] be led safely across the fearful ambush of the Bardo;
> And may [I] be placed in the state of the All-Perfect Buddha-hood."

---

[20] Walter Y. Evans-Wentz, P. Sambhava, P. Sangay, and C.G. Jung, *The Tibetan Book of the Great Liberation: Or the Method of Realizing Nirvana Through Knowing the Mind*, Oxford: Oxford UP, 1968, 97.
[21] Ibid., 95.

Praying thus, in intense humble faith, [thou] wilt merge, in halo of rainbow light, into the heart of Vairochana, and obtain Buddhahood in the Satnbhoga-Kāya, in the Central Realm of the Densely-Packed.[22]

Removing this dimension of the *Tibetan Book* to create the *Bardo* means, of course, further reducing the immediate religious aspect. The deceased repeating the words of the reader indicates that the deceased has faith in the teachings and hierarchy of the religion. Hughes's Solo, on the other hand, is more detached, unable, for whatever reason, to enter into such an understanding with the reader of the *Bardo* and, consequently, with the world of the original *Tibetan Book*. Instead, like perhaps like Hughes himself, Solo incapable fully of entering into communion with the reader of the text and the world the reader represents. On the other hand, the *Tibetan Book* assigns colors to different parts of the afterlife: "dull white light" signifies the land of the Devas[23]; "dull, smoke-coloured light" signifies Hell,[24] and so on. Hughes will adopt this color symbolism exactly, and this, as we will see, draws Hughes's libretto close to the conventions of Chinese drama. The move allows Hughes further to cut the *Bardo* adrift from the religious world of Tibet while retaining the spiritual and literary facets of the *Tibetan Book*.

We noted that Evans-Wentz's book pays close attention to time. In fact, the book is divided into 14 days. On each day a different event takes place; for instance, the Wrathful deities appear on the eighth day. But it is not necessary that the soul spend every day in the Bardo. The soul may take the chance at liberation on day one or day nine. Obviously, if Hughes wants to use material from the entirety of the *Tibetan Book*, he cannot allow the Solo to achieve liberation on the first day. Rather, Hughes has taken the material from all 14 days and compressed it into a single occurrence. Of course, there is still the suggestion of time in Hughes's *Bardo*. The deities still appear in succession. But the amount of time that passes is ambiguous. The audience has no indication that two weeks are passing on stage.

We also mentioned the *Tibetan Book*'s distinction between "noble" and "common" souls. The book further distinguishes between "those who have meditated much" and those who have been "limited" in their "religious practices."[25] The more the departed "meditated" on religion in life, the easier it will be to achieve enlightenment. In other words, while in the Bardo the soul can recall knowledge of the Bardo obtained while alive, Hughes's Solo seems to have no knowledge of the Bardo. He is overwhelmed by surprise and horror. Hughes has given us a character that is at the furthest extreme of ignorance, and whose ignorance perhaps mirrors the audience's lack of knowledge of the Bardo and the *Tibetan Book*. On top of that, he has given no sign to his audience that the *Tibetan Book* encourages stratification along lines of class and education.

Hughes has remained faithful to the diction, symbolism, and overarching themes of the *Tibetan Book*. He has ignored those features of the book that would have given his

---

[22] Ibid., 107,
[23] Ibid., 124.
[24] Ibid., 109.
[25] Ibid., 151.

libretto a more dramatic element. He has eschewed notions of class, education, and society, and has marginalized the passage of time. Reducing his characters to pure types existing in a formless space, Hughes emphasizes the spiritual content of the *Tibetan Book*. That is to say, he makes it less a piece of dramatic entertainment and more a window into the religious world described in Evans-Wentz's text. To understand how Hughes interpreted the world of "Tibetan" Buddhism, we first need to pass again through Yeats.

The *Bardo*'s Networks

What I have in mind is not so much Yeats's understanding of the *Tibetan Book* but his broader comprehension of East Asian art, particularly Nō, or rather the way in which Yeats makes the world of Nō intelligible to his own theater. The reason for the following exposition of Yeats's view of Nō is twofold. It gives us a sense of how Hughes's literary idol solved the problem of integrating East Asian theater with the English language and dramatic tradition. Given Hughes's enthusiasm for Yeats, we might even surmise that Yeats's experiments with Nō would have informed the completed *Bardo* project. Yet the more important reason for looking at Yeats's "Noh" plays is that the way in which he attempted to make Nō theater cohere into his own literary universe parallels what Hughes does with the *Bardo* and the idea of Asian culture. Essentially, both writers first construct an imagined shared history between parts of "Western" literature and "Asian" literature, then use this premodern affinity to structure and support a new transnational literary world.

Yeats's first encounter with Nō came through his amanuensis, Ezra Pound. Sanehide Kodama explains that, in 1914, Pound had gotten hold of Ernest Fenollosa's rough translations of several Nō and, at the request of Fenollosa's widow, Mary, turned them into more literate pieces for publication in literary journals.[26] Yeats wrote the introduction for Pound's *Certain Noble Plays of Japan* (1916), wherein he says that the plays will help him "to explain a certain possibility of the Irish dramatic movement."[27] That "possibility" was realized that same year with the inaugural performance in London of *At the Hawk's Well*. Yeats imagines his Cuchulain, hero of Irish myth, wearing a mask as in Nō and in Greek Drama. By "wearing this noble half-Greek half-Asiatic face," the figure of Cuchulain, Yeats writes, "will appear perhaps like an image seen in revery by some Orphic worshiper."[28] Nō conjures up in Yeats's mind Greek theater, and this correspondence between two foreign, ancient art forms allows him to express a myth belonging to a language he does not speak. Indeed, as a mythic figure of the Irish people, Cuchulain is even further removed from Yeats, a Protestant Anglo-Irishman whose ancestors were not of those people among whom the myth first arose.

---

[26] Sanehide Kodama, *American Poetry and Japanese Culture*, Hamden, CT: Archon Books, 1984, 99.
[27] W. B. Yeats, "Introduction," in *Certain Noble Plays of Japan from the Manuscripts of Ernest Fenollosa*, ed. Ezra Pound, Dublin: Cuala Press, 1916, i.
[28] Ibid.

We find out, though, that in Yeats's view Greece itself is "half-Asiatic." These Asiatic influences represent the antithesis of what European theater by the early twentieth century had become: rational, realist, naturalist, fixated on the idea of progress in the arts.[29] For Yeats, art should speak a different language from that of everyday speech. "Realism was created for the common people," Yeats contends, "and it is the delight today of all those whose minds educated alone by school-masters and newspapers are without the memory of beauty and emotional subtlety."[30] Against the depiction of the banal and the naturalist reduction of life to mechanistic processes, Yeats, as both Kodama and Akiko Manabe mention,[31] envisioned an "aristocratic" theater "having no need of mob or press to pay its way."[32] Yeats envisions a theater with minimal setting and music, where the actors speak with "slight variations upon old cadences and customary words, all that high breeding of poetical style where there is nothing ostentatious, nothing crude, no breath of parvenu or journalist."[33] There is no better form, Yeats thinks, than the Japanese Nō, which he believes is a purely aristocratic form, performed for and occasionally played by nobles, in a language that the common people and the middle classes do not understand, with highly stylized movements and speech that are far away from the conventions of public entertainment and media—a theater whose very name means "accomplishment." This is no ordinary accomplishment; rather, "it is [the nobility's] accomplishment and that of a few cultured people who understand the literary and mythological allusions and the ancient lyrics quoted in the speech or chorus, their discipline, a part of their breeding."[34] Both the form and the history of Nō accord with Yeats's ambitions for a new and aristocratic European theater.

Thanks to Yeats's mistrust of progress, it is the antiquity of Nō that attracts him. It is not that Yeats believes that everything new is poor. But he imagines that the further European art moved from its sources, the more it lost its noble and spiritual core, of which the shift from Shakespeare's high poetic drama to the prose drama of Dryden is exemplary.[35] Yeats charges that this movement toward prose and the mundane is tied to the increasingly rational mind-set of Europeans, and had modern Europeans "been Greek, and so but half-European, an honourable mob would have martyred though in vain the first man who set up a painted scene, or who complained that soliloquies were unnatural, instead of repeating with a sigh, 'we cannot return to the arts of childhood, however beautiful.'"[36] Japanese Nō's sparse props, exemplified by the representation of "a fruit tree by a bush in a pot," suggest to Yeats "a child's game become the most noble

---

[29] Cf. Claudel's distinction between the French and Japanese temperaments in Chapter Four.
[30] Yeats, "Introduction," viii.
[31] Kodama, *American Poetry*, 100; Akiko Manabe, "W. B. Yeats and Kyogen: Individualism and Communal Harmony in Japan's Classical Theatrical Repertoire," *Études anglaises* vol. 68, no. 4 (2015): 4
[32] Yeats, "Introduction," ii.
[33] Ibid., ix.
[34] Ibid., xi.
[35] Ibid., vi.
[36] Ibid., vi–vii.

poetry."³⁷ The childlike simplicity has the effect of encouraging the audience to use its imagination; the Nō playwright, unlike the realist, does not break the magic of the theater by "[setting] before us all those things which we feel and imagine in silence."³⁸ The antiquity of the theater means that it has retained the affective childlike aspect of art that has been cast aside by the progress of rationalism in Europe, and so Yeats values the antiquity of Nō, because he may set it against all that he deplores in modern European art and society.

There is a third aspect of Yeats's interest in Nō: the perceived proximity of Shintō to Irish myth. Yeats notes that Nō grew from ritual Shintō dancing before "receiving its philosophy and its final shape perhaps from priests of a contemplative school of Buddhism."³⁹ He states that in Nō a "god, goddess, or ghost reminds me at times of our own Irish legends and beliefs, which once it may be differed little from those of the Shintō worshipper."⁴⁰ He then proceeds to draw more parallels between the Nō tales he has read and the Irish myths to the study of which he had devoted much of his life. Of course, Ireland did not have a native theater like Japan. But because Irish and Japanese native beliefs are close in Yeats's mind, he can use the Japanese theatrical genre to express Irish myth. That is to say, because Irish and Japanese myths are, he thinks, at root so similar, the Nō Theater that acts as a vessel for the one can easily act as a vessel for the other. This helps Yeats to solve the problem of adapting Irish myth for the European theater, a problem which he says he had long struggled with.⁴¹ Yeats goes even further, in fact, in claiming that among the medieval Nō playwrights and theatergoers "some would have understood the prose of Walter Pater, the painting of Puvis de Chavannes, the poetry of Mallarmé and Verlaine."⁴² This is because in Nō, and in all ancient Japanese art, Yeats finds "the most vivid and subtle discrimination of sense and the invention of images more powerful than sense; the continual presence of reality."⁴³ He sees in Japanese art the answer to the question that occupied Mallarmé and other modern European artists: how to create art in "an industrial age" dominated by "a mechanical sequence of ideas" and in which people are unable fully to experience life and art because they can no longer enter into a "confusion of the senses" in which the rational mind stops working.⁴⁴

The similarities between that which Yeats tries to do with Nō and Hughes with the *Bardo* are striking. In effect, both Hughes and Yeats make heavily Buddhist worlds of art intelligible by reducing them to a prehistorical shared origin with European, particularly Celtic, myth. What Hughes and Yeats highlight in making this analogy differs—Hughes, as noted earlier, doesn't share Yeats's enthusiasm for "nobility"—but the ways in which

---

[37] Ibid., xiii.
[38] Ibid.
[39] Ibid., x.
[40] Ibid., xiv.
[41] Ibid., xv.
[42] Ibid., xix.
[43] Ibid., xviii.
[44] Ibid., xviii–xix.

both poets set about crafting new worlds from an Asian 'original' resemble one another greatly.

To this end, perhaps the most important legacy Hughes received from Yeats was an interest in "shamanism" and non-Christian spirituality. Yeats himself knew something of Evans-Wentz's *Tibetan Book* and had a copy of it in his library.[45] In an article from 1964 entitled "Regenerations," (included in the 1994 collection *Winter Pollen*) Hughes writes: "Traces and variations of shamanism are found all over the world, but it has developed its purest and most characteristic procedures in north-eastern and central Asia."[46] He mentions that shamanism "flourishes alongside and within the prevailing religion" and that "[the] Buddhist influence on Asiatic shamanism is strong."[47] Because of this intertwining of Buddhism and shamanism, Hughes feels justified in concluding that the *Bardo Thödol* is essentially shamanistic. While in the text, though, "the geography and furnishings of the afterworld are Buddhist,"

> the main business of the work as a whole, which is to guide the dead soul to its place in death, or back into life—together with the principal terrific events, and the flying accompaniment of descriptive songs, exhortation to the soul, threats, and the rest—are all characteristically shamanic. This huge, formal work has long ago lost contact with any shaman, but its origins seem clear.[48]

He goes through the various tasks of the shaman, mentions that "[the] calling is not exclusively male: in some traditions (Japanese) women predominate," and argues that "[in] a shamanizing society, *Venus and Adonis*, some of Keats's longer poems, *The Wanderings of Oisin*, *Ash Wednesday*, would all qualify their authors for the magic drum."[49] By the early 1960s, Hughes was familiar with the history of shamanism, including Japanese "shamanism," identified shamanism as a Central and East Asian phenomenon, understood its role in relation to Buddhism, viewed the *Bardo* at its core as shamanistic, and tried to reinterpret some of his favorite English poets by casting some of their monumental works as shamanistic. Hughes's work on the *Bardo* appears to have convinced him of the fitness of shamanism as a poetic guide, just as he was losing enthusiasm for Yeats. The *Bardo* allowed him to rationalize the appearance of authentic or "whole" poetic texts in an England increasingly suffering from a "disassociation of sensibility" as manifestations of a suppressed shamanistic spirit, which Hughes undoubtedly thought was manifested in himself.

In exploring Hughes's debt to Yeats, Rand Brandes points out that the central text in Hughes's dialogue with the Anglo-Irish poet is *The Wanderings of Oisin*, of which the

---

[45] Francis Wilson, *Yeats and Tradition*, New York: Macmillan, 1958, 49.
[46] Ted Hughes, *Winter Pollen: Occasional Prose*, ed. William Scammell, London: Faber and Faber, 1994, 56.
[47] Ibid., 56.
[48] Ibid.
[49] Ibid. 58.

"circular structure begins and ends in the same moment."⁵⁰ In a letter from December 16, 1992 in which he describes his teenage development, Hughes himself writes:

> I was looking one day in the School library for more poems in those same long rhythms, when I came across the last part of *The Wanderings Of Oisin*, by Yeats. It so happened, my particular craze, in folklore and mythology, was the Irish (very rich, as you know). So here was an Irish myth and my special verse metre all in one. I then read the whole poem—for the legend. Then I searched Yeats for more—not tramping rhythms but—folklore made into poems. So I was swallowed alive by Yeats. From that point, my animal kingdom, the natural world, the world of folktales and myth, and poetry, became a single thing—and Yeats was my model for how the whole thing could be given poetic expression. It all happened pretty quickly. I simply tried to learn the whole of Yeats (and eventually did learn the complete poems). (*Letters* 624)

Brandes does not say so, but in the "circular structure" of *Oisin* we can find an aspect of Yeats's work that would have appealed to Hughes in his search for poetry that embodies "wholeness." Circularity goes against teleology; it suggests that its subject exists outside of time, that is, that its subject is transcendent. If something is outside of time, it cannot change. When Brandes asserts that shamanism "is the master metaphor / narrative of Hughes' thinking and writing," when he says that Hughes saw shamanism as the root of all religion, including Christianity, he is highlighting Hughes's investment in the transcendent and the essential.⁵¹ He continues: "The shaman brings together East and West, ancient and modern."⁵² Searching for a belief system that could give wholeness to a world characterized by difference and conflict, Hughes would have been interested not only in the subject matter of *Oisin* but also in its form. This aspect of *Oisin* would influence the structure⁵³ Hughes gave to his *Bardo*, while the Irish aspect would become important as a way of bringing together East and West in Hughes's mind through the uniting trope of "shamanism."

I think that the role of the *Bardo* in Hughes's career is clear. It helped him to transfer from the English poetic tradition with which he had grown dissatisfied to a global, but principally Central and East Asian, "shamanistic" tradition. At the same time, it confirmed his indebtedness to Yeats. Since Yeats would always be the poet who introduced Hughes to shamanism, Hughes's conception of shamanism would always be built on top of a structure that he inherited from the Anglo-Irish poet. Hughes's work on the *Bardo* was a catalyst for change and retrenchment of his youthful interests.

In addition to being a personal project for a young English poet growing beyond his spiritual apprenticeship under Yeats, Hughes's *Bardo* is also an exercise in translation in cooperation with a Chinese American composer that exhibits sporadic fidelity to its source

---

⁵⁰ Rand Brandes, "Mercury in Taurus: W. B. Yeats and Ted Hughes," *South Carolina Review* vol. 43, no. 1 (2010): 205.
⁵¹ Brandes, *Mercury*, 202–3.
⁵² Ibid., 204.
⁵³ Circular structure figures often in modernism (*Finnegans Wake*) and early to mid-twentieth century theater (*Endgame*).

material. Before getting into the Chinese and Japanese elements of Hughes's *Bardo*, we should mention the possible influence of "Asian" theater, broadly defined, on the opera. Doing so fleshes out the possible "network" of influences, in the sense described by "weak theory," that might have been Hughes's or Chou's during the composition of the *Bardo*. It further aids us in seeing how the *Bardo*, as an East–West text, relates back to the worlds of older English and East Asian theater. Such work elucidates the "network" of the *Bardo* in the sense given by Paul Saint-Amour and his "weak theory" interlocutors in the previous chapter: it shows how the *Bardo* is implicated in a constellation of rhetoric and languages, in translation or otherwise. But it also begins to indicate the multidimensionality of this network, as ontologically vague elements of older literary works and traditions begin to be exploited to construct a new, coherent world for the *Bardo*.

To this end we could turn to the books in Hughes's library. Hughes did not habitually leave notes in his books. The critic's task is therefore more difficult in connecting the books in Hughes's library to his works than it is in *Samuel Beckett's Library* (2013), for instance.[54] Going by the publication dates of the books Hughes owned that are related to his later work, that is, books the publication of which predate certain of Hughes' works, we can conjecture a relationship between what Hughes read and what he produced. But as we cannot conclusively state lines of influence, we must proceed with caution through this survey.

In his library is Faubion Bowers's *Theater in the East* (1956). Bowers had specialized in Japanese and Indian theater before writing *Theater in the East*, in which he took on not only Japanese and Indian but also Chinese and Southeast Asian performance art. The book was the first of its kind and was well received at the time of publication. We can reasonably surmise that Hughes acquired his copy before or, more likely, during his work on the *Bardo* and used it as reliable reference to construct his "Asian" play. If so, then in accordance with the general perspective of Hughes's studies, the English author would have had access to information on a wide variety of national Asian theaters when writing the *Bardo*. Earl Ernst describes the information Hughes might have absorbed:

> To make matters somewhat easier for the Western reader, he distinguishes between dance and drama, drawing a line which, except with reference to the imported realistic theatre, the native of the Orient has not drawn. There is no time to discuss the apparently universal Asian aptitude for dance, nor to consider explicitly the deleterious influences which the realistic theatre and film have already exerted upon traditional forms of expression.[55]

Bowers's book would not have conveyed the niceties of "Oriental" theater to Hughes, but it would have encouraged him to think of "Asian" drama as symbolic and musical.

---

[54] Dirk Van Hulle and Mark Nixon, *Samuel Beckett's Library*, Cambridge: Cambridge UP, 2013. The book is an "attempt to interpret Samuel Beckett's reading traces" left in the margins of all of the books he read and kept (3).

[55] Earle Ernst, "Theatre in the East: A Survey of Asian Dance and Drama. By Bowers, Faubion. New York: Thomas Nelson, 1956. Xi, 374. Illustrations, Bibliography, Index. $7.50," *Journal of Asian Studies* vol. 16, no. 1 (1956): 115.

The very attributes that, as we will see in this chapter and the next, Yeats and Claudel thought were essential to Nō might, to Hughes, have been presented as less a part of the Japanese theatrical genre and more vaguely "Asian." A specialist in subcontinental and Southeast Asian theater would be able to say more on the possibility of such influence on Hughes's *Bardo*. Here, let us simply say that the presence of *Theatre in the East* in Hughes's library suggests the multiplicity of influences that might have fed into the *Bardo* opera; and it indicates the intellectual climate into which the *Bardo* would have been released.

The link is, however, imperfect. A much more persuasive reason for thinking about the *Bardo* in relation to Asian, particularly Chinese, theater, is Chou's role in the project. When he met Hughes, Chou had just read the *Tibetan Book* and found it "fascinating." According to Chou, the project did not work for two reasons. First, both Chou and Hughes became overwhelmed with work after Yaddo, when Chou's academic and Hughes's poetic career blossomed. But there is another, more interesting reason: Chou believed that composing a score based on the original text, a score that could encapsulate the meaning of the original, would be immensely difficult. Though Chou regretted not tackling these obstacles and finishing the opera, the labor involved in making the *Tibetan Book* intelligible in another form combined with other work stopped the project short.[56] The apparent fervor that Chou brought to the project makes it worthwhile for us to think of the *Bardo* as an extension of Chou's interests at the time, and to examine it in light of Chou's own obsession with fusing Eastern and Western art.

Shortly before meeting Hughes, Chou composed *Soliloquy of a Bhiksuni*, a composition "based on a scene in a sixteenth-century Chinese drama, in which a Bhiksuni (Buddhist nun) worships before statues of Buddhas."[57] Peter M. Chang elaborates: "The piece is for solo trumpet and wind ensemble is based on a scene from a sixteenth-century Chinese drama, the famous *kunqu* tune, Si Fan. Initially, Chou planned to use this material for a one-act opera and wrote most of the libretto but later decided to compose an instrumental piece instead."[58] The *Bihksuni*, or 比丘尼 (mandarin: *bǐqiūnǐ*), is Sekong from the *kunqu* play *Si fan*, translated as *Longing for Worldly Pleasures*.[59] Having just reached maturity, Sekong sings five arias in which she states her sexual desire, her fear of damnation, her attraction to a young monk, and ultimately her decision to leave the monastery. As does the *Bardo* with Solo and the fantastic images he describes, *Si fan* relies strongly on "acting, chanting, dancing, and singing" to make "Sekong's staged desire is more realistic and sensual (i.e. more wanton) than what her words alone convey." Sekong's dress,

---

[56] The information in this paragraph is based on private correspondence with the Chou Wen-chung estate in 2015.
[57] Eric Chiu Kong Lai, *The Music of Chou Wen-Chung*, London: Ashgate, 2009, 206.
[58] Peter M. Chang, *Chou Wen-chung: The Life and Work of a Contemporary Chinese-Born American Composer*, Lanham, MD: Scarecrow Press, 2006, 68. For more on *Si Fan*, see Andrea S. Goldman, "The Nun Who Wouldn't Be: Representations of Female Desire in Two Performances of 'Si Fan,'" *Late Imperial China* vol. 22, no. 1 (June 2001): 71–138.
[59] Joseph Lam, "Musical Seductresses, Chauvinistic Men, and Their Erotic Kunqu," in *Wanton Women in Late Imperial Chinese Literature: Models, Genres*, ed. Mark Stevenson and Wu Cuncun, Leiden: Brill, 2017, 86.

her "acting-dancing with her eyes, lips, limbs, and torso," and her "long and extended melodies [in] a clear and pure voice, enunciating intimate words with eloquent precision" all count nearly, if not as much as the words themselves in making *Si fan*'s story work.[60] Though the subject matter differs, the use of a Buddhist story, communicated through extended soliloquys, with descriptions of the torments of Buddhist hell and the indecision of a protagonist before them, and the particular reliance on staging decisions to complete the performance, does recall the material of Hughes's libretto. This in turn suggests that there is a strong connection between these two unrealized projects of Chou's, and, I think, a reason for looking in more detail at the possible lines of communication between the *Bardo* and the Chinese theater on which the complete opera would almost certainly have drawn for characterization and staging, if not for the verse form that Hughes uses.

Just as Japanese theater began in ritual, Chung-wen Shih writes, so Chinese drama began in shamanism before itself spawning light entertainment, puppet theater, shadow plays, and opera.[61] The "Golden Age" of Chinese drama occurred in the Yuan period (1271–1368). During this period, China was ruled by a Mongol class that disliked Confucianism and Classical Chinese. Moreover, the civil service exams were suspended from 1237 to 1314. Scholars who previously could have taken the exam and made a career in government had to find other ways to support themselves and many turned to writing plays. These scholars had an audience in an emergent middle class wishing to be entertained.[62] From these fortuitous circumstances emerged a drama that was more populist than the Nō. Being more populist, Chinese drama is also less tragic. The language may still be poetic; the content is never tragic, and the suggestiveness that characterizes Nō differs from the totality of Chinese drama. In Chinese drama, goodness is rewarded, badness is punished, and everything rectified according to the logic of a just cosmos. Here the influence of Confucianism, whatever opposition it faced from the Yuan dynasty itself, is felt, as is the taste of the merchant class, and encourages a lack of interest in psychological conflict. Shih writes that "great Western tragedies are largely dramas of personality, while Yüan plays are dramas of events and their meanings."[63] One of the most celebrated of Yuan dramas is *The Romance of the Western Chamber* by Wang Shifu (1250–1337). The play derives from a short story of the Tang epoch (618–907) by Yuan Zhen (779–831). The short story has a tragic ending, but the play is not tragic, for as Shih puts it, the tragic "would have been too sophisticated and disappointing for a popular audience."[64] In a social structure in which every member of society is supposed to know his or her place, the focal point is generally how well characters uphold their social obligations.

---

[60] Ibid., 89.
[61] Chung-wen Shih, *Golden Age of Chinese Drama: Yuan Tsa-Chu*, Princeton: Princeton UP, 2015, 10.
[62] Ibid., 18–20.
[63] Ibid., 41.
[64] Ibid., 16.

Chinese opera is not tragic either, not in the European sense of tragedy.⁶⁵ It relies heavily on theatrical conventions and symbolism, and it presupposes that the audience is familiar with the story taking place on stage:

> Over several centuries, Chinese opera has developed a series of stage conventions that has become familiar to regular theatre goers. They know when they see the oily white-faced actor that they have a villain before them. When they see the actor walk in a circle they know that he or she has made a journey. Knowing the conventions of this stage language means the new audience is no longer excluded from the rich theatrical experience of Chinese opera. The centre of all these conventions is the actor. Traditional Chinese opera has focused its attention upon the actor rather than the lighting, scenery, or even the director. The audience already knows the stories well. They come not to see what happens, but rather how highly trained actors present that familiar story in their singing and their mastery of stage technique. In other words, the real pleasure in store for a new audience to the Chinese opera is savouring how the actors unfold the story through their mastery of stagecraft.⁶⁶

There are a variety of different operas in China, with the various styles "connected to [the] places" in which they are performed in terms of dialect and conventions.⁶⁷ Peking opera is the most famous version in the West, but Chou Wen-chung was not a fan of it. The reason is that Peking opera blends Chinese and European instruments, whereas Chou preferred to use Western instruments to perform traditional Chinese music in order, in the words of Eric Lai, to achieve a "kind of cultural fusion."⁶⁸ Simply combining the outward form of music, the instruments, is not enough for Chou, and perhaps some of this mind-set was communicated to Hughes. Perhaps here Hughes has combined his interest in Yeats's circular *Oisin* with passing knowledge of the highly stylized nature of Chinese drama and opera. The problem, though, is that Hughes and Chou had no audience accustomed to such theatrical conventions. Taking inspiration from a tradition that relies on the audience's knowledge of an array of generic types allows for theatrical innovation in English; yet it presents formidable obstacles when only the creators of the piece are certain to be aware of the conventions. The conundrum is likely another reason for the failure of the *Bardo* project.

There are a few other aspects of Chinese theater worth mentioning. Earlier, we saw that one of the recurrent features of the Evans-Wentz translation and Hughes's *Bardo* is color symbolism. The various supernatural entities are associated with a particular color: for example, a "white woman," a "woman of yellow," a "red-woman, a black woman," and a "dark-green woman" arise before Solo to teach him about "earthly existence" (*Bardo* 16). Color symbolism also serves to differentiate the paths that Solo may take out of the Bardo. Solo notices the "brute world" thanks to a "mild blue light" (*Bardo* 12).

---

[65] The absence of tragedy in the European sense in China is a much-noted phenomenon. See Jennifer Wallace, "Tragedy in China," *Cambridge Quarterly* vol. 42, no. 2 (2013): 99–111.
[66] Wang-Ngai Siu and Peter Lovrick, *Chinese Opera: The Actor's Craft*, Hong Kong: Hong Kong UP, 2014, 1.
[67] Ibid., 2.
[68] Lai, *Music*, 40.

"Hell," on the other hand, is mentioned after the "land of the Asuras" with its "fiery circles flaming in opposite directions," and is described by B as having:

> [...] black roads leading
> Over low hills, by windowless houses:
> Heat and cold to and fro
> Make it their battleground and wailings
> Come through the windowless black walls.
> (*Bardo* 23)

Likely, these colors would have been illuminated on stage as A spoke. Chinese opera employs colors in its complex symbolism. When the audience sees a particular color in the actor's face paint or costume, they gain an instant understanding of the character's personality. Red, for example, signifies strength, while black signifies loyalty.[69] Hughes does not adopt the symbolism of the Chinese opera; even if Hughes knew of this facet of Chinese theater, his Western audience would likely not have understood Chinese conventions. Yet much of the color symbolism found in Evans-Wentz's translation already works well with Western symbolism; for example, the "fiery circles flaming in opposite directions" make for an infernal setting, and are thus in fortuitous agreement with Western depictions of fire and brimstone representing Hell, quite like what we found in the *Tibetan Book*. Given his knowledge of Chinese theater, Chou would have realized that the color symbolism of the *Tibetan Book* would have translated easily into Chinese drama. A final production may have seen these colors represented on the characters themselves according to Chinese convention. Regardless, there is no indication that Hughes was aware of this. At most, we can say that this resemblance to Chinese theater is a coincidence.

More concrete are the Shakespearean elements of the *Bardo*. Shakespeare was so important to Hughes that we could convincingly argue that nothing Hughes wrote was unaffected by Shakespeare.[70] But the *Bardo* has a specific allusion, namely, to the famous line in *King Lear*: "Then, kill, kill, kill, kill, kill, kill" (IV.vi), and the line "Never, never, never, never, never!" (V.iii).[71] In Part 2 of Hughes's *Bardo*, the chorus joins Solo's description of the horrors before him:

C1: SLAY! SLAY! SLAY! SLAY! SLAY!
C2: Om Mane Padme Hum (Continuing under what follows)

Solo: Clashing armaments of bone
Braying through their thigh-bone trumpets

---

[69] For a discussion of shadow theater and its continued relevance, see Lisa Kronthal, "Conservation of Chinese Shadow Figures: Investigations into Their Manufacture, Storage, and Treatment," *Journal of the American Institute for Conservation* vol. 40, no. 1 (2001): 1–14.

[70] For a recent study of Hughes and Shakespeare, see Neil Corcoran, *Shakespeare and the Modern Poet*, Cambridge: Cambridge UP, 2010, especially 181–241.

[71] William Shakespeare, *King Lear*, 1606. Shakespeare.mit.edu.

Treading to drums and to skull-timbrels
Bannered with whole hides of Rakshasas
Pennons of man-skin, man-skin canopies

C1: SLAY! SLAY! SLAY! SLAY! SLAY!
C2: Om Wagi Shari Mum (Continuing under what follows) (*Bardo* 12)

Chorus 1's "SLAY! SLAY! SLAY! SLAY! SLAY!" deliberately echoes *Lear*. In fact, when Hughes wrote *Eat Crow* (1971), a closet drama that also draws heavily on his knowledge of the *Bardo Thödol*, he directly mentions *Lear*:

MORGAN: "Never, never, never, never, never!"

MORGAN PRODUCER (after long pause): It won't do, will it. You see, here the king is using this word NEVER like a knife, to carve up his own insides. This is Hara-kiri on the astral plane. He's forcing it down into the last, deepest cellars and underground resistance of his life—illusion murdering himself: once—not enough, no visible effect, he's in full strength: twice—and still he's missed, but the wave hits him and suddenly it's horrible; three times—and it's agony, but he's gone too far to stop; he'll have to finish it, quick; so four times—and he still hasn't got it, he's wild, he's already out of the world, he's a beast, a god, but alive—so five times—and relief! Relief! He's cracked open the foundations—the light floods in. You see, here, he dies, two or three lines later. End of the old king. Got it. Now. Go.[72]

As the division between Morgan and Morgan Producer indicate, *Eat Crow* is a psychological exploration of a man's descent into madness following the fracturing of his psyche into different personas. The exclamation "Slay!" comes from Evans-Wentz's translation: "Thick awesome darkness will appear in front of thee continually, from the midst of which there will come such terror-producing utterances as 'Strike! Slay!' and similar threats. Fear these not."[73] Hughes takes this note and transforms it into an allusion to Shakespeare. In 1971, working alone, Hughes drew more openly on Shakespeare, but we can see that the influence was already quietly present in his *Bardo*.

In summary, Hughes's *Bardo* sources material from Hughes's own English literary tradition and resembles the theater of China as refracted through the insight he could have gained from his own reading of literature from or studies of these traditions, possibly through correspondence with Chou, possibly through Yeats's early experiments with Nō. Because the opera was never finished, there is much of which we are ignorant. We do not know how Chou and Hughes would have solved many of the staging problems presented by Hughes's narrative-driven and often fantastical script. We also do not know whether some of the resemblances with Chinese theater originated with Hughes or Chou, or what role Chou had as Hughes wrote his script. But these epistemological

---

[72] Hughes, *Eat Crow*. Page Proofs. Box 118. Folder 10. Emory University, 12.
[73] Evans-Wentz, Sambhava, Sangay, and Jung, *Tibetan Book*, 476.

problems aside, we are certain that much in Hughes's libretto is amenable to elements of Chinese theater. However, the *Bardo* appears to mix influences from various different "Western" and "Eastern" theatrical forms together with subtle influences from English theater. This heterodox script suggests that the usual meaning of words and ideas have undergone a change in aspect as they have been wrenched out of their old contexts and placed into a new one.

The *Bardo* and Its Worlds

I turn to the internal coherence of the world of the *Bardo*. The libretto draws from a variety of sources and liberally combines them. How each of these possible sources would be realized in performance depends on the way in which Chou would have finished the music and staging. Both Chou and Hughes would have been constrained by their Western audience's familiarity with the source material and with the many fountains of inspiration which both men dipped into. Considering this heterogenous background, the problems of collaboration, and the difficulties of translation across languages and cultures, the final opera would have difficulty accommodating any one of its sources. Is it possible to find *internal coherence* in the world of this libretto? To answer this question, I will first look at Chou's own thoughts on the possibility of "cultural fusion," and return to some of the mutations that familiar generic elements have undergone after having been transferred to the world of the *Bardo*.

A way to classify works that draw upon multiple foreign genres is to call the work a "hybrid."[74] Perhaps the most influential work on this is "Rhetorical Hybrids: Fusions of Generic Elements" by Jamieson and Campbell. The article argues that works of hybrid genre are more capable of drawing attention to the individual elements of the literary work: "a generic critic recognizes the combination of recurrent elements that forms a hybrid, but, on the other hand, such a critic can perceive the unique fusion that is a response to the idiosyncratic needs of a particular situation, institution, and rhetor."[75] Though I agree that works that draw from more than one genre may help to foreground the generic elements present in the work and the social situation of the writer, the term "hybrid" suggests a radical newness that so-called hybrid works do not possess. What is this work that is inspired by Elizabethan, Irish, and Chinese theater? Well, it is a hybrid. Notice that this assumes that the subgenres from which the hybrid takes are "pure," even if we protest otherwise. It would be a tautology to say that the combination of

---

[74] For a recent discussion of the domain of hybridity in genre studies, see Anneleen Masschelein, Christophe Meuree, David Martens, and Stephanie Vanasten, "The Literary Interview: Toward a Poetics of a Hybrid Genre." *Poetics Today* vol. 35, no. 1–2 (March 2014): 1–49, doi:10.1215/03335372-2648368. They define a hybrid genre as a "genre belonging to different domains and performing different functions" (39). For a consideration of East–West collaborations as hybrid or contrapuntal in strict postcolonial sense, see Olga Taxidou, *Modernism and Performance*, London: Palgrave Macmillan, 2007, 118–47.

[75] Kathleen Hall Jamieson and Karlyn Kohrs Campbell, "Rhetorical Hybrids: Fusions of Generic Elements," *Quarterly Journal of Speech*, vol. 68, no. 2 (1982): 157, doi: 10.1080/00335638209383600.

hybrid genres gives us a hybrid genre. Things in the past were pure; things in the present and things in the future will be hybrid. Naturally, historic subgenres were not pure but themselves grew from various influences. Nō, for instance, has roots in agricultural celebrations, Buddhist and Shintō rituals, and Chinese performance, not to mention its debt to earlier Japanese poetry, which itself borrowed from Chinese poetry. Here, the term "hybrid" assumes that East–West cross-pollination is new, when in fact the process is old hat.[76] Now, it is true that the term has a special application in postcolonial criticism; but Hughes's work can hardly be read as postcolonial. Haun Saussy has already called attention to the limits of the concept of hybridity in comparative literature. The *Bardo* collaboration draws attention to the peculiar methods of analogy that go into constructing an East–West work. These methods give the resultant work an identity that, though of diverse origins, is more specific than the term hybrid might suggest; as Saussy puts it, "hybridity as such often becomes a one-size-fits-all term good for blotting out specific interactions."[77] The *Bardo* project serves as an example in support of Saussy's claim. What I want to show is that these works, or worlds, have unique identities because creating them requires an intricate process of making analogies between a source and a target set of information, in this case between "East" and "West." The process of analogy allows for the creation of a literary world that seems to access both the source and target sets, and so serves as a relay point between the two. I will first outline what those elements might be in more detail, then elaborate on the nature of this process of making worlds through analogies.

Is there anything of Yorkshire in the *Bardo*? There is definitely not in the language. Curiously, despite Hughes's commitment to his Yorkshire identity and accent, the language of his poetry in general is, well, *general*. Because Hughes was always turned toward the past, his diction approximates Yeats and Shakespeare, two models well integrated into the consciousness of most English language speakers who read poetry. We can contrast this with the practice of another late modernist, Basil Bunting (1900–1985), in whose poetry was strongly expressed the Northumberland dialect. We can term Hughes's diction here *traditional*, insofar as it is distant from the diction of most of his contemporaries. On the other hand, the *Tibetan Book* with which Hughes is working is modern. The sources from which Evans-Wentz drew to make the *Tibetan Book* may be old, and Evans-Wentz may adopt antiquated diction. However, from Hughes's point of view, and that of the English-speaking world, the *Tibetan Book* is modern because it emerged only in 1927. This old book becomes something new and groundbreaking as "tradition" is transformed in a transnational collaboration.

---

[76] As Chou mentions, cross-cultural (and cross-aesthetic) interaction "has always taken place wherever and whenever individuals of different cultures have come into contact — whether along the so-called Silk Road or in the course of the spice trade." Chou is assuming that each of these cultures is, in itself, a stable entity, but his notice that hybridity is not a particular feature of the modern era is important. See Chou, "US-China Arts Exchange: A Practice in Search of a Philosophy," *Intercultural Music Studies* Vol. 2, International Institute for Comparative Music Studies and Documentation (1989): 144–64.

[77] Haun Saussy, "Exquisite Cadavers Stitched from Fresh Nightmares," in *Comparative Literature in an Age of Globalization*, Baltimore: Johns Hopkins UP, 2006, 29.

What of Chou and Chinese music? We have seen that the "Chinese" elements of the *Bardo* are varied. I touched earlier on Chou's interest in fusing East and West. According to Chou, the modern Chinese diaspora further frustrates efforts to single out a particularly "Chinese" experience or concern:

> Who is a Chinese? It depends on whether the term is defined ethnically, politically or culturally. There are those from mainland China, Taiwan, Hong Kong, Singapore and throughout Southeast Asia, and, of course, overseas Chinese on every continent. And what about mainland Chinese now settled in the West or elsewhere? All of them have different political, cultural and even ethnic identities, and yet most Chinese assume every other Chinese has the same cultural heritage as theirs. And this is also an assumption of Westerners. The truth is no assumption can be made that all Chinese are the same politically, culturally and ethnically in view of the fact that Chinese culture historically embodies a large number of indigenous ethnicities. Today, much depends on when they were born, where they spent their childhood or formative years, where they were educated and where they now live.[78]

In other words, the term "China" or "Chinese" masks a wealth of diversity. As a mainland Chinese expatriate in the United States, Chou brings a set of concerns and experiences that direct his attention to certain elements of Chinese and East Asian culture, but these are not necessarily essential elements of a trans-historical entity called "China." Therefore, we need to take a more fine-grained approach, or an approach capable of detecting minute differences, to understand what is happening in this fusion of "East" and "West" in the *Bardo*.

However, even as Chou argued against a single Chinese identity, he tried to find essential differences between Chinese and Western composers:

> An even greater difference between [Chinese and Western composers] is that the Western composer traditionally is considered a genius without any social or political responsibility, whereas his Chinese counterpart is never referred to as a composer and has never enjoyed the public recognition accorded to his Western colleague, nor is he compensated. Instead, he (and sometimes she) is an all-round philosopher-artist (wenren, 文人), who composes idealistically about nature and larger issues rather than personal emotions, and often shares a moral responsibility for, as well as influence over, the society with scholars, painters, calligraphers and poets.[79]

It seems contradictory that, in the space of a single article, Chou moves from arguing that there is no single Chinese identity to finding an irreducible disagreement between the historical roles of Chinese and Western composers. There is no attempt here to look more sensitively at what is meant by "Chinese" and "Western." In fact, the opposing term to "Chinese" varies across Chou's articles. At times it is Europe, at others the "West," at still others "Western Europe." At other times, Chou slips between talking about China and about Asia more generally.[80] The reason may be the restrictions of comparison: when

---

[78] Wen-chung Chou, "Whither Chinese Composers?" *Contemporary Music Review* vol. 26, no. 5–6 (October 2007): 501, doi:10.1080/07494460701652939.

[79] Ibid., 503.

[80] See, for example, Wen-chung Chou, "Asian Concepts and Twentieth-Century Western Composers," *Musical Quarterly* vol. LVII, no. 2 (1971), doi:10.1093/mq/LVII.2.211.

Chou talks about China itself, he feels free to complicate the term, to draw out its various senses and contradictions. But in order to compare Chinese music and art to that found in Europe and the United States, he relies on broader terms that obscure the differences that he elsewhere underlines.

This process of simplifying terms when comparing between East and West helps us better to understand the motives behind the *Bardo* project. Chou chose the *Bardo* in part because it was a text of some renown outside of East and Central Asia. As he would later claim:

> I am attracted to these classics of the East that have come to be fairly well-known in the West, not only because of the dramatic impact of their multicolored content and the universal appeal of their humanistic message at a time like ours, but also because of their polygenetic and polymorphous history. It is my belief that these qualities will afford me opportunities to carry out some of my own ideals—musical or otherwise.[81]

What are these ideals? Throughout his career, Chou desired the *"confluence* of musical cultures, which aims at inner representation, and not *influence,* which shows only the outward experience."[82] To achieve this, he believed that both Eastern and Western music must understand their deep-rooted differences.[83] "Turkish Marches" should be abandoned, Chou says, in favor of music that, should it go "East" for inspiration, looks critically at the philosophical foundations underpinning the art and music of that community. Musicians inspired by China, therefore, would do well to learn from Daoism, Buddhism, and the *I-Ching* as these are, Chou argues, the philosophical roots of Chinese music. When these roots are cut away, Chinese music loses its sense.[84]

It seems intuitive enough for Chou to say that a fusion of East and West is a deep-level combination of the philosophical histories of the two. Yet Chou gives a more concrete rationale. Part of his reasoning is that philosophy affects musical composition. He writes that "inimitable performances by the great Fukeshu shakuhachi master, Watazumido Shuso, are but one example, though exceptional, of how deeply music can affected by the state of mind on the part of the performer—in this case under the influence of Zen and Tao."[85] Chou's theory suggests that he was interested in the *Bardo* as a *religious* text, an ancient *Buddhist* text that could contribute to deep-level fusion between East and West.

As we have seen, however, Hughes was convinced that the shared term that would allow for fusion of East and West is shamanism. In other words, an ancient shared heritage between East and West justifies cross-cultural collaborations and overreaching like those of the *Bardo* project. In fact, this is also Chou's reasoning. His fusion of East and West is in fact a "re-merger of Eastern and Western musical concepts and practices," for

---

[81] Nicolas Slominsky, *Writings on Music: Russian and Soviet Music Composers,* ed. Electra Slominsky Yourke, Abingdon, UK: Routledge, 2003, 3.
[82] Lai, *Music,* 20 (emphasis in the original).
[83] Wen-chung Chou, "East and West, Old and New," *Asian Music* vol. 1, no. 1 (1968): 20, doi:10.2307/834006.
[84] Ibid., 22.
[85] Ibid., 21.

Chou believes "that the traditions of Eastern and Western music once shared the same sources and that, after a thousand years of divergence, they are now merging to form the mainstream of a new musical tradition."[86] The logic here is the same as Hughes's, only Hughes goes further in giving these "shared sources" a name and a lineage in shamanism.

If this work has been arguing literary worlds in translational literature arise through analogies targeting vague elements of both the original work and the target culture, it is time to look in more depth at the process of analogy itself. In *By Parallel Reasoning: The Construction and Evaluation of Analogical Arguments*, Paul Bartha goes through what makes analogies work. He argues that analogies rely on horizontal and vertical relations. Vertical relations are between properties within a term; horizontal relations are relations between terms. These are the source and target domains. If there are horizontal relations between a source and target domain, then we can infer properties in the target domain based on what we know about the source. Bartha gives the example of sound and light. In the seventeenth century, Dutch physicist Christiaan Huygens drew vertical relations between the two: just as sound echoes, so light reflects; sound bends around corners and light refracts through slits; sound has volume, light brightness; sound pitch, light color. Knowing that sound travels through either the medium of air or water, Huygens concluded that light too must pass through a medium, which he concluded was ether.[87] That Huygens was incorrect is not at issue. We can take Bartha's formalization of analogical arguments to understand Chou and Hughes's logic. In essence, both Chou and Hughes are drawing on the inherent vagueness of the source text to make both horizontal and vertical analogies; what each does with this vagueness, however, differs the one from the other. The process accords well with Klein's distinction between vertical and horizontal relations—indeed, the process appears almost identical. Bartha's utility to this discussion then is to provide a clearer heuristic model that highlights the role of analogy in Klein's horizontal/vertical schema, and how the "horizontal" elements are made to fit with submerged "vertical" ones in order to enter a new literary and linguistic constellation.

What happens in the *Bardo*? More exactly, what has happened to all of the elements that have been pooled together to create the *Bardo*? I present a passage already considered:

> Solo: Others, others. Who are these others.
> A&B: Recognise Vajra Heruka, the blood-drinker;
>   Recognise Vajra Krotishaurima:
>   Recognise Ratna Heruka, the blood[-]drinker;
>   Recognise Ratna Krotishaurima;
>   Recognise Padma Heruka, the blood-drinker;
>   Recognise Padma Krotishaurima;
>   Recognise Karma Heruka, the Blood-drinker;
>   Recognise Karma Krotishaurima.

---

[86] Ibid., 19.
[87] Paul F. A. Bartha, *By Parallel Reasoning: The Construction and Evaluation of Analogical Arguments*, New York: Oxford UP, 2010, 14.

Solo: I am blown like a breath through the Bardo.
B: Evil Karma drags you further, further and deeper into the Bardo.
Solo: I am blown like ashes through the Bardo.
B: Evil Karma catches you from yourself and from Liberation
A&B: Recognise these forms for your own mind.

(Bardo 16)

Here is the source of this episode in the Evans-Wentz translation:

On the Tenth Day, the blood-drinking [deity] of the [Precious]-Gem Order named Ratna Heruka, yellow of colour; [having] three faces, six hands, four feet firmly postured; the right [face] white, the left, red, the central, darkish yellow; enhaloed in flames; in the first of the six hands holding a gem, in the middle [one], a trident-staff, in the last [one], a baton; in the first of the left [hands], a bell, in the middle [one], a skull-bowl, in the last [one], a trident-staff; his body embraced by the Mother Ratna-Krotishaurima, her right [hand] clinging to his neck, her left offering to his mouth a red shell [filled with blood], will issue from the southern quarter of thy brain and come to shine upon thee. Fear not. Be not terrified. Be not awed. Know them to be the embodiment of thine own intellect.[88]

Evans-Wentz's archaic diction and use of hyphenated words encourages Hughes to think of the *Bardo* as akin to an early or pre-modern English text, one brimming with Anglo-Saxon rather than Latinate words. This is in turn helps Hughes to connect the *Bardo* to the more mystical non-Latinate civilization that he identifies with pre-Christian Britain, and so on to shamanism. But for this to occur, something must happen to the words themselves.

In short, the *aspect* of the words changes even as the words retain their original meanings as tokens of word types. For instance, putting aside its possible source in the Tibetan language, "blood-drinker" in the context of the *Bardo* serves not only as an epithet that describes a trait of a Buddhist deity and through inflated language elevates it; it also points to the "pre-modern" aspects of the *Bardo*. Hughes turns Evans-Wentz's adjective "blood-drinking" into the hyphenated noun "blood-drinker." Yet "blood-drinker" cannot help but remind us of kennings, medieval rhetorical devices in which a circumlocutive phrase metonymically associated with an object is used in place of that object's name.[89] Accordingly, the aspect of the term changes in the *Bardo* as Hughes tries to draw out not only whatever meaning he believes lies in the *Tibetan Book* but also the early English and "shamanistic" meaning that he believes is latent in the *Bardo*. Moreover, if Chou is correct, then the "Buddhist" nature of the terms must take on a heightened importance in the *Bardo*. "Vajra Krotishaurima" would refer not simply to a Buddhist deity, but also, now that this name is appearing not in the context of Tibetan ritual but an opera written by an Englishman and a Chinese expatriate, refer back to the very *Buddhist* aspect of that word. Taken from its original context, the deities' names highlight their

---

[88] Evans-Wentz, Sambhava, Sangay, and Jung, *Tibetan Book*, 141.
[89] E.g., "sea-wood" for "ship."

own status as Buddhist names in a way that they could not do in a purely Tibetan or Buddhist context. At least in this case, translation forces words to change in aspect purely by them being placed in a new social and aesthetic context, and this change allows words and the pieces of literature that they form to *cohere* within the literary universe into which they are shifted.

Had the opera been completed, there may have been a musical correlative to Hughes's medievalism. In the 1950s and 1960s, while studying medieval composition at Columbia and Greek composition in his spare time, Chou was experimenting with composition that could express the ideas of the *I Ching*. He devised a system called variable modes, which attempts to blend Chinese, Indian, and Greek modes of composition.[90] The experimentation, evident in *Metaphors* (1960) and fully expressed in *Pien* (1966), was another of Chou's attempts to find a common ground on which to fuse Eastern and Western music,[91] and it is not difficult to imagine that the modal techniques Chou employed, hearkening as they do back to medieval compositions such as those of the Gregorian chant as well as Chinese compositional practices, was such a shared source. Indeed, Eric Lai suggests that in the 1950s Chou's search for a common source attracted the Chinese American composer to "ancient Greek, Medieval, and Renaissance music, in particular the topic of modal theory, for he discovered certain affinities between European modal principles and ancient Chinese music theory."[92] The heterogenous influences from which Hughes crafted his libretto would likely have been mirrored in the Chou's music. The odd associations Hughes made would have gone beyond his libretto and been expressed in conceivably every facet of the *Bardo*.

Here is *multidimensionality*. The text and the figures, religious ideas, and rhetoric in it have different extensions depending on the contexts into which they have been placed. I have been referring to the contexts as the universe, constellation, and world of a society, author, and text. But it is not just the text that changes in aspect. The senses of "English," "Chinese," "Asian," "European," "Buddhist," and so on are not quite the same in the *Bardo* or in a comparative context generally.

Chou's source domain is the Chinese composer, a philosopher-artist who is defined by being socially engaged, retiring, and unpaid. The target is the Western composer, who is a celebrated amoral genius who is dedicated to one craft and is remunerated. There is, he says, a vertical relation between these traits and Daoism and Buddhism in China. Since there are no horizontal relations between China and the West at the top level, any fusion between the two must be a deep-level philosophical combination. This, I think, is the reason Chou stresses the need to attend to the philosophical foundations of China and the West in comparative and collaborative musical projects.

---

[90] A more detailed explanation is in Yayoi Uno Everett, "Calligraphy and Musical Gestures in the Late Works of Chou Wen-chung," *Contemporary Music Review* no. 26, vols. 5–6 (2007): 569–84.

[91] Sau Woon Au, "I Ching in the Music of John Cage, Chou Wen-chung (周文中) and Zhao Xiaosheng (趙曉生)," PhD Dissertation, Chinese University of Hong Kong, 2013, 67, 68.

[92] Lai, *Music*, 13–14.

Hughes follows the same logic, but his terms differ. He traces a lineage for himself to an ecstatic, occult, and premodern "English" literature that achieved fruition in then languished after Shakespeare. This is his source category. He then constructs a broadly "Asian" target category that is also ecstatic, occult, and premodern, epitomized by the *Bardo*. There is a one-to-one correspondence at the top level, and since the target domain already has vertical relation between these three items and "shamanism" (Hughes thinks) the same vertical relation should exist within English literature. Hughes has carried out the process Chou aspires to complete, but does so by changing the deep-level term in the target domain from Buddhism and Daoism to shamanism, and by focusing less on analogies between artists East and West as on analogies between the texts themselves. This is a haphazard process with an essentialist reading of English and Tibetan and Asian literature and religion, yet it allows Hughes to give an internal coherence to the world he was trying to construct out of the *Bardo* and to his own poetic universe.

My interpretation of the *Bardo* does not claim to find a unique process that led to its development or a unique feature of East–West literature. But I do claim that focusing on this deep-level reasoning aids us in discovering what counts and what must be overcome in order to make a "fusion" of "East" and "West" take place. It reminds us why East and West often merit the inverted commas in which I have yet again put them, and to doubt the apparent naturalness of the two categories that the term "fusion" suggests. The "Tibetan" source of the *Bardo* is not exactly Tibetan, and Chou and Hughes's treatment of it pushes Tibet further into the background. In turn, Britain and China swell in importance for the *Bardo* as the text becomes an experiment in bringing East and West closer together. Yet even Britain and China, and East and West, are categories molded during the process of fusion. Chou and Hughes need an East and a West that *can* be combined, and this requires highlighting certain dimensions to the disadvantage of others. Both Chou and Hughes suggest a primordial sameness between East and West that allows for fusion. Chou leaves ambiguous the terms that will be used in bringing the two regions together, while Hughes identifies a single term, "shamanism," as the essential source of art East and West. The need to find a deep-level horizontal relation between the two things Hughes tries to make one in his libretto explains the strange features of the text and of his few commentaries upon it.

The process leaves us with an East and West in the *Bardo* that are not identical with the totality of cultures, languages, and literatures in two independently existing regions but possible arrangements of elements mainly pulled from the unstable categories of Chinese, Japanese, Tibetan, and British literature. The categories of East and West, then, and indeed all of the national subcategories used for the *Bardo*, are *images,* possible states of each of these categories as made to cohere in a particular constellation of belief. Think back to the ternary relation introduced in the last chapter: x is at least as close to y, in F-relevant aspects, as it is to z. Because there is no precise application of "Eastern" or "Western" or even "Chinese" and "British," their applications are fixed by focusing on a relevant aspect of one that brings it as close to the other as it is to a third category. For Hughes, the concept of shamanism, or the predicate "evinces Shamanic roots," brings Old English literature at least as close to Chinese and "Asiatic" literature as it is to post–Civil War English literature. In treating these categories as if they were vague predicates,

Hughes establishes a common ground that allows him to handle a large amount of material from ontologically inconsistent traditions. Looking at his libretto now, and the work and comments that he and Chou left during and after the *Bardo* project, we begin to see how important the ontological vagueness of texts and literary traditions themselves are to comparative literature and world literature, in which the *Bardo* project might be considered an exercise.

Chapter Three

WHAT WE DISAGREE ABOUT WHEN WE DISAGREE ABOUT NŌ

「能楽の自由な空間と時間の処理や、
露わな形而上学的主題などを、
そのまま現代に生かすために、
シチュエーションのほうを現代化したのである」[1]

C'est la vie telle que, ramenée du pays des ombres,
elle se peint à nous dans le regard de la méditation ;
nous nous dressons devant nous-mêmes, dans
l'amer monument de notre désir, de notre doleur
et de notre folie. [2]

Nō fascinated several writers through the early and mid-twentieth century, but for Paul Claudel and Mishima Yukio 三島由紀夫 the "exposed metaphysical themes" that are "brought back from the land of shadows" were the chief fascination of the Japanese theatrical genre. The focus on the spiritual or metaphysical aspects of Nō provides an interesting point of contact between Claudel's and Mishima's drama, a point of contact especially fascinating to find between two writers separated by time, religion, ethnicity, and language. This chapter will consider how these points of divergence between Claudel and Mishima affect the use of their shared concern for the spiritual as a *tertium comparationis* between the two modern writers and classical Nō.

To tighten the scope of comparison, and to make for a clean triangulation, I will focus on Claudel's and Mishima's adaptations of one classical Nō play, *Kantan* 邯鄲. I begin with an overview of *Kantan* and Nō theater. I then compare Claudel's and Mishima's

---

[1] "To adapt classical Nō's free use of time and space and take the exposed metaphysical themes while modernizing the situations." (230) In this afterword to the *Kindai Nōgakushū* from which this quote of Mishima's comes, Donald Keene contrasts Mishima's "modern" Nō with the "modern" Nō of Meiji-era writer Kōri Torahiko 郡虎彦. According to Keene, while Kōri dispenses with the medieval worldview of the Nō, he keeps the Medieval setting, which results in Nō like Oscar Wilde's *Salomé*. Mishima's Nō have the opposite intention. Donald Keene, "Kaisetsu," in Yukio Mishima, *Kindai nogakushū*, Tokyo: Shinchōsha, 1968, 229.

[2] "It is life such that, brought back from the land of shadows, it reveals itself before us in the vision of meditation; we stand before ourselves in the bitter monument to our desire, our sadness, and our folly." Paul Claudel, *Oeuvres en prose*, ed. Jacques Petit and Charles Galpérine, Paris: Gallimard, 1965, 1171. Subsequent references to this work will be made in-text and use the abbreviation *Pr.*

critical reflections on Nō: Claudel's famous essay "Nô" and his impressions recorded in his journal of the Nō he saw in Japan; and Mishima's comments on Nō and Japanese literature in various essays, letters, and interviews. With this background in place, I set Mishima's *Kantan* 邯鄲 against the "Guardian Angel" scene of Claudel's *Le Soulier de Satin*, which Ayako Nishino has shown is likely inspired by *Kantan*,[3] a classic Nō piece by an unknown author, sometimes purported to be Zeami, the greatest author of classical Nō. My attention here will not only be on how Claudel and Mishima treat the same source material, but also on how Claudel, Mishima, and the original Nō author relate to one another in their use of what Mishima calls the "exposed metaphysical elements" of Nō.

When thinking of world literature, translation, and weak theory here, we again refer to Wai Chee Dimock's call for a "lower-level kind of theorizing" that does not try to prioritize any genre or system above any other and makes "no prediction about being the last word."[4] Taking a play from the Nō genre and two responses to it as a case study, and thinking of the *religious* framework of the genre and the three plays, we see essentially why Dimock is correct to caution us. As I will demonstrate, a "weak" approach is notably useful in dealing with translations and adaptations that span not only languages but also ontologies founded on religious belief. The message, to borrow the words of G. E. R. Lloyd speaking about the importance of differences in spiritual practices in the concept of rationality across cultures, is that, in studying different cultures, "We should learn to attune ourselves to unfamiliar ideas and unfamiliar ways of expressing them."[5] Lloyd's advice holds not only for the direct study of spiritual practices but, we will discover, even for reading literary texts all of which seem to owe a lot to a common root.

Comparing Charles Baudelaire's "Une Charogne" with Xu Zhimo's translation of it into Chinese, Haun Saussy notes that translation, rather than being a one-to-one correspondence between a term "A" in the source language and an equivalent "B" in the target language, rather assimilates fragments of the original in a process of digestion. "Rather than equivalence," Saussy writes of Xu Zhimo's translation, we get "appropriation; rather than asserting new identities between separate and independent things,

---

[3] Nishino notes that the influence is most acute in the 1943 version, thanks to stage directions that recall the Nō *Kantan*. Yet Nishino notes that the affinities between *Soulier* and *Kantan* are restricted by the fact that in the original "la rêve s'avère une expérience philosophique qui mène à l'éveil bouddhiste" (the dream reveals a philosophical experience that leads to Buddhist enlightenment). See Ayako Nishino, *Paul Claudel, le nô et la synthèse des arts*, Paris: Classiques Garnier, 2013, 519. It is uncertain how much the stage directions owe to Claudel's collaborator Jean-Louis Barrault, whom Nishino also concludes likely knew of *Kantan* ahead of the 1943 version of *Soulier* (521–22). Although the dialogue is slightly different in the 1942 version, and the fact that Dona Prouhèze sees her life pass before her in a dream is more evident, the significance of the action is the same as in the original Claudel wrote in Japan.

[4] Wai Chee Dimock, "Weak Theory: Henry James, Colm Toibin, and W. B. Yeats," *Critical Inquiry* vol. 39, no. 4 (June 1, 2013): 733.

[5] G. E. R. Lloyd, *The Ambivalences of Rationality: Ancient and Modern Cross-Cultural Explorations*, Cambridge: Cambridge UP, 2018, 91.

this translation breaks down and recycles bits of those things."[6] It should be obvious that I am in agreement with Saussy, who is in many ways the theoretical protagonist of this chapter, if not this book. Moreover, the digestion metaphor Saussy uses has currency elsewhere in the study of world literature, as when Paul Giles, treating Anthony Powell's novels in the context of modernism, says that he does not "suggest that modernism is simply ignored by Powell; rather, its disruptive force is ingested, masticated, and then ultimately expelled."[7] In this chapter, I want to see what happens to these "bits." A good way to do that is to look not at translations per se but at adaptations or appropriations, literary works that attempt to disassociate something essential in the original text from the language in which it is expressed (which is, after all, the very conceit of translation). It is good, moreover, to look not only at translations across languages—those "horizontal" translations Klein discusses—but within a language across time—the "vertical" relations. Doing so can show us that the bits that are digested and processed are often themselves changed as they are cut loose from their cultural moorings and made to flow into the mold of a new cosmology. If the last chapter was about fusion, this chapter is about exercises in disassociation.

A sustained comparison of Claudel's and Mishima's adaptations of Nō theater has never appeared. Though the two playwrights feature in mentions of the reception of Nō in the twentieth century, their views and uses of classical Nō have not been critically compared. Certainly, there is reason for this oversight. Claudel and Mishima were from different parts of the world, born nearly 60 years apart, wrote in different languages, and had different aesthetic concerns. A comparison between the two might seem, at first blush, to uncover far more differences than similarities and thus not be worth the trouble. Yet, despite the many personal differences between them, Claudel's and Mishima's relationships to the Nō theater resemble one another strikingly. Though Claudel, the staunch Catholic, would not mention Buddhism by name in his reception of the Nō theater, we can show that the "metaphysics" that he valued in Nō appear close to those dear to Mishima. And while Claudel died before he could become aware of Mishima, Mishima was aware of Claudel. In a speech he delivered in English, Mishima mentions Claudel's essay on the Nō:

> When the French poet Paul Claudel came to Japan, he was deeply moved by the Noh and wrote a beautiful essay. For a foreigner to appreciate the Noh, I imagine Claudel must have been a very unusual person. Even for a Japanese, if for example, a young man were to invite his girl friend to see the Noh, I would imagine that nine out of 10 would refuse to go. Not only does Noh last for a couple of hours, but also there is hardly any movement on the stage, which results in many of the spectators falling fast asleep.[8]

---

[6] Haun Saussy, *Translation as Citation: Zhuangzi Inside Out*, Oxford: Oxford UP, 2017, 39.
[7] Paul Giles, *Backgazing: Reverse Time in Modernist Culture*, Oxford: Oxford UP, 2019, 190.
[8] Yukio Mishima, "Influences in Modern Japanese Literature," in *Mishima Yukio Zenshū*, ed. Jun Ishikawa and Shōichi Saeki, Dai sanjyū maki, Tokyo: Shinchōsha, 1973, 22.

For his part, Mishima believed that "Noh has a wonderful characteristic that cannot be found in any other of the forms of dramatic art," that of opposing on stage "the conscious and the unconscious in the individual."[9] Mishima's opinion of Nō brings him in turn close to Claudel, his fellow "strange" admirer of traditional Japanese theater. The resemblance between the two is perhaps less surprising when we recall that, though Mishima and Claudel were born far apart, Claudel did not come to Japan and encounter the Nō until later in his life, only two years before Mishima was born. And though Claudel began work on *Soulier* in the 1920s, the gap between the first performance of *Soulier* in 1942 and Mishima's *Kantan* is only eight years. In the history of the reception of Nō in the twentieth century, Claudel's and Mishima's interpretations of Nō are close not only aesthetically but temporally as well.

Three *Kantans*

Kantan 邯鄲 is based on the famous Chinese story of the Pillow of Kantan, Shen Jiji's *Zhenzhong ji*, which we met in Chapter One, that allows someone who rests on it to see her entire life pass in the duration of one sleep. In the Nō, a traveler who professes to have wasted his life so far, Rosei, the *shite*, comes to an inn in the Chinese region of Kantan. As the female innkeeper, the *waki*, prepares him a bowl of millet, Rosei sleeps on the pillow. Rosei dreams that he rises to become the king of Chu and reigns gloriously for five decades. On the 50th anniversary of his reign, Rosei is feted with dancers and a feast. His minister offers Rosei a cup made by an ascetic that will allow Rosei to live for a thousand years. Here the dream ends. As the mistress wakes him, Rosei realizes that his reign of 50 years only lasted the time it takes to cook a bowl of millet. With this insight into the brief and illusory nature of life, Rosei achieves enlightenment and returns home. This Nō belongs, according to the traditional classification of the theater, to the third category of "miscellaneous Nō." According to the modern classification it is a "*mugen* Nō" 夢幻能 or "dream Nō," as opposed "*genzai* Nō" 現在能 or "present-time Nō."

Though Claudel did not see a performance of *Kantan*, Ayako Nishino has shown that Claudel probably knew the piece thanks to English translations by Basil Hall Chamberlain (1880) and a more faithful version by Arthur Waley (1921).[10] Moreover, *Kantan* was in vogue among "intellectuals and people involved in theater in the West in the 1920s" (parmi les intellectuels et les hommes de théâtre du monde occidental), and in 1924 Jacques Copeau planned to bring Waley's version to the stage, a failed attempt, but one which Claudel was aware of.[11] As for Mishima, a version of *Kantan* in 1950 was his first attempt at modern Nō or *shinksakunō* (新作能). Because it takes place within a dream, with a rapid succession of characters and locations, Mishima's *Kantan* is more surreal,

---

[9] Ibid., 23.

[10] Chamberlain titled his translation "Life Is But a Dream," which, as Nishino indicates, recalls Calderon's 1635 *Life Is a Dream*. See Nishino, *Synthèse*, 517–18. Waley's translation is titled *Kantan*.

[11] Nishino, *Synthèse*, 518.

and, with its masks and chorus, retains more elements of Nō than his later attempts at the genre. Of course, the chief difference between Claudel's and Mishima's reception of *Kantan* is that Mishima could understand the Japanese of the original *Kantan* whereas Claudel, ignorant of Japanese, had to rely on translations. The translation on which he relied came in two forms. First, he read translations of Nō into English, mostly those of Chamberlain and Waley, and, in French, of Noël Péri, Michel Révon, and Georges Renondeau.[12] Second, he viewed several Nō performances during his time as ambassador to Japan, for which his assistants provided notes explaining the significance of the action on stage. As a major non-Japanese writer in the early twentieth century, Claudel occupied a rare position insofar as he saw authentic Nō performances yet still needed to have recourse to translation: he gained far greater familiarity with the form than, say, W. B. Yeats, but never achieved the proximity that Mishima enjoyed.

That does not mean, however, that Mishima's Nō, as *shinsaku nō*, are naturally closer to the genre. At the core of his *Kantan*, like the original Nō and the *Zhenzhong ji*, is a dream sequence; the events of the dream, or rather the ways in which the protagonist, Jirō (次郎), reacts to them is at odds with the original scenario. Jirō returns from the city to the home of his nursemaid, Kiku (菊). Kiku's husband has long since deserted her. In the city, Jirō heard a rumor surrounding Kiku's husband's disappearance according to which the husband's personality changed after he slept on a mysterious pillow. Upon awakening, the husband departed instantly, and the flowers in Kiku's garden have not bloomed since. Jirō is nihilistic: he uninterested in all aspects of life, and is emblematic of the general sense of youthful angst in postwar Japan. If we think of the Nō upon which Mishima's *Kantan* is based, we notice that Jirō's state of mind resembles Rosei's after Rosei achieves enlightenment. But Jirō takes no solace in Buddhism or any other religious view. His disenchantment with life is purely negative, not pointing to a higher spiritual order that would give his apathy meaning. The interest of the play is both in the presence of the supernatural in modern Japan, and in the way in which supernatural or Buddhist themes take on a different significance as Mishima transplants them from the Middle Ages to postwar Japan.

Once Kiku yields the pillow to Jirō and he falls asleep, the stage gives way to his dreamscape. *Kantan* is unusual among Mishima's Nō for its use of masks and chanting. Mishima's retention of these features of classical Nō may owe to this being Mishima's first take on the genre. His intention to retain only the "exposed metaphysical themes" and not the props and songs of Nō would, perhaps, emerge as he grew more confident in adapting the genre. But the chanting and the masks are perhaps also appropriate to a Nō that explicitly represents a dream. The chorus and mask mark the shift from the

---

[12] For an in-depth discussion of Claudel's literary sources, see Dominique Millet-Gérard, "Claudel et le nô: Sources, méditations, intuitions," in *La Fleur cachée du nô*, ed. Catherine Mayaux, Paris: Honoré Champion, 2015, 125–40. The most thorough treatment is found in Nishino, *Synthèse* , and the most in-depth comparison of Claudel's reception of Nō relative to other Western writers is in Ayako Nishino, "L'Histoire de la réception du nô en Occident (XVIe—XXe siècles) et son Adaptation par Yeats, Pound, Claudel, et Brecht," in *La Fleur cachée du nô*, ed. Catherine Mayaux, Paris: Honoré Champion, 2015, 55–74.

actual world to the world of the dream, as well as the movement between the different phases of Jirō's dream. Thus, to mark the initial shift from dream to reality, Kiku leaves to fetch Jirō the pillow, and the chorus chants a short song. Afterward, a masked woman appears on stage.

(ーーこの間、無言劇。次郎、上着を脱ぎて床に入る。菊、枕を挙げもって登場。これを次郎の頭にあってがって退場。合唱をはる。正面より美女を登場・仮面を着す。ロングスカートの洋装なり)

美女　次郎さん……次郎さん。。。。
合唱　起きなさい！起きなさい！
美女　次郎さん。。。。次郎さん。。。。
合唱　起きなさい！起きなさい！
次郎　（眼ざめて上半身を起す）何だい。誰？ あ、君は誰？ ずいぶん美人だね。

During this time [as the chorus chants], a dumb show. Jirō takes off his coat and gets in the bed. Kiku returns onstage with the pillow. She places it under Jirō's head and exits. The chorus ceases. A masked beauty (美人) *appears. She wears a long skirt in the Western style.*

Beautiful woman: Jirō, Jirō.[13]
Chorus: Awaken! Awaken!
Jirō: (Waking and rising half his body) Huh? Who's there? Ah, who're you? You're really beautiful, aren't you?[14]

The *bijin* 美人 or beautiful woman's "name," insofar as we can call it that, in the play appears to come from Jirō directly. Jirō refers to her as "really beautiful" (ずいぶん美人 *zuibun bijin*) upon first seeing her. He never bothers to learn what she is actually called, if anything. Hence, her most salient feature for him (being a beautiful woman) becomes the most salient mark of her identity for us in the text, her name. This could be both a critique of Jirō's chauvinism and the apparent chauvinism of the medieval world against which the source text was reacting, in which simply having a beautiful wife *as such* is a token of good fortune and happiness, a token which the original Nō *Kantan* showed, through the experiences of Rosei, was illusory. Or it might also give us a glimpse into Mishima's own fraught stance toward women, which, as Hashimoto Osamu has indicated, takes as its prototypical woman a fleetingly beautiful yet, at the

---

[13] There's no way to preserve the softness of the beautiful woman's speech in translation, since English does not distinguish so sharply between Jirō's rough speech and the beautiful woman's, indeed between male and female speech patterns, as does Japanese, a difference missed by Waley in his review of Keene's translation. Though Keene's translation is commendable, I have chosen here to translate the play myself in an effort to capture more fully the important linguistic markers in Mishima's original. For Keene's version, see Yukio Mishima, *Five Modern Nō Plays*, trans. Donald Keene, New York: Vintage International, 2009.

[14] Yukio Mishima, *Kindai nōgakushū*, Tokyo: Shinchōsha, 1968, 21. Subsequent references to this work will be made in-text and use the abbreviation *Kindai*.

same time, severe and dangerous type. Beneath a soft and enigmatic appearance lurks a certain hard dignity,[15] though, as we will see, the beautiful woman's soft exterior hides not dignity in this case but the emptiness characteristic of the original Nō. Whatever the case, having her called "beautiful woman" gives her a generic belonging to that medieval Nō world of *Kantan*, in which a beautiful woman is necessary for the temptation and subsequent enlightenment of the protagonist, Rosei. This medieval Nō world cannot quite enter into equal dialogue with the world of modern Japan.

The chorus functions as a third person. But for whom is it speaking, if anyone? It may be speaking for the beautiful woman, for the author, for the audience; or it may be another spectral entity within the pillow. That the beautiful woman wears a mask is also significant, for, as we saw, the *shite* alone wears a mask. There are, I think, two nonexclusive ways to interpret the mask here. Since the mask breaks with the realism of the opening part, it marks a clear split between dream and reality. As such, the mask preserves a sense of realism as it keeps the dreamscape distinct from the reality of Kiku's house. However, the division further marks the division between Mishima's Nō and classical Nō, for, if we keep in mind that the *"mugen"* aspect of Nō only became important in classification in the twentieth century, the divide between dream and reality suggests a dichotomy not present in the Japanese original. Moreover, Jirō does not act like Rosei; his dream neither seduces nor impresses him. His action is purely negative, a rejection of that which passes before him. Now, by making the beautiful woman wear a mask and be introduced and, depending on our reading, supported by a chorus, Mishima has identified her with the world of classical Nō. That is to say that by using the chorus only during the dream sequence and the mask only for a dream figure, Mishima has drawn the figures of Jirō's dream close to the world of classical Nō, whereas Jirō, with his rough modern speech and rough modern dress, and with his inability to be roused by the scene that passes before him, embodies the "modern" or *kindai* element of Mishima's modern Nō. At the same time, however, the fact that she wears a skirt "in the Western style" makes the beautiful woman herself look contradictorily both modern and "Western" and medieval and "Japanese." Though the mask and the chorus pull her toward the world of classical Nō, the dress signals that this world too has been affected by modernity. Just as we ourselves cannot have perfect access to the actual world of a literary text, as I argued in Chapter One, but have to modify that world to make sense of it in our current constellation of belief, so the world of classical Nō that Mishima brings before our and Jirō's eyes is already made self-contradictory. Mishima's *kindai* Nō not only dramatizes the clash between the world of classical Nō and modernity, but the reorganization of the very world of classical Nō that has taken place in the modern era.

The beautiful woman shows Jirō their life together. They go on honeymoon, she cooks for him, and a child is born. Jirō remains detached. When offered a drink, he complains that he hates being drunk; when cooked an egg, he caustically tells the beautiful woman

---

[15] Osamu Hashimoto, *Mishima Yukio to ha nanimono dattanoka*, Tokyo: Shinchō Bunko, 2002, 261–62.

that her cooking is like that of any woman: it is either too sweet, too spicy, too raw, or overdone. When asked to kiss, he wonders how he is to breathe. When told to breathe through his nose, he fusses that he hates breathing like that (*Kindai* 24–28). Unlike Rosei, Jirō finds all of the sensual things he is offered dull.

Often, his thoughts arrive immediately at the moral of the original *Kantan*. For instance, looking into the beautiful woman's eyes, he notices something terrifying within their comeliness:

次郎　あ、今君の目のなかをこはいものがとほりすぎた。
美女　こはいものって何が？
次郎　女の目のなかにはね、ときどき狼がとほりすぎるんだよ。
美女　おほかたシェパアドのまちがひだわ。(*Kindai* 23)

Jirō: Ah, something terrifying just passed by in your eyes.
Beautiful woman: Something terrifying?
Jirō: Sometimes in a woman's eyes a wolf passes by.
Beautiful woman: Surely it's really a large sheepdog.

Unlike Rosei, Jirō sees hollowness in beauty immediately. We might, thinking again of Hashimoto's description of Mishima's ideal woman, imagine Jirō as seeing immediately past the soft exterior that Mishima thought was essential to feminine allure, and in the process ruining the whole effect. Admiring the beautiful woman's face, he decides to kiss her. Just as quickly, his thoughts turn morbid:

次郎　君、きれいだね。
美女　やっと目がさめたわね。
次郎　僕、お面にキッスされたやうな気がした。
美女　女のキッスってみんなそんなものよ。
次郎　君ってほんとにきれいだ。でも皮をむけば、やっぱり骸骨なんだ。
美女　え？
次郎　皮をむけば、やっぱり骸骨なんだよ。
　美女　あらいやだ、あたくしそんなこと考へてみたこともないわ。（思はず顔にさはってみる）
次郎　骸骨に美人なんてあるかい
美女　そりやあ、あるでせうよ、きっと。
　次郎　すごい自信だな。でも今キッスされたときね、君の頬っぺたの下でね、君の骨が笑ってゐるのが、僕にはわかったわよ。
美女　顔が笑へば、骨も笑ふわよ。
　次郎　ふん、あんなことを言ってる。かう言はなくちゃいけないよ。顔が笑ふとき、骨は笑ってゐるんだ、それはたしかさ。しかし、顔が泣いてゐるときも顔の骨は笑ってゐるんだ。骨はかう言ってるんだよ、笑はば笑へ、泣けば泣け、今に俺の天下が来るんだ、ってね。(*Kindai* 25–26)

Jirō: You really are beautiful.
Beautiful woman: Your eyes have finally opened, huh?
Jirō: It feels as if I was kissed by a mask.
Beautiful woman: Everyone feels that way about a woman's kiss.
Jirō: You're really, really beautiful. But peel off your skin, and you're just a skeleton.
Beautiful woman: Eh?
Jirō: Peel off your skin, and you're just a skeleton.
Beautiful woman: How coarse! I've never thought of such a thing. (Unconsciously she strokes her face).
Jirō: Don't beautiful people also have skeletons?
Beautiful woman: Well, of course, yes.
Jirō: What confidence! But when I gave you a kiss just now, there underneath your cheek your bones were laughing—I know it.
Beautiful woman: If the face laughs, then the bones laugh.
Jirō: Ah, of course you say that. You have to say that. Naturally, when the face laughs the bones laugh. But when the face cries, even then the bones are still laughing.

The mask (お面) is mentioned in passing, but plays an interesting mediatory role between the face and the skeleton (骸骨). Though the mask is something durable, that can be passed from person to person and serve the same function, it does not suggest that the mask, or, by extension, art and Nō theater itself, belongs to a world that transcends death. Rather, the hardness and impersonality of the mask connects it to the skeleton, and so to a transcendent world of death. Mishima suggests no such world in this scene; quite the opposite. We might think of this as a difference with Claudel; Claudel's characters, as we will discover in a moment, exist against the backdrop of an eternal Christian world of life after death. Trying to divert Jirō's thoughts, the beautiful woman keeps flattering him and introducing new aspects of their life together. Yet even the revelation of their child displeases Jirō. Desperate, the beautiful woman even suggests killing the child to make Jirō happy. Of course, this does not bring him happiness either. Eventually, the beautiful woman relents, and rather than seducing Jirō is subdued by him.

We can contextualize Jirō's apathy by comparing it with the general atmosphere in which the original Nō *Kantan* emerged: What "exposed metaphysical themes" is it trying to ferry across? Medieval Japan saw the development of the concept of *mappō*, "the latter days of the Buddhist Law," according to which "after the death of Gautama, some five centuries BCE, Buddhism would pass through three great ages: an age of the flourish of the law, of its decline, and finally of its disappearance in the degenerate days of *mappō*," thought to commence "by Japanese calculations" in 1052.[16] *Mappō* expressed the pessimism of the war-torn era. With the decline of the royal court, different shogunates competed for supremacy. Among them were, of course, Zeami's first patron, the shogun Ashikage Yoshimitsu, and Yoshimitsu's son and successor, Ashikage Yoshimochi, who exiled Zeami in the artist's declining years. Not until the Tokugawa shogunate

---

[16] Paul Varley, *Japanese Culture*, Honolulu: U of Hawaii P, 2000, 70.

brought all of the competing dynamos under its rule in 1603 did over 400 years of turmoil end.

During the Middle Ages new Buddhist sects emerged, including Pure Land Buddhism and Zen Buddhism. These sects had different ideas of salvation, but they generally agreed in their mistrust of worldly phenomena and in their occasionally apocalyptic visions.[17] The mountain hut and the recluse became important tropes in Japanese art and, in effect, became "medieval ideals," acting as "[metaphors] for the Buddhist idea of impermanence."[18] The simple rustic life, connected to the *yamabushi* 山伏, an itinerant Buddhist monk who lived an ascetic lifestyle alone in the mountains to achieve enlightenment, was a source of refuge in a country torn by war. From this desire for simplicity arose the modern version of the tea ceremony or *chanoyu* 茶の湯. Varley writes that, "even when the teahouse was situated in a city, such as Kyoto or Nara, it was styled as though—and provided with natural surroundings to give the impression that—it was in a remote 'mountain village' (*yamazato*)."[19] The teahouse bore rush matting or *tatami* 畳 and strove in every respect to fulfill the ideal of "deprived beauty."[20] Meanwhile, iconographic sculpture met with disapproval from some Buddhist sects and declined.[21] In art, the trope of the traveler gained ground, since "[to] the medieval Japanese, traveling symbolized the Buddhist sense of impermanence (*miyo*) that was felt so deeply during this age; and travelers, conceived of as men who leave society behind to wander to distant, lonely places, were thought to experience more fully the nature of life itself."[22] Finally, in this environment the concept of *aware* (or *mononoaware* 物の哀れ) appeared. The concept casts the "human condition [as] essentially one of loneliness [*sabi*]," but provides "some consolation" in the beauty of the evanescence of things, as might be seen in "such things as a desolate field or a monochromatic, withered marsh" as depicted in the monochromatic painting that dominated the age.[23]

What can we identify as crucial to medieval Nō? We can identify historical, religious, and stylistic elements. I will focus on the role of religion. As J. Thomas Rimer tells us, Zeami's plays and his critical writings owe a great deal to Buddhism. The metaphysical underpinnings of Zeami's Nō works are often Buddhist,[24] and his insistence on the need for "intuitive understanding on the part of the actor" corresponds to Buddhist ideas of the transmission of knowledge.[25] Though Nō has origins in Shintō ritual, especially the harvest ritual, the material and philosophy of Nō are overwhelmingly Buddhist. But we must be precise about what we mean when we talk about Buddhism in the Japanese context.

---

[17] Ibid., 101–4.
[18] Ibid., 92.
[19] Ibid., 93.
[20] Ibid.
[21] Ibid., 94. For Claudel's response to Japanese Buddhist sculpture, see the next chapter in this book.
[22] Ibid., 96.
[23] Ibid.
[24] J. Thomas Rimer, "The Background of Zeami's Treatises," in *On the Art of the Nō Drama: The Major Treatises of Zeami*, Princeton: Princeton UP, 1984, xxi.
[25] Ibid., xxii.

Buddhism divides into a variety of sects in Japan. The influence of Buddhism upon Zeami and Nō varies with the sect. Zen interested Zeami the most, as Ayako Nishino shows. A characteristic feature of Zen is "son refus d'expliquer la réalité ou l'essentiel par un système scientifique" (its refusal to use a scientific system to explicate reality or the essential).²⁶ Zeami was a practitioner of Sōtō Zen, a belief system marked by paradoxical reasoning and Daoist elements, particularly the idea of yin and yang, or of complimentary opposites that become harmonious in a "superior synthesis."²⁷ Zen's presence is felt in one of Zeami's critical pieces, *The Mirror and the Flower* or *Kakyō* 花鏡. According to Nishino, *Kakyō*, stressing paradox, the ineffable, "non-interpretation," and the "nonconscious" ["*non-conscience*"] is "somewhat foreign" to European thinking that "privileges clairvoyant logic."²⁸ The Zen concept *kyakurai* 却来 epitomizes this way of thinking. *Kyakurai* "exprime le retour au point de départ après avoir atteint un certain niveau de conscience" (expresses the return to the point of departure after having obtained a certain level of consciousness).²⁹ Nishino hears echoes of *kyakurai* in one of Zeami's famous maxims from *Kakyō*: "Forgetting the result, regard the Nō; forgetting the Nō, regard the actor; forgetting the actor, regard the spirit; forgetting the spirit, understand the Nō."³⁰ We will shortly see the influence of this maxim on Claudel. For the moment, we agree with Nishino that Zeami's adage displays paradoxical Zen thinking. To understand Nō, the spectator must first forget Nō and look at the actor's technique and intention. Forgetting these in turn, the spectator comes to understand Nō. This "affirmation in negation" that Zeami espouses indicates the influence of the Zen upon Zeami's approach.³¹ Nishino concludes:

> Contrairement au théâtre occidental fondé sur la tradition aristotélicienne qui offre au spectateur « la délectation logique », assurée par l'agencement raisonné de l'action, le nô propose au spectateur le plaisir émotionnel créé par l'accomplissement le plus parfait de la technique. S'absorber dans la beauté onirique, tel est l'état idéal pour le public du nô.³²

As Haruo Nishino informs us, one of Zeami's contributions to the formation of Nō theater was "établ[ant] un type de Nô onirique, centré sur le récit rétrospectif d'un héros unique" (establishing a sort of dreamlike Nō, centered on the retrospective narrative of a single

---

²⁶ Nishino, *Synthèse*, 354.
²⁷ Ibid., 355–56.
²⁸ Ibid., 357.
²⁹ Ibid., 359.
³⁰ Ibid., 358.
³¹ Ibid.
³² "Contrary to Western theater founded on the Aristotelian tradition that offers to the spectator [according to Claudel] 'delectation in logic,' assured by the rational development of the action, Nō proposes to the spectator the pleasure of perfect technical accomplishment. Absorption in a beautiful dreamlike atmosphere, such is the ideal state of the Nō audience" (Nishino, *Synthèse* 358). Shinbo Satoru advances a similar interpretation of Zeami's thought. See Shinbo, *Nihon shisōshi Shohan*, Kyōto-shi: Kōyō Shobō, 1989, 162–78.

hero).³³ However, Zeami's texts are not the sine qua non of Nō theater: the actor has an equal, if not greater, significance. For the Nō actor, in Haruo Nishino's estimation, the stage and life itself are one and the same:

> Son but est de rendre une scène constamment attrayante. Sa plus grande joie est de parvenir, par l'excellence de son jeu, à toucher le cœur des spectateurs. Le succès dépend à la fois de la perfection de l'œuvre et de la perfection de l'interprétation, et le problème majeur est de savoir comment étreindre le cœur des spectateurs.³⁴

Zeami himself states that a Nō performance requires the "concordance" of the author, the actor, and the audience.³⁵ To describe this concordance and the way in which the actor can attain it, Zeami uses the metaphor of the flower. The flower "désigne l'état dans lequel l'acteur et le jeu suscitent l'émotion du spectateur" (designates the state in which the actor and his performance elicit the spectator's emotion).³⁶ Here, Zen once again inspires Zeami. Especially important are the concepts of absence and *yūgen*幽玄, or profundity in simplicity.³⁷ An actor who has grasped the "flower" of Nō has entered into the emotion of the performance. He is not an actor imitating the passions of another person, nor is he himself seized by emotion. Rather, he embodies the emotion; and the disappearance of the actor allows for the triangulation of the text, the performance, and the audience. Taking the Nō *Kinuta* as an example, Nishino writes that the epitome of Zeami's style is the "[transmission d'] un sentiment de profonde tristesse qui franchit le temps et l'espace" ([transmission] of a profound sadness that goes beyond time and space).³⁸

Though Zen was crucial to Zeami's criticism of Nō theater, Zen seldom makes its presence felt in Nō itself. Instead, the Tendai 天台, Shingon 真言, and Hokke 法華 sects are the most prevalent. Tendai and Shingon began in the Heian era. Tendai is a "secte ésotérique de la Sutra du Lotus, prêchant la possibilité de salut universel" (an esoteric sect based on the Lotus Sutra, preaching the possibility of universal salvation) while Shingon is a "secte ésotérique de la Vraie Parole, respectant le symbolisme et la magie, caractérisée par le panthéisme et polythéisme" (an esoteric sect of the True Word, valuing symbolism and magic, characterized by pantheism and polytheism).³⁹ Around the turn of the twelfth century, Amidism, a movement proclaiming salvation for all those who simply call the name of Amida, quickly gained followers. In 1253, to

---

[33] Haruo Nishino, "Le Poète dramatique Zeami, ses œuvres et ses théories artistiques," *La Fleur cachée du nô*, ed. Catherine Mayaux, Paris: Honoré Champion, 2015, 12.

[34] "His aim is to render the scene constantly attractive. His greatest joy is to succeed, through the excellence of his acting, in touching the hearts of his spectators. The success [of a performance] depends on the perfection of the text and the perfection of the interpretation, and the principal problem is to know how to seize the hearts of the audience." Nishino, "Le Poète dramatique Zeami," 13.

[35] Ibid.

[36] Ibid., 14.

[37] Ibid., 14–15.

[38] Ibid., 20.

[39] Nishino, *Synthèse*, 267.

counter Amidism, Nichiren, a Tendai adept, established the Hokke school, which "insiste sur la retour respectif au Sûtra du Lotus" (insists on a return to the Lotus Sutra).[40] The presence of these three sects in Nō is a consequence of the preoccupations of writers like Zeami. Writing Nō was not simply an expression of the playwright's ideas. On the contrary: "Les auteurs du nô traitent simplement de sujets en vogue, et par conséquent, le contenu et la forme du nô se colorent de bouddhisme" (The writers of Nō simply treated subjects in vogue, and consequently the content and the form of Nō took on the color of Buddhism).[41]

There is a modern form of classification that divides Nō plays according to their treatment of Buddhist themes. In 1942, Masaharu Anesaki combed through 200 Nō plays and grouped them according to whether or not they touched on Buddhist ideas. Of the 200 plays, 39 do not treat Buddhism at all, 41 delve briefly into Buddhist themes, and 120 directly "reflect" Buddhist ideas.[42] The 120 pieces divide further into ones that reveal general Buddhist themes and ones that concern one of the Buddhist sects that flourished during the era. Of these, 51 fall in the former camp, while 9 in the latter. Regarding the 69 pieces indebted to particular Nō sects, Anesaki attempted to disentangle Hokke, Amidism, and Shingon by having recourse:

> à une comparaison en rapport avec les saisons: des pièces imprégnées de la pensée de l'école de Sûtra (*Hokke*) sont comparées au paysage gracieux du printemps et au point cardinal de l'est où se lève le soleil, puisque la secte *Hokke* promet le salut à tous les êtres animés ou inanimés ; des pièces d'intérêt amidiste sont assimilées à la tristesse de l'automne et au point cardinal de l'ouest, puisque cette école console le défunt par l'invocation de prières silencieuses ; à propos des pièces reflétant le bouddhisme ésotérique de *Shingon* est invoquée la foudre de l'été, puisque la secte livre un combat implacable contre l'esprit maléfique. D'après Anesaki, c'est cette dernière secte, le bouddhisme ésotérique de *Shingon*, qui caractérise le plus la vision bouddhiste du nô. En fait les pièces imprégnées de la pensée Zen sont peu nombreuses, malgré la domination de la secte à l'époque de la constitution du nô. C'est sous la forme du spectacle et dans la philosophie fondatrice de l'art que l'on peut trouver des reflets directs du Zen plutôt que dans le récit raconté: le Zen exerce une influence sur la théorie de Zeami concernant la technique du nô (la Forme), alors que la Fable des pièces est imprégnée de la pensée bouddhique d'autres sectes, telles que le *Hokke*, l'amidisme ou le *Shignon*.[43]

---

[40] Ibid., 267.
[41] Ibid., 266.
[42] Ibid., 267–68.
[43] "recourse to a comparison concerning the seasons: pieces impregnated with the thought of the Sûtra School (Hokke) are compared to the graceful countryside of springtime and to the cardinal point of the East where the sun rises, since the Hokke sect promises salvation to all beings living or inanimate; pieces connected to Amidism are assimilated to the sadness of autumn and to the cardinal point of the West, since this school consoles the deceased through the invocation of silent prayer; as for those pieces reflecting the esoteric Buddhism of Shingon is invoked by the lightning of summer, since the sect leads an implacable fight against the spirit of evil. According to Anesaki, it is this last sect, the esoteric Buddhism of Shingon, that most characterizes the Buddhist vision found in Nō. In fact the pieces impregnated with Zen thought are few in number, despite the domination of the sect during the epoch in which Nō

A variety of Buddhist currents feed into Nō, yet Zeami's theory of Nō is indebted to a sect, Zen, that plays a marginal role in furnishing the material of Nō theater.

To determine whether we can see bits of medieval, particularly Buddhist, thought in Mishima's *Kantan*, we can compare it with Claudel's take on the medieval Nō in *Soulier*. Claudel's *Soulier* is not an adaptation of *Kantan*. Only one scene develops the themes and techniques Claudel discovered in the original Nō. Nonetheless, the scene provides several points of comparison with Mishima's *Kantan*.

Divided into four "days" or *journées* after the fashion of Spanish *autos*, *Soulier* shows the impossible love of Dona Prouhèze and Don Rodrigue. After falling in love at first sight, the two are separated for more than ten years by a series of unfortunate circumstances. Rodrigue is in Panama, Prouhèze in Northern Africa. Despairing, in *Journée III, Scene VIII* Prouhèze receives a visit in her sleep from her guardian angel. The scene commences with Prouhèze watching "the blue image of the terrestrial globe" revolve behind her. The image is projected on a screen placed on the bottom of the stage. The globe keeps turning until "on the horizon of the extreme curve begins to appear the long sinuous line of the Isthmus of Panama behind which starts to shimmer the waters of another ocean."[44] Quickly, the image of Panama passes from the screen, and boundless ocean returns. From behind the screen, Rodrigue calls Prouhèze's name twice. Twice she responds, but receives no other reply. Continuing to call after Rodrigue, Prouhèze expresses her wish to become pure spirit and fuse with Rodrigue. Still, no response comes from behind the screen.

The globe on the screen turns again, and the Japanese archipelago appears. Prouhèze, who has never seen the islands, is taken aback:

DONA PROUHÈZE.— [...] Quelles sont ces Iles là-bas pareilles à des nuages immobiles et que leur forme, leurs clefs, leurs entailles, leurs gorges, rendent pareilles à des instruments de musique pour un mystérieux concert à la fois assemblés et disjoints?

J'entends la mer sans fin qui brise sur ces rivages éternels! Près d'un poteau planté dans la grève je vois un escalier de pierre qui monte.

Les nuages lents à s'écarter, le rideau des pluies,

Permettent à peine de distinguer de temps en temps des montagnes atramenteuses, une cascade aux arbres mélancoliques, le repli de noires forêts sur lesquelles tout à coup s'arrête un rayon accusateur!

A la torche de la lune répond le reflet des feux souterrains et le tambour sous un toit de paille s'unit à la flûte perçante.

Que signifient aussi par moments ces nuages de fleurs où tout disparait? l'or inouï de cette consommation annuelle avant que la neige descende?

---

took shape. It is in the form of the spectacle and in the foundational philosophy of the art more than in the stories themselves that one can find direct reflections of Zen: Zen exercises and influence upon Zeami's theory in terms of the technique of Nō (the Form), while the Fable of the plays is impregnated by the Buddhist thought of other sects, such as Hokke, Amidism, and Shingon." Nishino, *Synthèse*, 268.

[44] Paul Claudel, *Théâtre* Tome XII, ed. Robert Mallet, Paris: Gallimard, 1958, 183. Subsequent references to this work will be made in-text and use the abbreviation *Th*.

Par-dessus les montagnes et les forêts il y a un grand Ange blanc qui regarde la mer.

La grande Ile du Japon peu à peu s'anime et prend la forme d'un de ces Gardiens en armure sombre que l'on voit à Nara.

L'ANGE GARDIEN.—Ne me reconnais-tu pas?
DONA PROUHÈZE.—Je ne sais. Je ne vois qu'une forme incertaine comme une ombre dans le brouillard. (*Th.* 184–85)

DONA PROUHÈZE.—
What are these islands other there, that look like immobile clouds, and whose form, cliffs, gashes and gorges seem like musical instruments for a mysterious concert at once cohesive and disjointed?
I hear the boundless sea that breaks against these eternal banks!
Close to a post planted in the shore I see a stone staircase that rises.
Clouds slow to separate, the curtain of rain,
Permitting to barely distinguish from time to time atramental mountains, a cascade of melancholy trees, the fold of black forests on which all of a sudden stops an accusatory ray of sunlight.
To the torch of the moon responds the reflection of underground fires and the drum under a roof of straw merges with the piercing flute.
What signify these clouds of flowers where at times everything disappears? The unheard gold of this annual consummation before the snow descends?
Above the mountains and the forests, there is a great white angel who watches the sea.
The great Island of Japan little by little becomes alive and takes the form of one of these Guardians in dark armor that one can see at Nara.
THE GUARDIAN ANGEL: Do you not recognize me?
DONA PROUHÈZE: I don't know. I see nothing but an uncertain form like a shadow in fog.

We find little here that overlaps with Mishima. Among the similarities, we note the dream-vision in which both Prouhèze and Jirō come across spectral beings. The appearance of the guardian angel does resemble the formalized masked figures that we encounter in Mishima's *Kantan*. Yet, crucially, the angel does not wear a mask, which, if we think of the mask as perhaps the most recognizable signifier of Nō theater, is a greater departure than Mishima has made. On the other hand, the angel and Prouhèze engage in a dialogue on the meaning of Prouhèze's life and life and general. Though Prouhèze and Jirō are distinct in their opinions on life, like Mishima Claudel takes this theme directly from the original *Kantan*.

We notice that Prouhèze and her guardian angel speak in the same register. The gap between formal and informal speech we find in Mishima's play is absent. Both the angel and Prouhèze use the familiar second person "*tu*" to address one another. In one sense, the two are close. Yet the scene is concerned with the idea of difference, the difference between proximity and distance, perfume and sound, being and nothingness, and the "frontier" between all of these things. Even though the intervention of the guardian angel suggests a mingling of this world and the spiritual world, the dialogue throws into relief the gaps between the two: the power of the scene comes from the fact that the spiritual world, the world of being and eternal life, is not the world that Prouhèze and Rodrigue currently inhabit. The frontiers or gray areas between opposites, of which the dream is one such area between this world and the next, exist to make the oppositional categories more strongly felt. This introduces a way of conceiving the relations between the mundane and the spiritual that is not present in the original *Kantan* or in Mishima's *Kantan*.

The two adaptations of the original *Kantan* strive to retain the same bits while dispensing with different elements of the original, not to mention the original words. The identity of those bits becomes vague, however, as the ways in which they can be interpreted opens to multiple possibilities depending on what we use to "fix" the reading: the ontology of the original Nō play, or that of the adaptation, or something else entirely. This is not a case of context-sensitivity in which, if we narrow down the context, we arrive at a correct, and final, answer. Reading Claudel's play, for instance, as open, despite Claudel's intentions, to the original's Buddhist metaphysical themes, is perfectly viable. Yet if we chose to read the play in this way, the identity of the angel changes: it can no longer fit securely in the Catholic cosmology Claudel thought he fashioned, and that many elements in *Soulier* sustain. This is, in other words, a true case of ontological vagueness borne through "translation"—translation here not of words but of ideas, or "exposed metaphysical themes."

Mishima Yukio's World

Let us return for the moment to Mishima, and try to fix his context, much as we did for that of the medieval Nō. When Mishima wrote his "modern Nō" plays in the early 1950s, he had only recently become interested in the Japanese literary tradition. Mishima had spent much of his youth fascinated by European literature. He liked romantic writers, with Yeats and Novalis being singled out specifically in his 1968 book *Sun and Steel* (太陽と鉄; *Taiyō to tetsu*). In a vein that is, after all, thoroughly modernist, Mishima came to identify his early, sickly years with romanticism and the night and his later, vigorous years, exemplified by his muscular body and tan skin, with the sun and with Japan.[45] This statement chimes with T. E. Hulme's distinction between the "dry hardness" of classicism and "damp" romanticism.[46] Mishima would likely have been familiar with Hulme and modernism generally. In a letter to Kawabata Yasunari 川端康成 dated July 18, 1945, Mishima, still called Hiraoka Kimitake 平岡公威, tells the older writer: 「文学の本当の意味の新しさといふことも考へる折が多いのですが」 (Often I ask myself what it really means to "make it new" in the domain of literature),[47] suggesting a deep affinity

---

[45] Yukio Mishima, *Taiyō to tetsu*, in *Mishima Yukio Zenshū*, ed. Jun Ishikawa and Shōichi Saeki. Dai sanjyūsan maki, Tokyo: Shinchōsha, 1973, 517–21.

[46] T. E. Hulme, "Romanticism and Classicism," *Speculations: Essays of Humanism and the Philosophy of Art*, ed. Herbert Read, London: Routledge & Kegan Paul, 1960, 126–27.

[47] Correspondence with Kawabata Yasunori. Yukio Mishima, Jun Ishikawa, and Shōichi Saeki, *Mishima Yukio Zenshū*, Dai sanjyūhachi maki, Tokyo: Shinchōsha, 1973, 237.

with the modernist movements in Europe.[48] The way the Western dichotomy between classicism and romanticism differs from Mishima's opposition between the night and the sun lies in the difference between what is foreign and what is native for him. In northern Europe, romanticism grew out of a desire to return to a natural native art that southern, Latinate classicism was thought to have suppressed. This is pronounced in the German distinction between *Kultur* and *Zivilisation*. *Kultur* represents the local achievements and inscrutable inner life of a group of people, an ethnos, while *Zivilisation* stands for "something which is indeed useful, but nevertheless only a value of the second rank, comprising only the outer appearance of human beings, the surface of human existence."[49] In its concern for the local "genius," *Kultur* is romantic. When Hulme rejects romanticism, as Goethe did before him, they ask to return to an ancient, and more foreign, pan-European tradition—the classicism of ancient Greece and Rome. To both writers, classicism is of course a part of their cultural heritage as Europeans, but it is still a more foreign heritage according to the nineteenth- and early-twentieth-century division between classicism and romanticism.

For Mishima, the opposite is true. The night stands for the European. His early devotion to it was, he tells us, a contrarian rejection of Japanese nationalism during the Second World War. Indeed, in the 1940s Mishima, "while working in an aircraft factory, translated *At the Hawk's Well* into a kind of classical Japanese and considered the project as one of his most useful during the war years."[50] It is interesting to remark that, at a time when Mishima described himself as fleeing from Japanese tradition toward Europe, he translated an English appropriation of Japanese classical literature into the very vernacular of classical Japanese. The exercise indicates not only Mishima's familiarity with modernist experimentations, but also his early desire to reconcile his European interests with the literary tradition to which he was an heir. The sun is for Mishima specifically Japanese; it symbolizes the inscrutable life of his inner Japanese being. When Mishima appeals to the sun, he is embracing the local, particular, and quasi-mystical. Receptiveness to the sun is enshrined in Mishima's very body in its ability to tan. Mishima has taken the European division between classicism and romanticism and turned a crucial part of it on its head.

We need not accept Mishima's division of his life into two parts. He was writing two years before his death, looking back over the early years of his life, trying to interpret his interests and actions then in order to make them accord with him interests and actions in the late 1960s. When he says that he rejected romanticism, it does not mean that he rejected European literature, or that Yeats and his early interests ceased to influence him. The act that cemented his movement toward the "sun," his taking up of bodybuilding, did not occur until after he had mostly written his Nō plays. We expect that the influence

---

[48] I think here of course of Ezra Pound's *The Cantos*, "Canto LIII." See *The Cantos of Ezra Pound*, London: Faber, 1975, 262–74.
[49] Norbert Elias, *The Civilizing Process*, Oxford: Blackwell, 1978, 6–7.
[50] Aoife Assumpta Hart, *Ancestral Recall: the Celtic Revival and Japanese Modernism*, Montreal: McGill-Queen's UP, 2016, 241.

of Yeats and other European artists was still strong when Mishima wrote his Nō, but, at the same time, we understand that his identification as a Japanese man was growing in strength.

A letter to Kawabata on September 10, 1951, reveals the heterogeneous materials Mishima was consulting. He mentions finishing Heinrich Heine's *The Romantic School* and states his interest in Heine's assertion that Goethe's art, and all art, is essentially "sterile" or *fumō* 不毛. "目下、" Mishima writes, "コルトオの「ショパン」を読んでゐますが、これもおもしろうございます" (I am in the process of reading Cortot's *Chopin*, which is also a very interesting work).[51] In the following paragraph, Mishima tells Kawabata:

> 舞踊劇を二つ書きました。一つは柳橋の通りのためで、「競近松娘松娘」、一つは青山圭男氏の新作日本バレエで、「姫君と鏡」で、後者は落窪物語のバレエ化です。前者は十月末明銀座で、後者は十一月末帝劇でいたします。[52]

There is already a great deal of heterogeneity in these theatrical pieces Mishima was writing: using Chikamatsu to make modern dance theater, working with the materials of a modern Japanese choreographer to stage a "classical dance" piece, and both works to be performed at major modern Japanese theaters. When we add to this the fact that Mishima's personal interest still tended toward northern European romanticism, we see that he was still caught between Japan and the foreign, the new and the old, as he constructed his *shinsaku* Nō. Furthermore, in the 1950s Mishima was presented with the opportunity and greatly interested in the possibility of traveling to the United States, the Caribbean, and South America.[53] His interest in the foreign was in full swing as he wrote his Nō. These Nō are modern, not only in updating Nō for a modern Japanese audience but also in the cosmopolitanism that we might expect in postwar Japan.

With this in mind, we ask whether Nō presented a religious or political undercurrent to Mishima as it did to Claudel and other European writers who tackled Nō including Pound and Yeats. Unlike these Western writers, Mishima was intimately acquainted with Nō from an early age.[54] By his late teens Mishima had written an essay praising the literary punning device *kakekotoba*, through which famous lyrics are incorporated into

---

[51] Correspondence with Kawabata Yasunori. *Mishima Yukio Zenshū*, Dai sanjyūhachi maki, 84.

[52] "I have written two pieces for dance theater: one called *Coquettish Duel between the Girls of Chikamatsu*, for the dances of Yanagibashi, the other, *The Princess and the Mirror*, for Japanese ballets by Aoyama Yoshio. In the latter case, the work is an adaptation, for classical dance, called *Tale of the Cellar*. The first piece will be performed at the Meiji Theater at the end of October, the second at the Imperial Theater at the end of November." *Mishima Yukio Zenshū*, Dai sanjyūhachi maki, 270.

[53] In a March 18, 1950, letter, Mishima tells Kawabata that visiting Europe—especially Germany, Italy, and Greece before their postwar reconstruction was complete—was his dream, and that the United States held no attraction for him, though he would happily visit the United States if invited (Ibid., 266–67).

[54] Naoki Inose, *Persona: A Biography of Yukio Mishima*, trans. Hiroaki Sato, Berkeley: Stone Bridge Press, 2012, 68.

Nō dialogue.⁵⁵ For Mishima Nō appears to be embedded in a cultural framework that differs substantially from Claudel's—a French writer who never learned Japanese and encountered Nō in his fifties. So any superficial similarities between any "Nō" plays written by the two men might hide deep-level differences.

In order to flesh out this background, we can look at how Mishima viewed Nō as a part of his own tradition, and how he modified that tradition to suit his interest in foreign literature. As we did with classicism and romanticism, we are charting the opposite movement here: Nō is the native; the European is the foreign. The dynamic is similar, though, and understanding how Nō functioned for a postwar Japanese writer like Mishima could, by way of contrast, illuminate how it functioned for Claudel—and vice versa.

In the letter to Kawabata quoted earlier, in which Mishima reflects on a concept similar to Pound's injunction to "make it new," Mishima imagines a literature that "transcends" the ancient and modern:

言葉、文学、様式等のすべてに於て今までの概念の古さも新しさも超越した新しさ（即ち、嘗てあった、と嘗てなかった、といふことを新旧弁別の唯一の基準とする態度をこえて）も考へられるのではないかと存じます⁵⁶

Mishima goes on to describe his desire to write stories in the "old style" that are, nonetheless, vibrant and lauded. He also details his hope for "あの古代の壮麗な大爬虫類が、峻厳な自然淘汰の手で絶滅に瀕した時代" (a time when those great old magnificent lizards suddenly find themselves on the verge of extinction thanks to the rigors of natural selection).⁵⁷ We could easily interpret Mishima's desire to be liberated from the tyranny of the influence of past masters and of the demand for novelty in terms of Harold Bloom's famous concept of the "anxiety of influence." Mishima's wish for a transhistorical valuation of literature and his interest in foreign literature would then reveal his own neuroticism under the weight of tradition. But a more sensitive approach would be to see whether Mishima's Nō plays put into practice this desire to escape from history.

An English appraisal of Mishima's Nō works is hindered by the paucity of critical work done on these plays. One of the earliest critical notices is Arthur Waley's review of Donald Keene's translation of *Five Modern Nō Plays*. Waley had met Mishima in London when the Japanese writer visited the city with his wife in 1958. Waley heaps praise upon the book. Waley notes the variety of sources from which Mishima has drawn; he points out that *Aoi no ue* 葵上 takes more from *The Tale of Genji*, of which Waley was the first, and in the 1950s still the only, translator into English, than from the classical

---

⁵⁵ Ibid., 121.
⁵⁶ "Is it not equally possible to imagine in every domain: that of words, of style, or of form, a newness that transcends the concepts of 'old' and 'new' as they have been used up until the present (in brief, that goes beyond the distinction between 'that which existed' and 'that which did not exist' previously—the only criterion used to judge the 'old' and the 'new')?" Mishima, *Mishima Yukio Zenshū*, 238.
⁵⁷ Ibid., 35.

Nō *Aoi*. Meanwhile, *Hanjo* 班女, Waley says, takes so little from the original Nō that the play avoids the "problem" of "the integration of the legendary and the actual." Regardless of the extent to which Mishima relies on tradition, according to Waley, the plays' "impact is enormously increased (especially in the case of [*Sotoba*] *Komachi* and *Aoi*) by having the old stories hovering at the back of one's mind."[58] Waley further conjectures that

> these plays are undoubtedly easier to translate than the old Nō plays, in which the sharp contrast between the prose dialogue and the sung parts, which are in a totally different kind of language, is very hard to bring out in English, whereas Mishima uses the same kind of quite modern and familiar language throughout. Nor is the translator of these modern plays faced with literary allusions, plays on words, or other ornamental devices.[59]

These Nō, to Waley, are radically different from "older Nō," yet in Waley's mind the older works are critical to the great pleasure the *Five Modern Nō Plays* can give. A review of Marguerite Yourcenar's French translation of Mishima's Nō, *Cinq nô modernes*, describes the newness of Mishima's Nō in more detail:

> They are fascinating, hypnotic, unique. Referred to as Nō, they do not, however, retain the ritual quality of this composite art form, which dates back to fourteenth-century Japan. There are no painted pine trees or bamboo accessories, nor are there five musicians seated on the stage, sung recitatives, gestural language or hieratic stances. Moreover, both women and men perform in these plays; and out of forty characters featured in his stage pieces, only five wear traditional Japanese clothes.[60]

We might wonder what makes these pieces Nō plays, bereft as they are of the most readily identifiable signs of the theater. Mishima's "plays deal with everyday situations," writes Knapp, "but their essence is Nō."[61] This "essence" is "beings [who] inhabit a spaceless area in a cyclical time scheme" and "a fluid, vaporous and dreamlike atmosphere"; "Dreamlike realities are transformed into tension provoking moments as past incidents are integrated into present realities, bringing into existence a whole metaphysical—sacred—climate."[62] Like Waley, Knapp argues that this "dreamlike" and "sacred" impression relies heavily upon familiarity with the original Nō plays that Mishima has

---

[58] Arthur Waley, "Five Modern Nō Plays. By Yukio Mishima. Translated from the Japanese by Donald Keene. New York: Knopf, 1957. xvii. 201, Illustrations. $4.00," *Journal of Asian Studies* vol. 17 no. 3 (1958): 487, doi: 10.2307/2941447.
[59] Ibid.
[60] Knapp, Bettina L. "Review of Yukio Mishima. *Cinq nô modernes.* Marguerite Yourcenar and Jun Shiragi (Silla), eds. & trs. Paris. Gallimard. 1984. 172 pages. 85 F." *World Literature Today* vol. 58, no. 4 (1984): 666–667, 666.
[61] Ibid.
[62] Ibid.

subtly woven into his work. Still Knapp writes that "Mishima does not seek to renew what was but rather to impress new amalgams upon his audience."[63]

In the West, the most famous, or at least the most critically appraised, of Mishima's Nō is *Aoi*. Partly, this fame must owe to the familiarity of the source material. As Waley pointed out, *Aoi* draws both from the Nō *Aoi no Ue* and from the tale of Lady Aoi and Lady Rokujo in *The Tale of Genji*. Because the matter of *Aoi* originates in the most famed piece of Japanese literature, it is natural that Western critics would feel most comfortable when criticizing the play. Nancy J. Barnes treats the Buddhist significance of the Aoi tale and of Mishima's *Aoi* in particular. Barnes writes:

> With a particular affinity for ghostly tales, Nō dramas may partly derive from ancient shamanistic rituals for summoning numinous beings and spirits of the dead. The plays unmistakably preserve elements of spiritual worship. Nō as a dramatic form, however, arose in a Buddhist tradition.[64]

It is no surprise then that the original *Aoi no Ue* is, in Barnes's view, "much more dogmatically Buddhist" than *Genji*.[65] However "dreamlike" a reader like Knapp may find Mishima's adaptation, if the otherworldliness of Mishima's *Aoi* is not overtly Buddhist, it deviates from its source material.

Barnes affirms that, though the play is "dramatically compressed," Mishima has "certainly preserved much of the weird, unearthly character of the original."[66] Nonetheless, Barnes writes that the Buddhist atmosphere is "excised," so "there is no healing for any of the three main characters. They remain helpless victims of their personal fantasies and supernatural forces."[67] Barnes finds Mishima's treatment of psychoanalysis "ironic," as it shows that Western medicine is unable to touch the irrational, yet in *Aoi* the salvific power of Buddhism is also "rejected."[68] According to Barnes it is not Mishima who rejects Buddhism. Rather, "Buddhism is very much at the heart of Mishima's thought," and the play's "recognition that it is one's own mental attitudes that generate health and success or misery and failure" is, she claims, quintessentially Buddhist.[69] Once more we have a critic who stresses the importance of the worlds of the source texts in framing our interpretation of Mishima's very eccentric Nō. Here, however, the implication is that in departing from the source material Mishima aims to uphold the worldview of the original texts. By showing a world without traditional spirituality, Mishima is powerfully arguing for the value of Buddhism in modern life. Yet, acute as Barnes's analysis is, the

---

[63] Ibid. For an in-depth treatment of the relation between classical Nō and one of Mishima's other modern Nō, *The Damask Drum* or 綾の鼓, see Bettina L. Knapp, "Mishima's Cosmic Noh Drama: 'The Damask Drum,'" *World Literature Today* vol. 54, no. 3 (1980): 383–87.
[64] Nancy J. Barnes, "Lady Rokujō's Ghost: Spirit Possession, Buddhism, and Healing in Japanese Literature," *Literature and Medicine* vol. 8, no. 1 (1989): 114, doi: 10.1353/lm.2011.0101.
[65] Ibid., 116.
[66] Ibid., 118.
[67] Ibid., 119.
[68] Ibid.
[69] Ibid., 120.

situation is less clear-cut than she presents it. If in his new Nō plays Mishima suggests that Buddhism has relevance in modern life, it is not quite Buddhism as it was in the time of Zeami. It is rather a conception of Buddhism that differs from its medieval counterpart thanks to the passage of time and the necessity of contending with other ideas introduced from abroad since the Meiji era.

Anne Lande Peters compares Mishima's *Hanjo* and Henrik Ibsen's *The Lady from the Sea* with a focus on the formal and affective similarities and differences between Mishima's and Ibsen's works.[70] Her insightful critique aims to demonstrate how culture determines the ways in which a writer can construct and an audience can interpret a piece of literature, the role of culture being evident in the case of *Hanjo* and *The Lady from the Sea* because the two plays deal with the same "universal themes" in different ways.[71] In contrast to Ibsen's psychological realism, Mishima's worldview is "mystical," opening onto "a beautiful, unreal world."[72] Peters asserts that even though Mishima's *Aoi* is psychologically "more realistic" than the original, the weight of tradition drives Mishima's *Aoi* toward the supernatural.[73] We might worry about the determinism implicit in this argument, but Peters writes that this is not because of a necessary Japanese drive toward the "mystical" but a reaction against the *shingeki* (新劇) or New Theater Movement that had arisen in the first half of the twentieth century. Originating in the 1900s, *Shingeki* tried to grow a new Japanese theater using the seeds of European realism. Mishima wrote his Nō at a time some years before the so-called Little Theater Movement took shape. The Little Theater Movement was among other things a reevaluation of traditional Japanese theater and popular entertainment. In this context Mishima's plays anticipated, if not helped to usher in, a new and original, Japanese style into the modern theater.[74]

From this brief overview, the tensions inherent in Mishima's Nō are clear. His theater is backward-looking, yet part of an exciting new trend in Japanese theater; it deals with the problems of postwar Japanese society, yet attempts to retain the spiritual cast of classical Nō; it is at once deeply traditional and deeply inflected by Western innovations. These contradictions are not only Mishima's; their counterparts riddle Claudel's conception of Nō as well.

Paul Claudel's World

As consul in New York in the 1890s, Claudel became entranced by the performances in the city's Chinese Opera House, Bernard Hue tells us, and came to believe "qu'on ne pouvait rien voir de plus beau que le théâtre chinois" (nothing could be as beautiful as

---

[70] Peters highlights that Mishima is connected to Yeats through the two dramatists' shared interest in *Aoi no ue*, but does not pursue the point. "The Longing Women of Mishima and Ibsen: A Reflection on "Hanjo" and "The Lady From the Sea,'" *Ibsen Studies* vol. 5, no. 1 (August 2006): 4–18. Yeats's "Irish Nō" is discussed in the previous chapter of this book.
[71] Ibid., 16.
[72] Ibid., 12.
[73] Ibid., 13.
[74] Ibid., 15.

Chinese theater).[75] Yet, the theater he found as ambassador in Tokyo captivated him even more. Japanese theater appeared to him to contain "formes dramatiques foncièrement originales, alliant, outre les mérites du théâtre grec, les qualités de la poésie, de la musique et de la danse" (profoundly original dramatic forms, allying, aside from the merits of Greek theater, the qualities of poetry, music, and dance).[76] For Claudel, acolyte of Stephane Mallarmé and admirer of Richard Wagner, the union of word and music, of drama and music, was one of the objectives of his theater; and it was in the theater of Japan, in Nō, kabuki, and bunraku, that he found a way to realize his vision:[77]

> Il n'avait encore entrevu que certaines possibilités; il avait vu dans l'opéra classique occidental un échec, dans le drame wagnérien une erreur ; il lui restait, grâce à la grande révélation japonaise, à réaliser, avec le concours d'un artiste merveilleusement fait pour comprendre, D[arius] Milhaud, le modèle même du nouveau drame, répondant à toutes les exigences que, durant quarante ans, il n'a cessé de dégager et de chercher à résoudre. Il a enfin compris que la musique dramatique est celle qu'emploie un dramaturge, non un musicien, « ayant en vue non pas la réalisation d'un tableau sonore, mais la secousse et le train à donner à notre émotion par un moyen purement rythmique ou timbré, plus direct et plus brutal que la parole ». Dans les circonstances où, en Europe, on utiliserait tout un orchestre, au Japon, un « coup unique et caverneux répété d'abord à longs intervalles, puis plus fort et plus précipité, […] suffit sans orchestre et sans partitions à nous placer dans l'ambiance voulue ». Le musicien japonais participe à l'action avec plus liberté que son homologue européen. « Il suit le drame et l'œil et le ponctue librement au moment voulu à l'aide de l'instrument […], ou simplement de la voix, car c'est là un élément magnifique du théâtre japonais ».[78]

Japanese theater allowed Claudel to pare down that which he needed for his ideal theater, to dispense with unnecessary musical accompaniment while fulfilling an aesthetic inherited from the grandiose schemes of the nineteenth century. Though throughout his career Claudel was interested in the possibility of a totalizing theater, it was in Japan, André Vachon says, that Claudel began seeking a way to show the "rapports

---

[75] Bernard Hue, *Littératures et arts de l'Orient dans l'œuvre de Claudel*. Paris: Klincksieck, 1978, 307.
[76] Ibid., 307.
[77] Ibid., 334–38.
[78] "He had but seen some possibilities in passing; he had seen an impasse in Western opera, in Wagnerian drama an error; he was left, thanks to the great Japanese revelation, to realize, with the help of an artist marvelously suited to understand, D[arius] Milhaud, the model of the new drama, responding to all of the demands that, for forty years, he had not ceased to liberate and tried to resolve. I finally understood that dramatic music is that which employs a dramaturge, not a musician, 'having in view not the realization of a sonic tableau, but the agitation and the path to deliver to our emotion by a rhythmic or timbrous method, more direct and more brutal than words.' In circumstances in which, in Europe, an entire orchestra would be used, in Japan, 'a single and cavernous blow repeated at first at long intervals, then more strongly and more precipitously, […] suffices without an orchestra and without a partition to place us in the desired atmosphere.' The Japanese musician participates in the action with more liberty than his European counterpart. 'He follows the drama and the eye and punctuates it freely at the desired moment with the aide of the instrument […], or simply with the voice, for that is a magnificent element of Japanese theater.'" Ibid., 338.

qu'entretiennent entre eux le visible et l'invisible" (relations that hold between the visible and the invisible).[79] But whatever inspiration Claudel drew from Japanese theater—and he drew a considerable amount—his interpretations inevitably lead back to his fundamental interests. Claudel ultimately saw *Soulier* as an exegesis of the Bible. Claudel, of course, did not hope to explain the Bible by representing its content in more lucid words. Rather, he hoped to express the "sense" of the Bible through theater.[80] Such a direct presentation of the sense of the Bible is possible because, "pour Claudel, les événements de la Bible se passent à la fois dans l'éternité et dans l'actualité de la vie humaine" (for Claudel, the events of the Bible pass at once in eternity and in actual human life).[81] Furthermore, manifest in Claudel's theater, Thomas Pavel argues, is the desire, "as [it is] for the Jesuits for whom the motto is *Ad maiorem Dei gloriam*, [for] the unity of the world [that will] make visible the glory of God."[82] The faith in progress gives Claudel's theater a marked optimism in the future and the effects of globalization.[83] *Soulier*, with its figures drawn not only from the West but, when considering characters like the painter Daibutsu, from the East as well, might stand as an allegory for this unity, of the exciting mix of many different groups of people on the world stage. If Claudel's *Soulier* adapts Japanese theater to express a biblical sense, with the Japanese being part of a pessimistic medieval period and the biblical interpreted as expressing a resolutely positive message, how does the one serve as the vehicle of the other?

The question takes us to the heart of Claudel studies, in which the extent to which Claudel understood Japanese art remains a point of contention.[84] Ayako Nishino shows

---

[79] André Vachon, *Le Temps Et L'espace Dans L'oeuvre De Paul Claudel,* Collection Pierres vives, Paris: Éditions du Seuil, 1965, 384. Vachon also notes that, as he wrote *Le Repos du septième jour,* Claudel had some knowledge of Chinese cosmology and writing. But he cautions that Claudel's understanding of Chinese writing and of Daoism was as "approximate" as his knowledge of Thomism. "Claudel would never have been faithful to anything but himself, and his 'borrowings' themselves always have, let us say, something of Claudel in them" (Claudel n'aura jamais été fidèle qu'à lui-même, et ses « emprunts » eux-mêmes ont toujours, si l'on peut dire, quelque chose de claudélien) (193). Claudel's own opinions on Chinese writing, in which he perceived a fixity and transcendence lacking in Western writing, can be found in the preface to *Cent Phrases* and in "La figure, le mouvement et le geste dans l'écriture en Chine et en Occident." See Claudel, *Œuvre Poétique*, ed. Jacques Petit. Paris: Gallimard, 1967, 699–701, and *Œuvres complètes Tome XVIII,* ed. Pierre Claudel and Jacques Petit, Paris: Gallimard, 1961, 454–57.

[80] Vachon, *Le Temps Et L'espace,* 404.

[81] Ibid., 405.

[82] Thomas Pavel, "L'unité du monde dans le théâtre de Claudel," *Critique* vol. 774 (November 2011): 859.

[83] Ibid., 859, 862.

[84] The point will be discussed in more detail in the next chapter, but for the moment note that among important works not discussed in depth in this chapter considering the role of Catholicism in Claudel's interpretation of Japanese art are Maurice Pinguet, *Le Texte Japon,* Paris: Seuil, 2009, 79–107; Akane Kawakami, *Travellers' Visions: French Literary Encounters with Japan, 1881–2004,* Liverpool: Liverpool UP, 2005, and Christopher Bush, *Ideographic Modernisms: China, Writing, Media,* Oxford: Oxford UP, 2010.

that Claudel, despite his original and sensitive reception of Nō theater, in his essay "Nô" cannot help but introduce concepts that are not present in the original Japanese. For instance, in his essay "Nô" Claudel describes the *shite* as "the Ambassador of the Unknown" and the *waki* a generic figure from this world—as a representative of the invisible and the visible, to parse the claim in Vachon's terms. "Or," writes Nishino regarding *mugen nō*,

> d'après l'interprétation japonaise, entre ces deux délégués de deux univers différents, il n'y a ni drame intime ni opposition directe, au sens occidental du terme: le nô est concentré sur l'action du protagoniste et le drame réside dans l'histoire du passé déjà vécu par le *shite*.[85]

Claudel's misinterpretation of Nō allows him to bring Nō within his constellation of belief. The process illuminates Hue's and Vachon's readings of Claudel's theater. If Claudel finds Nō an ideal vessel through which to communicate his aesthetic vision, it is because Nō in his mind is not quite the same as Nō as it is orthodoxly interpreted in Japan. It is a resolutely Catholic interpretation of Japanese art.

However, it would be unfair to claim that Claudel was hostile toward or simply uninterested in Japanese practices on account of his Catholic faith. His interactions with Buddhism in Japan in particular are distinct from his previous negative encounters with the religion. The reason is that Claudel found certain schools of Japanese Buddhism congenial to his own faith. In the 1920s, he came to esteem Amidism and Zen Buddhism. Whereas Indian Buddhism disturbed him with what he perceived as its garish idolatry, Amidism and Zen, and much of the Buddhism he found in Japan, fitted well with his tragic conception of temporal life, of *visible* life:

> Le bouddhisme en Chine ne m'a pas spécialement intéressé, je dirai. Le bouddhisme tel que je l'avais vu à Ceylan m'avait profondément répugné, ça je dois le dire. Ces énormes bouddhas étendus, couchés dans des autels obscurs, dans des temples obscurs, m'avaient répugné. Le bouddhisme chinois ne m'avait pas beaucoup plu non plus. Le bouddhisme sous sa forme japonaise m'a beaucoup plus intéressé. Dans ce bouddhisme japonais, il y a une espèce de mélancolie amère et profonde qui est vraiment intéressante. Sous sa forme japonaise, la forme amidaïste du bouddhisme m'a plu davantage que le bouddhisme chinois.[86]

---

[85] "But according to the Japanese interpretation, between these two delegates from two different universes, there is neither intimate drama nor direct opposition, in the occidental sense of the term: Nō is concentrated on the action of the protagonist and the drama resides in the story [*histoire*] of the past that the *shite* has already lived." Nishino, *Synthèse*, 86–87.

[86] "I will say that Chinese Buddhism did not particularly interest me. I must say that Buddhism as I saw it in Ceylon profoundly repulsed me. These giant Buddhas stretched out, lying on dark altars, in dark temples, repulsed me. Chinese Buddhism pleased me no more. I found Buddhism in its Japanese form much more interesting. In this Japanese Buddhism, there is a type of bitter and profound melancholy that is really interesting. In its Japanese form, the Amadist form of Buddhism pleased me much more than Chinese Buddhism." Paul Claudel, Jean Amrouche, and Louis Fournier, *Mémoires Improvisés*, Paris: Gallimard, 1969, 165.

Claudel's apology for Japanese Buddhism recalls some of the Catholic meditations on the nature of this world found in his journal. For him, this world naturally declines. Only Armageddon may redeem what exists in this life. For instance, on February 26, 1922, he writes that the "feu dernier, solution, résolution, dissolution ineffable de tout dans le sein du Créateur. Tout lui a été rendu finalement comme au Jour de la Création il a tout donné" (final fire, solution, resolution, ineffable dissolution of all in the breast of the Creator. Everything given up to him as at the Day of Creation everything was given by him).[87] The same day, he jots down that "[l]a nature peut aller du plus au moins, mais non du moins au plus—évo[lution]—remonter. On ne se transforme qu'en perdant q[uel]q[ue] ch[ose]" (nature can go from more to less, but not from less to more—evol[ution]—return. Things cannot transform without losing something).[88] He recorded these thoughts at the start of his time in Japan, a few years before writing *Soulier*. We can see why he felt parts of Japanese Buddhism and the medieval spirit of Nō congenial to his own philosophy. Naturally, his interpretation of Japanese art and religion was ultimately a Catholic one, and often entailed distorting Japanese ideas by wrenching them out of their original context. Yet his conviction that Japanese religion was close to his Catholicism left him more open than usual to non-Christian beliefs.

As Nishino indicates, Claudel was hardly a blank slate when he encountered Nō as ambassador. In scenes from the *IIe Journée*, Claudel portrays certain supernatural figures such as the Double Shadow or *l'Ombre Double* that Nō also seems to have inspired. However, "ces scènes de la IIe Journée ont été écrites *avant* que Claudel n'assiste pour la première fois à un spectacle de nô, le 22 octobre 1922. L'auteur aurait donc pu trouver à travers le nô une confirmation de sa propre idée de mettre en scène le monde spirituel" (the scenes were written *before* Claudel saw a Nō performance for the first time on 22 October 1992. The author would therefore have been able to find in Nō a confirmation of his own ideas of how to put the spiritual world on stage).[89] However, through the many Nō plays he saw, and the many pieces of information on Nō he read in Japan, Claudel entered into a rare conversation with the Japanese theatrical form. We can see his fascination with Nō most clearly in his essay by the same name, in which, stressing the supernatural and irrational nature of Nō, he casts Nō as a confrontation between this world and the other, symbolized by the confrontation between the *waki* and the *shite*. Claudel even paraphrases in his essay Zeami's famous maxim: "Par un étonnant paradoxe, ce n'est plus le sentiment qui est à l'intérieur de l'acteur, c'est l'acteur qui se met à l'intérieur du sentiment" (Through a stunning paradox, it is no longer the sentiment that is inside the actor, but the actor who is inside of the sentiment) (*Pr.* 1170.) In the final version of *Soulier*, Nishino suggests, we can see the fruits of his dialogue with Nō. The many performances he saw, and translations he read, tested and refined his original ideas for his long play. His labor brings his work closer to Nō, but also brings Nō closer to his original

---

[87] Paul Claudel, *Journal Tome I*, ed. François Varillon and Jacques Petit, Paris: Gallimard, 1968, 541.
[88] Ibid., 541.
[89] Nishino, *Synthèse*, 506.

work. Nō in Claudel's eyes is essentially a "materialized dream" (rêve matérialisé) sparked by a visitor from the other world, whom Claudel terms "l'Ambassadeur de l'Inconnu" or the "Ambassador of the Unknown" (*Pr.* 1169).[90] With his folding fan, the *shite* sweeps away ordinary time and space places us in another dimension (*Pr.* 1170). The mask, "le sceau définitif de ce qui n'est plus capable de changer" (definitive seal of he that which can no longer change), acts as an unbroachable barrier between this world and the world of the *shite* (*Pr.* 1175). This view of Nō makes *mugen nō* the theater's essential type with *genzai nō* forgotten, and gives an implicit Catholic spin to modify both the original material and Claudel's source material, a deformation that allows both to exist harmoniously in Claudel's constellation of beliefs.[91]

The difficulty of approaching Claudel's work goes beyond the Japanese influences. The Catholic "universe" of *Soulier* may be prohibitive for French and broader Western audiences as well. Discussing the play with Claudel, Jean Amrouche asks whether "l'intervention des Saints et des Anges devait requérir, de votre spectateur, je ne sais quelle croyance à l'existence réelle de ces personnages" (the intervention of saints and angels should require, of your audience, some sort of belief in the real existence of these personages).[92] Claudel responds:

> Je ne demande à mon spectateur que la croyance à mon propre drame quand il le regarde, je ne sors pas de là, je ne fais pas métier d'apologiste, bien que *Le Soulier de Satin* ait joué un rôle, à ce qui paraît, pas négligeable de ce côté-là. Je cherche seulement à fournir un ensemble délectable, comme font tous les artistes quels qu'ils soient. Et si les personnages surnaturels entrent dans la composition, c'est que leur présence m'a paru artistiquement nécessaire, de même que dans l'*Iliade* l'absence des personnages représenterait quelque chose d'absolument inconcevable, et sans lesquels cette magnifique épopée n'existerait pas. On ne demande pas plus à mon spectateur la croyance à mes Anges ou à mes personnages surnaturels qu'un lecteur de l'*Odyssée* ou de l'*Iliade* n'a besoin de croire à Pallas ou à Jupiter.[93]

Amrouche presses Claudel further by suggesting that, if the supernatural entities of *Soulier* can be taken in the same way as a modern reader of Homer takes Greek deities, then the dramatist seems to want his audience to interpret his Catholic figures as mythic figures.

---

[90] Ibid., 506, 508.

[91] Analyzing *Tête d'Or*, Millet-Gérard also discusses the superficial similarity between Claudel's early theatrical ideas and his mature interpretation of Nō. See Millet-Gérard, "Claudel et le nô," 135–40.

[92] Claudel, Amrouche, and Fournier, *Mémoires,* 292.

[93] "I do not ask my spectator to share my beliefs when he watches my drama; I don't go further than that; I am not about to become an apologist, even if *The Satin Slipper* played a non-negligible role in that regard. I try simply to furnish a delectable ensemble, as do all artists regardless of who they are. And if supernatural personages enter into the composition, it is because their presence seemed artistically necessary to me, just as in *The Iliad* the absence of [these kinds of] personages would be inconceivable, since without them that magnificent epic would not exist. No one asks my spectator to believe in my angels or in my supernatural personages any more than a reader of *The Odyssey* or *The Iliad* needs to believe in Pallas or in Jupiter." Claudel, Amrouche, and Fournier, *Mémoires,* 292.

Claudel, however, disagrees. The concept of myth, he says, does not quite account for the approach the audience should have to entities in which it does not believe. In a way strikingly reminiscent of Thomas Pavel and subsequent theorists of literary worlds, Claudel continues:

> Je dirai simplement qu'une œuvre d'art forme un monde à part, qui n'est pas du tout le monde de la théologie ou de l'apologétique, qui a simplement pour objet la délectation du spectateur, délectation qui est loin d'être mauvaise et d'être nuisible et qui, au contraire, peut être d'un grand profit et d'un grand avantage, même spirituel, à ceux qui le regardent. Les personnages surnaturels dont vous parlez et qui répondent, bien entendu, comme je suis chrétien, pour moi, quand je fais ma prière, à des réalités concrètes tout à fait réelles et véritables mais quand ils sont portés sur la scène c'est un monde à part qui s'adresse au public et n'interviennent plus que comme éléments de délectation, que comme fournissant un ensemble de beauté et de joie pour celui qui les contemple.[94]

As the problems with conceiving of literary works as belonging to discrete worlds took up the first chapter of this thesis, I will not argue the point further here. Amrouche himself asks Claudel whether there is not "une relation entre cet élément de beauté, de délectation, de joie dont vous parlez, et la manifestation d'une vérité" (a relation between this element of beauty, of delectation, of joy of which you speak, and the manifestation of a truth).[95] Claudel demurs, and, finally, Amrouche poses the question that is at the heart of this thesis. He says that many readers feel that, if they are not Christian, they "n'entrer[ont] pas dans ce monde, [ils] n'enter[ont] pas dans le monde qu'il a construit" (will not enter into this world, [they] will not enter into the language of Claudel, [they] cannot enter into the world that he has constructed).[96] He adduces the example of André Gide, Claudel's erstwhile correspondent, who, having been interested in Claudel's oeuvre for years, found *Soulier* impenetrable. In Amrouche's words: "Bref, tout se passe comme si une porte qui était demeurée ouverte jusqu'à quelques années de là, s'était tout à coup fermée, et qu'il ne pouvait plus pénétrer dans cet univers" (In short, a door that had been slightly ajar for a few years seems suddenly to have shut, and he could no longer enter into this universe).[97] Claudel's response? "Eh ben, c'est son affaire!" (Well, that's his problem!).[98] He stresses once more that one need not be Christian to access his dramatic world; but then he relents a bit, and concludes,

---

[94] "I would say simply that a work of art forms a world apart, which is not at all the world of theology or of apologetics, which aims simply to delight the spectator, delight which is far from being bad and being harmful, and which, on the contrary, can be very profitable and very advantageous, even spiritually, to those who watch. The supernatural personages of whom you speak and who correspond, of course, as I am a Christian, for me, when I pray, to concrete realities entirely real and true, but, when they are brought onstage, it is a world apart that addresses the public and have no role other than as objects of delight, that act as an ensemble of beauty and joy for those who contemplate them." Ibid., 292–93.
[95] Ibid., 293.
[96] Ibid., 294.
[97] Ibid.
[98] Ibid.

Eh ben, un homme qui regarde *Le Soulier de Satin* n'a pas besoin d'être chrétien *complètement* convaincu, mais il y a besoin certainement d'avoir un désir d'autre chose, un désir de surnaturel, d'avoir des sentiments profonds qu'il a à exprimer, et il en trouve le lieu, le paysage, si vous voulez, dans ce drame où beaucoup de choses lui échappent mais qui, cependant, lui paraît adapté comme peut être une serre, par exemple, au développement de certains sentiments inarticulés qu'il portait en lui-même.[99]

In a few words, Claudel's insistence that *Soulier* belongs to another world that can be contemplated disinterestedly by a non-Catholic observer gives way to the more restricted claim that the observer need not be "completely" convinced by Catholic doctrine, but must have some sort of "desire" for a "supernatural" beyond. This desire for the supernatural serves as the common ground that allows the audience to enter into the world of *Soulier*. But even this may be too much. The desire for a supernatural beyond is present in both the original *Kantan* and in Mishima's adaptation, but does this conception of a "spiritual" realm form a *tertium comparationis* connected to the spirituality of Claudel's play?

Degrees of Distance?

I move to comparing Claudel's and Mishima's plays according to the ontologies that structure them. My point will be that in order to make comparison between the two plays, we need to draw on some aspects of the plays while ignoring others. There is nothing prima facie surprising about this. Were we able to show total correspondence between two things, we would have not just similar but identical things. We also must remember that we can have two different descriptions of the same thing without having two competing descriptions. But my point is somewhat different. I mean to show that we need to suppress deep-level differences between the two plays in order to make a convincing argument for their similarity. The superficial correspondences *supervene* on the deep differences; that means we cannot deal with the one without accounting for the other.

I will focus on how we interpret the supernatural figures in both plays. I will show that although Claudel, Mishima, and the author of the original *Kantan* bear superficial similarities to one another in the way they treat the category, they differ at a deep ontological level. Concomitantly, occasionally the three differ at a superficial level but agree at a deeper one. Understanding the ways in which these surface and deep strata interact across the three plays will in turn allow us better to map the connections between the plays, and to reveal what we assert when we assert "closeness" between literary works from different times and languages.

---

[99] "Well, look, a man who watches *The Satin Slipper* does not need to be *completely* convinced by Christianity, but he certainly needs the desire for something else, the desire for the supernatural, to have deep emotions to express, and he finds the place, the landscape, if you'd like, in this drama in which many things elude him, but that, nonetheless, seem to him like a hothouse to develop certain inarticulate sentiments that he holds within himself." (my emphasis), Ibid., 295.

The ending of both Claudel's scene and Mishima's play provide the most pertinent comparison. In *Soulier*, the Guardian Angel ultimately convinces Prouheze to commit suicide in order to be reunited with Rodrigue in the next life:

DONA PROUHÈZE.—Il m'aimera toujours?
L'ANGE GARDIEN.—Ce qui te rend si belle ne peut mourir
  Ce qui fait qu'il t'aime ne peut mourir.
DONA PROUHÈZE.—Je serai à lui pour toujours dans mon âme et dans mon corps?
L'ANGE GARDIEN.—Il nous faut laisser le corps en arrière quelque peu.
DONA PROUHÈZE.—Eh quoi! il ne connaîtra point ce goût que j'ai?
L'ANGE GARDIEN.—C'est l'âme qui fait le corps.
DONA PROUHÈZE.—Comment donc l'a-t-elle fait mortel?
L'ANGE GARDIEN.—C'est le péché qui l'a fait mortel.
DONA PROUHÈZE.—C'était beau d'être pour lui une femme.
L'ANGE GARDIEN.—Et moi je ferai de toi une étoile.
DONA PROUHÈZE.—Une étoile! c'est le nom dont il m'appelle toujours dans la nuit.
  Et mon cœur tressaillait profondément de l'entendre.
L'ANGE GARDIEN.—N'as-tu donc pas toujours été comme une étoile pour lui?
DONA PROUHÈZE.—Séparée!
L'ANGE GARDIEN.—Conductrice.
DONA PROUHÈZE.—La voici qui s'éteint sur terre.
L'ANGE GARDIEN.—je rallumerai dans le ciel.
DONA PROUHÈZE.—Comment brillerai-je qui suis aveugle.
L'ANGE GARDIEN.—Dieu soufflera sur toi.
DONA PROUHÈZE.—Je ne suis qu'un tison sous la cendre.
L'ANGE GARDIEN.—Mais moi je ferai de toi une étoile flamboyante dans le souffle
                        du Saint-Esprit!
DONA PROUHÈZE.—Adieu donc ici-bas! adieu, adieu, mon bien-aimé! Rodrigue,
                    Rodrigue là-bas, adieu pour toujours! (*Th.* 191–92)

DONA PROUHÈZE: He will love me forever?
GUARDIAN ANGEL: That which makes you so beautiful cannot die. That which
                    makes him love you cannot die.
DONA PROUHÈZE: I will be his forever in my soul and in my body?
GUARDIAN ANGEL: We need to leave the body behind a little.
DONA PROUHÈZE: What! He will not know this delight [*goût*] that I am?
GUARDIAN ANGEL: It is the soul that makes the body.
DONA PROUHÈZE: How did it make the body mortal?
GUARDIAN ANGEL: It is sin that made it mortal.
DONA PROUHÈZE: How good it was to be for him a woman.
GUARDIAN ANGEL: And I will make a star of you.
DONA PROUHÈZE: A star! That's the name by which he always calls me at night.
  And deep in my heart came a shiver when I heard it.
GUARDIAN ANGEL: Have you therefore not always been like a star for him.
DONA PROUHÈZE: Separated!

GUARDIAN ANGEL: Conductor.
DONA PROUHÈZE: Here I am, slowly fading on this earth.
GUARDIAN ANGEL: I re-illuminate the sky.
DONA PROUHÈZE: How will I shine if I am blind?
GUARDIAN ANGEL: God will breathe on you.
DONA PROUHÈZE: I am no more than a brand under the ashes.
GUARDIAN ANGEL: But I will make of you a flaming star in the breath of the Holy Spirit!
DONA PROUHÈZE: Goodbye therefore to this earthly world! Goodbye, goodbye, my beloved! Rodrigue, Rodrigue over here, goodbye forever!

The implication here is straightforward: Prouhèze's decision is predicated on this world being fleeting, but the afterlife, and her soul, being eternal. This is obviously contrary to the original Nō, in which all existence is revealed to be fleeting, without an eternal world behind the scenes intervening to guarantee the continued existence of whatever perishes on Earth. We also see that Prouhèze is in fact seduced to go over to this other world, a seduction reinforced by the call and response technique Claudel uses, with Prouhèze supplying essentially the first half of a couplet (for instance, "C'était beau d'être pour lui une femme") and the angel providing the second half ("Et moi je ferai de toi une étoile"). Prouhèze's desires are completed by being redirected by the angel from the temporal (the body of a woman) to a symbol of the timeless (a distant and constant star). The effect is a different one from that which we find in the medieval *Kantan*.

It differs as well from what we see in Mishima. Having become a despotic leader, Jirō is being persuaded to commit suicide by ghosts masquerading as officials and doctors. The scene is an inversion of the medieval Nō, though it does recall the despair we find in the Tang-era *chuanqi* from which all of this derives. Jirō refuses, leading to a final confrontation with the head "doctor":

老国手　いいかね、次郎、わしはあなたに納得させるよ。しづかにおきき。わしらは邯鄲の里の精霊だ。な、それはあんたも多分御承知だ。この枕で寝たものは、悟りをひらかねべならぬ定めになってゐる。むかしは粟のおだいの炊けるあひだに一生の夢を見て、現世のはかなさを悟ったわけだ。今もさうだ。夢を見てゐるあひだ、みんな徒順にすなほに生涯を生きた。本当に行きたのだよ。だから夢をさめぎはにはその一生のはかさをいやさらに身にしませるためにだ。帝王となった夢のなかで不老長寿の薬をすすめたもんだ。それがわしの役目だ。それだのに、あんたは何だ。はじめからあんたは生きようとしないぢやないか。あんたは素直さを欠いてゐる。あんたは夢のなかででも、人生に全部肘鉄をくらはした。わしは一部始終を見てをつたよ。

次郎　だって、おぢいさん、夢の中でだって僕たちは自由です。生きようとしたって生きまいとしたって、あなたの知ったことぢやないか。(*Kindai* 47–48)

Senior Doctor: Well now, Jirō, I'm going to make you understand. Listen well. I am a spirit from the village of Kantan. You probably already know that. When you sleep on this pillow, you must necessarily achieve enlightenment. Long ago, during the time it takes to cook millet, one man saw all of his life flash by in a dream. This was done to enlighten him of the truth of this world. Even now the same [event] happens. While dreaming, everyone passively and meekly lives an entire life. They really live. To make the experience truly impressive, right before they wake, in this dream in which they have become the ruler of a country, I entice them to drink medicine to give them eternal life. That is my role here. But what exactly are you? Did you not want to live from the start? You lack obedience. Even though you're in the middle of a dream, you rebuff everything. I've been watching the whole time.

Jirō: So what, old man? If we're in the middle of a dream then we're free to do whatever we want, aren't we? What do you know about living and not living?

We can note that the fusion that happens between Prouhèze and the angel never occurs here. Jirō's rough speech contrasts with the more sophisticated speech patterns we find in the "doctor's." Jirō's rejection of the dream world is not a rejection per se, but a refusal to care. It is, to put it differently, a championing of the postwar apathy Jirō represented at the start. After reiterating that, however uninterested he is in life, he wishes to live, Jirō wakes. Kiku enters. Worried that he will desert her as did her husband, she grows anxious. Jirō tells her to abandon all hope that her husband will return. At the same time, he assures her that he will stay with her. The two look out at the garden, where the flowers bloom for the first time since Kiku's husband departed. The difference with *Soulier* is not merely Jirō's refusal. Mishima's *Kantan* dramatizes its own incoherence: the final image of the blooming flowers suggests the efficacy of the dream in the "real" world, yet this only occurs thanks to Jirō refusing to hear the Buddhist message inside of the dream. As with the mask, which Jirō seems both to see and not to see in his earlier encounter with the beautiful woman, the play seems unable to decide whether the world of *Kantan* is merely a theatrical world with an ersatz "Buddhist" core, or a genuinely Buddhist play immanently relevant to postwar Japan. If *Soulier* appropriates the medieval *Kantan* and pretends like the Buddhist message was pointing toward Catholicism all along, Mishima makes this clash of ontologies the core of his adaptation.

Each of the critics discussed focus on Mishima's departure from and inevitable return to the Japanese tradition. It is worth noting that regarding Mishima's work as a whole the prevailing critical paradigm in Japan and in the West is "to interpret Mishima's works in light of Western aesthetics, specifically Western modernist influences."[100] Yoshie Endo divides the critical corpus into three categories. Aside from this "dominant" critical approach, there is an approach that "read[s] Mishima's works in the context of Japanese and Chinese classical literature" (seen, Endo notes, in the criticism of Donald Keene and David Pollack), which Endo argues "has served to neutralize the political nature of [Mishima's] works."[101] Endo says that the "third approach employs a comparative study between Mishima's controversial activities and his literary works in order to dig out the 'real' meaning of his works and death (Henry Scott-Stokes; John Nathan)."[102]

---

[100] Yoshie Endo, "Craving for the Absolute: The Sublime and the Tragic in Mishima Yukio's Theatrical Works," Dissertation/Thesis, ProQuest Dissertations Publishing U6, University of Pennsylvania, 2004, 2.
[101] Ibid.
[102] Ibid.

Ultimately, the best indicator of Mishima's worldview at the time of his experiments with Nō is the original afterword to *Kindai nogaku*. Critics such as Masaki Dōmoto have noted the paradox of a "modern Nō," with Dōmoto suggesting that Mishima must have been "smirking" (笑み) as he took up the project.[103] Yet the notion of a modern Nō is not necessarily paradoxical. In the afterword to *Kindai nōgakushū*, Donald Keene discusses that Mishima's intention was to take the "exposed metaphysical themes" of classical Nō and apply them to modern situations.[104] The problem that Mishima had to overcome, writes Keene, is the different beliefs of modern audiences and the medieval audiences of classical Nō. For the medieval spectator, ghosts (幽霊 *yurei*) were as real as the actors of the Nō performance; in other words, ghosts and living people were both part of the folk ontology of the average medieval Japanese person.[105] The modern viewer, however, does not believe in ghosts, and the dramatist who presents a specter onstage cannot dupe the twentieth-century audience into believing in the reality of ghosts,[106] for in modern folk ontology ghosts simply do not exist, at least not at the actual world. If Mishima wants to preserve the "metaphysical" structure of classical Nō, he needs to accommodate those entities that are no longer present in his modern folk ontology. Keene notes that Mishima drew "inspiration" from Greek theater. Just as European writers since at least the Renaissance have drawn upon Greek theater without necessarily sharing the worldview of Sophocles and Euripides, so Mishima could adapt Nō for modern Japanese audiences without possessing the ontology of Zeami.[107] So Keene asserts that both Mishima and whoever views the modern Nō plays can entertain medieval ideas without actually believing in them. We could say, then, that the haunting and often pessimistic ideas that run through classical Nō appealed to Mishima. But we cannot say that Mishima held the exact same ideas.

This gives us a tripartite division. Spirits appear in each play. The obvious difference between them is that the spirits of *Kantan*, both the original and Mishima's, are Japanese Buddhist whereas the angel of Claudel's *Soulier* is Christian. This is a trivial difference. The more pressing concern is finding that which allows us to state that all of these things, the specters contained within the Pillow of Kantan and the guardian angel, all belong to the same meta-category of "spirit." By meta-category, I mean a critical category part of a higher level ontology that encompasses both Claudel's Christian ontology and the Buddhist ontologies of Mishima and the medieval author of *Kantan*, or rather the Buddhist ontology of the medieval Nō and Mishima's pseudo-Buddhist ontology. In using this meta-category, we have a good idea of what we are talking about—we know we are dealing with some sort of immaterial being that is not alive but that is real, if only as a possible figure—but we need to be wary of the deep divisions between each conceptualization of this category.

---

[103] Masaki Dōmoto, *Gekiji Mishima Yukio*, Tokyo: Gekishobō, 1994, 165.
[104] Keene, "Kaisetsu," 257.
[105] Ibid.
[106] Ibid., 256.
[107] Ibid.

Since spirits appear in all the plays, let us use that category as our point of comparison. The obstacle to surmount is how we *weigh* each component that makes up the different concepts of "spirit." Surely some are more important and thus have more weight. For example, Claudel's notion of the spiritual world bears some similarity to that of the original *Kantan* since both *Soulier* and the classical Nō promote the idea that this world is somehow lacking, or that there is a grander scheme of things in which this world is an insignificant part. Surely this differs considerably from the concept we find in Mishima's more nihilistic take. But Claudel's notion of "spirit" is irreducibly Christian, whereas Mishima's is ostensibly Buddhist, even *if* Mishima himself does not believe in the reality of what he is representing! If we take the Christian aspect of Claudel's play seriously, then we bring in a great deal of ontological baggage that removes *Soulier* from the worldview of both *Kantan*s. Whatever we do, taking seriously the notion of a ternary relation and degrees of closeness helps to clarify what we are doing in making comparisons and how our comparands relate to one another. More than that, it helps us to break free from the somewhat simplistic assertion that everything is translatable or nothing is translatable; two things are either identical or nonidentical.[108] It helps us, that is to say, grasp not only the grand but also minute differences that exist between different literary works, and that determine the relations between the various pieces of comparative and world literature.

That sounds compelling, but what happens once we try to map degrees? Let us continue to say that the term we are dealing with is "supernatural" or "ghostly." I have already detailed some of the ways in which the supernatural figures differ between the three versions. But might the fact that they are there at all be significant? I will focus only on the effect the supernatural realm has on the actual world. I mentioned that in Mishima the flowers withered after the departure of Kiku's husband and bloomed again sometime during Jirō's dream or his awakening. This suggests that the supernatural world is not separate in this *Kantan* from the 1950s Tokyo in which Kiku and Jirō live. Even if Jirō remained apathetic throughout the dream, his desire to live, his rejection of the poison offered to him by the ghosts, appears to have had some effect on the actual world. Therefore, we can say that spirits are actual in the world of Mishima's *Kantan*, much as they are in the original.

The same is true, I think, in Claudel, but with important differences that cast the comparison into doubt. Of course, the obvious effect of the angel's apparition in Prouhèze's dream is her death. But the choice is Prouhèze's: Prouhèze is convinced to end her

---

[108] See Emily Apter, *The Translation Zone: A New Comparative Literature: A New Comparative Literature*, Princeton: Princeton UP, 2006, xi–xii. "Nothing is translatable" and "Everything is translatable" are the first and last of her "twenty theses on translation" that serve as the prologue to the book. Apter of course means that nothing is translatable if we want perfect correspondence between a source text and its target in translation, a proposition with which I naturally agree. My concern is rather that adopting this axiom flattens out the fine-grained or delicately wrought distinctions between different types of translations, between those translations that are separated from the original by many degrees and those which are only separated by a few.

life, and she herself takes it. This is not quite the manipulation of the nonhuman in the actual world by a supernatural party we find in Mishima. Indeed, the effect is a Christian one: Prouhèze, in accepting death, "saves" Rodrigue and becomes an "eternal star" for him, a guiding force in imitation of Christ. It is here that Claudel's Catholic vision becomes especially important; our only indication that the angel is real is the Catholic ontology to which Claudel subscribes. Everything is linked, everything has a purpose, even hardship and death, in the grand plan of God. Claudel's adaptation of Nō transfers the significance of the action into his own constellation of Catholic beliefs, and he demands that we entertain his vision of the world in order to make "real" the spiritual elements of his drama in a way that Mishima, with that final and vivid blossoming of the flowers in Kiku's garden, does not.

A final consideration: I have been talking about the supernatural in relation only to Claudel and Mishima, but it is worth passing by the classical Nō again. I can do justice neither to the complexity of medieval Buddhism in Japan nor the influence of the various schools on Nō theater and the critical writings of Zeami. But we can say that the supernatural elements fit differently into the ontology of medieval Japan in a way foreign to either of our modern versions. This is perhaps the reason for which the *mūgen* Nō classification is a modern one; the presence or absence of the supernatural takes on an exaggerated importance in the modern era after that original medieval understanding of the world was lost.

We might then map degrees between the two adaptations, considering how they relate to one another in terms of their conception of the supernatural. Whether we consider Claudel's Catholic ontology mutually intelligible with Mishima's indeterminate one is another matter. I have suggested elsewhere that such different ontologies do not access one another. But it seems like this might be a viable option. However, the very concept of the supernatural has a different place in the medieval Buddhist ontology of the original *Kantan*. Thus it seems that, as in the case of the various props mentioned earlier, degrees might suggest a similarity or even identity between the world of the original *Kantan*, its constellation of beliefs, and those of the twentieth-century adaptation. That, I think, would obscure rather than illuminate the texts.

The way to solve this is to think of certain categories as multidimensional, with senses accrued from the "original" and from the new constellation of belief into which it is placed. We need first to fix the constellation of belief, and then determine whether there is mutual intelligibility between these constellations. But whatever the case, perhaps if philosophical approaches to vagueness can teach us anything, and I would like to think they have much to teach us, it is just that idea that the components of a literary work in translation exist in a larger constellation. In comparing plays from the East and West, we should, I think, always consider how the significance of all that passes in the text supervenes on deep-level ontological differences; we can heuristically borrow from philosophical approaches to vagueness to help us to understand just what happens to literary works in their translation across time, space, and into new constellations of belief.

Of particular importance is the gap that exists not only between "East" and "West" but "East" and "East." There is nothing shocking in finding that Claudel, a French Catholic writing in the early twentieth century, deformed Japanese ideas in order to make them fit in his constellation of belief. From Pinguet and Bush to Millet-Gérard and Nishino, Claudel scholars have remarked this deformation so often that it is almost a cliché. Yet Mishima is a more interesting case, for, being himself Japanese, and having been exposed since childhood to traditional Japanese arts including Nō, he should be as well placed as anyone to understand Nō on its own terms; and he did understand Nō well, but that does not stop his *Kantan* from belonging to a different ontology from that of the original. I have suggested that the reason for Mishima's distance from the original *Kantan* is both his time of writing and his range of interests. Even if he were, like the writer or the audience members of the original *Kantan*, a Buddhist with a medieval worldview, capable of believing in ghosts and other supernatural entities as actual, the significance of his beliefs would differ from those of the medieval cohort simply by virtue of him believing in all of these things *despite* living in the mid-twentieth century. That is not to make a value judgement about the correctness or otherwise of medieval Japanese beliefs. It is only to say that the field, or to use the standard metaphor, constellation, in which those beliefs appeared in the Muromachi period necessarily cannot be replicated in the Shōwa as a subset of possible beliefs of the totality of beliefs of that era, whatever such a totality might look like. No more am I claiming that every person in the Muromachi or the Shōwa period held the same beliefs; differences in class, education, and experience, among other things, would affect what is believed and what is thought possible. What I am claiming is that the range of possibilities is different, and unequivocally so. The oppositional categories of, say, realism, scientific rationality, or Christianity, did not exist for the Muromachi person as they did for Mishima in 1950. We could say the same about Claudel; "Japan" and all of the senses that that noun held for Claudel did not exist in the constellation of belief of anyone writing centuries before him in France, much less for Zeami and other writers of classical Nō.

If a play like *Kantan* is intelligible across time and space but changes in aspect, what are we to understand it as? I suggested at the outset that entities in East–West literature are often images of the originals formed in the process of comparison between "East" and "West." This definition, I think, works well for *Soulier* and the *shinsaku nō Kantan*. But what if Mishima and Claudel were put into dialogue in 1951 and began speaking about *Kantan*? What makes it so that both of them are speaking about the same thing, if their comprehension of it is different, and Claudel is speaking of something he might have witnessed but only could have read in translation? Are we to say that what Claudel means by *"Kantan"* is something different from what Mishima means? Or, more importantly, that what we as critics mean is something different from what is meant, in this case or in a multitude of others, by the writers we study?

The difficulty arises because *Kantan* seems to be both modally plastic and temporally plastic. The truth value of a modally plastic assertion varies depending on small changes in the situation in which it is uttered; that of a temporally plastic one varies across time.[109] For instance, "spirit" is modally plastic since the properties and relations it expresses, in

---

[109] This discussion of modally and temporally plastic terms and assertations and the subsequent consideration of how to deal with them relies on the work of Cian Dorr and John Hawthorne.

our critical metalanguage, change depending on the context in which we embed the term, be that context Claudel's, Mishima's, or Zeami's. We map it to different admissible sets of possible worlds in each case. But our own metalanguage is not itself outside of time. Were we to get a new set of information telling us that, in fact, Zeami and other writers of classical Nō were in fact familiar with Christianity and Aristotle's *Poetics*, our use of the word "spirit" would change. This is because we would embed it in a new context, the updated constellation of belief for the writer of Nō plays in Muromachi Japan. The same is true not just in the critical metalanguage but in the "regular" languages themselves. Mishima's *yūrei* 幽霊 means something different for him than it would have meant for an earlier writer, say one from the Tokugawa period whose only knowledge of Western ideas could have come through the Dutch materials that made their way into Japan during its period of isolation.[110] Temporal plasticity seems to present us with an altogether more difficult situation than modal plasticity, since it is easy to imagine lines between the ontologies of different cultures existing in different spaces of the globe but more difficult to imagine competing ontologies springing up in the same space at different times. The reason is that we are inclined to believe that there was a precise moment at which one ontology (a medieval one) ceases and another (a modern one) begins. But that also sounds strange, as we generally think of cultural change as something gradual, even in remarkable cases like the Japanese one of the late-nineteenth and early-twentieth centuries. And if two competing ontologies exist in a single culture, we begin to wonder what "culture" could mean. It begins to look dangerously opaque.

There is no easy way out of this impasse. At least there is no way that I can see to get rid of the imprecision surrounding our terms, be they modally or temporally plastic. Terms like "spirit" will shift in meaning depending on the contrast class that we use to fix them; Claudel's *Soulier* is not only a Christian vision of a Japanese scenario but also a Christian vision in spite of a Japanese scenario. This sounds evident enough, but the significance of that assertion becomes clearer once we use Mishima's *Kantan* to fix the boundaries of Claudel's work, as Mishima's interpretation shows the possibilities that are absent from Claudel's rendering and vice-versa. The contrast shows that Mishima's version, strange as it may be to the medieval vision of the original, occupies a space that is more indeterminate than is Claudel's. This shows that Mishima's *Kantan* is *relatively close* to the classical *Kantan*, but not absolutely. Relative closeness, as the result of our ternary relation, arises in contrast, and therefore cannot be deemed an intrinsic property of Mishima's play. Claudel's interpretation could itself be relatively close depending on the contrast used to fix it. What we deal with in East–West literature are these entities that emerge in comparison—these *arguments* in favor of a particular contrast class used to fix the identity of a given text.

See Dorr and Hawthorne, "Semantic Plasticity and Speech Reports," *Philosophical Review* vol. 123, no. 3 (2014): 281–338.

[110] For the effect of this transmission, and how they did in fact enshrine an idea of Greece in Edo Japan, see Michael Lucken, *Le Japon grec: culture et possession*, Paris: Gallimard, 2019, especially 76–87.

Since there is no fact of the matter according to which plays like *Kantan* and *Soulier* are definitely classifiable as certain entities, they are vague. Certainly, some comparisons, some contrast classes, some terms of comparison are better than others. The three *Kantans*, as we might call them, work in this case, as does the category of "spirit" as the shared term of comparison. However, another comparison focusing on masks might work just as well. We might then compare one of Yeats's "Irish Noh" plays with Mishima's *Kantan*, and perhaps triangulate them with another classical Nō that we think uses masks in a similar—or interestingly dissimilar—way. What is salient in the comparison depends on the contrast class with which we have to work. That is not to say that the reference frame is entirely up to the reader or translator. It is to say, though, that elements become vague in translation, such that ontologies clash and one point of reference leads to proximity and another to distance, or incompatibility. We have degrees of distance, but also multiple dimensions. There may be lines of communication along one dimension, but disconnections along another.

What this makes clear is that, when digested and assimilated in translation, the elements, or "bits," undergo modifications at a deep level, restructuring their very DNA. Rather than a biography, we have a lineage: rather than the original elements themselves achieving a new life in another language, they give birth to something that carries their genetic code but with important additions and subtractions. Hence, we have not identity but resemblance, yet resemblance that does go beyond superficiality to indicate something like parentage. In a sense, what we find is the product of the cross-fertilization between the horizontal and vertical aspects of a work. This is not normal parentage, however, but rather something like genetic engineering. Parts of the genetic code of the original are knocked out, new grafts from different sources are introduced. While bits from the original are there, the bits themselves may have been divided up, cut down, and different parts recombined with other bits entirely. This reminds us of the problem of the comparative study of religion as Lloyd summarizes it:

> The cross-cultural question has often been supposed to be a matter of definition. If we take "myths" to be traditional tales, they are to be found everywhere. But that leaves us with the question of how those traditional tales were viewed by those who told and performed them. Do the actors themselves draw a distinction—any distinction, indeed—between stories that tell of present-day events and those that deal with remote times, times quite different from those of today? Do they invoke some notion of the sacred to mark out some tales from other, profane, ones? If so, then it is a mistake to seek to homogenised discourse and have it all to be subject to an identical set of criteria for appropriateness, namely those that suit familiar, mundane transactions, though the question remains of how those other registers are understood and marked out by the actors themselves.[111]

The conundrum to which Lloyd brings our attention is essentially the same as the one involving the different spiritual entities of the three plays. Our situation is made more difficult still as, in each of the plays, the links to the sources from both the horizontal and vertical axes are themselves vague—how we determine closeness depends on what we

---

[111] Lloyd, *The Ambivalences of Rationality*, 89.

use for contrast—and this means that the entire "world literary system" is characterized by ontological vagueness. No matter how much information we have, we never reach a point of confidence or finality, a definite identity for texts or bits of texts in translation. There is always *some* line of communication, and we always understand a text to *some* extent, but we may exploit the vagueness of terms, or superficial similarities, in order to achieve a yet greater comprehension.

In some ways, this is quite the opposite of Nan Da's pronouncement that transnational studies pays too much attention to depth and too little attention to surfaces, or surface readings, too much attention to consequences and too little to events.[112] Or it is not at odds with Da, but orthogonal to her: superficial readings and events or encounters like Ted Hughes's and Chou Wen-chung's, surveyed in the last chapter, or Claudel's encounter with Nō and Mishima's encounter both with Nō and Claudel's "strange" interpretations of the medieval art, are immensely significant. At the same time, how we read them and the texts these events and encounters produce depends on deep-level processes of world creation that we can often not readily see. This gives another spin on Da's insightful reading of transnational "intransitivity," in line with my concept of asymmetry, of literary worlds that become inaccessible to later readers and have to be reconstituted according to a current cosmology. We only reach a point of clarity relative to a given ontological scheme, or set of interests. And this is why we deal not with "ambiguity" in the old post-structuralist sense of being open to multiple interpretations, but with vagueness, a lack of precision or clarity: ambiguity permits multiple interpretations, and we think of it, in the literary sense, as part of a general loss of faith in overarching truths.[113] As we have seen, nothing of the sort characterizes at least some of the works of world literature. Once the context is fixed, certain interpretations become impossible. We could not read Claudel's *Soulier* both as Buddhist and as Catholic, as that would lead to a contradiction, unless we ourselves employ a logic of contradiction like the one Graham Priest describes in Chapter One of this book—still, that itself is a way of fixing context to deal with vagueness, even if it is one more congenial to the tastes of many literary critics today.[114] Hence, we have degrees of distance in some contexts, but multiple contexts, or, better, to highlight the ontological incommensurability, multiple dimensions in which to map our degrees. This bottomless vagueness is not a flaw of world literature, but its very constitution.

---

[112] Nan Da, *Intransitive Encounter: Sino-U.S. Literature and the Limits of Exchange*, New York: Columbia UP, 2018, 220.

[113] See Thomas G. Pavel, *The Feud of Language: A History of Structuralist Thought*, Oxford: Blackwell, 1989.

[114] See Jan Alber, "Logical Contradictions, Possible Worlds Theory, and the Embodied Mind," in *Possible Worlds Theory and Contemporary Narratology*, ed. Alice Bell and Marie-Laure Ryan, Lincoln; London: U of Nebraska P, 2019, 157–76. Alber argues that we accept contradictions as natural in fiction. But this overlooks a major point of this book: *we* (whoever that is) might accept contradictions in fiction and delimit fiction from the actual world in which we believe there are no contradictions, but many ontologies, particularly Buddhist ones, might differ on this last point. Since the way we interpret the fictional world depends on our interpretation of the actual world, this is a significant point.

Part 3
POETIC WORLDS

Chapter Four

PAUL CLAUDEL AND KUKI SHŪZŌ IN THE 1920S: FRANCE, JAPAN, AND THE WORLD

見はるかす山々の頂
梢には風も動かず鳥も鳴かず
まてしばしやがて汝も休はん[1]

Voyageur!
旅 *app roche*
et respire enfin
cette odeu r
人 *qui guérit de tout*
mouvement[2]

In 1929 the Japanese philosopher and poet Kuki Shūzō travelled to Washington, DC, to pay a visit to the French Ambassador to the United States, the dramatist and poet Paul Claudel. After eight years of study in France and Germany, during which time he befriended the German philosopher Martin Heidegger (1889–1976) and took as his language instructor the young French thinker Jean-Paul Sartre (1905–1980), Kuki was returning to Japan to take up a position at the Imperial University of Kyoto at the behest of the eminent founder of the so-called Kyoto School of philosophy, Nishida Kitarō (1870–1945). Claudel himself had only been appointed ambassador to the United States in 1927. For six years before that, he had served as ambassador to Japan, and had arrived in Tokyo the very year that Kuki departed for Europe. Though we do not know what caused Kuki to go out of his way to see Claudel in Washington, the meeting marks a fitting end to the 1920s for both men; for each man, as a modern traveler, had spent the better part of the decade working in the other's homeland, and each

---

[1] "Gazing over the mountain crests / In the treetops neither wind stirs nor bird sings. / Wait awhile, and at last you too shall rest." Nishida Kitarō's inscription on Kuki's grave in Kyoto. The inscription is a Japanese translation of Johann Wolfgang von Goethe's "Wandrers Nachtlied," and possibly translated by Nishida himself. See Sakurai Shōichiro, *Kyōto gakuha suikoden* 京都学派水故伝, Kyoto: Kyoto UP, 2017, 338. This is the second poem bearing this title that Goethe wrote. Both were set as lieder by Schubert.

[2] "Traveler! / approach / and breathe in at last / this smell / that cures your need for any /movement." Paul Claudel, *Oeuvre Poétique*, ed. Jacques Petit, Paris: Gallimard, 1967, 707. Subsequent references to this work will be made in-text and use the abbreviation *Po.*

had labored arduously to make ideas from the other's tradition fit with his deeply held native beliefs.

I compare works written by Claudel and Kuki in the 1920s that attempt to fuse Japanese and European literature and philosophy. I will go through the ways that both men framed one another's traditions, with particular reference to how each writer related the foreign culture he encountered to parts of his native philosophical and religious ideas—Catholicism for Claudel; Buddhism, the moral code of Bushidō, and Shintoism for Kuki. Blending Japanese and European aesthetics, philosophy, and moral precepts allowed the poets to create a space of indeterminacy between Europe and the Far East, a space in which they could work, as writers cast between native traditions to which they were deeply committed and foreign cultures they were enamored but of which they felt they could never fully be a part. What I want to stress here are impossible worlds, which have often been claimed not to be a problem for literary worlds since anything that is conceivable is, we hear, possible.[3] Though this is true in one sense, it glosses over the ways in which writers grapple with literary worlds that are fascinating but, taken as a whole, cannot sit coherently in the writer's constellation of belief. Graham Priest develops this argument in *Towards Non-Being*. As he notes, something being conceivable does not entail that it can be imagined visually: "I cannot form a visible image of a chiliagon (a regular 1,000 sided figure), even though there is nothing impossible about this. Conversely, I can picture a state of stationary motion, even though this is contradictory."[4] Here I want to think of impossible worlds as worlds that, thanks to strongly held beliefs, are particularly inaccessible to a writer. Impossible worlds require great ontological reshuffling and recasting of bits of the original to fit into a new constellation of belief, to make parts of the original appear to merge seamlessly into the ontology of the new literary world.

Building upon what we saw of the *Kokin Wakashū* 古今和歌集, the first imperial collection and the Heian era Japanese cult of the four seasons, this chapter will focus on how the *Kokinshū* in particular assisted in structuring Claudel's and Kuki's ideas of Japanese poetry. As discussed in Chapter One, the *Kokinshū*, is, in form and content, founded on Buddhism; in the words of Kimiko Sata, the collection, "from its expressions to the arrangement of its poems," gives us good reason to see it against a Buddhist background.[5] There are, of course, other ways of reading the *Kokinshū*, and the exegesis of it given in its famous Japanese or *kana* preface 仮名序 by Ki no Tsurayuki 紀貫之 (879 – 945). Donald Keene sees the preface as a statement akin to the poetics

---

[3] See Lubimir Doležel, *Heterocosmica: Fiction and Possible Worlds*, Baltimore: Johns Hopkins UP, 1998.

[4] Graham Priest, *Towards Non-Being*, Oxford: Oxford UP, 2016, 193.

[5] Kimiko Sata, "*Kokinwakashū* shunka-ka Tsurayuki no rakka no uta ni tsuite -- 'sange' to no kakawari no kanōsei"『古今和歌集』春歌下 貫之の落花の歌について--「散華」との関わりの可能性, 中古文学 no. 73 (2004): 10. The Buddhist element she looks at is *sange* 散華, the practice of commemorating the Buddha by scattering flower petals, especially those of the lotus, while chanting sutras.

of the American transcendentalists, with the transcendent power of nature, not gods, as the focus. Tsuneya Okamura disagrees with Keene, stressing instead what he calls the "humanistic" (人間主義) tendencies of the preface.⁶ All the same, the Buddhist and Sinitic cosmological aspects, broadly conceived, of Japanese literature are what cause the most tension in both the Japanese poet's and the French poet's consideration of the *Kokinshū*, and are that which is most informative when thinking about the formation of their literary worlds. This too has roots in the *Kokinshū*, the preface of which, as Wiebke Denecke has shown in her landmark book on "classical" world literatures, "constructed a timeless and universal 'Way' (道Ch.*dao*, J.*michi*) of poetic composition" and thus "made poetry into an even more powerful entity by implanting it into a cosmological discourse emerging from the beginning of heaven and earth."⁷ To this end, I will pay attention to the significance of the seasons in Claudel's and Kuki's poetry relative to one another and to the imperial collection. Thus, we will see both how Claudel and Kuki, who knew one another's hometowns intimately, responded not only to modern French and Japanese life, but also to classical Japanese literature. This will enable us to see how the horizontal and vertical elements of translation intersect in the decade of transnationalism, both physical and literary.

Claudel and Kuki have encountered similar criticisms of their work. Kuki was accused by some his peers of being a "traditionalist" phobic of modern thought and, on account of his nationalism, Kuki dropped out of favor following Japan's defeat on the Pacific front during the Second World War.⁸ More recently, Ryōsuke Ōhashi has questioned whether Kuki was cognizant enough of his own cultural biases in trying to interpret Japanese things by way of Western philosophy.⁹ Meanwhile, Claudel caught the ire of fellow *japoniste* Andre Malraux (1901–1976), who found Claudel's understanding of Japan "idiotic,"¹⁰ a view echoed, though much more moderately, by Akane Kawakami when she says that at first Claudel took an authoritarian and a partial view of Japan and Japanese culture.¹¹ According to Shigemi Inaga Kuki too felt ill at ease at the Imperial University of Kyoto and dreamed of being back in "the European world of philosophers"; indeed,

---

[6] Tsuneya Okamura, "Kaisetsu," in Tsurayuki Ki, *Kokin wakashū*, ed. Tsuneya Okumura, Tōkyō: Shinchōsha, 1978, 405 – 7. Okamura is discussing Donald Keene's, *Nihon no bungaku*, trans. Kenichi Yoshida, Tokyo: Chikuma Shobō, 1963; this is in turn a translation of Keene, *Japanese Literature: An Introduction for Western Readers*, New York: Grove Press, 1955.

[7] Wiebke Denecke, *Classical World Literatures: Sino-Japanese and Greco-Roman Comparisons*, New York: Oxford UP, 2014, 69 – 70.

[8] Michael F. Marra, "Words in Tension: An Essay on Kuki Shuzo's Poetics," in *Kuki Shuzo: A Philosopher's Poetry and Poetics*, ed. and trans. Michael F. Marra, Honolulu: U of Hawaii P, 2004, xvii.

[9] Ryōsuke Ōhashi, "Kuki Shūzō and the Question of Hermeneutics," *Comparative and Continental Philosophy* vol. 1, no. 1 (2009): 36.

[10] Tadao Takemoto and Olivier Germain-Thomas, *L'âme japonaise en miroir: Claudel, Malraux, Levi-Strausse, Einstein*. Paris: Entrelacs, 2016, 12.

[11] Akane Kawakami, "Claudel's Fragments of Japan: Co-naissance of the Other in *Cent Phrases pour Éventails*," *French Studies* vol. L.II, no. 2 (1999): 177, doi: 10.1093/fs/LIII.2.176.

Inaga says that Kuki even felt maladroit when writing philosophy in Japanese, so fully had he given his mind over to European thought.[12] Claudel's lifelong admiration for Japan and interest in various aspects of Japanese culture have been well documented by, among others, Jacques Petit, Michel Wasserman, Bei Huang, and Pamela Genova;[13] even Kawakami, despite her reservations about Claudel's attitude to Japan, commends the Frenchman's attempt in *Cent Phrases pour Eventails* (One Hundred Movements for Japanese Fans) (1942), in which Claudel's poems on Japanese themes sit beside kanji that Claudel could not read chosen by a calligrapher, to enter sincerely into a language and tradition he did not fully understand.[14]

We see that two problems are identified in the works of both Claudel and Kuki: a way of thinking subordinated to narrow nationalism, and an occasionally naïve engagement with foreign thought. Concomitantly, we find that critics have remarked that Claudel and Kuki alike held the foreign in high esteem and were willing to experiment with ideas not connected to their native countries.

Now, there are important differences between Claudel and Kuki. While Claudel never learned to speak Japanese, Kuki was proficient in French and German. For the Catholic Claudel, all men were essentially equal as creatures of God, and any differences between people could be resolved by acceptance of the Catholic faith. On the other hand, Kuki's unique blend of Japanese and East Asian philosophical concepts led him to believe that each locality has its own being, its own unique character, and he "appeals to the idea of tension between two entities whose individuality and specificity should not be offered as victims to the god of harmony."[15] There was an imbalance of power between the French Claudel and the Japanese Kuki: though by the 1920s Japan had become a world power and a League of Nations member, Kuki, like so many other intellectuals of his era, felt that he had to travel to and study in Europe to become a true philosopher. The same could not be said of Claudel or indeed of any other major French thinker of the interwar era, which is why Kawakami argues that Claudel's play on Japanese art forms could be seen as an abuse of his status as "honored Westerner,"[16] and why

---

[12] Shigemi Inaga, "Japanese Philosophers Go West: The Effect of Maritime Trips on Philosophy in Japan With Special Reference to the Case of Watsuji Tetsuro (1889–1960)," *Japan Review: Journal of the International Research Center for Japanese Studies* vol. 25 (2013): 121.

[13] See Jacques Petit, "Préface de Connaisance de l'est suivi de L'oiseau noir dans le soleil levant," in *Paul Claudel: Connaissance de l'Est: suivi de, L'oiseau noir dans le soleil levant*, Paris: Gallimard, 1974; Michel Wasserman, "L'ambassadeur poète: Paul Claudel au Japon (1921–1927)," 立命館国際研究 *Ritsumeikan Journal of International Studies* vol. 19, no. 1 (2006): 197–208; Bei Huang, *Segalen et Claudel: Dialogue à travers la peinture extrême-orientale*, Rennes: Presses universitaires de Rennes, 2007; and Pamela Genova, "Knowledge of the East?: Paul Claudel and the Equivocal Nature of Intercultural Exchange," *L'Esprit Créateur* vol. 56, no. 3 (2016): 104–19.

[14] Kawakami, "Co-naissance," 186.

[15] Marra, "Words in Tension," 3. We might recall here the tension, mentioned in Chapter One, that David Damrosch says characterizes a piece of world literature, or the feeling that translation produces, according to Haun Saussy, of being "at odds with—askance from—our former selves" (*Translation as Citation: Zhuangzi Inside Out*. Oxford: Oxford UP, 2017, 22).

[16] Kawakami, "Co-naissance," 179.

Michael Marra and Leslie Pincus dwell on Kuki's nationality and race when analyzing his work.[17]

Simon Ebersolt argues that this imbalance continues in philosophy in Japan, where "Japanese philosophy" seems a less natural term than "Japanese literature" or "Japanese art."[18] Philosophy, he says, whether in Japan, Europe, or elsewhere, is "considered fundamentally occidental."[19] Here a contradiction becomes apparent: philosophy is supposed to be a universal exercise, but also seems anchored in Europe. At the same time, talk of a "Japanese philosophy" sounds illegitimate because it infringes upon that desire for universal application.[20] Shōichiro Sakurai suggests that Kuki's efforts to find peculiarly Japanese personality traits are not reducible to the imperialist ideas that dominated 1930s Japan, but rather are responses to globalization. If Western ideas were pushing into Japan, Kuki wanted Japanese ideas to push into the West and the entire world,[21] although, as Masakatsu Fujita reminds us, Kuki believed that each country possessed a particular cultural essence.[22] Naturally, this sounds imperialistic, but, as Sakurai points out, we can see it as a more benign form of global cross-fertilization than the more nationalistic ideas that Kuki might have advanced closer toward the end of his life.[23] This is the very problem that we addressed at the start of this book when we considered the incompatibility of different logical and ontological schemes and their implications for comparative literature. As we will see, both Claudel and Kuki were preoccupied with this apparent contradiction, and their work in the 1920s and 1930s are contemporaneous attempts to resolve it.

Historical Conditions in Paris and Tokyo and Critical Background

The 1920s were a time of great upheaval in Paris and Tokyo alike. Paris was a hub of modernism in the arts. James F. English affirms that Paris was "the great-power center of literary modernity."[24] Paris not only attracted many of the most famous modernist artists but also was home to critics, publishers, and translators, so that it was "virtually impossible for a writer to achieve world-recognition, that is, a reputation extending beyond her own national and linguistic field, without the intercession of these symbolic underwriters."[25] Living in Paris in the 1920s, Kuki was at ground zero of the revolutions

---

[17] See Marra, "Words in Tension", and Leslie Pincus, "In a Labyrinth of Western Desire: Kuki Shuzo and the Discovery of Japanese Being," *Boundary 2* vol. 18, no. 3 (1991): 142–56.
[18] Simon Ebersolt, "Contingence et Communauté: Kuki Shûzô, philosophe japonaise," PhD Thesis, INALCO, Institut national des langues et civilisations orientales 2017, 9.
[19] Ibid., 10.
[20] Ibid., 11–13.
[21] Sakurai, *Kyōto gakuha suikoden* 京都学派酔故伝, 329–31.
[22] Masakatsu Fujita, *Kuki Shūzō: richi to jōnetsu no hazama ni tatsu "kotoba" no tetsugaku*, Tokyo: Kōdansha, 2016, 177–78.
[23] Sakurai, 京都学派酔故伝, 331.
[24] James F. English, "Cultural Capital and the Revolutions of Literary Modernity, from Bourdieu to Casanova," in *A Handbook of Modernism Studies*, ed. Jean-Michel Rabaté, Chichester, UK: John Wiley & Sons Inc, 2013, 364.
[25] Ibid., 373.

occurring in the arts in the interwar period. He was deeply interested in the philosophy of Henri Bergson (1859–1941), whom he met in the autumn of 1928.[26] That same year, Kuki even participated in and spoke at the *Décades de Pontigny*, an annual gathering of critics and intellectuals in a former Cistercian abbey in Pontigny, France. The year that Kuki delivered his lecture saw in attendance none other than the eminent novelist André Gide, and André Malraux.[27] We will have more to say later on Kuki's speech at the *Décades*, but for now suffice it to say that Kuki was admitted to the inner circle of French intellectual life, and most certainly would have had knowledge of the movements and ideas swirling around the artistic world of 1920s Paris, and, moreover, that many of his aesthetic and philosophical preoccupations overlapped with those of famous Western modernists.

Claudel, meanwhile, lived through a time in which Tokyo was undergoing a sweeping cultural change.[28] Despite the modernization occurring around him, Claudel was ultimately not interested in modern Japan, at least not as an object for art. Claudel was rather concerned with images and ideas that originated before the end of the Tokugawa era. The Japan that appears in his essays and poetry is premodern and gives little indication of the sweeping changes affecting the Japan in which he lived. When he depicts Japan, he is mostly drawn to nonurban scenes. Claudel was also not enamored by the images and theories of the Far East that were current among many modernists. In *Ideographic Modernisms: China, Writing, Media*, Christopher Bush discloses the disparity between the theories of the Anglo-American imagists led by Ezra Pound (1885–1972) and informed by Ernest Fenollosa (1853–1908) and Claudel's personal approach to East Asian art. Thanks to a misreading of the features of Chinese characters and the Chinese language, the imagists celebrated the Chinese character for its pictorial quality, insofar as the character or "ideogram" was thought to image primitive sketches of phenomena, and for its privileging of the verb over the noun, insofar as ideograms were thought not to denote concepts but to depict events.[29] Claudel, conversely, found the allegorical potential of the ideogram enticing.[30] In the French symbolist tradition of Stéphane Mallarmé (1842–1898)—and to this we should add, as Bei Huang does, Arthur Rimbaud (1854–1891), famous for his ideas of identity and alterity, the state of becoming estranged from oneself in poetry, and for his notion of the poet as a seer deciphering the signs of nature[31]— Claudel was preoccupied by metaphor and absence. As Bush puts it, "the complexities of Imagist poetics emerge from its approach to the instant, [while] those of Claudel emerge

---

[26] Simon Ebersolt, "Le Japon et la Philosophie Française du Milieu du XIXe au Milieu du XXe Siècles," *Revue Philosophique De La France Et De l'Étranger* vol. 137, no. 3 (2012): 378.

[27] Jan Hokenson, *Japan, France, and East-West Aesthetics: French Literature, 1867–2000*, Vancouver: Fairleigh Dickinson UP, 2004, 337. Hokenson claims that Claudel himself was in the audience, but I have not been able to confirm this elsewhere.

[28] For an overview of Tokyo and the arts in the 1920s, see Seiji M. Lippit, *Topographies of Japanese Modernism*, New York: Columbia UP, 2002, especially 1–36.

[29] Christopher Bush, *Ideographic Modernisms: China, Writing, Media*, Oxford: Oxford UP, 2010, 37.

[30] Ibid., 41.

[31] Huang, *Segalen et Claudel*, 153.

from its relationship to the eternal."[32] The imagists saw in the Chinese sign a way to elude the abstraction of the European alphabet and to enter into the dynamism of the present, whereas Claudel believed the Chinese sign could remove phenomena from the confusion and flux of time and fix them forever in poetry.[33]

We see that Kuki and Claudel differed in their approaches to modernity changing the foreign lands in which they were working. Kuki took a great deal of pleasure in modern Paris, from which he took inspiration for numerous essays and poems. Claudel, however, appears to have found modern Japan of little aesthetic interest and turned his eyes toward a premodern, or pre-Meiji, rural Japan of which he could never have had direct experience. Yet, for Kuki, modernization was enjoyable so long as it was happening elsewhere. Though he enjoyed Paris and Europe, he did not wish to see Tokyo become culturally colonized by the West. As did Claudel, he turned his eyes to the past to find the essence of Japanese identity, and in the 1930s worked to safeguard what he believed to be "real" Japanese life against the encroaching influence of America and Europe. For both men, Japan was essentially pre-Meiji.

Let us look in more detail at the ways Claudel and Kuki understood the art and philosophy of Japan and Europe. In "La Poésie française et l'Extrême-Orient" (French Poetry and the Far East) Claudel tries to discern the foundations of intercultural communication:

> Je veux dire qu'entre les divers peuples, entre les diverses civilisations, il y a un contact psychologique plus ou moins avoué, un commerce plus ou moins actif, un rapport comme de poids et de tensions diverses qui se traduit par des courants et par des échanges, par cet intérêt qui ne naît seulement de la sympathie, mais de la réalisation d'un article idéal, dont la conscience d'une certaine insuffisance en nous fait naître le besoin, un besoin qui essaye plus ou moins gauchement de se traduire par l'imitation. Tantôt la balance dont je viens de vous parler se traduit par un actif et tantôt par un passif. Tantôt un peuple éprouve la nécessité de se faire entendre, et tantôt—et pourquoi pas en même temps?—celle de se faire écouter, celle d'apprendre et de comprendre.[34]

Claudel refers to this "psychological contact" as "interpsychic" (*Pr.* 1037). But it is not exactly clear how a writer can comprehend foreign and deeply heterogenous cultures. Claudel takes China as an example. We speak as if there were one China, but in fact

---

[32] Bush, *Ideographic*, 41.
[33] Ibid., 42.
[34] "I want to say that between the diverse peoples, between the diverse civilizations, there is a psychological contact more or less avowed, a commerce more or less active, a rapport like diverse weights and tensions translated by currents and by exchanges, by this interest that is not born only from sympathy, but that is the realization of an ideal item, of which the consciousness of a certain insufficiency gives rise in us to the need, a need that tries more or less maladroitly to be translated by imitation. Sometimes the balance of which I have just spoken to you is translated actively, sometimes passively. Sometimes a people feels the necessity to make itself heard, and sometime—and why not at the same time? — to listen, to learn and to understand." Paul Claudel, *Œuvres en prose*, ed. Jacques Petit and Charles Galpérine, Paris: Gallimard, 1965, 1036. Subsequent references to this work will be made in-text and use the abbreviation *Pr.*

there are several, including a "Regence China, a *boucher* China, a China of Saxe, a Silk China, one of porcelain [...]" (*Pr.* 1038–39). Each of these "Chinas" is a version of the actual "China" viewed from a different aspect, with each one possessing its own internal coherence and relations with other constellations of belief such as Claudel's constellation of French poetry. It is the same, let us say, for "Japan" and Claudel's poetry, as well as for "Japan" and Kuki's. We are not dealing with a single Japan, but with a vision of Japan, a *possible* Japan that is in fact a constellation. And within this possible Japan is a set of possible worlds that make up Japanese poetry. Each of these sets is composed of different elements, but the same, or nearly the same, elements may appear across different sets. Let us call these sets, for the moment, the Japanese constellation of Kuki and the Japanese constellation of Claudel. How is each of these constellations logically coherent?

According to Kuki in his speech at Pontigny, the "most eminent characteristic" of Japanese art is "the expression of the infinite."[35] This "expression" is an attempt to recuperate finite time by trying to "break through time, to live in the eternity that is the beautiful" (*Zs.* 268). Time here is a time that repeats, a circular time, that runs its course in a universe with "bottomless metaphysical chasms" (*Zs.* 268). It opposes the linear time of Christianity and takes as its foundation "pantheistic mysticism" (*Zs.* 269), be it that of Bushidō, Indian mysticism, or Zen Buddhism (*Zs.* 282). The eternity of which Kuki speaks does not possess a reality of its own since everything in Kuki's conceptual universe hovers above nothingness or "le vide," in contrast to strands of Western and Christian thought, such as Claudel's, which takes being or the Holy Spirit as the origin of all things. As for *tanka* and *haiku*, the two poets give interpretations of the two poetic genres that sometimes align, sometimes separate. In Kuki's estimation, tension between harmony and dissonance is the essence of *tanka* and *haiku*:

> Cette suite de cinq, sept, cinq syllabes d'un *Haikai*, ainsi que le tercet initial du *Tanka*, trouve sa beauté originale dans la possibilité de différentes combinaisons subjectives, à la fois en cinq-sept et en sept-cinq. L'union trop harmonieuse des cinq-sept est troublée par la présence d'un troisième terme. Le heptasyllabe du milieu, tout en gardant la fonction de suivre le pentasyllabe du début, a acquis, en même temps, celle de précéder le pentasyllabe qui la précède et, en se retournant, elle se hâte d'une marche sautillante vers celui qui suit. La beauté irrésistible de la mélodie rythmique du *Haikai* consiste précisément dans cette fluidité changeante, dans cette coquetterie enchanteresse. Et par cette forme asymétrique et fluide, l'idée de l'affranchissement du temps mesurable s'est réalisée. (*Zs.* 276)[36]

---

[35] Kuki Shūzō, *Kuki Shūzō zenshū* dai ichi maki, ed. Amano Teiyū, Omodaka Hisayuki, and Satō Akio, Tokyo: Iwanami Shoten, 1981, 269. Subsequent references to this work will be made in-text and use the abbreviation *Zs.*

[36] "This succession of five, seven, five syllables of *haiku*, as well as the initial tercet of *tanka*, finds its original beauty in the combination of different subjective combinations, at once five-seven and seven-five. The too harmonious union of the five-seven is troubled by the presence of a third term. The medial heptasyllable, as it retains its function as follower of the initial pentasyllable, has acquired, at the same time, that of preceding the pentasyllable that precedes it and, as it returns, hastens with a bouncy walk towards that which follows. The irresistible beauty of the rhythmic melody of *haiku* consists precisely in this changing fluidity, in this enchanting

Like Kuki, Claudel highlights the differences between Japanese and French poetry. In "A Travers la littérature japonaise" (Across Japanese Literature), he cites at length extracts from the preface to the *Kokinshū* to make his readers "comprendre comment les gens là-bas entendent la poésie" (understand how the people over there comprehend [*entendent*] poetry) (*Pr.* 1161). The extract tells his readers that:

> La poésie du Yamato a pour semence le cœur humain, d'où elle se développe en une myriade de feuilles de parole [...] Sans effort, la poésie émeut le ciel et la terre, touche de pitié les dieux et les démons invisibles ; elle sait rapprocher l'homme de la femme, et elle apaise le cœur des farouches guerriers. Cette poésie existe depuis l'ouverture du ciel et de la terre. (*Pr.* 1161–62)[37]

The passage highlights the role of human emotion in creating poetry and, in turn, affecting the sentiment of humans, deities, and spirits alike. Claudel, however, does not devote much attention to the pantheistic origin of the *Kokinshū*'s emotive theory of poetry affect. Having provided his readers with this insight into the Japanese aesthetic mind, he declares:

> Les japonais apportent dans la poésie comme dans l'art une idée très différente de la nôtre. La nôtre est de tout dire, de tout exprimer. Le cadre est complètement rempli et la beauté résulte de l'ordre que nous établissons entre les différents objets qui le remplissent, de la composition des lignes et des couleurs. Au Japon au contraire sur la page, écrite ou dessinée, la part la plus importante est toujours laissée au vide. Cet oiseau, cette branche d'arbre, ce poisson, ne servent qu'à historier, qu'à localiser une absence où se contemplait l'imagination. (*Pr.* 1162)[38]

If French literature, motivated by "le désir passionné de l'exactitude" (the passionate desire for exactitude) (*Pr.* 1121), aims to illuminate everything, "la révérence, le respect, l'acceptation spontanée d'une supériorité d'un intelligence inaccessible à l'intellect" (reverence, respect, the spontaneous acceptance of a superiority inaccessible to the intellect), which is nothing other than "notre existence personnelle en présence du mystère qui nous entoure, la sensation d'une présence autour de nous qui exige la cérémonie et la précaution" (our personal existence in presence of a mystery that encircles us, the sensation of a presence all around us that demands ceremony and precaution), impregnates Japanese literature (*Pr.* 1123). Despite the fact that Claudel thinks that the origin of this

---

coquetry. And by way of this fluid and asymmetric form the idea of breaking through measurable time is realized."

[37] "The seed of Yamato poetry is the human heart, from which it develops into a million leaves of words. [...] Without effort, poetry moves the sky and the earth, touches the pity of gods and invisible demons; it knows how to reconcile man and woman, and to calm the heart of savage warriors. This poetry has existed since the opening of the sky and the earth."

[38] "The Japanese have in their poetry as in their art an idea very different from ours. Ours is to say everything, to express everything. The beauty results from the composition of lines and colors, from the order that we establish between the different objects that make up the completely filled cadre. In Japan, on the contrary, on the page, in writing or in drawing, the most important part is always left empty. This bird, this tree branch, this fish, serve only to describe, to localize an absence where the imagination contemplates itself."

"reverence" is in Shintō, he believes that "pour le Japonais traditionnel la Création est avant tout l'œuvre de Dieu, encore toute pénétrée d'influences divines" (for the traditional Japanese, Creation is before all the work of God, still completely penetrated by divine influences), in contrast to the modern European who is interested only in "un domaine destiné à son agrément ou à son profit" (that which pleases or profits him) (*Pr.* 1125). And the (translated) *Kokinshū*'s emphasis on poetry that can move gods and spirits is lost. The "seed" mentioned in the "Preface" becomes "une touche sur l'eau déserte destinée à propager d'immenses cercles concentriques" (a touch on still water destined to produce immense concentric circles), "une semence d'émotion" (a seed of emotion), and "la corde où le musicien avec le doigt fait vibrer une seule note qui peu à peu envahit le cœur et la pensée" (the cord on which a musician with his finger makes vibrate a single note that little by little invades the heart and the mind) (*Pr.* 1162).[39] The shift in intention from that of the original under Claudel's pen is slight, but perceptible.

This deviation from the spirit of the *Kokinshū* aside, the intersections between Claudel's and Kuki's conceptions of French and Japanese literature are clear. Both see a gap between the French mind-set and the Japanese mind-set and the arts that they produce. Both think that the thought and the arts of modern France are rational and mechanic, while those of "traditional" Japan, to borrow Claudel's terminology, are full of mysticism and demand an appreciation beyond words and beyond thought. Both underscore the importance of nothingness or "le vide" in interpreting Japanese poetry. Yet, despite these agreements, a gulf opens between the two concerning the relation between Christianity and the indigenous religion of Japan, Shintoism.

In effect, Claudel thinks that Shintoism makes the Japanese peculiarly open to Christian doctrine, while Kuki declares that Europeans can never understand traditional Japanese thought nourished by Shintoism, so long as they remain under the influence of Christian metaphysics. As we have seen, in his paper at Pontigny, Kuki forms an alliance between Japanese thought and the philosophy of "pagan" and pre-Socratic Greece. Thus, both writers try to establish mutual intelligibility between the thought, the art, and especially the poetry of Europe and Japan, but the categories they use to link these various traditions differ. Consequently, the signification of their aesthetics differs, because the entirety of their conceptual universes differs.

Before pressing on to Claudel's and Kuki's poetry, our focus should shift again back to the *Kokinshū*. Significant in Claudel's and Kuki's evaluations of the *Kokinshū* as the epitome of Japanese poetry is what they do not mention. The *Kokinshū*, as we have seen, draws on ideas transmitted from China. The idea of an imperial collection came, as

---

[39] In *Connaissance de l'est*, Claudel uses a similar metaphor to explain his theory of mind in "Sur la cervelle": "La sensation n'est point un phénomène passif; c'est un état spécial d'activité. Je le compare à une corde en vibration sur laquelle la note est formée par la juste position du doigt. Par la sensation, je constate le fait, et je contrôle, par le mouvement, l'acte. Mais la vibration est constante" (Sensation is not at all a passive phenomenon ; it is a special state of activity. I compare it to a vibrating cord on which the note is formed by the correct positioning of the finger. Through sensation, I test that which is before me, and I control, by movement, the action. But the vibration is constant) (*Po.* 105).

Ozawa Masao notes, from Japanese understanding of the *Shijing* 詩経, in Japanese *Shikyō*, known in English as *The Book of Odes*. Confucius was the reputed compiler of the *Shijing*, made up of poems and folk songs from various provinces collected by bureaucrats; the idea of the *Shijing*, as it existed in Japanese thought of the Heian period, was one of peaceful accord among various people in China through the celebration of each group's art. Emperor Daigo 醍醐天皇, whose imperial decree (宣命) initiated the compilation, drew upon this idea of the *Shijing* when he declared his wish to collect poems that exemplified the *kokufū* 國風 of his people. *Kokufū* might mean national customs, but it is more polysemous in Daigo's use. In Ozawa's words, we might define *kokufū* variously: "最も広く解釈すれば「諸国の産業・人民の生活」の意味であるが、もう少し狭く解釈すれば「国々の風俗」を意味し、もっと狭くすれば「地方的な民間芸能」を意味する(To offer the widest interpretation, it is "the produce of various kingdoms, and the activities of the people"; to give a slightly narrower interpretation, it is "the customs of various kingdoms"; to go narrower still, it is "regional folk performing arts").[40] At first glance, this fits with both Claudel's evaluation and Kuki's of the *Kokinshū*, but there is a caveat. Though there is a tendency to read the Japanese imitation of this model as a proto-nationalist declaration of the Japanese state, Ozawa argues that such a consciousness did not in fact develop until the Edo period, when scholars attempted to contrast the *Kokinshū* with Chinese and, indeed, Dutch models in order to arrive at a peculiarly Japanese essence in poetry.[41] Hence, in their rather essentialist readings of the *Kokinshū*, both Claudel and Kuki appear to join in a discourse that antedates the imperial collection by several centuries, and itself emerges through a process of contrast with China and a vague notion of the culture of Holland. As such, the "world" of the *Kokinshū* as it appeared to both Claudel and Kuki was itself an amalgam of the influence of (pre-Buddhist) Chinese poetry passed through Japanese scholarship, and worked over for centuries by Japanese scholars until it emerged as a candidate for the origin of Japanese literature and perhaps the very concept of "Japan" itself.

Of course, the *Shijing* was not the only example of Chinese poetry influential on the *Kokinshū*. From the early Heian period, the classical Chinese influence waned, and poetry from the Six Dynasties and the Tang grew prominent in the Japanese literary imagination.[42] The constellation of belief was different from that of the first Japanese poetry collection, the *Manyōshū* 万葉集, which, though it too was "born of the intersection between, on the one hand, native song and ritual and, on the other, Chinese script, poetry, and ideas about the political role of literature,"[43] and incorporates Buddhist and Confucian themes, is arguably more heterogenous than the first imperial collection, being composed over a longer period, and looking back to pre-Heian government and literature.[44]

---

[40] Masao Ozawa, *Kokinshū no sekai*, Tokyo: Hanawa Shobō, 1961, 12.

[41] Ibid., 14 – 15.

[42] Ibid., 21.

[43] H. Mack Horton, "Man'yōshū," in *The Cambridge History of Japanese Literature*, ed. Haruo, Tomi Suzuki and David Lurie, Cambridge: Cambridge UP, 2015, 84.

[44] Ozawa, *Kokinshū no sekai*, 22.

The early Heian, on the other hand, saw the rise of *Kanbun* 漢文 and the solidification of Confucianism at the Heian court in imitation of the Tang.[45] Naturally, Confucianism in Japan existed before the *Manyōshū*, and Buddhism persisted after the time in which the collection was created —as we have seen, Buddhism helped to give a sense of order to the *Kokinshū* and its progression through the four seasons. But the importance of the four seasons in the imperial collection also reflects the way in which poems were composed for important events in an agrarian society with four distinct seasons, in which, in other words, the progression of the seasons had a practical as well as a cosmological dimension.[46] In short, the *Kokinshū* does not stand in a seamless world of "Japanese" thought, but is also the product of compromise between the horizontal and vertical, foreign and native elements, as well as composed of religious and secular dimensions that are difficult to disentangle. Indeed, though the Japanese preface that Claudel and Kuki both refer to focuses on the *waka* as "Yamato verse" or *yamato uta* 大和歌, the Chinese preface is more wide-ranging and "attributes a wide array of metrical structures to *waka*" and closely follows the poetics of the *Shijing*.[47] This is a rough overview of the *Kokinshū*, and cannot do justice to its multifaceted and rich world. It does, though, give a sense of the process of selection that Claudel and Kuki are engaged in before we even arrive at the poetry. It gives a sense of how Claudel and Kuki needed to construct their own versions of the world of the *Kokinshū*, certain dimensions of which were highlighted while others passed over, in order to rationalize the inspiration they drew from it in their poetry, regardless of whether Japanese or French, native or foreign.

Claudel, French Ambassador–Poet in Japan

Claudel made his first trip to Japan in 1898, when he was French consul in Shanghai. The voyage inspired conflicting emotions in the French poet. In "Ça et Là" ["Here and There"], he describes visiting a Buddhist temple. He ruminates on the "Satanic" features of Buddhism. He castigates the Buddha for refusing "à reconnaitre l'être inconditionnel" (to recognize the unconditional being) and in the place of God making "le Néant" or "the Void" the absolute substratum of human existence. Without an Absolute Being to guide its faithful, Buddhism, Claudel continues, encourages its practitioners to become nihilistic and to engage in self-gratification or "jouissance" (*Po.* 90).

Bush sums up Claudel's feelings: "The Buddha is 'satanic' because not only does he not strive for the beyond but his immobility is a mocking imitation of God's, the temporal imitating the eternal: he confounds Nothingness and being."[48] Because Claudel felt that the telos of human existence was union with God in the afterlife, he was scandalized by Buddhism's rejection of an Absolute Being. As Bush writes, Claudel, in the tradition of

---

[45] Ibid., 24.
[46] Gustav Heldt, "*Kokinshū* and Heian Court Poetry," in *The Cambridge History of Japanese Literature*, ed. Haruo, Tomi Suzuki and David Lurie, Cambridge: Cambridge UP, 2015, 112.
[47] Ibid., 115.
[48] Bush, *Ideographic*, 43.

Saint Augustine, saw nature as God's handiwork, as valuable in signifying the glory of God; but to Claudel Buddhism seemed to take nature itself as divinity and was locked in self-satisfaction or "jouissance."[49] Claudel concludes that the Buddha is emblematic of "le silence de la créature retranchée dans son refus intégral, la quiétude incestueuse de l'âme assise sur sa différence essentielle" (the silence of a creature trapped in its integral refusal [to join with a higher being], the incestuous quietude of a soul seated on its essential difference) (*Po.* 90). Bush's analysis of the religious dimension of Claudel's engagement with Buddhist art is perceptive. Still, as I will show, his critique would benefit from increased attention to the aspects of Japanese spirituality, especially of Shintoism, that Claudel strove to incorporate into his Catholic aesthetic.

If Claudel disliked Buddhism, he loved, according to Pamela Genova, Japan and its landscapes and art.[50] Genova states that "Claudel plunged into Asia with a gusto rarely witnessed in other European envoys" as he "sought every opportunity to discover new cultural (and natural) landscapes, exploring many cities independently of his diplomatic duties."[51] He went on walking tours, partook in "touristic activities, tried new foods, and explored other unfamiliar cultural traditions relating to religions, philosophies, and general culture."[52] Though Claudel's inability to speak Japanese would certainly have affected his understanding of Japanese art and culture, Genova posits that the language barrier may actually have been a boon to Claudel, since it would have forced him to learn of Japan "through his own direct experiences" rather than through literature alone.[53] Not that Claudel enjoyed every aspect of Japanese life: both Genova and Jacques Besineau describe Claudel's disdain for the niceties of Japanese customs. And, like Kawakami, Genova mentions that Claudel's "brusqueness" could be interpreted as "a dominating orientalist stance, thus casting Claudel's involvement with Far-Eastern culture in ambivalent terms."[54] But, according to Besineau, "le conquérant fut conquis. Le repos, l'immobilité, le silence aussi telle est la grande leçon que Claudel sut retirer de son séjour en Extrême-Orient" (in effect, the conqueror was conquered). [The importance of r]est, immobility, and silence as well: this is the grand lesson that Claudel took from his sojourn in the Far East).[55]

Bush's theory is that Claudel approached Japan as he would an exegesis of the Bible: he emptied Japanese culture and language of its content and made it so that what he encountered in Japan would be read as signs pointing to eternity and to God.[56] He writes: "Just as Moses might be a figure of Christ but never the other way around, so too East Asian writing and thinking are redeemed from Satanic self-satisfaction only by being

---

[49] Ibid.
[50] Genova, "Knowledge of the East?," 104.
[51] Ibid.
[52] Ibid., 105.
[53] Ibid.
[54] Ibid., 107.
[55] Jacques Besineau, "Claudel au Japon: Souvenirs et documents inédits," *Etudes*, vol. 94, no. 311 (1961): 345.
[56] Bush, *Ideographic*, 48.

emptied of their original historical content in order to signify a truth that is universal and eternal—for Claudel."[57] This is true to an extent. As we will see in relation to *Cent phrases*, Claudel's major collection of Japanese-inspired poetry, Claudel uses Japanese aesthetics as a vehicle for his own Catholic ideas. However, to say that Claudel "emptied" Japanese aesthetic forms and ideas of their content and filled them with a Christian message goes too far. On the contrary, Claudel combines Japanese ideas with Catholic ones, and this tension allows him to reconcile his love of Japan with his faith.[58]

Other critics, mainly French and Japanese, have noted such a tendency in Claudel's writing. Michel Wasserman remarks that Claudel's sensibility is Shintoist in his "amour de la nature, sens du génie et de la spiritualité du lieu, bref cet animisme qui est au fond de la mentalité shintoïste" (love of nature, sense of the genius and the spirituality of the spot, in brief the animism that is at the bottom of Shintō mentality), even though Claudel rarely uses the word "Shintō."[59] Regarding Claudel's collaboration with the painter Tomita Keisen (1879–1936) on *Cent phrases* and other poetic projects, Bei Huang remarks that, while the two artists shared an interest in an aesthetic realm in which calligraphic ink highlights an artistic "sensibility for nature," it would be too much to say that the Catholic Claudel and the Buddhist and Daoist Keisen have the same vision of nature.[60] The two men, Huang says, were able to rally around evocative images and themes common to both their spiritual backgrounds, such as water, an image of transcendence for Claudel, but of the eternal spontaneity of life for Keisen.[61] But even if Keisen drew from Buddhist and Daoist images of water, according to Machiko Kadota, Claudel's association of water with transcendence is ultimately Shintoist.[62] It seems likely that Claudel was more accepting of Shintō, not only because it echoed his own love of nature and had employed similar images in its texts, but also because, unlike Buddhism, Shintō is not a universal religion but a folk religion without a central deity like the Buddha. Indeed, as Sukehiro Hirakawa has shown, early British visitors to Japan, remarking Shintō's lack of scripture and a clear moral code, did not consider Shintō to be a religion at all; before 1945, the Japanese government held the same opinion.[63]

Criticism of Claudel's Japanese work often remarks the same difficulty of intercultural interaction, but the Claudelien attitude, with Christianity as its motor, is more positive and integrationist than is Kuki's. Michel Truffet observes that in *Cent phrases*, the "format, la mise en pages, l'architecture et le graphisme des textes, tout est 'autre.' Étrange ou, plus

---

[57] Ibid., 53.
[58] We saw in the previous chapter that Claudel's disdain for Buddhism weakened in Japan, as he came to appreciate the somber and austere aspects of the religion there.
[59] Michel Wasserman, "Claudel et le shintoisme," *Bulletin de la Société Paul Claudel* vol. 210 (2013), http://www.paul-claudel.net/bulletin/bulletin-de-la-societe-paul-claudel-n°210.
[60] Huang, *Segalen et Claudel*, 131.
[61] Ibid., 132.
[62] Machiko Kadota, "L'image d l'eau chez Paul Claudel et dans Cent phrases pour éventails," *Journal of the Faculty of General Education*, vol. 25 (1991): 205.
[63] Sukehiro Hirakawa, *À la recherche de l'identité japonaise: le shintō interprété par les écrivains européens*, Paris: Harmattan, 2012, 14–15.

simplement, étrangère?" (format, the *mise en page*, the architecture and the graphism of the text, everything is "other." Strange or, more simply, foreign?)[64] Yet the Claudel of *Cent phrases* is not content to let Japan rest purely as "strange" or "foreign." While Dominique Millet-Gérard, like Genova, points out the conflict between Claudel's brusque temperament and the refined manners that he encountered in his diplomatic work in Japan, she asserts that, in *Cent phrases*:

> Claudel reste fidèle à ses inspirations antérieures, à ce don d'observation qui est le sien, mais il montre aussi l'extraordinaire capacité d'assimilation dont son intelligence est capable, plus par intuition que par compréhension logique.[65]

The attempt at integration characterizes Claudel's attitude toward the art and culture of Japan. Even if, unlike Kuki, speaking French, German, and the antique languages of Europe, Claudel did not speak any Japanese, he attempts to fuse that which pleases him in Japan with his own aesthetic. In the poems of *Cent phrases*, short and often enigmatic, Claudel adds his Christian belief in the "essential failure of all human words" to the "Japanese" silence and the absence that can nonetheless signal, *via negativa*, the presence of the divine. The tension between two opposites, the "paradox," that the reader of *Cent phrases* finds everywhere, opens the mind to a more profound presence.[66] The religions that Claudel found in East Asia undergo the same treatment. Françoise Lachaud demonstrates that Claudel reinterprets the religions of China and Japan by transforming them into avatars of Catholicism. With this rapprochement in mind, Lachaud concludes that "Claudel ne pouvait pas entrer en conversation avec le bouddhisme" (Claudel could not enter into conversation with Buddhism), for he was not capable of understanding East Asian religions on their own terms. The *Dao* becomes Jesus, and the teachings of Zen on the importance of silence are brought under the umbrella of the ineffability of the Christian divine.[67] Given this, it was impossible for Claudel to have an encounter with "the Other," only a "mis-encounter" (*mérencontre*).[68]

Four years after his first trip to Japan and his condemnation of Buddhism, Claudel translated into French the myth of the sun goddess Amaterasu. Representing an older vein of Claudel scholarship, Moriaki Watanabe describes how Claudel adheres closely to multiple translations of the Japanese source texts, indicating a close study of the

---

[64] Michel Truffet and Paul Claudel, *Edition critique et commentée de Cent phrases pour éventails de Paul Claudel, Annales littéraires de l'Université de Besançon*, Paris: Les Belles-Lettres, 1985, 16.

[65] "Claudel remains faithful to his former inspirations, to this this gift of observation that he possesses, but he shows as well the extraordinary capacity of assimilation of which his intelligence is capable, one more intuitive than logical." Dominique Millet-Gérard, "Un grand Ange blanc qui regarde la mer," in *Claudel et le Japon: Cinquantenaire de la mort de Claudel. Actes du Colloque International et de la Table Ronde*, ed. Shinobu Chūjō et Takaharu Hasekura, Tokyo: Shichigatsudō 七月堂 Tokyo: Shichigatsudō 七月堂,2006, 36.

[66] Ibid., 52–53.

[67] François Lachaud, "Le poète et les buddhas: Claudel et la tradition religieuse asiatique," *Claudel et le Japon: Cinquantenaire de la mort de Claudel. Actes du Colloque International et de la table ronde*, ed. Shinobu Chūjō et Takaharu Hasekura, Tokyo: Shichigatsudō 七月堂,2006, 74–93.

[68] Ibid., 92.

legend.⁶⁹ This is evident in Claudel's accurate description of the tools used in the Shintō ceremony and their relation to the Amaterasu myth: the *gohei*, the *sakaki*, the *shimenawa*, and the mirror.⁷⁰ Watanabe points out that Claudel sometimes keeps the original Japanese word when describing the Shintō relics to his readers, as he does with the *gohei*, but at other times translates the items into something easier for his European audience to understand, as he does when he transforms the *sakaki* into a tree "un autre arbre, plus familier aux Occidentaux, et après tout lié étroitement à l'imagerie shintoïste, «le pin »" (more familiar to Westerners, and after all closely related to Shintō imagery, "the pine").⁷¹ Elsewhere, Watanabe says, Claudel diverges from the original narrative as he multiplies descriptions and makes the original conflict of the narrative, that between Amaterasu and her brother, the storm god Susanō, into a conflict between Amaterasu and human beings who have turned their backs on the sun deity.⁷² In this last modification we might see the influence of Claudel's Catholicism and his critique of Buddhism, with humans who, forgetting a higher power and focusing on their own pleasure, dismay a deity.

Watanabe explains Claudel's modification of the Amaterasu myth as the poet using raw Japanese materials to create a "personal myth" in which dichotomies of darkness and light, night and day, connect with Claudel's aesthetic and religious ideals.⁷³ Watanabe also notes that, in *Partage de Midi* (1906), a play Claudel wrote later in China, Claudel joins the Amaterasu story, particularly the location in which the myth is said to take place, Ise Shrine, with the figure of Isolde (or Yseult) from Richard Wagner's opera *Tristan and Isolde* (1859), to create the figure of Ysé.⁷⁴ The Germanic legend of Tristan and Isolde, set in a Europe transitioning from paganism to early Christianity, and the Japanese Shintō myth of Amaterasu, fuse in Claudel's mind to create a new narrative. In part this validates Bush's claim that Claudel empties Japanese ideas and fills the lacunae with his own meaning. However, Claudel has not so much emptied the Amaterasu myth as fused parts of it with his own ideas. It is in this sense that his narrative, like his play, is a "personal myth": indeterminate, the narrative is somewhere between the original Japanese and Claudel's European tradition.

We can see this indeterminacy more clearly in *Cent phrases*. There is a poem that could bolster Bush's argument:

Une belle journée d'automne	est comme la vision de la justice (*Po.* 727)⁷⁵	A beautiful day in autumn	is like the vision of justice

---

⁶⁹ Moriaki Watanabe, "Le nom d'ysé: Le mythe solaire japonais et la genèse du personage," *Revue d'Histoire Littéraire De La France* vol. 69, no. 1 (1969): 76–77.
⁷⁰ Ibid.,148–49.
⁷¹ Ibid., 84.
⁷² Ibid., 86.
⁷³ Ibid.
⁷⁴ Ibid., 75.
⁷⁵ Michel Truffet's note to this poem in his critical edition of *Cent phrases* suggests that Claudel alludes here to Rimbaud's *Une saison en enfer:* "L'automne déjà! […] Le combat spirituel est

Donald Keene mentions that autumn holds a special place in Japanese poetry, because Japanese poets are peculiarly sensitive to the "brevity of beautiful things."[76] Yet rationalizing autumn as a "vision of justice" has a didactic element that is out of place in the Japanese poetry Claudel knew. Huang remarks Claudel's interest in the teachings the German mystic Meister Eckhart (1260–1328), according to which beings or creatures of God exist thanks to a loan of life force, meaning that all that exists on earth is negative, a privation of God's power.[77] With this in mind, we can see that for Claudel autumn is like "a vision of justice" because it represents the decline of that which is necessarily against God. The moral judgment that the decline of nature is "just" dampens the poem's pathos, for it suggests that the observer should not be saddened by the passing of the finite in the scheme of Christian cosmology. The poem fills a Japanese vessel with a non-Japanese message, and even though there is no "I" ("*je*") explicitly organizing the poem and drawing a link between autumn and Claudel's Catholic worldview, the introduction of Claudel's personal philosophy into this "Japanese" poem, and the use of simile to link the two halves of the poem together, signals the strong presence of a European subject and limits the meaning that the reader can find in the piece.

Claudel's approach is subtler elsewhere, especially in those poems that are hybrid artworks composed of Claudel's calligraphy and Tomita Keisen's paintings. A few of the hundred phrases were released to the public in a different fashion from those found in the complete French version. Unlike the hundred collected in the 1942 edition, the early poems were actually written on Japanese folding fans or *éventails* and distributed as *Le Souffle des quatre souffles* (*The Breath of the Four Breaths* or *The Breath of the Four Winds*). Each poem took one of the four Japanese seasons as its subject. On one half of each fan is Claudel's poem drawn by the ambassador himself with a calligraphic brush, while on the other half is a calligraphic drawing by Keisen. Huang writes that in creating with Keisen these hybrid artworks in which calligraphy and painting are joined, Claudel was trying to bring forth a "new poetic form," the "painted word."[78] Even more interestingly, Huang remarks that the inspiration for *Cent phrases* came from a long French poem, *Saint Geneviève*, extolling French women during the First World War and embellished with illustrations by Audrey Parr, which Claudel completed shortly before assuming his post in Japan. Claudel's first advances toward the "painted word" came in the poem *La muraille intérieure de Tokyo* (*The Inner Wall of Tokyo*), which, again featuring Keisen's art, served as the verso to the Japanese edition of *Saint Geneviève*. Huang notes that whereas the paintings that

---

aussi brutal que la bataille d'hommes ; mais la vision de la justice est le plaisir de Dieu seul" (Autumn already! [...] Spiritual combat is as brutal as battle between men; but the vision of justice is God's pleasure alone) See Truffet and Claudel, *Edition critique et commentée de Cent phrases pour éventails de Paul Claudel*, 108–9.

[76] Donald Keene, "Characteristics of Japanese Literature," in *The Blue-Eyed Tarōkaja: A Donald Keene Anthology*, ed. Donald Keene and J. Thomas Rimer, New York: Columbia UP, 1996, 188.

[77] Huang, *Segalen et Claudel*, 185.

[78] Ibid., 129.

accompany *Saint Geneviève* are secondary to the poem, the calligraphic painting for *La muraille intérieure de Tokyo* is as of as much importance as Claudel's words. The painting and the verses fuse together to form a multidimensional poem. From a specifically French Catholic starting point, *Saint Geneviève*, Claudel wound up creating with Keisen an experimental half-French and half-Japanese artwork. Let us take one of the *quatre souffles*, a poem evoking spring:

	Dans	*mêlé de*	In		
	le	*pailletes d'argent*		the	silver sequins
	brouillard	*l'ombre de la prêtresse*		fog	the shadow of the priestess
撒		*secouant son goupillon*			shaking her aspergillum
		de			of
鈴		*g*			ca
		relots et le semoir de son			scabels and the seeder of sound
			s (Po. 717)		s

On the left half of the fan for *Souffles*, Keisen has sketched a monochromatic image of a Shintō shrine with what appears to be a ceremony occurring inside. To the right is Claudel's poem. As with the Amaterasu narrative, in describing a Shintō ceremony, Claudel has made a few key changes. Recall that Watanabe argued that Claudel's knowledge of the Amaterasu myth and of Shintō was quite accurate. Claudel's more intensive study of Japanese culture and visits to Japanese cultural sites while he was ambassador would have deepened his knowledge of Shintō even further. Nonetheless, here Claudel does not use any Japanese words. He calls the *miko*, the Shintō shrine maiden, a "priestess" and her instrument, the *kagura suzu*, an "aspergillum." Indeed, the *kanji* here are *maku* or "scatter" as with seeds and *suzu* or "bell," consolidating the conceit of a bell with sounds that become material and fruitful. In the Catholic Church, an aspergillum contains holy water and is associated with purification during mass. A closer object to the aspergillum would be another purification device, the *gohei* that Claudel described in his Amaterasu. Yet Claudel has chosen to make the *kagura suzu* an aspergillum, and thereby to make the sound emitted by the bells the Shintō equivalent of holy water. Truffet writes that, in a diary entry from 1924, Claudel employs similar language in describing a Nō performance, where he sees "[un] esprit noir avec un sistre d'or qui est un goupillon et un semoir, les gouttes d'eau q[ui] se détachent remplacées par le son" ([a] black spirit with a golden rattle that is an aspergillum and a seeder, the drops of water that fly off replaced by sounds).[79] It appears then that the use of bells in the Shintō ceremony was bound up in Claudel's mind with the use of bells in Nō. He believes the ancient Japanese religion connects with the medieval Japanese art, and translates the two together into the religious language of the Catholic Church. In other words, Shintō becomes a vehicle for Claudel the Catholic poet as he tries out a Japanese aesthetic in *Le Souffle* and in *Cent phrases*; he does, as Bush says, empty out aspects of Japanese culture and fills them with his own European ideas, but only does so by remarking a similarity between religious ritual and dramatic art

---

[79] Truffet and Claudel, *Edition critique et commentée de Cent phrases pour éventails de Paul Claudel*, 93.

that is lacking in his native country. Claudel's Japan cannot be evacuated of its original significance; rather the Japanese and the European must sit in tension, with the boundary between them ill defined. Of course, Nō is far more connected to Buddhism than to Shintō, but it matters little here whether Claudel was aware of this. What matters is that Claudel views the scene as "Japanese," and tries to reconcile this Japanese scene with Catholic ceremony.

The final gesture to reconcile East and West is Keisen's painting. The poem describes a Frenchman's idea of a Shintō ceremony. The painting is a Japanese man's response to the Frenchman's poem. If Claudel takes the idea of Japan and draws it toward his native mind-set, tying East and West together in a poem, Keisen takes Claudel's union and draws it back toward Japan. The painting gives Claudel's poem an air of authenticity, suggesting that that which Claudel depicts in the poem is as concrete and real as the calligraphic work painted next to it. We might also say it makes the foreignness of Claudel's poem stand out, since Keisen has painted only a Shintō shrine. There are no priestesses, no subtle blending of Catholicism and Shintoism. Keisen's painting is "authentic"—it is a Japanese painting of a Japanese subject by a Japanese man. Compared to it, Claudel's poem, with its experimental form and allusions to European religion, appears more eccentric. However, as a member of the *Nihonga* movement, particularly the Kyoto school of painting 日本画壇 which developed in the Meiji era around Takeuchi Seihō 竹内栖鳳 and sought to combine Japanese and Western painting techniques, Keisen was himself already straddling the divide between Japan and Europe.[80] Because the poem and the painting form a single artwork, one *éventail*, we find the entire piece hard to classify. It is a French poem on a Japanese theme, and it is a Japanese painting inspired by that very Franco-Japanese poem. Kawakami writes that the presence of kanji next to each poem in *Cent phrases* signals Claudel's "invitation to the reader to enter, in ignorance if need be, into the linguistic system of the Other."[81] Looking at this *éventail*, we see an attempt to enter not only into the language of the Japanese "Other" but into a web of Japanese aesthetics and religion. Huang reminds us that the calligraphy, painting, and poetry were all done with a brush in Japan, just as are Claudel's poem and Keisen's painting here, and so may be traced back to a single art.[82] The single origin further urges us to unify the two pieces of the *éventail*. We are encouraged both to distinguish between the French and the Japanese parts of the fan, and to unite them as two variations on the same theme, both crafted with a brush, both part of a single Japanese tradition. The twin claims of identity and difference leave us once again in a state of indeterminacy.

---

[80] Michel Wasserman has investigated Claudel's relationship with the Kyoto school of painting. See Wasserman, "Paul Claudel et les peintres de Kyoto," *Bulletin De La Société Paul Claudel* no. 178 (2005): 59–61. For more on the School itself, see Tadao Ogura (director), *Kyōto No Nihonga 1910–1930: Taishō No Kokoro Kakushin to Sōzō*, Kyoto: Kyōto Kokuritsu Kindai Bijutsukan, 1986.

[81] Kawakami, "Co-naissance," 183.

[82] Huang, *Segalen et Claudel*, 103.

Kuki, Japanese Philosopher–Poet in Paris

In 1930, Kuki published his best-known work, *The Structure of Iki* (*Iki no kōzō*). Started in Paris in 1925, *Iki* attempts to find in the Japanese language a word that expresses the Japanese ethnic experience. His assumption is that "一の意味または言語は、一民族の過去および現在の存在様態の自己表明、歴史を有する特殊の文化の自己開示に外ならない" (a meaning or even an entire language is the self-expression of the past and present of a group of people, and is nothing other than the self-revealing of the history of a particular culture) (*Zs.* 8).[83] Kuki seeks a word that has no correlate in any European language and finds it in "*iki*," a word associated with Edo during the Tokugawa epoch and which Kuki ties to the geisha and the samurai of the pleasure quarters. He says "*iki*" may be understood as "chic," "refined," or "coquettish," but all of its connotations elude encapsulation in a single European word (*Zs.* 11–12). Kuki asserts: "従って「いき」とは東洋文化の、否、大和民族の特殊の存在様態の顯著な自己表明の一つであると考へて差支ない" (Hence, *iki* can safely be considered to be one of East Asian culture's—or, no, as a remarkable self-expression of a mode of being of the culture of the Yamato people) (*Zs.* 12).[84] Kuki further argues that *iki* reveals itself in heterosexual desire: in coquetry (媚態, *bitai*), born from the tensions between oneself and the opposite sex; in chic (意気地, *ikiji*), or resistance to the charms of the opposite sex; and in resignation (諦め, *akirame*), or the giving up of worldly desire following disappointment in the floating world of Edo. If desire is consummated, it ceases. Therefore, *iki* requires that the desirer not give into his attraction and be restrained by *ikiji* that is based on the idealism （理想主義）of *Bushidō* (*Zs.* 19). This "idealism" is in turn tempered by *akirame* that has "Buddhist a-realism as its background"(仏教の非現實性を背景とする「諦め」) (*Zs.* 22).[85] Kuki's idea of *iki* thus depends on tension between two aspects of Japanese tradition, Bushidō and Buddhism, as manifested in the pleasure quarters of Edo.

Kuki's attempt to unearth the "specific mode of being" of the Japanese people has attracted much criticism. Ryōsuke Ōhashi points out that the examples of Japanese culture Kuki presents in *Iki* come from a narrow range of Japanese history, namely the Bunka-Bunsei period (1804–1829), and questions whether this "decadent" period well represents Japan as a whole.[86] After asserting that Kuki's thought was founded on

---

[83] I have referred to Hiroshi Nara's excellent translation of *Iki no kōzō*, but have made some small changes. See Nara, *The Structure of Detachment: The Aesthetic Vision of Kuki Shuzo*, Honolulu: U of Hawaii P, 2004, 8.

[84] Ibid., 17.

[85] Ibid., 23.

[86] There is a fascinating overlap with Claudel here that goes beyond the limits of this chapter. In the 1940s, Claudel referred to French and English translations of *dodoitsu* 都々逸 to create his own versions of the Japanese poems. *Dodoitsu* refers to popular poetry that flourished between 1804 and 1852 and was especially current among women working in pleasure quarters. Claudel's collection of this poetry, *Dodoitzu*, highlights different features of the poetry from those which Kuki might have selected. Notably, he explains *dodoitsu* as "rustic" poetry (*Po.* 755), and a note to the collection in the *Oeuvre poétique* informs us that Claudel "a préféré d'ailleurs le dodoitsu paysan à sa forme plus élaboré" (preferred the peasant *dodoitsu* to its more elaborate form) (1154).

"European conceptual systems,"[87] Ōhashi mentions that *Iki* "had occurred to [Kuki] during his study in Europe simply as a favorable example, through which he could explain Japanese culture to a Western audience."[88] Considering these cultural biases latent in *Iki*, Ōhashi asks whether Kuki could have achieved the definitive study of the Japanese character at which he aimed. Leslie Pincus develops this line of reasoning and concludes that Kuki was coaxed into "insular" European philosophy and, after he realized he was "trapped" in a foreign conceptual system, had no choice but to "[construct] and imaginary place called Japan"[89]—a rather extreme view that robs Kuki of his agency and presupposes and inseparable line between European and Japanese thought. To these critiques we could add Roy Starrs's observation that Bushidō is largely a modern construction, insofar as it was a term not familiar to the majority of Japanese people before the Meiji era.[90]

But the validity of Kuki's thesis is not at issue here. Rather, we are focusing on the role Buddhism and Bushidō play in his attempt to rally European philosophy to interpret Japanese culture. The lecture Kuki delivered in 1928 at Pontigny expands on his ideas on Buddhism and Bushidō. Yasunari Takada analyzes Kuki's dichotomy between linear Christian time on the one side and circular ancient Greek and Buddhist time on the other. In the lecture, Kuki charges that the majority of Western philosophy presupposes a unitary self whose experience constitutes an orderly, irreversible horizontal time. Through consciousness as "will" or *volonté*, the subject is able to distinguish between varying moments and order them as past, present, and future (*Zs.* 295). The assumption is that the ordering subject is the same at every instance of time. Against this linear model, Kuki places the cyclical model of ancient Greece and Buddhism; in particular Kuki focuses on the latter's notion of the transmigration of the soul, where the same soul is reborn continuously in a variety of bodies (*Zs.* 294, 293). If time is cyclical, and if the same soul inhabits different bodies, then the logic of identity is disrupted, since the subject who creates time through her consciousness is constantly changing her physical identity and having her sense of past, present, and future reset. Takada writes that Kuki here presents a concept of time "through which the human existence has the theoretical possibility of opening itself to self-same but plural identities."[91] Despite Kuki's references to antiquity, and despite the notion of cyclical time having obvious links to the philosophy of Friedrich Nietzsche (*Zs.* 291), Takada argues that "Kuki's strategy at the Pontigny lecture was to place the eternal-return type in the Oriental camp while leaving the linear type in the opposite camp of Europe."[92] Of course, Takada ignores that Kuki aims to show that this "peculiar" logic is actually more rational than that which could

---

[87] Ōhashi, "Kuki Shūzō and the Question of Hermeneutics," 30.
[88] Ibid.
[89] Pincus, "In a Labyrinth of Western Desire," 156.
[90] Roy Starrs, *Modernism and Japanese Culture*, London: Palgrave Macmillan, 2011, 56.
[91] Yasunari Takada, "Shuzo Kuki: or, A Sense of Being In-between," in *Transcendental Descent: Essays in Literature and Philosophy*, Collection UTCP 2, University of Tokyo Center for Philosophy, 2007, 290.
[92] Ibid.

be found in twentieth-century Europe, and that it is in fact subject to the principle of identity, "A est A" (*Zs*. 293). Takada is also at odds with Obama Yoshinobu, who argues that Kuki rather attempts to across Western linear time with East Asian cyclical time to arrive at an "ideology of eternal return" ("永遠回帰の思想"), a process that relies on porous borders as much as if not more than on binaries.[93] But Takada is correct insofar as Kuki's reference to the logic of identity is an attempt to claim ancient Greek thought for "oriental" and Japanese, and that his notion of circularity through rebirth is one that would have been foreign to many of his French contemporaries, among them Claudel in his search for a "nouvelle Logique" of a different kind.[94]

As we saw in *Iki*, Kuki believed that Buddhist resignation needed to be checked by the willpower of Bushidō. In his Pontigny lecture, Kuki argues that Buddhist "pessimism" wants liberation from the cycle of death and rebirth and aims to achieve this by denying human will and human desire (*Zs*. 287). Contrarily, Bushidō affirms the will and denies liberation from the torments of earthly life (*Zs*. 287). Thus, Bushidō, Kuki says, inculcates "[une] bonne volonté infinie, qui jamais ne peut se réaliser entièrement, et qui est destinée à être toujours 'déçue,' doit toujours se renouveler sans effort" ([an] infinite good will, which can never be fully realized, and which is destined always to be frustrated, must always renew its effort) and which encourages adherents to face "la transmigration sans peur, vaillamment" (transmigration without fear, valiantly) (*Zs*. 286). He sees this "idéal moral du Japon" in the reconstruction following natural disasters such as the Great Kanto Earthquake. The new constructions will themselves be destroyed only to be rebuilt again, and it is this perseverance in the face of a cycle of growth and destruction that Kuki finds ethical (*Zs*. 284–85). Buddhism and ancient Greek thought join together to form an alternative to a European conception of time, but it is the specifically Japanese code that makes Kuki's formulation moral.

Takada states that Kuki's Bushidō "is a form of moral idealism which draws for support on no transcendental, absolute divinity but on one's inner god, a divinity of relativity." Consequently, without a transcendent divinity like Claudel's Catholic God, there is nothing to secure "all phenomena on the underlying principle of identity and necessity."[95] Using "European conceptual systems" to build a philosophy that joins ancient Greek and Buddhist thought, of which a Japanese moral code is the ethical engine: Is this not a way for Kuki to reconcile his Japanese and Far Eastern identity with the European "world of philosophers" that, according to Shigemi Inaga, Kuki felt more at home in than when he was among his compatriots? Takada seems to have this in mind when he says that Kuki was "in-between" Europe and the "peculiarities of his own culture."[96] The idea chimes with Graham Mayeda's statement that Kuki valued Bushidō more than Buddhism in order to have a "subjective point of view—a point of view of control"

---

[93] Yoshinobu Obama, "九鬼周造における「永遠回帰の思想」," *Risō* no. 698 (2017): 2–3.
[94] See Chapter One for more on Claudel and logic.
[95] Takada, "A Sense of Being In-between," 290.
[96] Ibid., 294.

when dealing with the cultural other.[97] Undoubtedly this vague position of Japanese identity and culture relative to Far Eastern and European thought owes to "Kuki's desire, as a young student from the 'Far East,' to explain to Europeans the soul and culture of Japan."[98]

The tension between Japan and France is evident in the poetry Kuki wrote in Paris. Marra contends that these poems show that "a meeting with the Other for Kuki was utterly impossible."[99] But the situation is more complicated than Marra suggests. The main schism between Kuki and Parisian life is that between Kuki, particularly his decadent lifestyle, and Christianity. We find an example of this just before halfway through Kuki's Paris *tanka* sequence, first in poems 62 and 63: "焼栗が巴里の辻にかをる宵立ちて栗食むイヴォンヌ、スザンヌ" (An evening when roasted chestnuts perfume the street corners of Paris—eating chestnuts stand Yvonne, Suzanne) (Marra 62) (*Zs.* 181); 秋の街ものほしげなるまじめになる顔を上げゆく加特力の僧 (The town in autumn—raising his craving, serious-looking face, a Catholic priest) (Marra 62)[100] (*Zs.* 181). Yvonne and Suzanne, as Marra tells us, are two of the "demimondaines or women of pleasure (*asobi onna*)" who abound in Kuki's *tanka*. The memory of these women would haunt Kuki later in Kyoto, where he would spend his "evenings in Gion, the district populated by clubs, parlors, coffee shops, and teahouses where Geisha performed their arts."[101] Kuki looks upon the prostitutes, attractive in his eyes, as they eat chestnuts. But the next poem replaces the poet's gaze with that of the Catholic priest, whose "craving" is tempered by his seriousness. The priest desires, but he restrains himself; he is the opposite of Kuki and serves to demarcate the boundaries of Kuki's world.

The divide between these "women of pleasure" and Catholicism is deepened in tanka 150 and 151. Let us start with 150: "鐘の音は聖心寺かさびしくも巴里の春の終わらんとする" (Is the sound of bells coming from Sacré-Coeur? How lonesome! Spring in Paris is going to end) (Marra 64) (*Zs.* 192). The passing of spring is the passing of Kuki's time in Paris, but what significance do the bells of Sacré-Coeur hold, and who is lonesome? Naturally, we must keep in mind that the emotions present in these poems are not necessarily identical with Kuki's own. Thoroughly knowledgeable of modern French poetry, especially that of Charles Baudelaire (1821–1867), whose decadent approach to modern life Kuki remarks is similar to the concept of *iki* (*Zs.* 79), it is possible that Kuki is here simply adopting the persona of a world-weary modern man in Paris, cut off from tradition. In that case, Kuki's poems would not be confessions but literary experiments

---

[97] Graham Mayeda, "Time for Ethics: Temporality and the Ethical Ideal in Emmanuel Levinas and Kuki Shūzō," *Comparative and Continental Philosophy* vol. 4, no. 1 (2012): 115.
[98] Ōhashi, "Kuki Shūzō and the Question of Hermeneutics," 30.
[99] Michel F. Marra, *Essays on Japan*. Leiden: Brill, 2010.
[100] The translations of Kuki's *tanka* in this section come from Michael Marra *Kuki Shuzo: A Philosopher's Poetry and Poetics*, ed. and trans. Michael F. Marra, Honolulu: U of Hawaii P, 2004. I have modified Marra's translation better to fit the original Japanese syntax, and have dispensed with the line divisions Marra adds that are not present in Kuki's originals.
[101] Marra, "Words in Tension," 26.

by a young philosopher-poet, and the bells would perhaps only signal a more common division between the sacred and the profane.

However, the next poem develops this dichotomy in a way that recalls that which we found in poems 62 and 63: "加特力の尼となりにし戀人も年へだたりぬ今いかならん" (Today I wonder, after so many years, how my lover who became a Catholic nun is doing) (Marra 64) (*Zs.* 192). Though there is no indication how Kuki lost contact with this "lover," her conversion to Catholicism and her entrance to a convent has severed all contact between them. Both Marra and Mayeda point out that the "Other" for Kuki is essentially feminine.[102] Marra ties this desire for the feminine Other more broadly to Kuki's desire for the West.[103] As we saw in the exposition of *Iki*, for Kuki heterosexual desire must always be subdued by "brave composure" in order to keep the self and Other distinct. Keeping in mind that tanka 151 comes right after the sensation of loneliness induced by the bells of Sacré-Cœur in tanka 150, we can surmise that Catholicism had become for Kuki a symbol of the antithesis of the floating world he occupied in Paris. The Catholic priest's worldview negates Kuki's, while the nunnery cuts ties between Kuki and one of the demimondaines with whom he had consorted. Kuki's inability to meet with the Other is thus in part an inability to reconcile his desire with the "seriousness" of the Catholic world from which he felt culturally and philosophically alien. The *ikiji* that he valued in Bushidō, could it not be a response to this unbridgeable gap that he felt between these two aspects of Parisian life? Kuki does not say so directly. Regardless, we can see that, as Catholicism was a stumbling block for Claudel in his relationship with the traditions of Japan and East Asia, it was an impediment for Kuki, a sign of a mysterious world he could not or would not enter into.

Claudel's and Kuki's Poetry on Autumn and Spring

So much for the general orientation of Claudel's and Kuki's poetry. I will now turn to their seasonal poetry. Both composed poems on the four seasons; both with an idea of traditional Japanese poetry in mind. I will begin with autumn, the season concerning which Kuki and Claudel diverge the most.

Claudel tries to eliminate from autumn the sense of sadness, even though in Japanese literature this season is most representative of doleful emotion. Certainly, some of the poems of *Cent phrases* express sadness. As we have seen in the previous chapter, Claudel was open to Japanese Buddhism because of its "bitter and profound melancholy." But behind the waning nature of autumn he glimpses the hand of God and the eternal. He writes: "L'automne aussi / est une chose / qui commence" (Autumn too is something that commences) (*Po.* 723). We have already seen that Claudel thinks of autumn as "justice," because it suggests the ultimate power of God over the temporal realm. Combining that poem with the one cited earlier, we can imagine that because the end of *this* life is the commencement of the life eternal for the Catholic Claudel, and because all that passes

---

[102] Marra, *Essays on Japan*, 179–81; Mayeda, "Time for Ethics," 108.
[103] Marra, "Words in Tension," 71.

on Earth leads to God's final judgment, Claudel sees in autumn the machinations of the Christian divine. Observing the Japanese countryside, Claudel feels moved by the fragile beauty of the changing seasons, but he refuses to allow this pleasurable melancholy to destabilize his positive Christian vision. Consequently, he cannot view autumn as a season of sadness as the writers of the *Kokinshū* could, for such an emotion would evince a lack of respect toward God.[104]

In contrast, for Kuki, autumn is the season par excellence of *kanashisa* and *sabishisa*. Throughout *Parī Shinkei*, Kuki takes pleasure in expressing his sorrow about autumn, and fall is the vehicle by which Kuki expresses his sentiment of melancholy and isolation in Paris where even his happy moments promise rupture, particularly between Kuki and a love interest. The following poem evinces this tendency: "初夏に君と踏みつる並木道おち葉する日にただ一人ゆく" (At the start of summer I walked with you along the tree-lined path; now as the leaves fall I walk alone) (*Zs.* 176).[105] Just as the green leaves of early summer must fall, so must Kuki and his beloved separate. If Claudel substitutes the stabilizing presence of God for the sadness of autumn in Japan, Kuki sees even in the happy loving moments of the prime of the year the melancholic sentiment of autumn. The subject matter is the same, but the message is the inverse.

The treatment of autumn here reminds us perhaps of the poetry of Paul Verlaine as captured in poems such as "Chanson d'automne," in which autumn expresses the poet's feelings of loss and isolation.[106] But he does not simply imitate Verlaine, for Kuki's treatment of fall refers back to the interpretation of the "Japanese spirit" laid out in *Iki*. Since consummation always leads to the end of love and even attraction, Kuki recommends the stoic resistance of Bushido and the pessimistic resignation of Buddhism as bulwarks against desire. But resistance and resignation themselves guarantee isolation, for Kuki's philosophy prohibits him from indulging in pleasure whenever it finds him. Thus, contra Verlaine, Kuki is not simply mourning lost youth and love but expressing a worldview that sees even in youth and love a bottomless emptiness. For this reason, aspects in his poetry that might recall Claudel—for instance, Kuki's apparent silent meditation on the natural world—are loaded with implications that recall *Iki*. Silence for Kuki

---

[104] To explain *Soulier de Satin*, Claudel paraphrases Saint Augustine to claim that all things, including dissatisfaction and suffering, conspire toward goodness. See Paul Claudel, Jean Amrouche, and Louis Fournier, *Mémoires Improvisés*. Paris: Gallimard, 1969, 283.

[105] The translations of Kuki's poems in this section are my own, based on the translations from Japanese to French used in Johnson, "La Poésie de Paul Claudel et de Kuki Shūzo durant les années 1920," *Cahiers d'études françaises* vol. 23 (2018): 31–46, which was the foundation of this chapter.

[106] Early in his career, Claudel wrote his own poem entitled "Chanson d'automne" and sent it to Mallarmé. The poem makes its symbolist influences palpable as nature evokes parting and fracture ("L'appel sombre du cor inconsolable / A cause du temps qui n'est plus, / Qui n'est plu à cause de ce seul jour admirable / Par qui la chose n'est plus") (*Po.* 433–34). But even in this poem Claudel's focus rests not on himself but on the natural world, and the allusions to gold and votive candles move Claudel's thoughts from the human to the divine and place Claudel's somber poem firmly within his Catholic universe.

is not a way of indicating the ineffable divine, but rather his self-respect and Buddhist-influenced fortitude before the pleasures of Paris: "言はざるを掟としたる僧のごと巴里の秋に默すひねもす" (An autumn day in Paris I keep silent like a monk) (*Zs.* 179). This monk (僧) is the Buddhist monk of *Iki*,[107] and his silence is a tool for resisting abandonment to love, not for comprehending God, or for purely expressing the sadness of autumn.

In the poems that treat spring we find the same tendency. Let us consider once more the poem of spring from *Souffle des quatre souffles*:

Une belle journée d'automne	est comme la vision de la justice (*Po.* 727)	A beautiful day in autumn	is like the vision of justice

Expanding on Truffet's analysis, Ayako Nishino explains that this poem stems from the "memory of the sacred agrarian dance" found in the Nō *Okina*, and that it is "probably an amalgam of other memories of a Shinto ceremony" that Claudel saw performed.[108] She says that in his notes Claudel mentions "a golden sistrum that is a goupillon and a seeder"; this seeder "likely corresponds to the bellflower used specially for *Okina*," while the goupillon is, of course, the instrument of the Christian liturgy: all of these terms suggests a confusion through which "the poet attributes to this Japanese object liturgical and / or agrarian significances."[109] Nishino's argument supports that which I have been arguing throughout this book: that Claudel's Catholicism transforms not only the Japanese countryside but also its indigenous theater and religion. Once more to return to Bush, then, we see that Claudel does fill Japan and Japanese things with his Christian vision. However, it is more exact to say that Claudel *adds* a new sense to Japanese objects, a Christian sense that permits him to integrate elements of Japanese art in his own aesthetic universe without disturbing the internal coherence of this universe.

For Kuki, springtime, to which he devotes the most energy in *Parī Shōkyoku*, is sometimes happier than autumn. Kuki warmly welcomes spring: "春の朝おとぎばなしの世にいきん願もてきぬブロオニュの森" (A spring morning—to Bois de Boulogne I carry with me the wish to live in a world of fairy tales) (*Zs.* 183). There are also tranquil poems that resemble the poetry of *Cent phrases*, such as 66: "マグダレナ御寺の柱やはらかにほのぼのとして春の雨ふる" (The spring rain falls softly on the columns of the church of Saint Magdalena), or 67: "ドビュシイが夢みるごとき音色より巴里の空の春ひろがる" (To the resonance of the music of which Debussy dreamed listens the sky of springtime Paris) (*Zs.* 182). His vision is less pessimistic here. He conveys his perceptions

---

[107] It is important to stress that 僧 (*sou*) indicates a Buddhist monk not a Christian one, so he could not have in mind, say, a Trappist monk.
[108] Nishino, *Synthèse*, 97.
[109] Ibid., 96–97.

of France without explicit dolor. He is still alone, but the world of Paris enchants him, the church emits a tranquil ambiance, the music of Debussy joins with the sky to form a dreamlike image. As such, the Paris of Kuki in spring draws close to Claudel's magical Japan. All the same, the promise of spring is like a fairytale (おとぎばなし): it concerns another world (世), that of fiction, not the world in which Kuki actually lives. Indeed, the suggestion is that the happy moments of spring are only a dream, one from which Kuki must inevitably awake. Only by emphasizing the transience of spring joy can Kuki make his happy moments in Paris accessible to his poetic universe.

A final remark on the interesting rapport between spring and autumn: in Claudel's poems of spring, we find that which Truffet calls the "accord of different senses."[110] This accord is found in the following poem: "A l'un des bouts de ce segment de cercle le printemps qui commence poursuit à l'autre bout l'automne également qui commence" (At one of the ends of the segment of this circle spring is commencing and pursuing to the other side the equally commencing autumn) (*Po.* 740). The poem indicates that Claudel too links spring to autumn, but that he does not suggest the circularity in which Kuki believes. The two seasons are for him points from which something can commence. His vision goes toward the future, and therefore, even as Claudel speaks of circularity, he emphasizes a starting point and the notion of progression rather than repetition. By stressing the commencement of both seasons, Claudel avoids the notion of decline dear to Kuki and inserts in his poems *à la japonaise* a positive Christian notion: the Buddhist concept of circularity is evoked to be undermined, for even autumn is a season of progress in Claudel's Christian universe running on teleological time.[111] This, it seems, is why Truffet speaks of tension between the world of Japanese aesthetics, as Claudel understands them, and the world of his Catholic faith. It is the tension between the Japanese countryside and seasons, long described by Japanese poets such as those of the *Kokinshū*, and the new Catholic interpretation that Claudel proffers. The tension here shows the difficulty of integrating elements drawn from diverse worlds into a coherent poetic constellation. Even if there are superficial similarities between Claudel's and Kuki's poems of spring, the metaphysical differences are profound.

Worlds, Constellations, and Universes of Belief

Paying special attention to seasonal poems influenced by the *Kokinshū*, I have described the differences between Claudel's poetry *à la japonaise* and Kuki's Parisian poetry. Claudel's vision is optimistic while Kuki's is pessimistic. This divide owes to each writer's philosophy, more precisely each's constellation of beliefs. The Catholic Claudel cannot doubt God's designs, and therefore cannot permit himself to indulge in feelings of sadness as he looks

---

[110] Truffet and Claudel, *Edition critique et commentée de Cent phrases pour éventails de Paul Claudel*, 99.
[111] One of Claudel's negative evaluations of East Asian ("*orientales*") civilizations charged that, in opposition to Christian societies that move toward the future, East Asian civilizations run in cycles and, consequently, never improve. See Claudel, Amrouche and Fournier, *Mémoires Improvisés*, 280.

at nature waning in autumn. That which matters for him is the ultimate victory of the eternal soul. For this reason, he inserts in his poetry on autumn elements that indicate the omnipresence of God, and the ultimate redemption of corruptible matter in the incorruptible body of God. The emotions of *kanashisa* and *sabishisa* are foreign to his poetry *à la japonaise*. Moreover, because he directs his thoughts toward God, he does not pay attention to Japanese *people* in his poetry on the seasons. Nature personified becomes his companion all throughout *Cent phrases*. In contrast, that which is important for Kuki is contingency and the tension latent in desire between the sexes. He rejects metaphysical necessity and the existence of a supreme being. His rejection of linear time that leads to eternal life after a final judgment bends to his pessimistic vision of the world, in which each being only declines toward death. And since he believes that desire disappears as soon as it is consummated, he underlines the necessity of self-restraint and resignation in amorous relations. Consequently, his *tanka* overflow with the sensation of solitude and heartbreak, a dignified sadness that recalls more fully the aesthetic effects of the *Kokinshū* and Kuki's interpretation of life in the pleasure quarters of late Edo Japan.

The process of constructing a coherent poetic world demands this divergence between Claudel's and Kuki's poetry. Claudel, avid reader of the *Kokinshū* in translation, in contact with the traditional arts of Japan during his time in the country, subsequent "translator" of *dodoitsu* into French, had at his disposal models of Japanese poetry that would not have been dissimilar in theme to Kuki's poignant verse. Yet, for Claudel, God is a necessary being. A world in which God does not exist is for Claudel an impossible world. He can imagine such a world, but he places this world outside of his constellation of possible worlds. Thus for Claudel, the worlds of traditional Japanese art are also impossible worlds, for the notion of God, the Catholic God, is not present. But since he ascertains certain elements of Japanese art and philosophy resembling that which is familiar to him in Catholic art and thought, he is able to translate these elements into his constellation of possible worlds by reinterpreting them according to his Catholic beliefs. Certainly, this translation is also a mutation, but it opens up to him versions of the worlds of Japanese art and allows to pass between the two a communion of ideas.

The world of Kuki, the poetic world, is structured according to his conception of the Japanese spirit limned in *Iki* and in his speech at Pontigny. He is more open than Claudel to foreign elements thanks to his understanding of metaphysical contingency. According to him, he may very well have been born a French Catholic like Claudel. Being Japanese is not necessary to his being. Superficially, the Christian world is more intelligible to him than the worlds of Japanese Buddhism and Shintō are to Claudel. All the same, in his poetry and philosophy the positive vision *à la Claudel* is absent. He cannot accept the Claudelian faith in an eternal kingdom that will redeem all of the contingent and corruptible things of the actual world. As such, Claudel's poetic world, his entire poetic and philosophical universe, is impossible for Kuki. In place of a rational and reassuring divinity, Kuki perceives in all possible worlds contingency and the breaking up of that which seems complete and stable. This is the reason that Kuki tries to link the philosophy of Japan to that of ancient Greece. In order for the world of Europe to be intelligible to him, it is necessary for him to translate Europe's foundational civilization, as a fellow "pagan" civilization, into the ontology that structures his constellation of possible worlds.

That translation too is a mutation, for it erects a strong barrier between East and West that, by distancing Kuki from a part of the European experience, further contributes to his sense of isolation in Paris. The process indicates the correctness of Priest's assertion that possibility and conceivability are distinct: there are many conceivable elements in the history of French and Japanese literature for Claudel and Kuki, but because those worlds clash with their belief systems they become impossible, inaccessible. To make the past intelligible to the present, Claudel and Kuki both need to translate them into not merely a conceivable but an accessible world, to create a duplicate literary world for, say, the *Kokinshū* before they can use the idea of the *Kokinshū* to structure their own twentieth-century poetry.

Does that mean that the worlds of Kuki and Claudel are impossible, relative to one another? Not exactly. Different ontologies do structure the two. All the same, it is in this process of comprehending another world while being caught between two distinct cultures that we discover an accessibility relation between the two. In one of the poems of *Parī Shinkei*, Kuki catches the scent of the fragrant olive, which reminds him of his hometown: "木犀のほのぼの匂ふ故郷を秋の晴るれば戀しとぞ思ふ" (The scent of the fragrant olive makes me yearn for my hometown) (*Zs*. 64). Though this might remind us of Claudel's "accord of different senses," the mixture of sight and smell recalls the techniques of the *Kokinshū*, where, for instance, the sight of blooming *sakura* and the smell of incense might lead the reader to transcend the scene and arrive at a higher (Buddhist) message that adds a subtle asceticism to an otherwise pleasurable image.[112] Thanks to the presence of this same tree in France and in Japan, Kuki is able, if only for an instant, to break the barrier between the worlds of France and Japan: he can be in France yet feel as if he were in Japan. In this confused state, he is mentally in one place yet physically in another. Like Claudel, poet of the "accord of different senses," Kuki tries to find an accord between the world of Paris and the world of Japan, despite the fact that their interpretations of the two cities conflict, and to form a new literary world in which his visions of France and Japan, Orient and Occident, can coexist. The latent idea in this, that a poet comes vested with a literary tradition, or a set of worlds, and a nationality, or a constellation of belief, takes this book to its final triangulation, featuring the multidimensional traditions envisioned by Bei Dao and Ted Hughes.

---

[112] See Sata, "*Kokinwakashū* shunka-ka Tsurayuki," 2.

Chapter Five

TRADITION EAST AND WEST, ENGLISH AND CHINESE: THE CROSS-CULTURAL POETRY OF BEI DAO AND TED HUGHES

In the last few years, there's been a certain rediscovery of tradition outside of China. It's like blood calling to blood: at a certain moment you're suddenly aware of it. Compared to an individual's poor powers and scanty accomplishments, the breadth and beauty of the tradition [are] like a huge wind pressing down on a tiny sail, a sailor has to know how to use the wind if the boat is going to go far. And the problem is that the tradition arises from causes as complex as those that produce the wind—you can seek them but you won't find them, you can feel them but not know them.[1]

庭前有白露　　　暗滿菊花團[2]

I have been concerned with the problem of communication between East Asian and Western traditions, namely, of what it entails for poets to draw upon foreign traditions, and how critics can make sense of the resultant literary works. In this chapter, I will focus on how interacting with foreign literature can affect a poet's conception of his or her native tradition. However, some earlier themes persist. I will again here be concerned with the problem of identity, not the identity of a literary work or a genre, but of an entire tradition. It has become increasingly common to "problematize" identity and to conceive of identity as fluid. In place of the Aristotelian logic of identity we find hybridity. I have been arguing throughout that the identity of a literary work supervenes or depends on the ontology and social network in which it is placed and by way of which it is interpreted. I will continue with this argument here. But my focus will fan out from a single text or manageable set of texts to the very concept of tradition itself. It should be understood that I am not trying to define a literary tradition, Chinese, English, or any other. My concern is for tradition as Bei Dao 北島 and Ted Hughes have viewed it, in relation to their work and identity. Doing so shifts the focus of this work from relations between literary worlds to the relations between literary worlds and the traditions in which authors and readers place them. My aim will be to show that poems attempting to bridge the gap between China and the West become a compromise between terms

---

[1] Xiaodu Tang, "An Interview with Bei Dao," trans. Haun Saussy, *World Literature Today* vol. 82, no. 6 (November 2008): 28.

[2] Du Fu, 初月. "Lucent/frost dusts the courtyard, chrysanthemum/blossoms clotted there with swollen dark" (trans. David Hinton, *Awakened Cosmos: The Mind of Classical Chinese Poetry*, Boulder, CO: Shambhala. 2019, 57).

ostensibly common to "East" and "West." Yet this generic transnationalism goes much deeper in both Chinese and Western traditions, and the extent to which we attempt to resolve the tensions opened by these often incompatible dimensions determines how we read "East–West" poetry.

My discussion delves into what has been called the supposed "intellectual divide between East and West."[3] According to one theory, there is no essential difference between Eastern and Western thought, or rather between Eastern and Western thinkers, insofar as these differences can be traced to actual structural differences between "Eastern" and "Western" minds. But there is a real divide between Eastern and Western ways of thinking that owes to a difference in metaphysics.[4] Thus current differences between Eastern and Western ways of thought are explained by examining historical metaphysical ideas, those of Confucius and Laozi or Aristotle and Augustine, and by then comparing traditional Eastern and Western metaphysics to show how the assumptions of past thinkers persist in the modern East and West. This theory is often not only descriptive but also normative: it suggests, as Ming Dong Gu and Jianping Guo hint, that bridging the gap between East and West is not only possible but desirable.[5]

Beneficial as this approach is, it implies that a state of critical impartiality can be reached. Fan Meijun and Wang Zhihe state that "[i]n place of either/or West- or East-consciousness binary thinking, it is time to develop a 'we consciousness.'"[6] Even if we presume that such integration could take place, how could we carry it out? As Gu and Guo put it: "For East and West to meet intellectually, it is certainly necessary for Western thinkers and scholars to relinquish their (un)conscious sense of superiority and adherence to Western-centrism; so also is it necessary for Eastern thinkers and scholars to reject Eastern-centrism and their (un)conscious sense of intellectual inferiority."[7] In the concept of "-centrism," it seems that two notions are confounded: chauvinism and inclination. Critics can be inclined toward a particular set of values without being chauvinistic. They would not be very good critics if they were unable to discern literary value, and such discernment requires a set of aesthetic criteria, even if those criteria are unconscious, and even if those criteria demand disinterestedness. Yet Gu and Guo seem to suggest that being inclined toward an intellectual tradition necessitates intolerance toward other traditions. The only way they see for East and West to "meet" is for both to become decentralized. However, this does not mean that there is no longer a center, only that the

---

[3] Ming Dong Gu and Jianping Guo, "How Can We Cross the Intellectual Divide Between East and West?: Reflections on Reading 'Toward a Complementary Consciousness and Mutual Flourishing of Chinese and Western Cultures: The Contributions of Process Philosophers,'" *Philosophy East and West: A Quarterly of Comparative Philosophy* vol. 65, no. 1 (2015): 298–315.

[4] Among the most astute, and persuasive, arguments in this vein is, again, Longxi Zhang, *The Tao and the Logos: Literary Hermeneutics, East and West*, Durham: Duke UP, 1992.

[5] Gu and Guo, "How Can We Cross the Intellectual Divide," 313.

[6] Fan Meijun and Wang Zhihe, "Toward a Complementary Consciousness and Mutual Flourishing of Chinese and Western Cultures: The Contributions of Process Philosophers," *Philosophy East and West* vol. 65, no. 1 (2015): 276–97.

[7] Gu and Guo, "How Can We Cross the Intellectual Divide," 312.

center is not located in either the East or the West but in a "world philosophical system."[8] According to the approach I have been developing throughout this work, texts and literary traditions are nestled in sets and constellations of belief; this nestling is not necessarily a bad thing—if I am correct, it is a neutral fact of literary production—but it does ask us to attend more to the vantage point from which we view literature. As intriguing as Gu and Guo's article is, it would benefit from accounting for the relations between a literary text, the actual world, and the set and constellation in which it is placed.

Gu and Guo's prescriptions imply that a dialogue between Eastern and Western scholars can lead to a weakening of the very idea of an East and a West. East and West are only oppositional terms; certainly, each contains distinct cultures, and even though there is perhaps no clear boundary between the two, we can refer to "Eastern ideas" and "Western ideas" and find real differences between the two. But a world philosophical system, in the sense of a single, unified world, would require the melting away of the oppositional terms East and West. Yet, this is not what Gu and Guo have in mind. They ask for "a variation neither of cultural relativism nor of cultural hybridity" that asks Chinese scholars to "creatively synthesize ideas from these cross-cultural texts into new forms of intellectual thought."[9] Throughout this book, we have been tracking the difficulties and potentialities of this fusion. Whenever writers attempt to "fuse" East and West, the structure of a literary constellation determines how a literary world coheres, which in turn leads to a unique fusion of ideas and scraps from various texts in a new literary world.

Motivated by his own status as a scholar of Chinese and Japanese literature, René Étiemble shared many of Gu and Guo's concerns. He wished to see comparative literature take a broader scope, by comparing not only between literatures within Western Europe but also between those of Europe and East Asia.[10] Since comparison between such distant languages and traditions might require a different methodology than requires comparison across the Rhine, Étiemble's evaluation of the state of the discipline left open the possibility that comparative literature could not take on such a task.[11] We can see here that East Asia serves both as a site of promise for comparative literature (it can rejuvenate the field) and as the ultimate check on the discipline (it presents materials for which the European discipline cannot account). The problem of East Asia for comparative literature has not faded. More recently, François Jullien has cast China as an indispensable foil to Western thinking and called for a "philosophy of the gap" between the West and China. When we find ruptures between Western and Chinese thinking, between, say, French and Chinese terms, Jullien asks that we "[n]e laissons pas recouvrir cet écart, car nous perdrions alors des ressources qui pourraient irriguer notre commune intelligence; ou, plutôt, faisons *travailler l'écart* de façon à ouvrir d'autres possibles dans la

---

[8] Ibid., 313.

[9] Ibid., 312.

[10] René Étiemble, *Comparaison n'est pas raison: la crise de la littérature compare*, Paris: Gallimard, 1963, 14–15.

[11] Ibid., 113–14.

pensée" (do not cover this gap back up, for we would lose resources that could irrigate our common intelligence; or, rather, let's make the gap work [*faisons travailler l'écart*] in such a way that it opens other possibilities for thought).[12] To his credit, Jullien asks us not only to make gaps work between China and Europe, but within Europe, or within whatever culture to which his readers might belong, as well. Thinking not of unity but of rupture would allow us to "frayer chaque fois un nouvel accès—ouvrir une nouvelle fenêtre—sur l'*impensé*" (clear each time [we think by way of gaps] a new access—open a new window—on the *unthought*).[13] For both Jullien and Étiemble, China can tear the non-Chinese thinker away from expected modes of thought and, by making thought break down, can open up new paths of enquiry and new modes of investigation.

In his most recent monograph, and in a chapter on literary worlds, David Damrosch points out that the old "binaries" of comparative literature have slowly morphed into multitudes. Once "East–West" studies had a sense of excitement and clarity—after all, how, if we think of the many "crises" in comparative literature of the postwar era, or even of the present work of someone like François Jullien, could we find a clearer binary than "East" versus "West"? Where once the "East" seemed like the negation of or, more positively, the ultimate test for the "Western mind" and its assumptions and methods, now both East and West are taken as complicated entities that only meld into coherent wholes with violence. Damrosch therefore takes it as a positive that the "lingering orientalism" of East–West studies has passed to a focus on the heterogenous communities with indistinct boundaries between them that form both sides of the binary.[14] Indeed, the very idea of national literature in practice comes under pressure when we consider that when "writers step back to theorize about their craft, they often draw on a range of world writers,"[15] as Bei Dao does and Ted Hughes did. Though I agree with Damrosch, certainly from a normative perspective, I wonder whether an important diction is not being glossed over here. While it is true that "East–West" studies presuppose and reifies a binary in practice, it is equally true that for many modern writers this term held much sway, and, in the case of Bei Dao and Ted Hughes, was a source of continued literary inspiration. To put it differently, if we think of "world literature" as a theory, then of course we would be remiss to divide the multitude of literatures, cultures, and beliefs of the Eurasian continent into two spheres. Doing so would be simply factually inaccurate. At the same time, we might also think of "world literature" in practice, as not only how texts move across borders and languages but how they are taken apart, finessed, and otherwise manipulated to fit into new environments. Then we might need to attend to how large categories such as "East–West" or "China–West" or "China–England" facilitate the integration of texts or bits of texts into new languages, new times, new places. We saw in Chapter Two how the concepts of East and West can aid in making analogies

---

[12] François Jullien, "Paris-Pékin, pour une philosophie de l'écart," *Le Débat* vol. 153, no. 1 (2009), 191, doi:10.3917/deba.153.0183.

[13] Ibid., 192.

[14] David Damrosch, *Comparing the Literatures: Literary Studies in a Global Age*, Princeton: Princeton UP, 2020, 266.

[15] Ibid., 269.

that help with understanding material in translation across time as well as place. In this chapter, I will return to this phenomenon. My aim will be to see how the idea of large-scale traditions, the very ones we balk at in theory, often imperceptibly structure modern world poetry. I will do so by tracing the ways in which Hughes and Bei Dao build up and tear down the "East–West binary" in theory and practice in order to translate elements of what they consider their native traditions into a world literary system.

Haun Saussy writes that saying "Western philosophy" or "Western civilization" rather than just "philosophy" or "civilization" is "a step towards self-knowledge (knowledge of oneself *as a self*)."[16] Again this is an intuitive idea, that the self comes to knowledge—comes into existence—through contact with other selves. And China is the ultimate other self because its civilization and philosophy developed independently of the West and "the Indo-European subject." China becomes "a way of learning about the relations of necessity and contingency, nature and culture, genus and example, sign and meaning."[17] The "problem of a Chinese aesthetic" is ultimately the pervasive otherness of Chinese thought for many Western scholars since at least Niccolò Longobardi (1559–1654) during the Chinese Rites controversy, a debate over the fitness of Chinese Confucian practices and the Chinese language for an understanding of Catholic doctrine, and the inevitable role of allegory in these European interpretations of China.[18]

However different China and Europe are, the extent of that difference depends upon our frame of reference. G. E. R. Lloyd mentions that Aristotelian substance, which clashes with parts of modern physics, is in discord with aspects of Classical Chinese metaphysics that focus on processes.[19] If we take Heraclitus, however, as our referent, the differences between Eastern and Western classical thought diminishes. In the end, the differences between East and West, or at least China and ancient Greece, are less significant than the fact that "both Chinese and Greek philosophers manifest an acute interest in what we may call cosmological questions, in the origin of things and in the world in general, in the current disposition of the earth on which we live, in change and coming to be."[20] This common ground, these "common, possibly universal, human concerns," furnishes the possibility of comparison between East and West.[21]

What I will be looking at now is how Bei Dao and Hughes conceive of their literary contexts, and how they imagine links forming between their literary traditions and what I have been calling their sets of possible worlds and constellations of belief and those of other writers. I will then look at some poetry from each that calls into question the situatedness of a literary work in each's "native" tradition. Working through these questions leads to the most grandiose questions of this work, but ones that have been

---

[16] Haun Saussy, *The Problem of a Chinese Aesthetic*, Redwood, CA: Stanford UP, 1993, 6 (emphasis in the original).
[17] Ibid., 7.
[18] Ibid., 38–46.
[19] G. E. R. Lloyd, "Notes on the Framework for Comparing Science and Philosophy across Civilizations," *Journal of Chinese Philosophy* vol. 40, no. S1 (2013): 43.
[20] Ibid., 42.
[21] Ibid., 45.

latent from the very beginning: What can East and West mean, and how could they possibly interact while retaining distinct identities?

Tradition According to Bei Dao and Ted Hughes

> But, as I say, one has only to look at our vocabulary to see where our real mental life has its roots, where the paths to and from our genuine imaginations run, clearly enough. It is false to say these gods and heroes are obsolete: they are the better part of our patrimony still locked up.[22]

So says Ted Hughes in a 1964 review entitled "Asgard for Addicts" (later included in Hughes's collection *Winter Pollen*) of E. O. G. Turville-Petre's *Myth and Religion of the North*. In this brief extract are two concepts to which we should attend. The first is that of the community implied by Hughes's use of the first-person plural. Who is this "we"? It is the people living in the Britain of the 1960s. But these people of Britain are united not by residency or even citizenship alone, but at a much deeper level by kinship. They are an "Anglo-Saxon-Norse-Celtic" people who share one "blood," yet who are heir to a heterogeneous culture.[23] This is the second concept to which we must pay attention. Hughes laments that only a small portion of Nordic and Northern European myths are available in English, which is

> a pity, because this particular mythology is much deeper in us, and truer to us, than the Greek-Roman pantheons that came in with Christianity, and again with the Renaissance, severing us with the completeness of a political interdict from those other deities of our instinct and ancestral memory. It is as if we were to lose *Macbeth* and *King Lear*, and have to live on *Timon* and *Coriolanus*; or as if the vocabulary drawn wholly from the Greek-Roman branch were to take over from our Anglo-Saxon-Norse-Celtic: there's no doubt which of these alternatives belong to our blood.[24]

In Hughes's implied community, there is a "genuine" culture, one that spontaneously arises from the "blood" of the people of Britain, and there is an imposed Latinate culture. The Latinate strain in Britain, be it in "blood" or language, may have been two millennia old by the time Hughes writes, but it remains in Hughes's opinion an addition to the British self, being that it is not Angle, Saxon, Norman, Celtic, or any of the strains he singles out as fundamental to British identity. And this appears to create multiple personae within the individual British person as embodied by the fused Latinate and Anglo-Saxon plays of Shakespeare. Here, Hughes posits a dichotomy between a genuine culture and an imposed culture that, it seems, cannot be overcome; for, if after all this time the Latinate remains foreign to Great Britain, then there is

---

[22] Ted Hughes, *Winter Pollen: Occasional Prose*, ed. William Scammell, London: Faber and Faber, 1994, 41.
[23] Ibid.
[24] Ibid., 40–41.

good reason to believe that the two will never be unified, with Greco-Roman culture being merely an additive to the "Anglo-Saxon-Norse-Celtic" blood of Hughes and his readers.

What is intriguing about Hughes's statements is that they appeared after his involvement in the *Bardo Thödol* project with Chou Wen-chung, after his intense study of comparative myth and his interest in the psychic unity of humankind. That is, even after his fierce inclination toward what we would now call "world literature," toward, to paraphrase Goethe, the best literature written by the best minds all over the world, Hughes was insisting on the ethnic and historical particularity of himself and his immediate British audience. The guiding fiction of his "imagined community"[25] remained strong despite his contact with literature and religion from around the world and his collaboration with the Chinese American composer Chou.

Toward the end of his life, Hughes would write *Shakespeare and the Goddess of Complete Being* in which he would try to bridge the gap between the Latinate and the northern European aspects of British history. I will return to this later. For the moment, let us remark that Hughes not only places himself within a clear line of descent, a clear tradition, that is not simply cultural but inherent within his very body and blood, but he places his audience, the British public, within this tradition. This tradition is total, as is the imagined community of which it is the corollary, encompassing genetics, literature, and language. As such, it prohibits a full meeting between British culture, literature, and people and anything from outside. The one will always be innate and natural, the other always something strange.

"Blood" and tradition are also mixed in Bei Dao's mind. However, his reference to "blood" is more complex than is Hughes's usage. Lucas Klein has touched on this topic in Bei Dao's poetry, and I will turn to Klein in a moment. First, I quote the first epigraph to this chapter in full:

In the last few years, there's been a certain rediscovery of tradition outside of China. [Tradition is just] like blood calling to blood: at a certain moment you're suddenly aware of it. Compared to an individual's poor powers and scanty accomplishments, the breadth and beauty of the tradition [are] like a huge wind pressing down on a tiny sail, a sailor has to know how to use the wind if the boat is going to go far. And the problem is that the tradition arises from causes as complex as those that produce the wind—you can seek them but you won't find them, you can feel them but not know them. The emphasis Chinese traditional poetry lays on imagery and poetic space is in the end our own wealth (sometimes it comes to us by twisted paths, as when we get it by way of the American Imagist school). When I do readings abroad, I sometimes feel that Li Bai, Du Fu, and Li Yu are standing right behind me. When I hear Gennady Aygi speak, I seem to sense Pasternak and Mandelstam standing behind him, not to mention Pushkin and Lermontov, even though the differences among them are very

---

[25] I am naturally borrowing this term from Benedict Anderson, though using it in a slightly modified way. For Anderson's masterful work, see *Imagined Communities: Reflections on the Origin and Spread of Nationalism*, London: Verso, 2006.

great. That's what tradition means. If we have the capability, we can enter into this tradition and enrich it; otherwise we're just failures.[26]

Each of the poets of Bei Dao's "blood"—Li Bai, Du Fu, and Li Yu—flourished during the Tang dynasty. Bei Dao's mixing of "blood" and tradition places him in a political line (Tang as ancestor to the modern Chinese state) and a racial line (Han Chinese).[27] Klein gives an illuminating reading of Bei Dao's use of wind or 風 (*feng*) as a metaphor for tradition in the Tang interview and in his poetry more widely. Though "wind" serves as a perfectly recognizable metaphor in translation, we might, either here or in Bei Dao's poetry, think of wind, or *feng*, as calling back to the origins of Chinese poetry: to the "Airs of the States" 國風 in the *Shijing*, where *feng* is not wind but a poetic genre. In Klein's words, "This is one way in which a poem can combine aesthetics translated from foreign literatures with the references translated from the Chinese literary past to place itself, via foreignization and nativization, both in world and Chinese literature at once."[28]

What complicates Bei Dao's use of the term "blood" is his reference to the Russian-Chuvash poet Gennady Aygi. Jacob Edmond has skillfully demonstrated the influence of translating Russian literature and Russian theory on Bei Dao's poetry; but what I am more concerned with is how Bei Dao imagines the networks in which "Russian" literature and "Chinese" literature are placed.[29] Just as Bei Dao feels the three Tang poets present in his psyche, so he sees "Pasternak and Mandelstam standing behind [Aygi], not to mention Pushkin and Lermontov."[30] While Boris Pasternak, Osip Mandelstam, Alexander Pushkin, and Mikhail Lermontov all wrote in Russian and were citizens of a

---

[26] Tang, "An Interview with Bei Dao," 28. I have made some minor changes from Saussy's translation. The original Chinese is: 这些年在海外对传统的确有了新的领悟。传统就像血缘的召唤一样，是你在人生某一刻才会突然领悟到的。传统博大精深与个人的势单力薄，就像大风与孤帆一样，只有懂得风向的帆才能远行。而问题在于传统就像风的形成那样复杂，往往是可望不可即，可感不可知的。中国古典诗歌对意象与境界的重视，最终成为我们的财富(有时是通过曲折的方式，比如通过美国意象主义运动)。我在海外朗诵时，有时会觉得李白、杜甫、李煜就站在我后面。-当我在听杰尔那蒂·艾基(Gennady Aygi)朗诵时，我似乎看到他背后站着帕斯捷尔那克和曼杰施塔姆，还有普希金和莱蒙托夫，尽管在风格上差异很大。这就是传统。我们要是有能耐，就应加入并丰富这一传统，否则我们就是败家子。See Zha Jianying, "Bei Dao" 北島, in *Bashi niandai fangtan lu* 八十年代訪談錄, Hong Kong: Oxford University Press, 2006, 74.

[27] Of course, just what counts as "Han" is not clear-cut. The use of the term now hides the ethnic diversity within China, both historically and actually, and owes in part to long-standing imperial ideology. For an overview of how ethnicity and identity worked in Han China itself, see Chun-shu Chang, *The Rise of the Chinese Empire: Frontier, Immigration, and Empire in Han China, 130 B.C – A.D. 15*, Ann Arbor: U of Michigan P, 2007, 249–56. For a consideration of how the process worked during the Tang, see Marc Samuel Abramson, *Ethnic Identity in Tang China*, Philadelphia: University of Pennsylvania Press, 2008, especially 150–63.

[28] Lucas Klein, *Organization of Distance: Poetry, Translation, Chineseness*, Leiden: Brill, 2018, 21.

[29] See Jacob Edmond, "Translating Theory: Bei Dao, Pasternak, and Russian Formalism," in *Chinese Poetry and Translation: Rights and Wrongs*, ed. Maghiel van Crevel and Lucas Klein, Amsterdam: Amsterdam UP, 2019, 135–57.

[30] Tang, "An Interview with Bei Dao," 28.

Russian state, each belonged to a community ethnically distinct from Aygi's. Mandelstam and Pasternak were Jewish, Pushkin part African, and Lermontov a Russian noble. None of them was of Chuvash ancestry or wrote in Chuvash. The sense in which Aygi shares "blood" with these four writers is, at first glance, less clear than it is in the case of Bei Dao and the Tang poets, or than in the case of Hughes and his "Anglo-Saxon-Norse-Celtic" brethren. Bei Dao's understanding of blood and tradition is considerably looser when he talks about Aygi than when he talks about himself. Nonetheless, the evocation of an essential sameness, a blood link, becomes a necessary correlate of Bei Dao's engagement with the past. Being part of a tradition becomes inevitable, and goes deeper than merely knowing the texts of a national canon, or making the right allusions in poetry.

When Hughes elaborated on the genealogy of the English tradition in the 1990s, he took into account the tension between communal and national meaning in "modern multi-cultural societies."[31] In "primitive groups, or in small nations that are still little more than tribal assemblies of ancient, inter-related families, where the blood link can still be felt, the conditions" for "shared group understanding" persist.[32] Hughes defines shared group understanding as "deeper shared understandings, [which emerge] through the tokens of the mythology that represents them, [and which when communicated to an audience strengthen] the unified inner life of the group."[33] In a society in which shared understandings are universal, Hughes says, such as they are among the remnants of the Hopi tribe, people "know so thoroughly the mythology of [their] system of shared understanding, which is the life of [the people]," that "nothing needs to be explained."[34]

In a "modern multi-cultural society," these groups with shared understandings become "sub-groups." The subgroup retains its language and myths, but it takes on a "second language," the language of the entire state, which "must by definition exclude the idiosyncratic shared understandings and mythologies of any of the federation's incorporated sub-groups, since it tolerates only what all can share."[35] The tension between the state and the subgroup language causes problems for the poet. The mythology of the poet's subgroup may mean nothing to a reader from a different subgroup, even though poet and reader alike speak the same language. Hughes gives the example of an American "urban poet"[36] who could not understand one of Hughes's poems because the poem focused on a wren. In the English poetic tradition, the wren is rich with connotations thanks to the fact that the wren is native to England and has featured in poems by renowned poets like John Keats and Thomas Hardy. But to the "urban poet" in America, the wren is not familiar. Hughes's poem failed to refer to anything familiar in the mythology of the urban

---

[31] Hughes, *Winter*, 311.
[32] Ibid., 310–11.
[33] Ibid., 310.
[34] Ibid., 311.
[35] Ibid.
[36] Hughes does not specify the writer's subgroup, but from the paragraph we can infer that the urban poet was Jewish American: "In Hebrew, I'm told, pretty well all birds are lumped together in one word: bird. In any case the wren was certainly no part of his mythos" (*Winter* 313).

poet's subgroup, so to the American the poem seemed senseless.[37] Were we to translate Hughes's argument into more familiar terms, we would say that, in a society with many subgroups, a person from one group may understand the reference of a word but not the sense attached to the word by the people of another group. We might say that this urban poet had no epistemic access to the literary universe in which Hughes's poem is situated.

In this essay not long before his death, Hughes has also moved away from his vision of a single English heritage. We might think that, because of his talk of modern multiculturalism, Hughes places the native English in one group and recent immigrants in other groups. In fact, Hughes says that his subgroup is that of Yorkshire. He is no longer claiming shared understanding based on the "blood" of the "Anglo-Saxon-Norse-Celtic" people. Now, his community is limited to a small region of northern England. It follows that Hughes conceives of his communal "mythology" as more particular than in "Asgard for Addicts". Consequently, problems of communication and shared understanding are not new to England or Britain but are, in Hughes's opinion, quite old, stretching back at least to the Norman invasion: "The technical form [of early English or Anglo-Saxon poetry] was brought into Britain by that pre-Conquest mingling of warrior peoples originating in Germany and Scandinavia."[38] For the Normans, the linguistic system was different:

> The King's Court, with its baronial aristocracy, held a peculiar position in England. Even after three hundred years, it still regarded itself, to some degree, as an army of occupation, racially distinct, centred on its defensive castles, still claiming rights to its ancestral possessions in France, still maintaining primary allegiance to French and Continental culture, and still, most important of all, speaking the language of superior status, the vocal code of the social and political ascendancy.[39]

To the Anglo-Saxons belongs the "two part, alliterative accentual line [that] served as a spinal column for the poetic organism that evolved among those interbreeding strains, finally emerging into the Middle English of Langland's *Piers Plowman* and of *Gawain and the Green Knight*."[40] To the aristocracy belong "strictly metrical, iambic, [and] rhymed" verses of Middle French and Italian.[41] Hughes applauds Chaucer for managing to fit the English language to these French and Italian verse forms. Chaucer was only able to accomplish this, Hughes says, because he "divined the human richness of this new double world coming to consciousness—probably because he belonged to both sides."[42] There is parity between the tension among subgroups in the modern multicultural society and the divide between Anglo-Saxons and Normans in the Middle Ages.

---

[37] Ibid., 313–14.
[38] Ibid., 366.
[39] Ibid.
[40] Ibid., 366.
[41] Ibid., 367.
[42] Ibid.

Chaucer's success did not mean the end of the divide between the two worlds of England. Hughes argues that, as the aristocracy dropped French, it made sure not to pick up "the strange Babel of English (Germanic) dialects" from the commoners; rather, the aristocracy adopted "King's English," which "had to display, as its most pronounced and obvious characteristic, that it did not derive from any corner of Englishness."[43] With the Restoration, the French model came back vigorously, and banished all remnants of the Anglo-Saxon from genteel discourse.[44] Romanticism attempted to bring it back, but failed. For Hughes this is the tragedy of English verse: the forgetting of one side of the English tradition.

Hughes's reconceptualization of English identity and the English tradition occurred as he was reconceptualizing his own identity. As Simon Armitage tells us, as Hughes aged he became more concerned with "mythologizing" himself as not simply a Yorkshire poet but a poet from the Calder Valley, even though Hughes spent the majority of his youth and adult life outside of the valley.[45] In other words, Hughes increasingly thought of himself as an outsider. The concept of "blood" in his 1964 essay, "Asgard for Addicts," guaranteed an essential sameness for all people in England. For this Hughes, if everyone shares the same blood then everyone has the same underlying identity. Consequently, regional differences are secondary: distinctions between a person from Manchester and one from Cornwall are obviated because both people are of Anglo-Saxon-Norse-Celtic blood. But later Hughes came to assert his difference from his English peers. Neil Roberts, discussing Hughes's time at Cambridge, notes that critics generally assume that,

> as one of a minority of working-class grammar-school boys [Hughes] was alienated from the social environment of the university; he hated the academic study of literature, which stifled his creativity, and therefore switched to Archaeology and Anthropology for the final year of his degree; despite publishing nothing under his own name while at Cambridge he had a reputation as a poet.[46]

Roberts contends that this "narrative constitutes a 'myth' of the creative individual struggling in a hostile academic environment: a romantic myth that suits Hughes' image as a poet" but which was largely exaggerated or "demonstrably untrue."[47] He finds that Hughes was admitted to Cambridge with a prestigious scholarship, did well studying literature, had friends from public schools, appeared happy, and published poems in small literary journals. The idea of Hughes as a Byronic force "at odds with the literary establishment" emerged later in Hughes's life and, Roberts says, is not an accurate description

---

[43] Ibid.
[44] Ibid., 370.
[45] Simon Armitage, "The Ascent of Ted Hughes: Conquering the Calder Valley," in *Ted Hughes: From Cambridge to Collected*, ed. Mark Wormald, Neil Roberts, and Terry Gifford, London: Palgrave Macmillan, 2013, 6–7.
[46] Neil Roberts, "Ted Hughes and Cambridge," in *Ted Hughes: From Cambridge to Collected*, ed. Mark Wormald, Neil Roberts, and Terry Gifford, London: Palgrave Macmillan, 2013, 17.
[47] Ibid.

of Hughes's undergraduate career.[48] Over time, Hughes's sense of his identity became increasingly narrow, just as his idea of Britain was broken down into a set of organic subgroups. And as Hughes's belief that he had to compromise his subgroup identity to communicate with other members of his nation or of the Anglosphere took shape, he made this problem central to the entire English literary tradition. Consequently, as Hughes's conception of a common English blood declined, his notion of conflict within the English tradition increased. He lost, that is, the sense of harmony implied by Bei Dao's definition of tradition as "blood calling to blood."

So far I have considered tradition in isolation, by which I mean I have discussed how Bei Dao and Hughes understood a tradition to be constituted but not how traditions interact with one another. I have touched on this with Hughes's investigation of the role of French and Continental poetry on English literature. But in that example, tradition is identifiable with a certain group, the Normans, who had taken up residence in Britain and was subsequently absorbed into what we now call the English people. In this case, the experience of a foreign tradition is inseparable from the physical existence of a group of people; and the mingling of the French and Continental models with the Anglo-Saxon *is* the mingling of the Anglo-Saxons of England with the invading Normans. But what of the modern encounter between Western European and East Asian traditions? Certainly, these encounters were driven by imperialism and war. However, the people of East Asia were not dissolved into the people of Western Europe, or vice versa, as the Normans were into the people of England. What does it mean, to put it in Bei Dao's terms, to "hear" blood calling to blood when dealing with a foreign tradition and when the "blood" is not the poet's own?

For Bei Dao, "the writer's task is to stand apart from the mainstream, and to regard it critically as well as with distrust." The contemporary writer is also a "witness to or participant in public life." The writer therefore has a "dual identity" that is "detached from and yet part of society."[49] We wonder why a writer must be part of a society yet remain skeptical of it: Of what is the writer to be skeptical? Surely the writer is not to be a skeptic for the sake of skepticism, whatever the conditions of society may be. In fact, the dual identity is a product of globalization:

> Currently, the complicity of globalization with money and power has replaced the tensions that existed between East and West during the Cold War; now, all forms of orthodox ideology are a potential threat to living an authentic life. Today's globalized world is more labyrinthine and unpredictable, and thus much more dangerous than in past decades. As such, a writer in our hyper-commodified era must be wary of so-called popular speech expressions, which feed on vulgarization emerging from the realm of entertainment. Under the flag of "democratization," the art of writing is reduced to simply a tool for profiteering. A writer must guard his multifaceted perspective, responding through his work and beyond.[50]

---

[48] Ibid., 30.
[49] Bei Dao, "Ancient enmity," *Manoa* vol. 24, no. 1 (July 2012): 3.
[50] Ibid.

The society Bei Dao describes privileges the present: instant gratification through the "infantilization" of the modern subject. Giving up his or her "authentic" subjectivity, the modern subject relies upon "the jargons of academia, business, politics, and such areas" and "the massive lingual and flotsam [that comes] from entertainment, the internet, and new media."[51] Jargon acts as a substitute for independent thought. In an economy that rewards sloganeering, the poet can easily rely on platitudes and yet become successful. This is the culture toward which Bei Dao claims the modern poet must be skeptical. What, then, is the culture to which the poet should feel connected? Considering Bei Dao's remarks on blood calling to blood, culture is a literary tradition that transcends history. Because of tradition, the poet can feel simultaneity with the poets of the past. Tradition acts as a referent for poet and audience alike. It allows the poet to communicate with his or her audience, while remaining vigilant against the desire to be popular and wealthy at all costs. Bei Dao says that many writers of his era were unable to remain steadfast in this regard:

> In other words, these artists and writers were no longer defying themselves, no longer competing against themselves. Truly, such self-defiance is the ultimate line of defense. If this defense falls, the writer simply surrenders completely to the world, follows its corrupt examples, and loses hope for salvation.[52]

Tradition, then, is an ideal that guides the poet and warns against the ready-made ideals and answers provided by mass culture.

We should historicize Bei Dao's position. The "jargon" that he rails against was an integral part of the Cultural Revolution in Mao's China. All poetry needed to point toward the glory of Mao and the inevitable victory of the proletariat. As Bei Dao puts it:

> For over three decades, since 1949, the Chinese dwelled in the dark shadow of an "official" language known as the "Maoist style." This official language restricted the content and form of people's thoughts and speech. It even tried to subvert the forms of love. In those years, words and their associations were tightly regulated, such that, for example, "sun" was always a reference to Mao Tse-tung, "red" meant revolution, and "mother" was homeland or the Communist Party. The means by which people resisted the prison-house of the official language— language that marched "in step with the executioners"—was precisely through underground modern poetry, which was able to transform and reinvigorate contemporary Chinese speech and writing.[53]

What Bei Dao does not mention is the role played by traditional Chinese poetry during this time. Haosheng Yang has observed the vicissitudes of traditional poetry in twentieth-century China. In 1919, the May Fourth Movement occurred. The movement was led by Beijing intellectuals, who protested against the government's inability to deal with

---

[51] Ibid., 3–4.
[52] Ibid., 4.
[53] Ibid., 3.

Western and Japanese imperialism and internal strife. From this came a group of writers including Lu Xun 鲁迅 (1881–1936), Zhou Zuoren 周作人 (1885–1967), Yu Dafu 郁达夫 (1896–1945), and Guo Moruo 郭沫若 (1892–1978) who remonstrated against the use of Classical Chinese in literature. Classical Chinese, also known as Literary Chinese, had been the language of Chinese literature since the 5th century BCE. This was despite the fact that Literary Chinese had been distinct from vernacular Chinese since at least the 2nd century CE. The May Fourth writers argued that Classical Chinese represented the backward and elitist Chinese culture that had fallen prey to Western and Japanese colonialism. The writers advocated imitating the West and writing literature in the vernacular so that Chinese culture could be reborn and no longer be vulnerable to colonial aggression. However, as Yang shows, each of the May Fourth writers mentioned earlier continued to write poetry in Literary Chinese. After Mao's triumph in 1949 and the crackdown on dissidents in the late 1950s, writing Classical Chinese poetry became an act of rebellion. For the later poet Nie Gannu 聂绀弩 (1903–1986), classical poetry became a way to deal with forced labor and the nightmare of the Cultural Revolution. In the span of half a decade, Classical Chinese poetry went from being retrograde to revolutionary; continuing the tradition of writing Classical Chinese poetry meant resisting the sloganeering of Maoism.[54] The universe of Classical Chinese accrued a new significance.

Even though Bei Dao does not write classical poetry, we can see why remaining close to tradition and distant from the official culture are important to him. Tradition is of course never a stable thing. It is constantly appropriated and redefined by various groups seeking to legitimize their rule or existence. Even as they persecuted practitioners of traditional poetry, Maoists claimed to be the champions of the Chinese people and of Chinese history in the face of Western and internal reactionary aggression. Yiching Wu notes that the Maoist government defined itself against the "imaginary universe of the old class—the bureaucratically codified class enemies defined mainly in terms prerevolutionary social positions."[55] "Invoking the traditional religious language of demonic invasion and the image of an ominous underworld populated by malevolent spirits," Wu writes, "discourses about old and new class enemies—each with distinct historical trajectories and structures of antagonism—became fused or confused."[56] From this invocation

---

[54] In the case of Guo Moruo, writing in Maoist jargon and classical poetry were not mutually exclusive. Yang points out that Guo "declared in the mid-1930s that he would like to be a 'slogan man' (*biaoyu ren/kouhao ren* 標語人/口號人) of the communist revolution rather than a poet who indulged in self-expression" (148). He and Mao exchanged classical poems: "While the two authors commonly followed traditional prosody's decorum, what they expressed are the typical concerns of modern Chinese authors regarding the rapid social, political, and cultural changes of the twentieth century" (182). But under Mao's rule Guo's poetry became increasingly constrained, and his Classical Chinese poems tailored to suit the contours of Maoist propaganda. See Haosheng Yang, *A Modernity Set to a Pre-Modern Tune: Classical-Style Poetry of Modern Chinese Writers*, Leiden: Brill, 2016.

[55] Yiching Wu, *The Cultural Revolution at the Margins: Chinese Socialism in Crisis*, Cambridge, MA: Harvard UP, 2014, 48.

[56] Ibid.

of traditional superstition, Mao's new elite both derived its legitimacy from and disguised its assumption of the very rigid class system it attacked.

To Maoism's version of the Chinese tradition, Bei Dao opposed his own version. Obscure poetry, or *menglong shi* 朦胧诗, arose, he claims, from "translation style":

> After the communist takeover of China, many very good writers and poets gave up writing and became professors, translators, and researchers of foreign literature, since some of them had a very good education and studied in foreign countries. They created a certain style—"translation form"—which was quite different from the official discourse. This translation form became mature just before the Cultural Revolution and formed a basis for the underground literature.[57]

Translations of Western literature enabled Bei Dao and other 1970s poets to escape the "dumb and wooden" official language. Eventually this influence became too pervasive, and Bei Dao and other Chinese poets "wanted to purify Chinese and say goodbye to this sort of translations style."[58] This modifies his later statement that "there has been a certain rediscovery of tradition outside of China." It is not simply that Bei Dao and other Chinese poets have come into touch with Chinese tradition by virtue of living in foreign countries; the rediscovery of Chinese tradition was concomitantly spurred by the surfeit of foreign influence in Chinese poetry.

We saw in Chapter Two that Hughes believed himself heir to a tradition of shamanism in English poetry that extended from Shakespeare to Yeats. Christopher Trinacty expands on this to include Hughes's treatments of Seneca and Ovid. Hughes's classical "translations were as much attempts to get at the heart of his own poetry as a conduit for another's voice."[59] In other words, Hughes came to translate the Latinate tradition into the same mythic universe of which he felt Yeats, Shakespeare, and the northern European tradition were an inextricable part. As his understanding of English tradition moved from the concept of England and Englishness as unified to one that was fragmented, and his own self as bound not to England as a whole but to a small region in Yorkshire, he laid claim to the Latin tradition from which he had previously excluded himself by virtue of his Anglo-Saxon-Norse-Celtic heritage. Yet, his interest in Ovid and Seneca was ultimately driven by his desire to understand Latin poetry as part of his personal mythic universe. In this sense, his retreat from the idea of a unified English nation did not mean that he was disinterestedly open to non-English poetry.

A year before his death, Hughes reflected on the changes in the English tradition occasioned by globalization:

> Has it modified British tradition? Well, it must have modified it one way: at least all young British poets now know that the British tradition is not the only one among the traditions

---

[57] Dan Featherston, "An Interview with Bei Dao," *University of Arizona Poetry Center Newsletter* vol. 24, no. 2 (1999), https://poetry.arizona.edu/blog/interview-bei-dao.
[58] Ibid.
[59] Christopher Trinacty, "Intertextual Translation in Ovid, Seneca, and Ted Hughes," *Classical Receptions Journal* vol. 8, no. 4, (2016): 502.

of the globe. Everything is now completely open, every approach, with infinite possibilities. Obviously the British tradition still exists as a staple of certain historically hard-earned qualities if anybody is still there who knows how to inherit them. Raleigh's qualities haven't become irrelevant. When I read Primo Levi's verse I'm reminded of Raleigh. But for young British poets it's no longer the only tradition, no longer a tradition closed in on itself and defensive.[60]

We find here the opposite of Bei Dao's idea of tradition. The tradition to which Hughes 30 years earlier believed he was tied by blood is now merely secondary. It appears powerless even to propagate itself. There are inexhaustible choices that the modern British poet can make; he or she need not even identify as British, but can be a part of as many or as few poetic traditions as desired. Even the locative identity that Hughes identified in his discussion of the genesis of the English tradition has dissolved. In this last formulation, the individual poet is in an unmediated relation with the universal.

For 30 years Hughes had worked to open English literature to foreign poetry. With Daniel Weissbort (1935–2013), he cofounded *Modern Poetry in Translation* in 1965. The journal introduced Central and Eastern European poets who were writing from the other side of the Iron Curtain including the Serbian Vasko Popa (1922–1991) and the Czech Miroslav Holub (1923–1988). It also published poets from non-Communist regimes, including Israeli poet Yehuda Amichai (1924–2000) and the French poet Yves Bonnefoy (1923–2016). The journal increasingly published and continues to publish poets from around the world, with several from China and East Asia. It is not just that Hughes acquiesced to the effects of globalism on English poetry. He actively encouraged them, and perhaps did more than any other poet in the latter half of the twentieth century to allow English readers to become acquainted with a variety of contemporary foreign poets.

Though the circumstances in China and England during the twentieth century were vastly different, there were for Bei Dao and Hughes many similarities. In both countries there was a flood of foreign literature that altered how Chinese and English were seen. In China, foreign literature was vaunted during the May Fourth Movement as an enlightened alternative model to Classical Chinese poetry. But many May Fourth writers eventually returned to Classical Chinese literature after the success of the May Fourth Movement lowered the status of traditional Chinese poetry. During the crackdowns of the 1950s and 1960s, translating and imitating foreign literature was a means to evade the strictures of the Maoist government. The success of Bei Dao and other "Misty" poets in the 1970s and 1980s, and Bei Dao's own forced exile, once again led to the overinfluence of foreign literature, and a "certain rediscovery of tradition outside of China" took place. In England, the triumph of liberalism opened England to foreign influence, both in the form of literary translations and immigrants from the Commonwealth. When Hughes wrote in the early 1960s, he could address his audience as if they all shared the same "blood" as him. He could also take for granted that the English tradition was self-generating, produced by the "Anglo-Saxon-Norse-Celtic" genetics of the English people. But his own work in introducing foreign

---

[60] Ted Hughes, Interview with Drue Heinz, "The Art of Poetry no. 71," *Paris Review* vol. 134 (1995), https://www.theparisreview.org/interviews/1669/ted-hughes-the-art-of-poetry-no-71-ted-hughes.

literature to the English public and the increase of immigrant communities with which he was in contact caused him to rethink the nature of English tradition and its value at the end of the twentieth century. For both Bei Dao and Hughes, the concept of tradition underwent several mutations in response to each poet's contact with foreign literature.

From here I will examine Bei Dao's and Hughes's efforts to integrate these foreign influences into their poetry. I will consider how this fusion of "East and West" modifies both the poet's concept of the foreign and of the native. I will attempt to show that, for both poets, it is not a question of either being cosmopolitan or being parochial; the native and the foreign exist in tandem, and a greater understanding of the one deepens the comprehension of the other.

A Chinese History of the Calder Valley

In the 1979 collection *Remains of Elmet*, Ted Hughes published "The Trance of Light." The poem is standard Hughes fare. A postindustrial setting, the Calder Valley, is suddenly overwhelmed and redeemed by premodern magic.

> The upturned face of this land
> The mad singing in the hills
> The prophetic mouth of the rain
>
> That fell asleep
>
> Under migraine of headscarves and clatter
> Of clog-irons and looms
> And gutter-water and clog-irons
> And clog-irons and biblical texts
>
> Stretches awake, out of Revelations
> And returns to itself.
>
> Chapels, chimneys, vanish in the brightening
>
> And the hills walk out on the hills
> The rain talks to its gods
> The light, opening younger, fresher wings
> Holds this land up again like an offering
>
> Heavy with the dream of a people.[61]

Hughes would later rewrite this poem as "Chinese History of Colden Water." I am first going to discuss the meaning of this poem and its relation to Hughes's idea of tradition.

---

[61] Ted Hughes, *Ted Hughes: Collected Poems*, ed. Paul Keegan, London: Faber & Faber, [2005] 2012, 459.

Then I will consider the transformations Hughes made in turning "The Trance of Light" into "Chinese History" and how the integration of China and England in the poem can deepen our understanding of East–West interactions in twentieth-century poetry.

The opening stanza of "Trance" sets up the land as Anglo-Saxon. The first lines are Yeatsian, with pantheistic overtones. The land is anthropomorphized, with a "face" and a finite body that can be "held up." The "mad singing" appears to be a direct quote from Yeats's 1922 drama *The Player Queen*, where Decima refers to her singing as "the song of the mad singing daughter of a harlot. The only song she had."[62] Decima ends up taking the place of the chaste queen at the end of the play, marking, as Otto Bohlmann argues, the reversal of the pure and the profane according to Yeats's notion of gyres.[63] The title *The Player Queen* is itself an allusion to "The Player Queen" of *Hamlet*, wherein the mad singing of Ophelia following her father's murder is well known. The line may also be yet another reference to *King Lear*, a text that, as we saw in Chapter Two, was crucial to how Hughes structured the *Bardo Thödol* opera. The reference in this case might be to the madness of Lear and the Fool upon the heath shortly before Lear's death. In each of these Shakespearean examples, mad singing is associated with the unjust deposition of a monarch and the establishment of a new order.

The old, pantheistic order here merely "falls asleep." The new order does not depose the old; it exists on top of the old. The new is a mix of technology and Christianity. Hughes signals the distance between the old and the new by breaking them into separate stanzas separated by the dependent clause "that fell asleep." He also changes the meter and the rhetoric. The first stanza is a series of trimetric and anaphoric noun phrases. The meter in the third stanza is 4-3-4-4 with several spondees, with the last two lines again anaphoric. We note that anaphora is especially associated with the book of Psalms. The use of anaphora throughout suggests the presence of Christianity in England and its conflict with pre-Christian pantheism. The anaphoric lines describe the lapse of pantheism, and reinforce the notion of struggle between the premodern and the modern, the pagan and the Christian. The repetition of "clog-irons" in the last two lines is anadiplosis, the repetition of the concluding phrase of one line at the start of the next line: "And gutter-water and *clog-irons* / And *clog-irons* and biblical texts." Anadiplosis is the first rhetorical scheme in the King James Bible: "In the beginning God created the heaven and the Earth. / And Earth was without form and void" (Gen. 1:1 and 2, KJV). The combination of anadiplosis and anaphora in stanza three mark as Christian the "migraine" that numbed the premodern elements of England. And it further encourages us to connect to Christianity the technological world that has overtaken the Calder Valley, a connection that strengthened in the sixth stanza, where "Chapels, chimneys, vanish" together "in the brightening."

We also note the use of metonymy in both the first and third stanzas. The *face* of the land and the *mouth* of the rain indicate that all aspects of nature are parts of a larger

---

[62] W. B. Yeats, *Plays in Prose and Verse: Written for an Irish Theatre, and Generally with the Help of a Friend*, London: MacMillan, 1922, 386.

[63] Otto Bohlmann, *Yeats and Nietzsche: An Exploration of Major Nietzschean Echoes in the Writings of William Butler Yeats*, London: Palgrave Macmillan, 1982, 184.

whole. To put it differently, everything we encounter in nature is like a part of a complete anatomy. But where nature is whole, the technological world is fragmented. Headscarves, clog-irons, looms, and biblical texts are all products of technology, especially if we think of texts in the context of the printing press. The products are listed and duplicated. They are placed beside one another, yet not unified by an overarching concept as the rain and the land are by nature. Metonymy in the first stanza points toward unification, whereas in the third stanza it indicates incoherence.

Stanza five gives us, at last, the predicate we have been awaiting since the first stanza. "The upturned face of this land / The mad singing in the hills / The prophetic mouth of the rain" now "stretches awake." The use of the third-person singular for the verb tells us that the land, singing, and rain are to be taken as one entity. The present tense of the verb also comes as a surprise; it is not that the pantheistic world is located in the past; rather, it is the "migraine" of technology that is past. The old world is in fact the world of the now. It is eternally present. That nature awakens from "Revelations / And returns to itself" shows that Hughes is recasting Christianity. Just as Revelations tells of the end of time and the return of humanity to its essence in God, so Hughes's poem tells of a nature that exists outside of time and the return of nature to its pretechnological state. We can say that Hughes's attack is not on Christianity per se—and Christianity has, after all, not fared well during the modern era—but on the mass production of religious verse. The religiosity that Hughes favors is revealed. The "rain talks to its gods." This is not religion mediated by scripture disseminated en masse, but direct communion with the divine. Hughes thus feels enabled to mix the pantheistic with the overt Christian imagery of the "wings" of light.

The final two lines are not anaphoric but alliterative. Hughes has changed the biblical scheme for the scheme most closely identified with Anglo-Saxon and Skaldic verse. In these alliterated lines we encounter "people." Not people in general, or "the people" of a state, but "a people." "A people" means one among many, and returns to Hughes's early declaration that the English people are a uniquely Anglo-Saxon-Norse-Celtic people. This group of people could also more narrowly be those of the Calder Valley. It is now they who sleep, "dream" of an "offering" made of the land spoiled by technology. That is, the restoration of nature in the Calder Valley appears to be the innate desire of its residents. There is a deep-rooted link between land and people.

"Trance of Light" accords with the axioms Hughes set down in 1964. People are bound by blood and by place. Blood and place are eternal, primary traits to which technology and the emergence of Christianity are secondary. Thus, the disappearance of technology and the reconfiguration of religion do not fundamentally change the people who live in the valley. That epoch was, after all, only a moment in the life of the land. The people exist so long as the land does. In this light, nature is supreme over culture.

Given this, why would Hughes change "The Trance of Light" into "Chinese History of Colden Water"? I will present the revised poem, then consider what Hughes has changed and what he has altered.

A fallen immortal found this valley—
Leafy conch of whispers
On the shore of heaven. He brought to his ear

> The mad singing in the hills,
> The prophetic mouth of the rain -
>
> These hushings lulled him. So he missed
> The goblins toiling up the brook.
> The clink of fairy hammers forged his slumber
>
> To a migraine of head-scarves and clatter
> Of clog-irons and looms, and gutter water
> And clog-irons and biblical texts.
>
> Till he woke in a terror, tore free, lay panting.
> The dream streamed from him. He blinked away
> The bloody matter of the Cross
> And the death's head after-image of 'Poor'.
>
> Chapels, chimneys, roofs in the mist—scattered.
> Hills with raised wings were standing on hills.
> They rode the waves of light
> That rocked the conch of whispers
>
> And washed and washed at his eye.
>   Washed from his ear
> All but the laughter of foxes.[64]

The word "trance" denotes a state of dread, a swoon or a cataleptic state, a state between sleeping and waking, ecstasy (OED). Hughes may have any or all of these meanings in mind as he wrote "The Trance of Light"; yet in the rewritten version the ontology of the ecstatic vision becomes questionable. In the original, the genuineness of the vision is presumed. The rhetoric of the poem accentuates the religiosity of the scene and makes the disappearance of technology a rapturous event. Moreover, the vision appears unmediated. Yes, we are looking at the "dream of a people," but we are given no reason to doubt the validity of that dream. Hughes, lifelong admirer of Yeats and Carl Jung, gives us direct access to the collective unconscious of the people of the Calder Valley. In this way, Hughes presents the scene as a morally just reclamation of nature, and indeed human nature, from the ravages of postindustrial modernity.

In "Chinese History," the dream element is amplified. We no longer find a land that falls asleep or a people who dream, but a Chinese immortal who enters a trance. Furthermore, the vision does not come from the immortal's unconscious, as a dream does. A "leafy conch" communicates the vision to the Chinese immortal. Whereas the origins of the vision are unquestioned in "Trance", here they have a material origin. Additionally, only the modern

---

[64] Hughes, *Collected Poems*, 738–39.

aspects of the original vision appear in the immortal's dream. The salvation of the land comes after we read that the immortal "woke in a terror, tore free, lay panting." Everything is now narrated in the past rather than the present tense. The transcendent time, the eternal now in which the land of the original poem lives, is now historicized. We have, in other words, a magical history rather than a divine vision, and the layers of mediation—the conch shell, the Chinese immortal, the narrator—conspire to make us aware of our distance from the events in the poem.

Gone are the "gods" and the anthropomorphized land and rain. Gone too is the "mad singing in the hills." Nothing can come back "to itself out of Revelations." The "hills" remain from the first poem, but now they have the "wings" that previously belonged to the "waves of light," and rather than having "hills walk out on hills" Hughes has hills "standing on hills." Though these are still hills with human characteristics, their human qualities are less pronounced: while the idea of hills walking on top of one another cannot be rationalized according to any common experience we have of hills or any other natural formation, the image of "hills standing on hills" could be a metaphor for hills rising behind hills, a commonplace image. The humanization of nature and the accentuation of a premodern, pantheistic bond between the residents of Calder Valley and the valley itself are less pronounced in the rewrite.

Finally, we notice that Hughes has altered his attitude toward Christianity. He no longer employs anadiplosis. The three lines of anaphora that start "The Trance of Light" have disappeared, as have the final two alliterative verses. Hughes has added "the Bloody matter of the cross / And the death's head after image of Poor." This implies a link between the poverty of the valley and organized religion. But, as we saw, pantheism is no longer offered as a natural alternative in "Chinese History." In "Trance," the residents of the Calder Valley are persecuted by technology and organized religion. The people's salvation comes when chapels and chimneys "vanish in the brightening." In "Chinese History," the people appear to be part of the problem. We read, "Chapels, chimneys, roofs in the mist—scattered." To the metonyms of religion and industry are added the generic "roofs," which could include the homes of the residents of the valley. The people appear complicit in the destruction of nature. This implies that the people of Calder Valley lack the essential innocent Anglo-Saxon-Norse-Celtic premodern identity that Hughes gave them in 1964 and played upon in "Trance." Further, the chapels, chimneys, and roofs do not "vanish" but are "scattered." The apocalyptic scene does not purify the land for eternity, but rather casts out that which is responsible for the postindustrial condition of the valley. Once more, the finality of the vision of "Trance" is undercut in "Chinese History." An exile can, after all, always return if there is a change in the land from which he or she was exiled.

Hughes leaves us with an enigmatic conclusion. Keith Sagar interprets "Chinese History" as the hope that modern civilization will pass as if "no more than the nightmare of a stranded immortal who will eventually wake to a world cleansed of humans."[65] Terry Gifford sees the conch as an indication of the "idyllic" preindustrial Calder Valley.[66] For

---

[65] Keith Sagar, *The Laughter of Foxes: A Study of Ted Hughes*, Liverpool: Liverpool UP, 2006, 168.
[66] Terry Gifford, "'Dead Farms, Dead Leaves.' Culture as Nature in Remains of Elmet & Elmet," in *Ted Hughes: Alternative Horizons*, ed. Joanny Moulin, London: Routledge, 2004, 27.

Gifford, the "laughter of foxes" is not to be separated from the "laughter of humans." Hughes does not believe that all human tendencies are bad, Gifford suggests, and the laughing foxes are an invitation to return to more harmonious relationship between man and nature, to that idyllic preindustrial valley that also contained humans.[67] As cogent as both critics' observations are, they take a limited reading of the final line. In truth, there are several elements in "Chinese History" that owe to Hughes's 35-year interaction with Chinese thought. Hughes owned many books on Chinese folktales including a copy of *Traditional Chinese Stories: Themes and Variations*, a seminal textbook discussing the motifs of Chinese fiction. Surely he would have been aware when writing a poem entitled "Chinese History of Colden Water" that foxes have an important supernatural function in Chinese letters. The Chinese fox spirit is invariably a woman, part of the overarching theme of the "supernatural maiden." Joseph S. M. Lau, one of the editors of *Traditional Chinese Stories: Themes and Variations*, instructs that the supernatural maiden is "usually an animal" that takes on "a human form after hundreds of years of self-cultivation in supernatural magic."[68] The maiden always falls in love with a young man, and this giving into her human side leads to her death. Perhaps because she is originally a part of nature, the maiden adheres much more to the moral codes of society than do normal human women. Regardless, because she is not human, she is almost always punished with death or reversion to her animal form. Only in P'u Sung-ling's *Liao Chai Chih-i* does the marriage between man and fox lead to uninterrupted conjugal bliss.[69] I am suggesting that, thanks to his amateur study of Chinese literature, Hughes's familiar fox motif has been partly Sinicized. This is still the English fox that bears witness to the ravages of industry, but it has accrued additional significance to which we must attend.

But the most important text to which Hughes alludes is the *Bardo Thödol*. Even though the *Bardo* is not Chinese, the *Bardo* filters Hughes's vision of China. Take the "leafy conch." In the Walter Evans-Wentz translation of the *Bardo*, the conch is mentioned as one of the instruments of the Tibetan death ceremony. Referring to a Tibetan illustration of a deceased man prepared for his passage through the Bardo Thödol, Evans-Wentz writes:

> Among other embellishments added by the artist are a sacred mirror (symbolizing form or body, which it reflects) near the trees on the left, and a sacred conch-shell trumpet of victory over the Sangsära (symbolizing sound) near the tree on the right; and, between the two Buddhas at the bottom, in two caves, yogīs, or holy men, in the Tibetan wilderness.[70]

---

[67] Ibid., 31.
[68] Joseph S. M. Lau and Y. W. Ma, *Traditional Chinese Stories: Themes and Variations*, Boston: Cheng & Tsui Co, 1986, 337.
[69] Ibid.
[70] Walter Evans-Wentz, P. Sambhava, P. Sangay, and C. G. Jung, *The Tibetan Book of the Great Liberation: Or the Method of Realizing Nirvana Through Knowing the Mind*, Oxford: Oxford UP, 1968, xxix.

The "sacred conch-shell trumpet of victory" is a familiar Buddhist symbol. It is used as a musical instrument in Tibetan drama and ritual to signify "auspicious moments."[71] In Chinese Buddhism there is the "Conch of the Law" (法螺 *faluo*). This conch is "a symbol of the universality, power, or command of the Buddha's teaching."[72] The conch has special significance in part because it resembles the curled or spiral-shaped hair of the Buddha in art.[73] The auspiciousness of the conch helps the departed soul through the trials of the Bardo as it is blown at the dead person's bedside.[74] These holy properties are what Hughes has in mind.

We observe this again in the location of the leafy conch in the poem: on the "shore of heaven." Planes of existence in Buddhism may be referred to as "shores." For instance, there is the "shore of nirvana" and the "shore of mortality."[75] In the Chou-Hughes *Bardo* discussed in Chapter Two, the Reader of the *Bardo* cautions Solo, the departed soul:

Balang-Chod has wealth walking as tall shining horses by water,
And their manes unfold abundance.
But be restrained:
It is a land
Without religion.[76]

In the Evans-Wentz translation of the *Bardo* from which Hughes drew material for his libretto, Balong-chod is described as "a lake adorned with horses, male and female, [grazing on its shores]."[77] On the same page, the Evans-Wentz translation mentions "the Northern Continent of Daminyan, a lake adorned with male and female cattle, [grazing on its shores], or trees, [round about it], will be seen."[78] Given Hughes's deep familiarity with Evans-Wentz's translation, we conclude that Hughes knew the significance of "shore" as a metaphor in Tibetan and Chinese Buddhism.[79]

---

[71] Alison Arnold, ed., "Himalayan Region," in *Garland Encyclopedia of World Music Volume 5—South Asia: The Indian Subcontinent*, London: Routledge, 1999, 345, 363.

[72] William Edward Soothill and Lewis Hodous, *A Dictionary of Chinese Buddhist Terms: With Sanskrit and English Equivalents and a Sanskrit-Pali Index*, London: Routledge Curzon, 2004, 272.

[73] Ibid., 462.

[74] The ritual surrounding the dead and the passage through the Bardo is discussed in detail in Chapter Two.

[75] Ibid., 250.

[76] Ted Hughes, *Bardo Thödol*. TS. Box 116, folder 2. Emory University, 23.

[77] Evans-Wentz, Sambhava, Sangay, and Jung, *Tibetan Book*, 516.

[78] Ibid.

[79] In Hughes's library is the Hawkes's translation of arguably the most famous Chinese classical novel, the *Hongloumeng* (紅樓夢). The novel is the story of a magical stone that has become a child of an aristocratic Chinese family. In its latest state, the stone sits on "the other shore," the shore of the afterlife, much as Hughes's conch lies on the "shore of heaven." The novel mixes historical and religious genres, and is famous for its multiple comments on the inextricability of truth and untruth in fiction and in human experience broadly. Hughes acquired this book after he wrote "Trance" but before "Chinese History." Regardless of whether the leafy conch and the shore refer to the stone and the shore of the *Hongloumeng*, the book was yet another occasion for Hughes to become acquainted with a variety of tropes related to Buddhism and

The mention of the conch and the shore of heaven tell us that Hughes is not lightly playing on Oriental tropes. Rather, he has made the cosmology of "Chinese History" agree with that which he has learned from study of the *Bardo*, the religion of Tibetan Bon, and Chinese Buddhism. What is remarkable is that Hughes has made this foreign material central to a poem that originally took Hughes's conception of a specifically English character and spirituality as its spiritual compass. Not only did Hughes's study of the *Bardo* come to inform his conception of Chinese religion, that Sino-Tibetan mix was used to sculpt an alternative history of his native Calder Valley. In this history, technology, organized religion, and indigenous folk beliefs have failed. They have been scattered, banished from the Valley. In their place arises a Buddhist cosmology. The change coincides with Hughes's changing definition of Englishness and the English tradition. When he wrote "Chinese History," he no longer believed in a coherent pan-British or pan-English identity. He began to conceive of Englishness as composed of several subgroups, of which his Calder Valley was one. Yet in "Chinese History" even the Calder Valley subgroup is impotent to redress the damage caused by industry. Therefore, Hughes calls upon Buddhism and the *Bardo*, and suggests that the valley may be reborn, with a conch shell announcing an auspicious rebirth. Buddhism functions as a path to a new beginning that elides the categories of Englishness that Hughes had previously set. It is fitting, then, that that which announces the rebirth of the Calder Valley should be the "laughter of foxes," the laughter of an animal central to English and Chinese literature. This fusion of East and West, however, comes at the price of humanity itself. That is, only by "scattering" the particulars of religion, culture, and people themselves—"Chapels, chimneys, roofs"—can this Buddhist recasting of Calder Valley be achieved. Ultimately, "Chinese History" is not a total reconciliation of East and West; the people who embody subgroups of East and West are done away with before the reconciliation can take place.

Bei Dao, Finding China as an Exile

Bei Dao's fame originated in the late 1970s with his role in the so-called *menglong shi* (朦朧詩) or misty or "obscure poetry" movement. A derogatory term chosen by critics of the movement, "misty poetry" sprung from Bei Dao's literary journal *Jintian* (今天) or *Today*, which ran from 1978 to 1980. Aside from Bei Dao, other famous "Misty" poets include Shu Ting 舒婷 (1952–), Yang Lian 楊 (1955–), and Duoduo 多多 (1951–). "Emphasizing polyvalent imagery, and irregular syntax," Chee Lay Tan explains, "Misty poetry engendered a multiplicity of meanings, often leading to interpretational indeterminacy."[80] "Indeterminacy" was important to the Misty poets because they emerged

---

Chinese literature that are present in "Chinese History." See Cao Xueqin, Gao E, and John Minford, *The Story of the Stone: A Chinese Novel in Five Volumes*, Volume I, trans. David Hawkes, New York: Penguin, 1973.

[80] Chee Lee Tan, *Constructing a System of Irregularities: The Poetry of Bei Dao, Yang Lian, and Duoduo*, Newcastle: Cambridge Scholars Publishing, 2016, 2.

during and just after the Cultural Revolution. Rejecting the fixed literary horizons of Maoism, Bei Dao and his peers introduced into Chinese poetry a polysemy without precedent.[81]

Tan has surveyed the reception of Misty poetry. In its early years, the Misty poets provoked the ire of the Chinese establishment:

> In general, the fury of orthodox critiques targeted Misty poetry's thematic opaqueness, which was seen as an ideological challenge to the dominant Maoist obsession with clarity and simplicity of meaning. In fact, the latter's covert motive was to limit the individual's control over his own interiority, and to undermine the writer's literary subjectivity, which has become a defense of both the autonomy of literature and human subjectivity against Mao's antihumanist injunctions an observation proposed by scholars such as Liu Zaifu.[82]

Preoccupied with the intangible and the "existential," Misty poets were labeled as "elitist" and reactionary.[83] While the Chinese establishment disliked Misty poetry, foreign critics have also attacked Bei Dao's work. Some, of course, have praised Bei Dao. Stephen Owen, for instance, draws a line between Chinese poetry meant for consumption abroad and that meant for appreciation in China, and favorably contrasted Bei Dao with Nobel Prize winner Gao Xingjian.[84] But Owen's praise of Bei Dao in 2003 partly reverses his earlier criticism of the Chinese poet. In his 1990 review of an English translation of *The August Sleepwalker* 八月的夢旅者, Owen charged that Bei Dao was currying favor with Western audiences "by writing a supremely translatable poetry" that uses images that have no particular attachment to China. As "international" poetry, Bei Dao's verse "achieves moments of beauty, but it does not have a history, nor is it capable of leaving a trace that might constitute a history."[85] This for Owen is bland literature that can fit in anywhere but be preeminent nowhere.

Tan in turn criticizes Owen. Considering that Bei Dao wrote the poems of *The August Sleepwalker* between 1970 and 1986, Tan argues that Bei Dao could not "have hoped to have [these poems] translated." He mentions that Owen's criticism aligns with W. J. F. Jenner's. Jenner too dismissed Bei Dao because Bei Dao broke with the conventions of Classical Chinese poetry and wrote in what Jenner considered degraded post–Cultural Revolution style. Tan writes:

> Owen and Jenner's accusations subscribe to a Western belief in a "monolithic China and Chinese language," created under the imagination of exotic Chineseness that Bei Dao avoids. The greater concept of "Chinese identity" or a totalizing supra-nationalism is so associated with the Chinese official discourse that Bei Dao has had to consciously escape its discourse.[86]

---

[81] Ibid., 15.
[82] Ibid., 16.
[83] Ibid., 17.
[84] Stephen Owen, "Stepping Forward, Stepping Back: Issues and Possibilities for 'World' Poetry,'" in *World Literature in Theory*, ed. David Damrosch, New Jersey: Wiley Blackwell, 2014, 245–59.
[85] Stephen Owen, "What Is World Poetry?" *New Republic* vol. 203, no. 21 (1990): 32.
[86] Tan, *Constructing*, 23.

I have already pointed out Bei Dao's own opinions on his Chinese identity. Regarding Bei Dao's early poetry, Tan is correct. Bei Dao was trying to escape the dominance of Maoist poetics. The vagueness of his early poetry is a consequence of the strictures of Maoism, which required that all poetry point to the glory of Mao and the inevitable victory of the Chinese proletariat. On the other hand, Tan overlooks the change that Bei Dao says he underwent while in exile. Once abroad, Bei Dao's circumstances changed, and along with them changed his perception of himself and his poetry. In exile Bei Dao "rediscovered" his Chinese identity. Any appreciation of Bei Dao's poetry as a whole has to take this change into account. We must take into account not only the Bei Dao who lived under Mao or who wrote in the era of 改革開放 (*gaige kaifang*), the 1980s period of "Reform and Opening Up" in Deng Xiaoping's China, nor only the Bei Dao who lived in America and Europe and taught at American universities as, in Dian Li's words, an ostensible "citizen of the world."[87] We must also keep in mind the Bei Dao who returned to Hong Kong and spoke of tradition as being like "blood beckoning blood."

What I want to do is see how Bei Dao's increasing awareness of his Chinese identity is manifested in his exile poetry. I aim to discover how Bei Dao's changing circumstances and places of residence affect the range of his identity. Is his identity dual? Plural? Or are all the experiences he has and materials he works with integrated into a univocal identity? In the end, I hope to see better what it means to be "Chinese" or "Western" in the era of globalization and "world literature." I will be drawing upon various previous critiques of Bei Dao, especially Owen's and Tan's, but I will distance myself from the recurrent argument that, because Bei Dao became an exile, his poetry, in Tan's phrasing, possesses "the ability to transcend cultural and national specificities."[88]

Bei Dao's poetry is hermetic. As Dian Li puts it, "The unending displays of paradoxes, whose power comes from an imaginative reordering of things and events, forms a key aspect of Bei Dao's poetic world."[89] Tan notes that Bei Dao often pairs "contradictory properties" to create ellipses.[90] For both Li and Tan, this opacity is a method by which Bei Dao attempts to express his alienation from society. Reading Bei Dao's 1983 *Notes from the City of the Sun* 太阳城札记, Tan notices the recurrence of "city-related objects such as street lights, railings, traffic lights, and nature-related images such as a valley, clouds, mist, sun, moon, stars, sea, river banks, far horizons, reefs, storms, shores, and shadow."[91] In translation, each of these images is generic. There is nothing especially Chinese about the moon or shadows; after all, they appear in the English poetic tradition already. Hence Owen's complaint:

> Success in creating a "world poetry" is not without its costs. Bei Dao has, by and large, written international poetry. Local color is used, but sparsely. Nor is such truly international

---

[87] Dian Li, "Paradox and Meaning in Bei Dao's Poetry," *Positions: East Asia Cultures Critique* vol. 15, no. 1 (2007): 115.
[88] Tan, *Constructing*, 92.
[89] Li, "Paradox," 116.
[90] Tan, *Constructing*, 83.
[91] Ibid., 74–75.

poetry merely the achievement of the translator, skillful as she is: most of these poems translate themselves. These could just as easily be translations from a Slovak or an Estonian or a Philippine poet. It could even be a kind of American poetry, though in this final hypothesis a question arises that must trouble us. If this had been an American poet writing in English, would this book have been published, and by such a prestigious press? We must wonder if such collections of poetry in translation become publishable only because the publisher and the readership have been assured that the poetry was lost in translation. But what if the poetry wasn't lost in translation? What if this is it?[92]

What Owen misses is that the interpretation of Bei Dao's poetry may vary between readers from Chinese and non-Chinese audiences. Dian Li suggests that paradox in Bei Dao is a direct descendent of paradox in Daoism. In Daoism, paradox points to the necessity of opposition. In the *Daodejing* 道德经, for example, we read: "When the people of the world all know beauty as beauty, / There arises the recognition of ugliness. / When they all know the good as good, / There arises the recognition of evil" (天下皆知美之為美，斯惡已。皆知善之為善，斯不善已).[93] Identity here is necessarily oppositional. Good and evil, beauty and ugliness, "Being and non-being produce" and then "complete each other."[94] Were these oppositions to be reconciled, both sides of the antagonism would cease to exist. Good could never triumph over evil, for a good without evil would have no sense. This gives rise to an intuitive philosophy. Because paradox is fundamental to human knowledge and identity, true knowledge, knowledge of the *Dao*, cannot be communicated in words. On the contrary, knowledge comes in flashes of inspiration, as in Zen (Chan) Buddhist koans. Li contends that we should understand Bei Dao's poetry as a part of this tradition; Li further argues that there are many images and illusions in Bei Dao's work that will resonate with Chinese people who are familiar with the sights and sounds of the Chinese city. Non-Chinese will not grasp these allusions purely because they have not walked repeatedly through the streets, for instance, of Beijing and seen the sites Bei Dao has in mind. According to this argument, Bei Dao's Chinese identity reveals itself obliquely, not through citing Classical Chinese literature or loudly proclaiming an interest in modern Chinese affairs, but by alluding to specific ideas and images that will resonate best with a Chinese audience.

The flaw here is that Li assumes a single Chinese audience which will inevitably resonate with Bei Dao's work, much as Bei Dao believes himself ineluctably drawn to the greatest poets of the Tang dynasty. But what if we take a translation one of those seemingly unproblematically traditional Tang poems and open it up to the same analysis given to Bei Dao? The poem is 初月, "New Moon," with David Hinton's 2019 translation to its side.

---

[92] Owen, "'World' Poetry," 31.
[93] The translation is from Wing-tsit Chan, *A Source Book in Chinese Philosophy*, Princeton: Princeton UP, 1963, 163; the original is found in Laozi, *Laozi quan yi*, Di 1 ban, ed. Shaohai Sha and Zihong Xu, Guizhou: Renmin chuban she, 1989, 3.
[94] Chan, *A Sourcebook*, 140.

光細弦豈上，	Thin slice of ascending light, radiant arc
影斜輪未安。	tipped aside bellied dark—the first moon
微升古塞外，	appears and, barely risen beyond ancient
已隱暮雲端。	frontier passes, edges into clouds. Silver,
河漢不改色，	changeless, the Star River spreads across
關山空自寒。	mountains empty in their own cold. Lucent
庭前有白露，	frost dusts the courtyard, chrysanthemum
暗滿菊花團。	blossoms clotted there with swollen dark.[95]

Note briefly that the poem contains the same apparently generic images—clouds, moons, mountains—that populate Bei Dao's poetry. Explaining his translation, Hinton, in a fashion that would bring a smile to Ezra Pound's face, highlights the significance of the pictorial quality of the Chinese title: 初, he says, is usually translated in this context to mean "new moon"; but a new moon can never be a crescent, and all of Du Fu's subsequent commentators seem simply to have gotten it wrong: the title should be "First Moon," and the substance about how through the "assemblage of things, reality appears as a single tissue—that magically generative source-tissue of Tao or Absence—within which the moon was not regarded as a bright distillation of, or embryonic origin of, *ch'i*-tissue."[96] He advises us to look at the radicals of 初, cloth 衣 and blade 刀, which ties with a "more primitive meaning" of 初, "of form cut from shapeless cloth."[97] Having made this connection, Hinton is free to say that the poem is about meaning-making and emblematic of "the mirror-deep perceptual dimensions of empty-mind that shape a typical Chinese poem with its focus on Ch'an-imagist clarity."[98] Hinton then joins Pound on his journey back to the Tang dynasty, although Pound's intolerance of Buddhism would perhaps have put him squarely at odds with Hinton's reading.[99]

My point in raising Hinton's translation and rather ingenious commentary is not to give a final word on Tang poetry. On the contrary, I wish to show how open such poetry is to different arrangements. If Hinton is convinced that Du Fu's poetry is ultimately Daoist and Chan Buddhist poetry, Lucas Klein, surveying other Du Fu's works, notes that Du Fu translates Buddhism, and the regulated verse that it brought with it into China, out of its Sanskrit origins and nativizes it as a peculiarly Chinese system and poetic form. In Klein's words, "by writing history in a form whose origins Victor Mair and Tsu-lin Mei asserted were 'equivalent to "Buddhist verse,' Du Fu is also historicizing Buddhism, bringing it into the Chinese conception of the historical along with the other representations of the foreign."[100]

---

[95] Hinton, *Awakened*, 58–59.
[96] Ibid., 61.
[97] Ibid., 60.
[98] Ibid., 61.
[99] For more on Pound's loathing of Buddhism and Daoism, see, most immediately, Canto 54: "war, taxes, oppression / backsheesh, taoists, Buddhists / war, taxes, oppressions." For a discussion of how these schools of thought influence Pound regardless, see Zhaoming Qian, "Ezra Pound's Encounter with Wang Wei: Toward the 'Ideogrammic Method' of The Cantos," *Twentieth Century Literature* vol. 39, no. 3 (October 1, 1993): 266–82.
[100] Klein, *Organization of Distance*, 181.

There are agreements between Klein and Hinton. Klein too highlights the Buddhist elements of Du Fu, only Klein is more interested in how Du Fu participated in making Buddhism and regulated verse ostensibly native elements of the Chinese canon by crossing them with Confucian sensibility. There is a subtle but important difference between Du Fu the Daoist/Chan Buddhist poet-sage and Du Fu the poet interested in Buddhism but aware of the compromises that must be made in translation.

The debate over Du Fu's poetry, beliefs, and indeed his "Chineseness" take us back to Bei Dao. Found in his most recent collection of poetry, Bei Dao's "Salt" (盐; yán) takes as its subject a poor industrial town. The poem ruminates on the photographer Chin-San Lang's 郎静山 *Saltworks* 盐厂.[101]

底片上暗夜的煤
变成人们每日的盐
一只鸟获得新高度
那些屋顶的补丁
让大地更完美

on the negative dark night's coal
turns into the people's daily salt
a bird attains new heights
patches of roofs
make the earth more perfect.[102]

We notice that, as in Hughes's "Chinese History" and "Trance of Light," there are no humans in the scene. Without the mediation of a worker, the coal "turns into the people's daily salt." The coal of course is the fuel for the factory. The couplet opposes energy to sustenance, night to day, and, in the image of the coal and the salt, black to white. The third line does not logically follow from the first two nor lead to the next couplet. It is a metaphor for the perspective of the photographer, whose picture gives a bird's-eye view of the saltwork. The "new heights" are the new relations between technology, art, and humans. Technology seems to become naturalized, and nature turned into technology. The camera becomes a bird, the factory runs autonomously. So in the final couplet "patches of roofs / make the earth more perfect." The naturalization of technology has made it so technology and nature are not in opposition. Or more precisely the opposition between technology and nature is now necessary. As in Daoism, the shabby factory roofs

---

[101] The scene Bei Dao describes was captured not only in "Saltworks" but in several of Lang's photos, for instance in the 1934 "Huaxi Salt Well" (華溪鹽井, *huaxi yanjing*). This Huaxi is located in Hunan province. Regardless of the photo, the following discussion of what the photograph can image versus what Bei Dao's interpretation brings to the scene would be the same.

[102] Bei Dao, 時間的玫瑰 (*The Rose of Time*), ed. Eliot Weinberger, trans. David Hinton, Bonnie S. MacDougall, and Eliot Weinberger, New York: New Directions Publishing Corporation, 2009, 256–57. Subsequent references to this work will be in-text and use the abbreviation *Rose*.

bring out the "perfection" (完美 *wanmei*) of the earth. The beauty of nature appears more beautiful because the roofs act as a foil. But the opposition also suggests a contrast between nature as it is and nature as it is perceived. "Perfection" is absolute; nothing can become more perfect. However, we can better perceive the perfection of nature through contrast. So to Bei Dao the roofs make nature appear "more perfect" (更完美 *geng wanmei*).[103] This is not so much a paradox as an elliptical way of indicating a change in perspective.

The atmosphere changes slightly in the second stanza:

烟高于树
正来自根的记忆
模仿着大雪
时间展示它的富足
从呼喊的盲井
溢出早晨的悲哀

smoke higher than the trees
it comes from the memory of roots
imitating a heavy snow
time displays its affluence
the blind wells of calling
spill over with morning's sorrow (*Rose* 256–57)

The opposition between nature and industry has turned to competition. The smoke rises *higher* than the trees and *imitates* a heavy snowfall. Smoke and snow are further tied together through their placement at the beginning and ending of the sentence.[104] Yet this makes their dissimilarity more apparent. Smoke rises as the emission of a salt refinery, while snow falls as natural precipitation; the former obscures the atmosphere while the latter covers the ground; smoke is associated with waste and opacity, while snow with purity. Smoke and snow are certainly not opposites. In the context of the poem, however, they do have a tense relationship, the one attempting to usurp the place of the other. The smoke comes from "the memory of roots," roots perhaps covered up by the snow. Taken together, the smoke and the snow form a single veil, blurring that which occurs above ground and that which is underfoot.

We cannot help but think of the massive industrialization of the Great Leap Forward, or of the "rehabilitation" of "reactionaries" during the Mao years, to accomplish which millions of Chinese citizens, including Bei Dao himself, were uprooted from their lives and sent to work on farms and industrial sites throughout the country. This massive

---

[103] *Wanmei* literally means "fully" or "completely beautiful," but signifies the perfect or ideal. The equivalent of the verb "to perfect" is 完善 (*wanshan*). "More perfect" is thus an accurate translation of *geng wanmei*, and my interpretation would be the same in either language.

[104] In Chinese, "salt" (*yan*) and "smoke" (煙, *yan*) are homonyms, though the tones are different. The assonance of "smoke," "snow" (雪, *xue*), and "sorrow" (悲哀, *bei ai*) in the English translation is not present in the original Chinese.

movement of people to what were often remote locations can be thought of as severing people from their roots, or indeed of separating China from its roots during the Great Leap Forward and the Cultural Revolution. Naturally, Chin-san Lang, who fled China for Taiwan in 1949, took no photos of Mao's China. But Bei Dao's response to Lang's photograph is not descriptive but emotive, and this emotional response is surely tied with his own experiences working in construction in rural China in the 1960s and 1970s. The veil of smoke and snow may be understood as hiding corruption in the present and covering up the realities of Maoist policies. But naturally the poem may simply be a comment on industrialization in general, in which case the uneasy relationship between nature and industry would point to a larger malaise of modernity.

As in the first stanza, there is a middle line that is not evidently connected to the others. "Time displays its affluence" if it is understood in the context of time determining labor and wages. Even if there are no workers, time has become reified, so that money becomes tied to time itself. As in the first stanza, the laborer has been excluded from the process. Bei Dao is dealing in abstractions, yet these abstractions, reified under the poet's pen, refer back to their own oddity. The abstraction here, contra Owen, points to the material existence of the worker, be it the Chinese worker under Mao, or more generally the laborer in a capitalist or communist state. We have in this line, then, two possible readings: one nebulous and applicable to any modernized country, the other specific not only to China but to the era in which Bei Dao first began to write.

The concluding stanza sees more personification, or, to use Li Zehou's terminology, humanization of nature and of material objects.[105] The atmosphere becomes more sinister.

沿东到西歪的篱笆
风醉倒在路旁
那穿透迷雾的钟声——
让这纸怦然心动

along the wobbling fence
the drunk wind falls on the roadside
the bell tolling through the mist
leaves the heart of the paper pounding (*Rose* 256–57)

The "drunk wind" that "falls on the roadside" suggests a downtrodden factory worker. In the photograph, the fence could appear uneven, but the "wobbling" is Bei Dao's invention, as is the presence of wind, as these movements could not be captured by Lang's still photograph. He has accentuated the instability of the factory and of nature. Both appear ready to collapse—a part of nature already has. The positive interaction between nature and technology in the first stanza gives way to competition in the second, and in the third

---

[105] Li Zehou and Jane Cauvel. *Four Essays on Aesthetics: Toward a Global View*, Lanham, MD: Lexington Books, 2006, 66.

both the natural and the industrial world are exhausted. The bell in the third line is yet another invention. A "bell tolling through the mist" could be either a temple bell or a bell signaling the beginning and end of factory shifts. In Dai Wangshu's 戴望舒 "A Fly in Autumn" or 秋蝇 the temple bell signifies a spiritual power that exceeds the existence of a single entity:

迢遥的声音，古旧的，
大伽蓝的钟磬？天末的风？
苍蝇有点僵木，
这样沉重的翼翅啊！ [106]

A distant, ancient sound—
The great temple bell? Wind from the ends of the earth?
The fly feels numb,
Its wings so heavy.[107]

The bell dwarfs the fly by magnifying the fly's small body and brief life. Were we to interpret the bell in Bei Dao's poem as a temple bell, the effect would be the same. The bell sound, which, again, could not be duplicated by Lang's photograph and is only heard from afar, would underscore the small amount of space occupied by the factory, as well as its limited existence as an entity in time. Whereas the temple bell as a concept has existed since antiquity, the factory is a new phenomenon and is already showing signs of decay, its structure "wobbling" as nature around it "falls down." And while the bell exists in a space beyond the borders of the picture, in the limitless space of the poet's imagination, the saltworks is visible, bound. Hence the "heart of the paper" palpitates as this signifier of a higher, more durable power spells out the unavoidable demise of the salt factory.

Yet if the bell belongs to the factory itself, the pounding heart might allude to the nervous worker being called to his post. Everything related to the worker has been omitted in the poem. His despair has been sublimated into the wind, and his fear now into the paper. The paper is that upon which the poem is being written. If it is pounding, then it means the spirit of worker is a part of the poem itself, embodied in the poem's materiality.[108] In other words, the worker, who has been conspicuously hidden throughout the poem, is in the end revealed to be the very paper that contains the poem. He is, like James Joyce's artist, to use a phrase invoked already in Chapter 1 of this work, "everywhere felt but nowhere seen." The generality with which Bei Dao has described this Chinese scene ends up making the ending more powerful. It causes the reader to engage more deeply with the meaning of "Salt" in order to understand the odd subjectivity that permeates the poem and leads to a heartbeat contained within paper. The abstraction of Bei Dao's

---

[106] Dai Wangshu, *Shiwenji*, Shenyang, China: Wan juan chuban gongsi, 2014, 66.
[107] Herbert Batt and Sheldon Zitner, *The Flowering of Modern Chinese Poetry: An Anthology of Verse from the Republican Period*, Montreal: McGill-Queen's UP, 2016, 195.
[108] It is important to recall here that the word for "heart" in Chinese, 心 (xīn), also means "mind" and "spirit," and is to be distinguished from the anatomical term for "heart," 心臟 xīnzàng.

poem, far from being a negation of Chinese identity and history, is in fact a rhetorical strategy. It allows Bei Dao to approach the issues of industrialization and exploitation in modern China without using the direct sloganeering language of Maoism.

All this, of course, relies upon the reader and, in the case of non-Chinese speakers reading Bei Dao, the translator picking up on the "right" reading of the poem. This in turn necessities sensitivity to context, resonances with and departures from older poems and movements, in short, the relationship between the world of a poem and the actual world. The process recalls what Michelle Yeh has called the "elective affinity" of translation, which denotes "the resonance, or a meeting of the minds, between the translator, at the intellectual, aesthetic, and personal levels."[109] In a technique that recalls the work of Zhaoming Qian, Yeh gives the example of Ezra Pound, upon inheriting Ernest Fenollosa's notebooks, reaching across the centuries to meet the minds of early Chinese poets, with "Pound's affinity with clean, crystallized visual imagery" making him ideally placed to become fixated on Chinese poetry.[110] Translations of *modern* Chinese poetry have an affinity, Yeh says, with the characteristic of "newness" itself. "Newness" could refer either to a shared fascination with the avant-garde, with, say, surrealist or modernist poetics, or it could refer to the "newness" of China itself after the opening up of the country in the 1980s. While I agree with Yeh to an extent, I do believe that paying more attention to the aspect of world formation in translation and interpretation could open up other dimensions in this process. When Hughes reads Chinese literature and philosophy in translation, however much of an affinity he might feel for sages like Zhuangzi, of whose *Daodejing* he appears to have purchased several copies across his life, he is making Chinese philosophy fit into a larger cosmos that affirms his idiosyncratic world vision; and this vision is not merely of world or Asian literature as we saw it in Chapter Two, but of English poetry as well. If Hughes's vision of English history and literature is inflected by his incorporation of a notion of "shamanistic Chineseness," then surely his notion of Chineseness too is altered by his odd vision of English poetry and history. One change in the constellation of belief affects all other points. The same is true of Bei Dao: even if Bei Dao wants to return to "tradition," his knowledge of world literature, his experience living abroad, his rejection of Maoist literature—which is, after all, now too a part of the Chinese tradition—all alter the elements of tradition for him and how they appear in his poem. As with our three *Kantans* in Chapter Three, what reference frame we have, what reference frame Bei Dao has, determines the "Chineseness" or not of his work.

The point that I wish to make is that there is nothing in "Salt," aside from the language in which it is written, that makes it specifically Chinese, yet we can abstract "Chinese" significance from it. This is aided by the poem being explicitly dedicated to Lang's *Saltworks*. However, if we did not have this dedication, would we dismiss this poem as being "vague" and "written for translation"? Would we castigate it for being apolitical

---

[109] Michelle Yeh, "Modern Chinese Poetry: Translation and Translatability," *Frontiers of Literary Studies in China* vol. 5, no. 4 (December 2011): 605.

[110] Ibid.

and eschewing the problems of modern China? Possibly. How "Chinese" a poem is depends largely on context: our context and the context or intention of the poet. That is not to say that there is no such thing as "Chineseness" or that any significance we find in a poem is arbitrary. Rather, it is to say that meaning is always a negotiation between the author and his society, the author and his audience, and, if the work is in translation, between the author's native society and the audience of the language into which the poem has been translated. At the same time, we can imagine that the author has a clear meaning in mind. Because of the dedication to Lang's photo, we are given rare insight into Bei Dao's motivations for writing a poem. We do not have to contend as much with the vagueness that usually characterizes our understanding of Bei Dao's poetry. Much of the contention surrounding Bei Dao's work may therefore owe not to ambiguity in the work itself but to epistemic vagueness, our own lack of knowledge of what was going on in the poet's mind as he wrote, which turns into *ontological vagueness*, as the boundaries of the poem, and the generic, transnational signifiers in them, ultimately become unfixable and in themselves vague. A top-down theory of world literature will miss such nuance, for it constrains interpretation by presupposing universal "modes." What modes we identify will always be partly tied to our own determined sociohistorical situation. Whatever meaning is in the poem will also be determined by the poet's intention. If we adhere to theories of world literature dogmatically, we will be less able to explain how conflicting identities can arise from poetry such as Bei Dao's, as "abstract" as it may be, as much of a "global citizen" the writer himself may be.

I am also proposing that the formal features of a work are not all that give it identity. Bei Dao's poetry is a radical break from Classical Chinese poetry. It is also, as Tan argues, a continuation of May Fourth Movement poetry.[111] And we may interpret certain images in his poems to connect them to classical literary allusions. Indeed, Bei Dao's ambiguity, his "mistiness," allows us to interpret him in a variety of ways. And it may be true, as Tan says, that "such ambiguity within poetic structure is still largely unprecedented in Chinese poetic history," marking Bei Dao's work as radically modern.[112] But that does not entail that his writings are without roots any more than the smoke in "Salt." Being "Chinese," or being "English," or being anything is not a conscious repetition of that which came before. According to Bei Dao himself, identity and tradition are spontaneous: "at a certain moment you're suddenly aware of it." Calling Bei Dao a Chinese poet should not mean that from close reading alone we can connect him to Li Bai, Du Fu, and Li Yu. It could involve his presence in the "cultural sedimentation" of China, to borrow another concept from Li Zehou, though proving this sedimentation and an author's presence in it is fraught, and assumes an unbroken line of cultural development.[113] The lines connecting one literary world to another do not necessarily proceed chronologically.

---

[111] Tan, *Constructing*, 11–12.

[112] Ibid., 15.

[113] Zehou and Cauvel, *Four Essays*, 152. Dian Li references this concept as well when arguing that Bei Dao would have been familiar with and inevitably incorporated into his poetry aspects of Daoism (119).

Bei Dao brings his world of Tang poetry into the present, but that doesn't mean he brings the nearly 1300 years of Chinese history between the Tang and the present with it. On the contrary, like Hughes with his loose combination of "Chineseness" with a similarly selective world of preindustrial, pre-Christian Britain, Bei Dao is choosing some elements from the past, and bringing them together with elements from the present to create a contemporary world that seems to contain an idea of the past, or an argument of what constituted the past, in it. Nor should his status as an exile relegate him to the nebulous field of world literature and global citizenry as a person who belongs everywhere and nowhere. Multiple levels of identity do not, I think, suddenly become flattened; assuming that something is either traditional or modern, global, national, or local, may blind us to the polysemy, the multidimensionality, present in poetry like Bei Dao's. In short, in approaching poetry like Hughes's "Trance of Light" and "Chinese History of Colden Water" and Bei Dao's "Salt," or indeed poetry like Du Fu's 初月"New Moon"/"First Moon," we should aim to understand the ways in which tradition, in literature and in personal identity, persist in the modern and coexist with the modern, and how the native and personal can accommodate the foreign. If this is not Hinton's "magically generative source-tissue of Tao or Absence," it certainly seems akin to the magically generative source-tissue of translation and literary worlds that await the translator in an imagined tradition like "chrysanthemum blossoms clotted there with swollen dark" (暗滿菊花團).

CONCLUSION

Concluding *Configurations of Comparative Poetics: Three Perspectives on Chinese and Western Literary Criticism*, Zong-qi Cai revisits his earlier considerations of similarities between Chinese and Western poetics and contends that

> with the ever increasing contact, interaction, and mutual influence across cultures, this area of resemblances will certainly expand substantially. In my belief, this expansion will not lead to the rise of "universals" at the cost of the waning or death of different cultural traditions. Quite the contrary, it will serve only to stimulate further development and enrichment of each indigenous tradition involved.[1]

Cai's hopeful message is a coda to a book dealing mostly with classical poetics. By looking at literary dialogues across East and West in the twentieth century, this book has, in a sense, picked up where Cai left off. Against "universals" and a "strong" view of world literature and literary worlds, I have advocated for weakness and bottomless vagueness. My work, however, needed to approach the topic in slightly different ways, to broach both the kind of East–West problems Cai addresses as well as more recent work in world literature, and indeed in logic, to evaluate the systemic questions, the calls for "strong" and "weak" approaches, current in the theory of world and comparative literature. This concluding chapter returns to the core problems addressed in the introduction and in Chapter One: How are we to understand the relations between the actual world and the world or worlds of the text; how are we to understand literary works and the entities that compose them in translation; and how are we to understand our role as critics and translators? I gave tentative answers to all of these questions in Chapter One, but, having examined four different configurations of translation across literatures East and West, it is time to see whether more precise answers are forthcoming.

Throughout this book I have underscored the role of impossibility and impossible worlds in the formation of East–West literature. When we think about fiction itself, impossible worlds are not static entities that exist outside of time. What makes a world impossible is its status in what I have been calling the writer's constellation of belief, which itself interacts with the larger universe of belief of the writer's society. Françoise Lavocat has drawn attention to this by asking for a "diachronic" understanding of impossible worlds. It is not only the bizarre worlds of postmodernism that we should think of as

---

[1] Zong-qi Cai, *Configurations of Comparative Poetics: Three Perspectives on Chinese and Western Literary Criticism*, Honolulu: University of Hawaii Press, 2002, 254–55.

impossible, Lavocat says; a conception of time that is not linear and that is at odds with Aristotle might seem perfectly possible to us, but it might have designated an impossible world for, say, the French *romanciers* of the seventeenth century.[2] But even then, Lavocat claims, fictional play with nonlinear time is present in seventeenth-century literature, in, for example, Marin Le Roy de Gomberville's *La Carithée*, in which something resembling time-travel is described.[3] But how to account for an impossible world in an era in which it should not exist—an era that seems open to everything? Lavocat's answer is that fiction often dramatizes its own impossibility, and audiences often intervene to "resolve" paradoxes, "soit en les ignorant, soit en tentant de toutes les manières de les resoudre" (either by ignoring them or by using all kinds of means to resolve them).[4] Lavocat's diachronic impossibility is, I think, mostly correct, but does not quite offer a full picture of how impossible worlds work in literature. The reason is that Lavocat is considering the contingency of impossibility on time, but not necessarily on place and language.

When we deal with languages we are dealing not only with words as such, but also with entire networks of belief and context. Making the context of the original fit with the constellation of belief into which it is transported means making analogies, as we saw in Chapter Two with the *Bardo* project; it means simplifying both the target and the source in order to create a third thing, a new set filled with simplified data, that stands apart from both of the original domains. The process is evident in Ted Hughes and Chou Wen-chung's opera, and is almost omnipresent in Paul Claudel's poetry and drama; but it can also be seen in Mishima Yukio's "modern" Nō, in Kuki Shūzō's Parisian writings, and in the exile poetry of Bei Dao. The world created by these analogies is an amalgam of source and target, and possibly many other things besides, that are made to cohere under the restrictions of what is possible in the target constellation. It is not a "hybrid" so much as an independent body with a discrete identity determined by the context in which it is placed. Of course, as Lavocat points out, the status of this new world, its possibility, is not fixed for readers. The original *Kantan* was itself a translation of a Chinese tale into the world of the Muromachi period Japanese Nō. Claudel and Mishima undertook a similar process of translation, both across languages and across constellations of belief, in order to make *Kantan* agree with what they believed was possible. And as Claudel's and Mishima's "modern" plays recede into the past, a similar process of translation becomes necessary to make each play intelligible to modern audiences.. Worlds can pass from the possible to impossible and, perhaps, vice versa, just as something can become non-actual over time. This is why East–West literature teems with new sets, new worlds.

This book splits into three sections, sections on theory, drama, and poetry. As I mentioned in the introduction, there were other options for how to split the book, according to author or according to language, for instance. The division I have given merely indicates the importance to the study of world literature of theory and media,

---

[2] Françoise Lavocat, "L'impossibilité des mondes possibles de la fiction," *Zeitschrift Für Französische Sprache Und Literatur* vol. 123, no. 2 (2013): 125.

[3] Ibid., 123.

[4] Ibid., 125.

of ideas and modes of expression that seem to cut across national borders and centuries. These things do travel across borders and do persist across time, but, as this book has shown, deep fractures can belie superficial points of contact. Hence, "world literature," "literary worlds," "dramatic worlds," and "poetic worlds" may furnish us with good starting points from which we can set off on our journey of comparison, and they may allow us to see the same writer differently, as Hughes and Claudel appear differently depending on the formal and theoretical questions they are asking and being asked in turn by their audiences. Yet, when we see that Claudel's idea of "*Kantan*" and Mishima's idea of "*Kantan*," or Hughes's "China" and Bei Dao's "China," appear to refer to both the same and different entities, we should also take care when assuming that "drama" and "poetry," or that favorite form of the study of world literature, the novel, refer to the same thing on both sides of our comparison, however "modern" and "cosmopolitan" the writers and texts with which we deal are. The vagueness inherent in these terms in world literature owes to the ways in which nigh invisible ontological assumptions persist in literary forms across time. These assumptions force writers and readers alike to manage the shock of the unfamiliar produced by the remnants of strange ontologies, and make the foreign seem both inscrutable and familiar, depending on how everything is made to cohere in the writer's or reader's constellation of belief.

Whether there is a characterization principle that identifies entities across different worlds, is a more difficult question. The spotlight in this work has not been on the trans-world identity of characters and things as such. We have, however, seen that the aspect of figures can change as different senses arise or are lost in translation. This is particularly true for the "Tibetan" Buddhist figures of the *Bardo* and the characters of *Kantan*. In order to claim that these characters take on different aspects, I have to assume that their identity is constant. Yet, there does not appear to be an individuation criterion of identity that would pick out, say, Rosei and the spirits of the Pillow of *Kantan* and the characters based on them. Determining trans-world identity has two steps. First might come the author's intentions: Chou's and Hughes's intentions are explicit, and Mishima, even if he modernizes the classical Nō, intends to refer to the same spirits within the Pillow. Can we say that intentionality alone is enough to ensure trans-world identity? It seems not. That would place identity entirely within the mind of the author and leave us without any way of verifying whether one fictional character is identical with another. Reference to fictional objects is a fraught matter. Some people, Russellians, would deny that fictional entities exist; others, Meinongians, would argue the contrary. But, in either case, we have no way to individuate fictional characters the totality of whose properties we do not know.[5] An interpretation of the *Kantan* specters that places them in opposition to the malaise of postwar Japan does not necessarily attribute qualities to the specters that they do not possess. As I suggested in the introduction, the response to this wide-ranging possibility of characterization is multidimensionality: we understand characters as possessing several dimensions, and we admit that later literary works may attribute to these characters new qualities . What this adds up to is multidimensional

---

[5] See Thomas G. Pavel, *Fictional Worlds*, Cambridge, MA: Harvard UP, 1986, 107–13.

vagueness: trans-world identity can mean similarity across certain dimensions (being specters in a dream) but not others (belonging to a Buddhist ontology). Assuming that not all dimensions are equal, as we probably find some characteristics more important than others, no "fact" tells us which "dimensions" carry the most weight.[6] This is where relative closeness and the ternary relation comes in: "x is at least as close to y, in *F*-relevant aspects, as it is to z."[7] The critic decides what *F* is relative to her interests, but in Chapters Two through Five I have continually suggested that deep-level differences, ontological gaps, may underlie superficial resemblances. Transferring a literary figure from a Christian ontology to a Buddhist one or vice versa *may* lead to such a translation across ontologies, and it is in cases like this, as in the poetry and drama of Claudel and the poetry of Kuki Shūzō, that we ought to say that we are no longer speaking about the same entity with different characteristics but different entities altogether. Identifying literary jumps across not only worlds but ontologies is not a simple matter, and we will not always get it right or agree when we think we have, but, if my analyses have been correct, it is something to strive for.

So, the final consideration: How do we account for our own position as critics? The question itself presupposes that literary criticism is made up of a homogenous "we," which is not at all the case. There are intramural differences as much as there are international ones. A single approach to comparative literature or East–West literature will never be agreed upon, but the very nature of "our" study, "our" here designating the group of people who believe they are engaged in comparative literature, thrives on competing perspectives. In Chapter Five, we saw how Ted Hughes's and Bei Dao's broadening horizons, their increasing knowledge of other cultures distant from their own, both increased their sense of the contingency of their own traditions and made them identify more clearly their places within them. The borders of our "native" traditions are no less blurry and multidimensional than those of the "foreign" traditions we study. Drawing comparisons across these sets of vague composition will not rid us of indeterminacy, but it can highlight aspects of both the source and the target, of our own constellations of beliefs and those of the other writers and groups of people we study, that would otherwise pass unnoticed. In G. E. R. Lloyd's words, "to suppose that our aim

---

[6] A nonliterary example is the concept of being "intelligent." "Intelligent" could be composed of a variety of regions (ability to think abstractly, ability to think quickly, possessing common sense, being observant; though *which* regions we think go here might be arbitrary and relative to our interests). As a thought experiment, we could imagine reducing a person's ability to think quickly until she no longer qualifies as intelligent in that domain. And we could simultaneously increase her common sense so that her "intelligence" is contradictory: She is intelligent and not intelligent, that is, intelligent in terms of common sense but not in terms of being a quick thinker. See Steven Verheyen and Paul Égré, "Typicality and Graded Membership in Dimensional Adjectives," *Cognitive Science* vol. 42, no. 7 (2018): 2250–86; Peter Gärdenfors, *Conceptual Spaces: The Geometry of Thought*, Cambridge, MA: MIT Press, 2000. We could do analogous things with the traits of literary characters, and I think that is what the writers examined across this book have done, to show how characters are composed of multidimensional vague predicates.

[7] Nicholas J. J. Smith, *Vagueness and Degrees of Truth*, Oxford: Oxford UP, 2008, 143.

should be to settle on a single definitive account is to prejudice the investigation and to ignore the possible multidimensionality of the phenomena in question."[8] As the writers we study and we ourselves forge new analogies, we will continue to find new dimensions and new worlds across literatures East and West. The proliferation of new qualities that East–West literature's vague composition makes possible will continue to encourage the development of older traditions, and, as different worlds in different constellations of belief come into being, open new universes of possibility.

As I said early on in this book, "weak" world literature attends as much to impasses as to bridges. But what counts as an "impasse" only comes before our eyes when we view literary works in light of the deep ontological assumptions that support them, and in contrast with incompatible ontological schemes from elsewhere. This is why I have been devoting much of my attention to the concept of tradition itself. I have been suggesting that "tradition" is multidimensional and should be treated as such: a poem can be Chinese and traditional in one sense but not in another. The reason we have such difficulty with these terms is that we hesitate before a contradiction. We do not want it to be the case that something both is and is not traditional, so we might draw arbitrary lines between the traditional and the modern, or, or perhaps *and* when such divisions are shown inadequate, contend that our terms are lacking in meaning. The latter move is, of course, that of deconstructionist theory. Though it continues to permeate our work in ways in which we are often not entirely aware of, such theory has, in its often hyperbolic rhetorical flourishes and overweening confidence in what cannot be known, left many scholars weary of the very term "theory": if there are contradictions at the heart of our terms, then our terms fail to possess fully either truth or falsity. This breakdown of binary logic in turn causes the deconstructionist to question whether logic and indeed the notion of truth itself are useful for literary criticism. I would venture that world literature's continued confidence in the unity of the world literary system, or that a gamut of worlds can exist side by side in a single frame, is a product of such theory's attack on "binaries," a phenomenon to which David Damrosch has recently drawn our attention.[9] An unremarked aspect of this fight is the fact that the very battle over binary thinking is itself, if scholars like Yasuo Deguchi, Jay Garfield, and Graham Priest are correct, inconsequential to other, particularly Buddhist views of the world. Binaries may underpin a logic based on the principle of noncontradiction, but a fourfold logic, be it Nāgārjuna's logic or that of the modern logician of paraconsistency, can accommodate contradictions. It is an interesting fact that debates over binary thinking in world literature and elsewhere are themselves framed in what we might call a provincial, or even "Eurocentric," logic, while developments in philosophical logic and elsewhere have long provided us with the tools to think through the implications of the often contradictory materials world literature gives us.

---

[8] G. E. R. Lloyd, "Fortunes of Analogy," *Australasian Philosophical Review* vol. 1, no. 3 (July 2017): 241, doi:10.1080/24740500.2017.1379867.

[9] David Damrosch, *Comparing the Literatures: Literary Studies in a Global Age,* Princeton: Princeton UP, 2020, 265–70.

As I have been trying to show throughout this book, just because terms do not admit of clear-cut application does not entail that they are not meaningful and cannot provide us with rich knowledge of that which we use them to describe. Because translation from one linguistic system to another requires entering into the universe of beliefs of the society that uses that language and the constellation of the writer and his or her immediate social milieu, the aspect of familiar words and ideas changes in order to cohere into new literary worlds. Therefore, we can have the elements of other traditions—and of other constellations—present in a literary world. However, since the aspect of those elements changes during the translation, since different dimensions are highlighted or added—we are not dealing with quite the same elements in both cases. If we expect the familiar in every case, with a clear-cut identity, then we will certainly be disappointed, and unable to deal with the contradictions that world literature presents us regularly. But if we value vagueness in practice and weakness in theory, we wind up with a richer understanding of the multidimensionality of world literature, of how worlds are born and how we modify these worlds in turn in our attempts to comprehend them. What is needed is more attention to how, at a deep ontological level, we structure our worlds in theory and how the writers we study structure theirs in practice.

When Kuki Shūzō died in 1941, as we saw in the epigraph to Chapter IV, Nishida Kitarō chose a few verses to inscribe on Kuki's stele. The poem Nishida chose was one that had been popular among the Kyoto philosophers earlier in the century, Goethe's *Wandrers Nachtlied*.

見はるかす山々の頂	Gazing over distant mountain crests
梢には風も動かず鳥も鳴かず	In the treetops neither wind stirs nor bird sings.
まてしばしやがて汝も休はん[10]	Wait awhile, and at last you too shall rest.

The stele stands not only as a monument to Kuki's life and his status as a long wanderer between Japan and the West. It stands as a monument to world literature itself. Its four sides are like the different dimensions of a literary text. Situated in Hōnen-in 法然院 just off the Philosopher's Walk in Kyoto, the stele presents itself from the front, where "Kuki Shūzō's grave" or 九鬼周造之墓 is inscribed, as a typical Buddhist grave in Japan. The other side of the stele pulls Goethe's poem into the orbit of the Japanese tradition as Nishida, or the translator, uses archaisms (汝 "nanji," for instance, from the heart of classical Japanese) to pull the poem into the orbit of *classical* Japanese literature, and make it look like it has belonged there all along. The informed viewer of this stele could not help but remember Kuki's own foreign life and inclinations, nor the other worlds of Goethe's poem, in its translations into Schubert's lieder or into the English of Henry Wadsworth Longfellow. As such, the two sides of the stele are overlaid with their own multiple significances, and four faces or dimensions of the stele, on the plane of significance, have vague relations to one another as they try to bring different traditions into contact. Yet the stele itself does form a coherent, unified object; its dimensions are bound

---

[10] See Sakurai Shōichiro, *Kyōto gakuha suikoden* 京都学派水故伝, Kyoto: Kyoto UP, 2017, 338.

together in a way that works for now, for Kuki, for Nishida. We can think of this small act of world formation as a synecdoche for world literature itself. Smaller worlds are brought together to form a stable monument to the process of understanding, or trying to understand, across cultures. But even as the literary world seems to give the process a sense of finality and the author time to rest, the larger world of world literature, like the world that surrounds Kuki's monument, keeps on going.

WORKS CITED

Abramson, Marc Samuel. *Ethnic Identity in Tang China*. Philadelphia: U of Pennsylvania P, 2008.
Akutagawa, Ryūnosuke. *Akutagawa Ryūnosuke zenshū*, Dai ni maki. Ed. Shin'ichirō Nakamura, Tōkyō: Iwanami shoten, 1964, 39.
Alber, Jan. "Logical Contradictions, Possible Worlds Theory, and the Embodied Mind." In *Possible Worlds Theory and Contemporary Narratology*. Ed. Alice Bell and Marie-Laure Ryan. Lincoln: U of Nebraska P, 2019, pp. 157–76.
Anderson, Benedict. *Imagined Communities: Reflections on the Origin and Spread of Nationalism*. London: Verso, 2006.
Apter, Emily S. *The Translation Zone: A New Comparative Literature: A New Comparative Literature*. Princeton: Princeton UP, 2006.
———. *Against World Literature: On the Politics of Untranslatability*. London: Verso, 2013.
Armitage, Simon. "The Ascent of Ted Hughes: Conquering the Calder Valley." In *Ted Hughes: From Cambridge to Collected*. Ed. Mark Wormald, Neil Roberts, and Terry Gifford. London: Palgrave Macmillan, 2013, 6–16.
Arnold, Alison, ed. "Himalayan Region." In *Garland Encyclopedia of World Music Volume 5 – South Asia: The Indian Subcontinent*. London: Routledge, 1999.
Arrowsmith, Rupert. *Modernism and the Museum: Asian, African, and Pacific Art and the London Avant-Garde*. Oxford: Oxford UP, 2010.
Au, Sau Woon Rebecca. "I Ching in the Music of John Cage, Chou Wen-chung (周文中) and Zhao Xiaosheng (趙曉生)." PhD Dissertation. Chinese University of Hong Kong, 2013.
Auerbach, Erich. "Philology and 'Weltliteratur.'" Trans. Maire Said and Edward Said. *Centennial Review*, vol. 13, no. 1 (Winter 1969): 1–17.
Barnes, Nancy J. "Lady Rokujō's Ghost: Spirit Possession, Buddhism, and Healing in Japanese Literature." *Literature and Medicine*, vol. 8, no. 1 (1989): 106–21, doi: 10.1353/lm.2011.0101.
Bartha, Paul F. A. *By Parallel Reasoning: The Construction and Evaluation of Analogical Arguments*. New York: Oxford UP, 2010.
Batt, Herbert, and Sheldon Zitner. *The Flowering of Modern Chinese Poetry: An Anthology of Verse from the Republican Period*. Montreal: McGill-Queen's UP, 2016.
Beckett, Samuel. *Endgame*. London: Faber, 1958.
Beecroft, Alexander. "World Literature without a Hyphen: Towards a Typology of Literary Systems." *New Left Review*, vol. 54 (November–December 2008): 87–100.
———. *An Ecology of World Literature: From Antiquity to the Present Day*. London: Verso, 2015.
———. "Eurafraisiachronologies: Between the Eurocentric and the Planetary." *Journal of World Literature*, vol. 1, no. 1 (2016): 17–28.
Bei Dao. 時間的玫瑰 (The Rose of Time). Ed. Eliot Weinberger. Trans. David Hinton, Bonnie S. MacDougall, and Eliot Weinberger. New York: New Directions Publishing Corporation, 2009.
———. "Ancient Enmity." *Manoa*, vol. 24, no. 1 (July 2012): 1–5.
Besineau, Jacques. "Claudel au Japon: Souvenirs et documents inédits." *Etudes*, vol. 94, no. 311 (1961): 345–51.
The Bible. Authorized King James Version. Oxford: Oxford UP, 1998.
Brandes, Rand. "Mercury in Taurus: W. B. Yeats and Ted Hughes." *South Carolina Review*, vol. 43, no. 1 (2010): 198–210.

Buruma, Ian. "The Sensualist: What Makes *The Tale of Genji* so Seductive?" *New Yorker* (July 13, 2015). https://www.newyorker.com/magazine/2015/07/20/the-sensualist-books-buruma.

Bush, Christopher. *Ideographic Modernisms: China, Writing, Media*. Oxford: Oxford UP, 2010.

———. "Modernism, Orientalism, and East Asia." In *A Handbook of Modernism Studies*. Ed. Jean-Michel Rabaté. Chichester, UK: John Wiley & Sons, 2013, 193–208.

Butler, John. "Review of 'Awakened Cosmos: The Mind of Classical Chinese Poetry' by David Hinton & 'The Selected Poems of Tu Fu', translated by David Hinton." *Asian Review of Books* (14 November 2019). https://asianreviewofbooks.com/content/awakened-cosmos-the-mind-of-classical-chinese-poetry-by-david-hinton-the-selected-poems-of-tu-fu-translated-by-david-hinton/.

Cai, Zong-qi. *Configurations of Comparative Poetics: Three Perspectives on Chinese and Western Literary Criticism*. Honolulu: U of Hawaii P, 2002.

Cao, Xueqin, Gao E., and John Minford. *The Story of the Stone: A Chinese Novel in Five Volumes*. Volume I. Trans. David Hawkes. London: Penguin, 1973.

Casanova, Pascale. *La république mondiale des lettres*. Paris: Éditions de Seuil, col. Points. 2004.

———. "Literature as a World." *New Left Review*, 31 (January–February 2005): 71–90.

Chan, Wing-tsit. *A Source Book in Chinese Philosophy*. Princeton: Princeton UP, 1963.

Chang, Chun-shu. *The Rise of the Chinese Empire: Frontier, Immigration, and Empire in Han China, 130 B.C – A.D. 15*. Ann Arbor: U of Michigan P, 2007.

Chang, Peter M. *Chou Wen-chung: The Life and Work of a Contemporary Chinese-Born American Composer*. Lanham, MD: Scarecrow Press, 2006.

Cheah, Pheng, and David Damrosch, "What Is a World (Literature)?" *Journal of World Literature*, 4, no. 3 (August 2019): 305–29.

Chou, Wen-chung. "East and West, Old and New." *Asian Music*, vol. 1, no. 1 (1968): 19–22, doi:10.2307/834006.

———. "Asian Concepts and Twentieth-Century Western Composers." *Musical Quarterly*, vol. LVII, no. 2 (1971): 211–29, doi:10.1093/mq/LVII.2.211.

———. "US-China Arts Exchange: A Practice in Search of a Philosophy." *Intercultural Music Studies*, vol. 2, International Institute for Comparative Music Studies and Documentation (1989): 144–64.

———. "Whither Chinese Composers?" *Contemporary Music Review*, vol. 26, no. 5–6 (October 2007): 501–10, doi:10.1080/07494460701652939.

Claudel, Paul. *Théâtre* Tome XII. Ed. Robert Mallet. Paris: Gallimard, 1958.

———. *Oeuvres complètes* Tome XVIII. Ed. Pierre Claudel and Jacques Petit. Paris: Gallimard, 1961.

———. *Oeuvres en prose*. Ed. Jacques Petit and Charles Galpérine. Paris: Gallimard, 1965.

———. *Oeuvre Poétique*. Ed. Jacques Petit. Paris: Gallimard, 1967.

———. *Journal* Tome I. Ed. François Varillon and Jacques Petit. Paris: Gallimard, 1968.

Claudel, Paul, Jean Amrouche, and Louis Fournier. *Mémoires Improvisés*. Paris: Gallimard, 1969.

Corcoran, Neil. "The Nation of Selves: Ted Hughes's Shakespeare." In *This England, that Shakespeare: New Angles on Englishness and the Bard*. Ed. Margaret Tudeau-Clayton and Willy Maley. London: Ashgate, 2010, 185–200.

Corcoran, Neil. *Shakespeare and the Modern Poet*. Cambridge: Cambridge UP, 2010.

Da, Nan. *Intransitive Encounter: Sino-U.S. Literature and the Limits of Exchange*. New York: Columbia UP, 2018.

Dai, Wangshu. *Shiwenji*. Shenyang, China: Wan juan chuban gongsi, 2014.

Damrosch, David. *What Is World Literature?* Princeton: Princeton UP, 2003.

———. "Toward a History of World Literature." *New Literary History*, vol. 39, no. 3 (Summer 2008): 481–95.

———. *Comparing the Literatures: Literary Studies in a Global Age*. Princeton: Princeton UP, 2020.

Davidson, Donald. "On the Very Idea of a Conceptual Scheme." *Proceedings and Addresses of the American Philosophical Association*, vol. 47 (1973): 5–20.

Deguchi, Yasuo, Jay L. Garfield, and Graham Priest. "The Contradictions Are True—And It's Not Out of This World! A Response to Takashi Yagisawa." *Philosophy East and West*, vol. 63, no. 3 (2013): 370–72.
Denecke, Wiebke. *Classical World Literatures: Sino-Japanese and Greco-Roman Comparisons*. Oxford: Oxford UP, 2014.
Dietz, Richard. "Comparative Concepts." *Synthese*, vol. 190, no. 1 (2013): 139–70.
Dimock, Wai Chee. *Through Other Continents: American Literature Across Deep Time*. Princeton: Princeton UP, 2009.
———. "Weak Theory: Henry James, Colm Toibin, and W. B. Yeats." *Critical Inquiry*, vol. 39, no. 4 (June 1, 2013): 732–53.
Doležel, Lubomír. *Heterocosmica: Fiction and Possible Worlds*. Baltimore: Johns Hopkins UP, 1998.
Dōmoto, Masaki. *Gekiji Mishima Yukio*. Tokyo: Gekishobō, 1994.
Dorr, Cian. "What We Disagree about When We Disagree about Ontology." In *Fictionalism in Metaphysics*. Ed. Mark E Kalderon. Oxford: Clarendon Press, 2005, 234–86.
Dorr, Cian, and John Hawthorne. "Semantic Plasticity and Speech Reports." *Philosophical Review*, vol. 123, no. 3 (2014): 281–338.
Ebersolt, Simon. "Le Japon et la Philosophie Française du Milieu du XIXe au Milieu du XXe Siècles." *Revue Philosophique De La France Et De l'Étranger*, vol. 137, no. 3 (2012): 371–83.
———. "Contingence et Communauté: Kuki Shûzô, philosophe japonaise." PhD Thesis, INALCO, Institut national des langues et civilisations orientales, 2017.
Edmond, Jacob. "Translating Theory: Bei Dao, Pasternak, and Russian Formalism." In *Chinese Poetry and Translation: Rights and Wrongs*. Ed. Maghiel van Crevel and Lucas Klein. Amsterdam: Amsterdam UP, 2019, 135–57.
Edmond, Jacob, Haun Saussy, and David Damrosch. "Trying to Make It Real: An Exchange between Haun Saussy and David Damrosch." *Comparative Literature Studies*, vol. 53, no. 4 (2016): 660–93.
Elias, Norbert. *The Civilizing Process*. Oxford: Blackwell, 1978.
Eliot, Thomas Sterns. *Selected Prose*. Ed. Frank Kermode. San Diego: Harvest Books, 1975.
———. "Tradition and the Individual Talent." *Perspecta*, vol. 19 (January 1982): 36–42, doi:10.2307/1567048.
Endo, Yoshie. "Craving for the Absolute: The Sublime and the Tragic in Mishima Yukio's Theatrical Works." Dissertation/Thesis, ProQuest Dissertations Publishing U6, University of Pennsylvania, 2004.
English, James F. "Cultural Capital and the Revolutions of Literary Modernity, from Bourdieu to Casanova." In *A Handbook of Modernism Studies*. Ed. Jean-Michel Rabaté. Chichester, UK: John Wiley & Sons Inc, 2013, 364–77.
Ernst, Earle. "Theatre in the East: A Survey of Asian Dance and Drama. By Bowers, Faubion. New York: Thomas Nelson, 1956. Xi, 374. Illustrations, Bibliography, Index. $7.50." *Journal of Asian Studies*, vol. 16, no. 1 (1956): 114–15.
Étiemble, René. *Comparaison n'est pas raison: la crise de la littérature compare*. Paris: Gallimard, 1963.
Evans-Wentz, W. Y. *The Fairy-Faith in Celtic Countries*, New Hyde Park, NY: University Books, 1966.
Evans-Wentz, W. Y., P. Sambhava, P. Sangay, and C. G. Jung. *The Tibetan Book of the Great Liberation: Or the Method of Realizing Nirvana Through Knowing the Mind*. Oxford: Oxford UP, 1968.
Everett, Yayoi Uno. "Calligraphy and Musical Gestures in the Late Works of Chou Wen-chung," *Contemporary Music Review*, vol. 5–6, no. 26 (2007): 569–84.
Faas, Ekbert. *Ted Hughes: the Unaccommodated Universe: With Selected Critical Writings by Ted Hughes & Two Interviews*. Boston: Black Sparrow Press, 1980.
Featherston, Dan. "An Interview with Bei Dao." *University of Arizona Poetry Center Newsletter*, vol. 24, no. 2, 1999. https://poetry.arizona.edu/blog/interview-bei-dao.
Friedman, Susan Stanford. *Planetary Modernisms: Provocations on Modernity Across Time*. New York: Columbia UP, 2015.

Fujita, Masakatsu. *Kuki Shūzō: richi to jōnetsu no hazama ni tatsu "kotoba" no tetsugaku*. Tokyo: Kōdansha, 2016.
Gadamer, Hans Georg. "Le Problème Herméneutique." Trans. J. -M. Fataud, *Archives De Philosophie*, vol. 33, no. 1 (1970): 3–27.
Gärdenfors, Peter. *Conceptual Spaces: The Geometry of Thought*. Cambridge, MA: MIT Press, 2000.
Geffen, Alexandre, and Sandra Laugier. *Le pouvoir des liens faibles*. Paris: Éditions CNRS, 2020.
Genova, Pamela. "Knowledge of the East?: Paul Claudel and the Equivocal Nature of Intercultural Exchange." *L'Esprit Créateur*, vol. 56, no. 3 (2016): 104–19.
Gifford, Terry. "'Dead Farms, Dead Leaves.' Culture as Nature in *Remains of Elmet & Elmet*." In *Ted Hughes: Alternative Horizons*. Ed. Joanny Moulin. London: Routledge, 2004, 23–31.
Giles, Paul. *Backgazing: Reverse Time in Modernist Culture*. Oxford: Oxford UP, 2019.
Goethe, Johann Wolfgang von, and J. P. Eckermann. "Conversations on World Literature." In *The Princeton Sourcebook in Comparative Literature*. Ed. David Damrosch, Natalie Melas, and Mbongiseni Buthelezi. Princeton: Princeton UP, 2009, 17–25.
Goldman, Andrea S. "The Nun Who Wouldn't Be: Representations of Female Desire in Two Performances of 'Si Fan.'" *Late Imperial China*, vol. 22, no. 1 (June 2001): 71–138.
Gu, Ming Dong. *Chinese Theories of Fiction: A Non-Western Narrative System*. Albany: U of New York P, 2006.
Gu, Ming Dong, and Jianping Guo. "How Can We Cross the Intellectual Divide Between East and West?: Reflections on Reading 'Toward a Complementary Consciousness and Mutual Flourishing of Chinese and Western Cultures: The Contributions of Process Philosophers.'" *Philosophy East and West: A Quarterly of Comparative Philosophy*, vol. 65, no. 1 (2015): 298–315.
Hart, Aoife Assumpta. *Ancestral Recall: the Celtic Revival and Japanese Modernism*. Montreal: McGill-Queen's UP, 2016.
Hashimoto, Osamu. *Mishima Yukio to ha nanimono dattanoka*. Tokyo: Shinchō Bunko, 2002.
Hashimoto, Satoru. "Afterlives of the Culture: Engaging with the Trans-East Asian Cultural Tradition in Modern Chinese, Japanese, Korean, and Taiwanese Literatures, 1880s-1940s." PhD dissertation, Harvard University , 2014.
———. "World of Letters: Lu Xun, Benjamin, and *Daodejing*." *Journal of World Literature*, vol. 1, no. 1 (2016): 39–51.
Hashimoto, Satoru and Karen Thornber. "Trans-Regional Asia and Futures of World Literature." *Journal of World Literature*, vol. 4, no. 4 (December 2019): 459–65.
Hawkes, David. *The Songs of the South: An Ancient Chinese Anthology of Poems by Qu Yuan and Other Poets*. Harmondsworth, UK: Penguin Books, 1985.
Hayot, Eric. *On Literary Worlds*. Oxford: Oxford UP, 2012.
———. *Chinese Dreams: Pound, Brecht, Tel Quel*. Ann Arbor: U of Michigan P, 2004.
Heldt, Gustav. "*Kokinshū* and Heian Court Poetry." In *The Cambridge History of Japanese Literature*. Ed. Haruo, Tomi Suzuki and David Lurie. Cambridge: Cambridge UP, 2015, 110–20.
Hember, Polly, Suzanne Hobson, Gareth Mills, and Jeff Wallace. "Weak Theory and Digital Modernism: A BAMS Workshop." *Modernism/modernity Print Plus*, vol. 4, cycle 2 (May 2019). https://modernismmodernity.org/forums/posts/responses-special-issue-weak-theory-part-iv.
Hibbet, Ryan. "Ted Hughes' 'Crow': An Alternative Theological Paradigm." *Literature and Theology*, vol. 17, no. 1 (2003): 17–31.
Hinton, David. *Awakened Cosmos: The Mind of Classical Chinese Poetry*. Boulder, CO: Shambhala, 2019.
Hirakawa, Sukehiro. *À la recherche de l'identité japonaise: le shintô interprété par les écrivains européens*. Paris: Harmattan, 2012.
Hokenson, Jan. *Japan, France, and East-West Aesthetics: French Literature, 1867–2000*. Vancouver: Fairleigh Dickinson UP, 2004.
Horton, H. Mack. "Man'yōshū." *The Cambridge History of Japanese Literature*. Ed. Haruo, Tomi Suzuki and David Lurie. Cambridge: Cambridge UP, 2015, 50–85.

Huang, Bei. *Segalen et Claudel: Dialogue à travers la peinture extrême-orientale.* Rennes: Presses universitaires de Rennes, 2007.
Hue, Bernard. *Littératures et arts de l'Orient dans l'œuvre de Claudel.* Paris: Klincksieck, 1978.
Hughes, Ted. *Bardo Thödol.* TS. Box 116, folder 2. Emory University.
———. *Eat Crow.* Page Proofs. Box 118. Folder 10. Emory University.
———. *Winter Pollen: Occasional Prose.* Ed. William Scammell. London: Faber and Faber, 1994.
———. Interview with Drue Heinz. "The Art of Poetry." *Paris Review*, vol. 134, no. 71 (1995). https://www.theparisreview.org/interviews/1669/ted-hughes-the-art-of-poetry-no-71-ted-hughes.
———. *Ted Hughes: Collected Poems* Ed. Paul Keegan. London: Faber & Faber, [2005] 2012.
———. *Selected Translations.* Ed. Daniel Weissbort. New York: Farrar, Strauss, and Giroux, 2006.
Hughes, Ted and Christopher Reid. *Letters of Ted Hughes.* Ed. Christopher Reid. London: Faber & Faber, 2007.
Hulle, Dirk Van and Mark Nixon. *Samuel Beckett's Library.* Cambridge: Cambridge UP, 2013.
Hulme, T. E. "Romanticism and Classicism." In *Speculations: Essays of Humanism and the Philosophy of Art.* Ed. Herbert Read. London: Routledge & Kegan Paul, 1960, 113–40.
Inaga, Shigemi. "Japanese Philosophers Go West: The Effect of Maritime Trips on Philosophy in Japan With Special Reference to the Case of Watsuji Tetsuro (1889–1960)." *Japan Review: Journal of the International Research Center for Japanese Studies*, vol. 25 (2013): 113–44.
Inose, Naoki. *Persona: A Biography of Yukio Mishima.* Trans. Hiroaki Sato. Berkeley: Stone Bridge Press, 2012.
Jamieson, Kathleen Hall, and Karlyn Kohrs Campbell. "Rhetorical Hybrids: Fusions of Generic Elements." *Quarterly Journal of Speech*, vol. 68, no. 2 (1982): 146–57, doi: 10.1080/00335638209383600.
Johnson, Ryan. "A Critique of Literary Worlds in World Literature Theory: Multidimensionality as a Basis of Comparison." *Journal of World Literature*, vol. 3, no. 3 (2018): 354–72.
———. "La Poésie de Paul Claudel et de Kuki Shūzo durant les années 1920." *Cahiers d'études françaises*, vol. 23 (2018): 31–46.
Jullien, François. "Paris-Pékin, pour une philosophie de l'écart." *Le Débat*, vol. 153, no. 1 (2009): 183–92, doi:10.3917/deba.153.0183.
Kadota, Machiko. "L'image d l'eau chez Paul Claudel et dans *Cent phrases pour éventails*." *Journal of the Faculty of General Education*, vol. 25 (1991): 199–207.
"Kantan." In *Utaibon Collection.* National Library of Japan Digital Collection. Kyoto, c. 1600.
Kawakami, Akane. "Claudel's Fragments of Japan: Co-naissance of the Other in *Cent Phrases pour Éventails*." *French Studies*, vol. L.II, no. 2 (1999): 179–88, doi: 10.1093/fs/LIII.2.176.
———. *Travellers' Visions: French Literary Encounters with Japan, 1881–2004.* Liverpool: Liverpool UP, 2005.
Keene, Donald. *Japanese Literature: An Introduction for Western Readers.* New York: Grove Press, 1955.
———. "Kaisetsu." Yukio Mishima. *Kindai nogakushū.* Tokyo: Shinchōsha, 1968, 228–35.
———. "Characteristics of Japanese Literature." In *The Blue-Eyed Tarōkaja: A Donald Keene Anthology.* Ed. Donald Keene and J. Thomas Rimer. New York: Columbia UP, 1996, 175–89.
Ki, Tsurayuki. *Kokin wakashū.* Ed. Tsuneya Okumura. Tōkyō: Shinchōsha, 1978.
Klein, Lucas. *The Organization of Distance: Poetry, Translation, Chineseness.* Leiden: Brill, 2018.
Knapp, Bettina L. "Mishima's Cosmic Noh Drama: 'The Damask Drum.'" *World Literature Today*, vol. 54, no. 3 (1980): 383–87.
———. "Review of Yukio Mishima. *Cinq nô modernes.* Marguerite Yourcenar and Jun Shiragi (Silla), eds. & trs. Paris. Gallimard. 1984. 172 pages. 85 F." *World Literature Today*, vol. 58, no. 4 (1984): 666–67.
Kodama, Sanehide. *American Poetry and Japanese Culture.* Hamden, CT: Archon Books, 1984.
Kripke, Saul A. *Naming and Necessity.* Oxford: Blackwell, 1980.
Kroll, Paul W. "Daoist Verse and the Quest of the Divine." In *Early Chinese Religion, Part Two: The Period of Division (220–589 AD)* (2 vols). Ed. John Lagerwey and Pengzhi Lü, Leiden: Brill, 2009, 953–85.

Kronthal, Lisa. "Conservation of Chinese Shadow Figures: Investigations into Their Manufacture, Storage, and Treatment." *Journal of the American Institute for Conservation*, vol. 40, no. 1 (2001): 1–14.

Kuhn, Thomas S. *The Structure of Scientific Revolutions*. Chicago: U of Chicago P, 1962.

Kuki, Shūzō. *Kuki Shūzō zenshū dai ichi maki*. Ed. Amano Teiyū, Omodaka Hisayuki, and Satō Akio, Tokyo: Iwanami Shoten, 1981.

———. *Kuki Shuzo: A Philosopher's Poetry and Poetics*. Ed. and Trans. Michael F. Marra. Honolulu: U of Hawaiì P, 2004.

———. *The Structure of Detachment: The Aesthetic Vision of Kuki Shuzo*. Trans. Hiroshi Nara, Honolulu: U of Hawaii P, 2004.

Lachaud, François. "Le poète et les buddhas: Claudel et la tradition religieuse asiatique." *Claudel et le Japon: Cinquatenaire de la mort de Claudel. Actes du Colloque International et de la table ronde*. Ed. Shinobu Chūjō et Takaharu Hasekura, Tokyo: Shichigatsudō 七月堂. Tokyo: Shichigatsudō 七月堂, 2006, 74–93.

Lai, Eric Chiu Kong. *The Music of Chou Wen-chung*. London: Ashgate, 2009.

Lam, Joseph. "Musical Seductresses, Chauvinistic Men, and Their Erotic Kunqu." In *Wanton Women in Late Imperial Chinese Literature: Models, Genres*. Ed. Mark Stevenson and Wu Cuncun. Leiden: Brill, 2017, 79–104.

Laozi, *Laozi quan yi*. Ed. Shaohai Sha and Zihong Xu. Di 1 ban, Guizhou: Renmin chuban she. 1989.

Lau, Joseph S. M., and Y. W. Ma. *Traditional Chinese Stories: Themes and Variations*. Boston: Cheng & Tsui, 1986.

Lavocat, Françoise. «Les genres de la fiction: État des lieux et propositions ». In *La Théorie littéraire des mondes possibles*. Ed. Françoise Lavocat. Paris : CNRS Éditions, 2010, 15–53.

———. "Le comparatisme comme herméneutique de la défamiliarasation." *Vox-Poetica*. April 5, 2012. http://www.vox-poetica.org/t/articles/lavocat2012.html#_ftnref45.

———. "L'impossibilité des mondes possibles de la fiction." *Zeitschrift Für Französische Sprache Und Literatur*, vol. 123, no. 2 (2013): 113–29.

Lewis, David K. *On the Plurality of Worlds*. Oxford: Blackwell, 1986.

Li, Dian. "Paradox and Meaning in Bei Dao's Poetry." *Positions: East Asia Cultures Critique*, vol. 15, no. 1 (2007): 113–36.

Li, Zehou, and J. Cauvel. *Four Essays on Aesthetics: Toward a Global View*. Lanham, MD: Lexington Books, 2006.

Lippit, Seiji M. *Topographies of Japanese Modernism*. New York: Columbia UP, 2002.

Lloyd, G. E. R. "Notes on the Framework for Comparing Science and Philosophy across Civilizations." *Journal of Chinese Philosophy*, vol. 40, no. S1 (2013): 39–46.

———. *Analogical Investigations: Historical and Cross-Cultural Perspectives on Human Reasoning*. Cambridge: Cambridge UP, 2015.

———. "Fortunes of Analogy." *Australasian Philosophical Review*, vol. 1, no. 3 (July 2017): 236–49, doi:10.1080/24740500.2017.1379867.

———. *The Ambivalences of Rationality: Ancient and Modern Cross-Cultural Explorations*. Cambridge: Cambridge UP, 2018.

Loizeaux, Elizabeth Bergmann "Reading Word, Image, and the Body of the Book: Ted Hughes and Leonard Baskin's 'Cave Birds.'" *Twentieth Century Literature*, vol. 50, no. 1 (2004): 18–58.

Long, Hoyt, and Richard J. So. "Turbulent Flow." *Modern Language Quarterly*, vol. 77, no. 3 (2016): 345–67.

Lopez, Donald S. *The Tibetan Book of the Dead: A Biography*. Princeton: Princeton UP, 2011.

Lucken, Michael. *Le Japon grec: culture et possession*. Paris: Gallimard, 2019.

Manabe, Akiko. "W. B. Yeats and Kyogen: Individualism and Communal Harmony in Japan's Classical Theatrical Repertoire." *Études anglaises*, vol. 68, no. 4 (2015): 425–41.

Marra, Michael F. "Words in Tension: An Essay on Kuki Shuzo's Poetics." In *Kuki Shuzo: A Philosopher's Poetry and Poetics*. Ed and trans. Michael F. Marra. Honolulu: U of Hawaii P, 2004.

———. *Essays on Japan*. Leiden: Brill, 2010.
Marx, Karl, and Friederich Engels. "The Communist Manifesto." In *World Literature: A Reader*. Ed. Cesar Dominguez, Theo d'Haen, and Mads Rosendahl Thomsen. London: Routledge, 2012, 16–17.
Masschelein, Anneleen, Christophe Meuree, David Martens, and Stephanie Vanasten. "The Literary Interview: Toward a Poetics of a Hybrid Genre." *Poetics Today*, vol. 35, no. 1–2 (March 2014): 1–49, doi:10.1215/03335372-2648368.
Mayeda, Graham. "Time for Ethics: Temporality and the Ethical Ideal in Emmanuel Levinas and Kuki Shūzō." *Comparative and Continental Philosophy*, vol. 4, no. 1 (2012): 105–24.
Meijun, Fan and Wang Zhihe, "Toward a Complementary Consciousness and Mutual Flourishing of Chinese and Western Cultures: The Contributions of Process Philosophers," *Philosophy East and West*, vol. 65, no. 1 (2015): 276–97.
Millet-Gérard, Dominique. "Un grand Ange blanc qui regarde la mer." In *Claudel et le Japon: Cinquantenaire de la mort de Claudel. Actes du Colloque International et de la table ronde*. Ed. Shinobu Chūjō et Takaharu Hasekura. Tokyo: Shichigatsudō 七月堂, 2006, 36–46.
———. "Claudel et le nô: Sources, méditations, intuitions." In *La Fleur cachée du nô*. Ed. Catherine Mayaux. Paris: Honoré Champion, 2015, 125–40.
Miner, Earl. *Comparative Poetics. An Intercultural Essay on Theories of Literature*. Princeton: Princeton UP, 1990.
Mishima, Yukio. *Kindai nōgakushū*. Tokyo: Shinchōsha, 1968.
———. "Influences in Modern Japanese Literature." In *Mishima Yukio Zenshū*. Ed. Jun Ishikawa and Shōichi Saeki. Dai sanjyū maki. Tokyo: Shinchōsha, 1973, 16–31.
———. *Taiyō to tetsu*. In *Mishima Yukio Zenshū*. Ed. Jun Ishikawa and Shōichi Saeki. Dai sanjyūsan maki. Tokyo: Shinchōsha, 1973, 506–84.
———. Correspondence with Kawabata Yasunori. Yukio Mishima, Jun Ishikawa, and Shōichi Saeki. *Mishima Yukio Zenshū*. Dai sanjyūhachi maki. Tokyo: Shinchōsha, 1973, 236–310.
———. *Five Modern Nō Plays*. Trans. Donald Keene. New York: Vintage International, 2009.
Monneret, Philippe. « Fiction et Croyance ». In *La Théorie littéraire des mondes possibles*. Ed. Françoise Lavocat. Paris: CNRS Éditions, 2010, 259–91.
Moretti, Franco. "Conjectures on World Literature." *New Left Review*, vol. 1 (January–February 2000): 54–68.
Nara, Hiroshi. *The Structure of Detachment: The Aesthetic Vision of Kuki Shuzo*. Honolulu: U of Hawaii P, 2004.
Nishino, Ayako. *Paul Claudel, le nô et la synthèse des arts*. Paris: Classiques Garnier, 2013.
———. "L'Histoire de la réception du nô en Occident (XVIe—XXe siècles) et son Adaptation par Yeats, Pound, Claudel, et Brecht." In *La Fleur cachée du nô*. Ed. Catherine Mayaux. Paris: Honoré Champion, 2015, 55–74.
Nishino, Haruo. « Le Poète dramatique Zeami, ses œuvres et ses théories artistiques. » In *La Fleur cachée du nô*. Ed. Catherine Mayaux. Paris: Honoré Champion, 2015, 11–22.
Numano, Mitsuyoshi. "Sekai (bungaku) to ha nanika." *Shisō*, no. 1147 (November 2019): 9–23.
O'Connor, Danny. *Ted Hughes and Trauma: Burning the Foxes*. London: Palgrave Macmillan, 2016.
Obama, Yoshinobu. "九鬼周造における「永遠回帰の思想」." *Risō*, no. 698 (2017): 2–16.
Ogura, Tadao. *Kyōto No Nihonga 1910–1930: Taishō No Kokoro Kakushin to Sōzō*. Kyoto: Kyōto Kokuritsu Kindai Bijutsukan, 1986.
Ōhashi, Ryōsuke. "Kuki Shūzō and the Question of Hermeneutics." *Comparative and Continental Philosophy*, vol. 1, no. 1 (2009): 23–37.
Okamura, Tsuneya. "Kaisetsu." In Tsurayuki Ki. *Kokin wakashū*. Ed. Tsuneya Okumura. Tōkyō: Shinchōsha, 1978, 389–410.
Owen, Stephen. "What Is World Poetry?" *New Republic*, vol. 203, no. 21 (1990): 28–32.
———. "Stepping Forward, Stepping Back: Issues and Possibilities for 'World' Poetry." In *World Literature in Theory*. Ed. David Damrosch. New Jersey: Wiley Blackwell, 2014, 245–59.

Ozawa, Masao. *Kokinshū no sekai*. Tōkyō: Hanawa Shobō, 1961.

Park, Josephine Nock-Hee. *Apparitions of Asia: Modernist Form and Asian American Poetics*. Oxford: Oxford UP, 2008.

Pavel, Thomas G. *Fictional Worlds*. Cambridge, MA: Harvard UP, 1986.

———. "L'unité du monde dans le théâtre de Claudel." *Critique*, vol. 774 (November 2011): 857–66.

———. *The Feud of Language: A History of Structuralist Thought*. Oxford: Blackwell, 1989.

Peters, Anne Lande. "The Longing Women of Mishima and Ibsen A Reflection on "Hanjo" and "The Lady From the Sea."" *Ibsen Studies*, vol. 5, no. 1 (August 2006): 4–18.

Petit, Jacques. "Préface de Connaisance de l'est suivi de L'oiseau noir dans le soleil levant." In *Paul Claudel: Connaissance de l'Est: suivi de, L'oiseau noir dans le soleil levant*. Paris: Gallimard, 1974.

Pincus, Leslie. "In a Labyrinth of Western Desire: Kuki Shuzo and the Discovery of Japanese Being." *Boundary 2*, vol. 18, no. 3 (1991): 142–56.

Pinguet, Maurice. *Le Texte Japon*, Paris: Seuil, 2009.

Pound, Ezra. *The Cantos of Ezra Pound*. London: Faber & Faber, 1975.

Priest, Graham. *An Introduction to Non-Classical Logic*. Cambridge: Cambridge UP, 2001.

———. *Beyond the Limits of Thought*. Oxford: Oxford UP, 2002.

———. *Towards Non-being*. Oxford: Oxford UP, 2016.

———. *The Fifth Corner of Four: An Essay on Buddhist Metaphysics and the Catuskoti*. Oxford: Oxford UP, 2018

Qian, Zhaoming. "Ezra Pound's Encounter with Wang Wei: Toward the 'Ideogrammic Method' of The Cantos," *Twentieth Century Literature*, vol. 39, no. 3 (October 1, 1993): 266–82.

———. *Orientalism and Modernism: The Legacy of China in Pound and Williams*. Durham: Duke UP, 1995.

Quine, W. V. O. *Word and Object*. Cambridge, MA: MIT Press, 2013.

Ram, Harsha. "The Scale of Global Modernisms: Imperial, National, Regional, Local." *PMLA. Publications of the Modern Language Association of America*, vol. 131, no. 5 (October 2016): 1372–85, doi:10.1632/pmla.2016.131.5.1372.

Rimer, J. Thomas. "The Background of Zeami's Treatises." In *On the Art of the Nō Drama: The Major Treatises of Zeami*. Princeton: Princeton UP, 1984.

Roberts, Neil. "Ted Hughes and Cambridge." In *Ted Hughes: From Cambridge to Collected*. Ed. Wormald, M., N. Roberts, and T. Gifford. London: Palgrave Macmillan, 2013, 17–32.

Rorty, Richard, and John Searle. "Rorty v. Searle, at Last: A Debate." *Logos: A Journal of Catholic Thought and Culture*, vol. 2, no. 3 (1999): 20–67.

Ross, Stephen. "Provocations on the Philosophy of Weakness." *Modernism/modernity Print Plus*, vol. 4, cycle 2 (May 2019). https://modernismmodernity.org/forums/posts/responses-special-issue-weak-theory-part-iv.

Sagar, Keith. *The Laughter of Foxes: A Study of Ted Hughes*. Liverpool: Liverpool UP, 2006.

Said, Edward W. *Orientalism*. London: Penguin, 1995.

Saint-Amour, Paul. "Weak Theory, Weak Modernism." *Modernism/modernity*, vol. 25, no. 3 (September 1, 2018): 437–59.

Sakurai, Shōichiro. *Kyōto gakuha suikoden* 京都学派水故伝, Kyoto: Kyoto UP, 2017.

Sata, Kimiko. "*Kokinwakashū* shunka-ka Tsurayuki no rakka no uta ni tsuite – 'sange' to no kakawari no kanōsei"『古今和歌集』春歌下　貫之の落花の歌について--「散華」との関わりの可能性," 中古文学 no. 73 (2004): 1–12.

Saussy, Haun. *The Problem of a Chinese Aesthetic*. Redwood, CA: Stanford UP, 1993.

———. "The Dimensionality of World Literature." *Neohelicon*, vol. 38, no. 2 (2011): 289–94.

———. *Great Walls of Discourse and Other Adventures in Cultural China*. Cambridge, MA: Harvard University Asia Center, 2001.

———. "Interplanetary Literature." *Comparative Literature*, vol. 63, no. 4 (2011): 438–47.

———. *Translation as Citation: Zhuangzi Inside Out*. Oxford: Oxford UP, 2017.
———. "Exquisite Cadavers Stitched from Fresh Nightmares." In *Comparative Literature in an Age of Globalization*. Ed. Haun Saussy. Baltimore: Johns Hopkins UP, 2006, 1–42.
Sayeau, Michael Douglas. *Against the Event: The Everyday and the Evolution of Modernist Narrative*. Oxford: Oxford UP, 2013.
Schleiermacher, Friedrich. *Hermeneutics: The Handwritten Manuscripts*. Trans. James Duke and Jack Forstman. Ed. Heinz Kimmerle. Atlanta: Scholars Press, 1977.
Scholes, Percy A. *The Oxford Companion to Music*, 10th edition. Oxford: Oxford UP, 1970.
Shakespeare, William. *King Lear*. 1606. Shakespeare.mit.edu.
Sharf, Robert. "Mindfulness and Mindlessness in Early Chan." *Philosophy East and West*, vol. 64, no. 4, October 1 (2014): 933–64.
Shen, Jiji. "Lü Weng." In *Taiping guangji*. Ed. Fang Li. Dai er ban. Beijing: Zhonghua shu ju, 1961, 527–28.
Shih, Chung-wen. *Golden Age of Chinese Drama: Yuan Tsa-Chu*. Princeton: Princeton UP, 2015.
Shinbo, Satoru. *Nihon shisōshi Shohan*, Kyōto-shi: Kōyō Shobō, 1989.
Shirane, Haruo. *Japan and the Culture of the Four Seasons: Nature, Literature, and the Arts*. New York: Columbia UP, 2012.
Shirane, Haruo, Tomi Suzuki and David Lurie (eds). *The Cambridge History of Japanese Literature*. Cambridge: Cambridge UP, 2015.
Siu, Wang-Ngai, and Peter Lovrick. *Chinese Opera: The Actor's Craft*. Hong Kong: Hong Kong UP, 2014.
Slominsky, Nicolas. *Writings on Music: Russian and Soviet Music Composers*. Ed. Electra Slominsky Yourke. Abingdon, UK: Routledge, 2003.
Smith, A. C. H. *Orghast at Persepolis: An Account of the Experiment in Theatre Directed by Peter Brook and Written by Ted Hughes*. London: Eyre Methuen, 1972.
Smith, Nicholas J. J. *Vagueness and Degrees of Truth*. Oxford: Oxford UP, 2008.
Smither, Howard E. *A History of the Oratorio*. Chapel Hill: U of North Carolina P, 1978.
———. "Oratorio and Sacred Opera, 1700–1825: Terminology and Genre Distinction." *Proceedings of the Royal Musical Association*, vol. 106 (1979): 88–104.
Soothill, William Edward, and Lewis Hodous. *A Dictionary of Chinese Buddhist Terms: With Sanskrit and English Equivalents and a Sanskrit-Pali Index*. London: Routledge Curzon, 2004.
Spivak, Gayatri Chakravorty. *Death of a Discipline*. New York: Columbia UP, 2003.
Starrs, Roy. *Modernism and Japanese Culture*. London: Palgrave Macmillan, 2011.
Steiner, George. "On Difficulty." *Journal of Aesthetics and Art Criticism*, vol. 36, no. 3 (Spring 1978): 263–76.
Stenberg, Josh. "Three Relations Between History and Stage in the Kunju Scene Slaying the Tiger General." *Asian Theatre Journal*, vol. 32, no. 1 (2015): 107–35.
Takada, Yasunari. *Transcendental Descent: Essays in Literature and Philosophy* Tokyo: Collection UTCP 2, 2007.
Takemoto, Tadao, and Olivier Germain-Thomas. *L'âme japonaise en miroir: Claudel, Malraux, Levi-Strausse, Einstein*. Paris: Entrelacs, 2016.
Tan, Chee Lee. *Constructing a System of Irregularities: The Poetry of Bei Dao, Yang Lian, and Duoduo*. Newcastle: Cambridge Scholars Publishing, 2016.
Tanaka, Koji. "On Nagarjuna's Ontological and Semantic Paradox." *Philosophy East and West: A Quarterly of Comparative Philosophy*, vol. 66, no. 4 (2016): 1292–306.
Tang, Xiaodu. "An Interview with Bei Dao." Trans. Haun Saussy. *World Literature Today*, vol. 82, no. 6 (November 2008): 27–29.
Tatsumi, Takayuki. *Modanizumu no wakusei*, Tokyo: Iwanami Shoten, 2013.
Taxidou, Olga. *Modernism and Performance*. London: Palgrave Macmillan, 2007.
Trinacty, Christopher. "Intertextual Translation in Ovid, Seneca, and Ted Hughes." *Classical Receptions Journal*, vol. 8, no. 4 (2016): 479–505.

Truffet, Michel, and Paul Claudel. *Edition critique et commentée de Cent phrases pour éventails de Paul Claudel, Annales littéraires de l'Université de Besançon.* Paris: Les Belles-Lettres, 1985.

Vachon, *Le Temps Et L'espace Dans L'oeuvre De Paul Claudel.* Collection Pierres vives, Paris: Éditions du Seuil, 1965.

Varley, H. Paul. *Japanese Culture.* Honolulu: U of Hawaii P, 2000.

Verheyen, Steven, and Égré, Paul. "Typicality and Graded Membership in Dimensional Adjectives." *Cognitive Science*, vol. 42, no. 7 (2018): 2250–86.

Wagner, Rudolf. "Can We Speak of East/West Ways of Knowing?" *KNOW: A Journal on the Formation of Knowledge*, vol. 2, no. 1 (2018): 31–46.

Waley, Arthur. "Five Modern Nō Plays. By Yukio Mishima. Translated from the Japanese by Donald Keene. New York: Knopf, 1957. xvii. 201, Illustrations. $4.00." *Journal of Asian Studies*, vol. 17, no. 3 (1958): 487, doi: 10.2307/2941447.

Wallace, Jennifer. "Tragedy in China." *Cambridge Quarterly*, vol. 42, no. 2 (2013): 99–111.

Warwick Research Collective. *Combined and Uneven Development: Towards a New Theory of World Literature.* Liverpool: Liverpool UP, 2015.

Wasserman, Michel. "Paul Claudel et les peintres de Kyoto." *Bulletin De La Société Paul Claudel*, no. 178 (2005): 59–61.

———. "L'ambassadeur poète: Paul Claudel au Japon (1921–1927)." 立命館国際研究 *Ritsumeikan Journal of International Studies*, vol. 19, no. 1, (2006): 197–208.

———. "Claudel et le shintoisme." *Bulletin de la Société Paul Claudel*, vol. 210, (2013). http://www.paul-claudel.net/bulletin/bulletin-de-la-societe-paul-claudel-n°210.

Watanabe, Moriaki. "Le nom d'ysé: Le mythe solaire japonais et la genèse du personnage." *Revue d'Histoire Littéraire De La France*, vol. 69, no. 1 (1969): 74–92.

Williamson, Timothy. "Logic, Metalogic and Neutrality." *Erkenntnis*, vol. 79, no. S2 (2014): 211–31.

Wilson, Francis A.C. *Yeats and Tradition.* New York: Macmillan, 1958.

Wu, Yiching. *The Cultural Revolution at the Margins: Chinese Socialism in Crisis.* Cambridge, MA: Harvard UP, 2014.

Yagisawa, Takashi. *Worlds and Individuals, Possible and Otherwise.* Oxford: Oxford UP, 2010.

Yang, Haosheng. *A Modernity Set to a Pre-Modern Tune: Classical-Style Poetry of Modern Chinese Writers.* Leiden: Brill, 2016.

Yeats, W. B. "Introduction." In *Certain Noble Plays of Japan from the Manuscripts of Ernest Fenollosa.* Ed. Ezra Pound. Dublin: Cuala Press, 1916, i–xix.

———. *Plays in Prose and Verse: Written for an Irish Theatre, and Generally with the Help of a Friend.* London: MacMillan, 1922.

Yeh, Michelle. "Modern Chinese Poetry: Translation and Translatability." *Frontiers of Literary Studies in China*, vol. 5, no. 4 (December 2011): 600–609.

Yu, Anthony C. *Comparative Journeys: Essays on Literature and Religion East and West.* Columbia UP, 2008.

Zachmann, Gayle. "Postcards from Japan: Asian Dissonance in Mallarmé, Zola, and Proust." Esprit Créateur, vol. 56, no. 3 (October 2016): 76–89, doi:10.1353/esp.2016.0030.

Zha, Jianying "Bei Dao." In *Bashi niandai fangtan lu* 八十年代訪談錄. Hong Kong: Oxford University Press, 2006, 66–81.

Zhang, Longxi. *The Tao and the Logos: Literary Hermeneutics, East and West.* Durham: Duke UP, 1992.

———. *Unexpected Affinities: Reading Across Cultures.* Toronto: U of Toronto P, 2016.

INDEX

"A Fly in Autumn" 186
à la japonaise 151–52
A Study in Scarlet 35
"A Travers la littérature japonaise" 133
AAP. *See* Asian Analytic Philosophy (AAP)
absence, concept of 94
Akutagawa, Ryūnosuke 37–39
Amichai, Yehuda 170
Amidism 94–95, 107
Amrouche, Jean 109–110
Anesaki, Masaharu 95
Anglo-Saxon-Norse-Celtic people 160–61, 163–65, 169–70, 173, 175
anxiety of influence concept 101
Aoi no Ue 101, 103
Apter, Emily 4
Aristotle 119, 156, 192
Armitage, Simon 165
"Asgard for Addicts" 160, 164–65
Ashikage, Yoshimitsu 91
Asian Analytic Philosophy (AAP) 23, 30–31
At the Hawk's Well 63, 99
The August Sleepwalker 179
Awakened Cosmos: The Mind of Classical Chinese Poetry 7–8, 17
aware, concept of, 92
Aygi, Gennady 162–63

Bardo Thödol 51, 74–82, 176–78
    Asian target category 81
    adaptation of 51
    aspects of words 79
    blood drinker 79
    Buddhist nature of terms 79
    Chineseness 51
    fusion of East and West 76, 81–82
    horizontal/vertical schema 78
    hybrid genre 74–75
    motives behind 77
    multidimensionality 80
    opera 172
    process of analogy 75
    project 161
    as religious text 77
    shared heritage 77
    Tibetan source of 81
    traditional 75
    variety of sources 74
    Westerness 51
    Yorkshire in 75
Barnes, Nancy J. 103
Bartha, Paul 78
Baudelaire, Charles 84, 147. *See also* "Une Charogne"
Beckett, Samuel 2
Beecroft, Alexander 10, 12, 23, 25–27, 32, 34–35
Bei Dao 1, 13, 154–89
    about blood and tradition in 161–62
    East Asian and Western traditions, communication between 154
    "infantilization" of 167
    "jargon" used 167
    as a poet in Exile 178–89
    term "blood", use of 162
    tradition, definition of 160, 166
    use of wind or (*feng*) 162
Bergson, Henri 130
Besineau, Jacques 137
Bhiksuni 69
Bian, Zhilin 36
Bible 106, 137
bijin (beautiful woman) 88–89
Bleak House 28
Bloom, Harold 101
Bohlmann, Otto 172
Bonnefoy, Yves 170
The Book of Odes 135
Bowers, Faubion 68
Brandes, Rand 66–67

Britain 22, 79, 81, 160, 164, 166, 189
Brook, Peter 56
Buddha 52, 136–138, 177
Buddhism 3, 7, 16, 18, 31, 37–38, 51–52, 63, 65–66, 77, 80–88, 85, 87, 91–93, 95, 103–4, 107–8, 117, 126, 136–40, 143–46, 148–49, 152, 177–78, 182–83
Buddhist Mass 53–54
Budhahood 52–53
Bunka-Bunsei period 144–45
Bunting, Basil 75
Bush, Christopher 118, 130, 136–37, 140, 150
Bushidō 126, 132, 144–46, 148
Butler, John 9

Casanova, Pascale 5, 9, 26–28, 32
Catholicism 108, 111, 126, 139–40, 143, 147–48, 150
Cent phrases 138–43, 148, 150, 152
Cent Phrases pour Eventails 128
Certain Noble Plays of Japan 63
Chamberlain, Basil Hall 86
Chan Buddhist 7–8, 32, 181–83
Chang, Peter M. 69
"Chanson d'automne" 149
Chaucer 164–65
chauvinism 88, 156
Cheah, Pheng 10
Chikamatsu, Monzaemon 100
China 13, 21–22, 38, 70–71, 73, 76–77, 80–81, 131–32, 135, 139–40, 155, 157–59, 161, 167, 169–70, 172, 178–89
Chinese Buddhism 176–78
Chinese drama, golden age of 70
Chinese opera 57, 71–72, 104
Chinese Yuan Drama 54
Chineseness 36, 51, 179, 183, 187–89
Chou, Wen-chung 12, 14, 51–82
    Buddhism and 79
    Chinese opera 57, 76
    color symbolism 72
    common source 80
    cross-cultural collaboration 55, 77
    on cultural fusion 74
    devised variable modes 80
    difference between Chinese and Western 76
    fusing Eastern and Western art 69, 75, 77, 80–81
    interest in East and West fusion 75
    letter from Hughes 60
    modal techniques 80
    music 54, 56, 77
    on philosophical roots of Chinese music 77, 80
    philosophical foundations of China 80
    preferred Western instruments 71
    on source of texts 78
    single Chinese identity 76
    trans-historical entity 76
    vertical relations 80
Christianity 67, 11, 118–19, 132, 134, 138, 140, 147, 160, 172–73, 175
chuanqi 36–37, 38
Cinq nô moderns 102
circularity 34, 43, 67, 146, 151
Classical Chinese poetry 168, 170, 179, 188
classicism 98–99, 101
Claudel, Paul 1, 12–14, 21–22, 41, 48, 69, 83–87, 91, 93, 96–98, 100–101, 104–120, 125–43, 147–53. *See also* Kuki Shūzō; *l'Art Poétique*; Mishima Yukio; *Soulier*
    Amaterasu, myth of 139–40
    Autumn and Spring, Poetry on 148–51
    Buddhist metaphysical themes 98
    calligraphy 141
    comparison with Mishima's plays 111–20
    criticisms of 127
    focus on spiritual or metaphysical aspects 83
    as French ambassador 125, 136–43
    German mystic, interest in 141
    "honored Westerner", status as 128
    Japan, depiction of 130
    Japanese and French poetry, differences between 133–34
    Japanese Buddhism, apology for 108
    Japanese culture, admiration for, 128
    Japanese identity, essence of 131
    Japanese-inspired poetry 126, 138
    modernity, approaches to 130–31
    Nô essay 84, 86
    notion of the spiritual world 116
    "nouvelle Logique", in search for 146
    performances in theater 104–6
    as poet in Japan 136–40
    rely on translations for Japanese 87
    Shintoism, view on 134
    staunch Catholic 85
    worked as ambassador to Japan 13
    works, problems identified in 128
color symbolism 62, 71–72

INDEX

Confucianism 3, 15, 70, 136
constellation of belief 13, 15, 17, 32–34, 42, 46, 48, 81, 89, 107, 109, 117–19, 126, 135, 151, 153, 187, 191–93
"Conversations on World Literature" 4
Copeau, Jacques 86
Corcoran, Neil 58–59
Crane, Hart 55
Cuchulain 63
Cultural Revolution 167–69, 179, 185

Dōmoto, Masaki 115
Da, Nan 40, 121
Dai, Wangshu 186
Damrosch, David 1, 4–5, 14, 158
Daoism 6–7, 16, 38, 77, 80–81, 181, 183, 188
Davidson, Donald 23–24, 34–35, 43, 46
"Dawn Landscape" poem 6–7. *See also The Selected Poems of Tu Fu*
Décades de Pontigny 130
Deguchi, Yasuo 30–32
Denecke, Wiebke 127
Dickens, Charles 28
Dimock, Wai Chee 10–11, 16–17, 84
Doležel, Lubomír 9–10, 12
Donne, John 33
Doyle, Arthur Conan 35
dreamlike realities 102–3
Du Fu 6–7, 9, 15, 17, 32, 36, 162, 182–83, 188–89
Duoduo 178
Dutch models 135

East Asian literature 1–4, 12–15, 17, 22, 26, 48, 57, 63, 66, 76, 130, 137, 139, 144, 146, 155. *See* Nō play
Eastern ideas 157
Eat Crow 73
Ebersolt, Simon 129
Edmond, Jacob 162
Edo period 135
Eliot, T. S. 41–42, 55, 57–59
Elizabethan drama 54
emotive theory 133
Emperor Daigo 135
Endgame 2
Engels, Friedrich 5
England 55, 58, 66, 163–66, 169–70, 172
English, James F. 129
epistemic access 25
Étiemble, René 157–58

Europe 1, 13, 27, 44, 65, 76–77, 99, 125–36, 128–39, 131, 134, 139–40, 143, 145–46, 152, 157–59, 163, 180
Evans-Wentz, Walter, 12, 35–36, 51, 54–55, 57, 61–63, 66, 71–73, 75, 79. *See also Tibetan Book*; Yeats, W. B.
antiquated diction 61, 75
archaic diction and use of hyphenated words 79
color symbolism 71
fascinated by Yeats 54–55
interpretation of Celtic myth 54
source materials 75, 79
translation of Tibetan text 12, 35, 57
Western symbolism 72

Faas, Ekbert 55
Fan, Meijun 156
The Fairy-Faith in Celtic Countries 54
Fenollosa, Ernest 22, 63, 130, 187
Fictional Worlds 25
Five Modern Nō Plays 101–2
France 13, 22, 56, 118, 125, 130, 134, 147, 151, 153
Franco-Japanese poem 143
French literature 133
Friedman, Susan Stanford 11, 47
Fujita, Masakatsu 129

Gannu, Nie 168
Gao, Xingjian 179
Garfield, Jay 30–32
gavagai (rabbit) 23–24
Genji Monogatari 1–3, 28–29, 101, 103
Genova, Pamela 128, 137, 139
Germany 13, 100, 125, 164
Gide, André 110, 130
Gifford, Terry 175–76
Giles, Paul 85
globalization 44, 75, 106, 129, 166, 169, 180
Glorious Revolution of 1688 55, 59
Goethe, J. W. von 4
gohei 140, 142
Greco-Roman culture 161
Gu, Ming Dong 156–57
Guo, Jianping 156–57
Guo, Moruo 168

haiku 8, 132
Hamlet 172
Hanjo 104

INDEX

Hardy, Thomas 163
Hashimoto, Satoru 4, 38, 88, 90
The Hawk in the Rain 52
Hayot, Eric 8, 10–12, 23, 25, 27–29, 32–35, 47
Heian Japan 29, 126, 135
Heidegger, Martin 27, 125
Heine, Heinrich 100
Heraclitus 159
Hinton, David 6–9, 15, 17, 32–33, 181–83, 189
  1989 version 8
  Chan Buddhism 7
  close to archetype of Chinese translation 7–8
  first translation 6
  imagism 8–9
  modern American poetry 8–9
  second translation 7
  yin and yang 6–7
Hirakawa, Sukehiro 138
Hiraoka, Kimitake 98. *See also* Mishima, Yukio
Hokke sect 94–95
Holub, Miroslav 170
Hopi tribe 163
The House of Taurus 57
Huang, Bei 128, 130, 138–39, 141, 143
Hue, Bernard 104
Hughes, Ted 1, 12–15, 58, 51–82, 154–89
  about British culture 161
  adapting East Asian religious text 57
  adopt color symbolism 62
  aims to bring contradictions 59
  approach to foreign art and literature 56
  Asian culture 56, 63
  attitude to Shakespeare 58, 72–73
  Buddhism 52, 63
  Colden Water, Chinese History of, 171–78
  on Chinese opera 57, 72
  Chou and 51
  Christianity, altered his attitude 175
  color symbolism 71
  commitment to Yorkshire 75
  cultural aspects of *Tibetan Book* 54
  diction 75
  East Asian and Western traditions, communication between 154
  eccentric vision of ideal English literature 58
  English identity, reconceptualization of 165
  enthusiasm for Yeats 54, 63, 71
  first poetry collection 52
  French and Continental poetry, investigation of 166
  "genuine" culture 160
  Guggenheim Fellowship 57
  heterogenous influences 80
  identification with rural 59
  imagined community, fiction of 161
  interest in shamanism 66–67, 81
  late modernist 58
  letters 60–61
  library 68–69
  libretto 52, 62, 70, 73
  medievalism 80
  modern multi-cultural societies 163
  moved to America 51
  operatic adaptation of *Bardo Thödol* 12
  poetic career 56, 69
  reference to *Bardo* 53
  shared sources 57, 73, 78
  subgroup language, problems in 163
  teenage development 67
  theater of China 73
  Tibetan text 12, 62–63
  traces a lineage of English literature 81
  tradition according to 160
  tried-and-true mold 53
  use of anaphora 172
  vision of China 13
  working with Chou 12
Hulme, T. E. 98–99
Huygens, Christiaan 78

I Ching 80
Ibsen, Henrik 104
idealism 42, 144
ideogram 130
Ideographic Modernisms: China, Writing, Media 130
imperial collection 136
impossible worlds 10, 13, 22, 26, 30–31, 126, 152
Inaga, Shigemi 127–28
Indian mysticism 132
integrationist 25
Irish Noh 119

Japan 3, 13, 29, 32, 46, 65, 84, 86–87, 89, 91, 93, 98, 100, 105, 107–8, 114, 117, 119, 125–53
Japanese Buddhism 108
Japanese literature 126–27, 129, 133–35, 148, 153, 157

Japanese philosophy 129
jargon 167
Jenner, W. J. F. 179
Jintian 178
jouissance 136–37
Joyce, James 58
Jullien, François 157–58
Jung, Carl 174

Kadota, Machiko 138
kakekotoba (literary punning device) 100–101
Kakyō 93
Kana 126
kanashisa 149, 152
Kanbun 136
Kantan 12, 14, 37–41, 47, 83–84, 86–98, 111, 113–20, 187, 192–93
Kawakami, Akane 127–28, 137, 143
Keats, John 163
Keene, Donald 101, 115, 114–15, 126–27, 141
Keisen, Tomita 138, 141–43
　artwork of 141–43
　Shintō shrine, painting of 143
　work with Claude's poem 142
Ki no Tsurayuki 126
Kindai nōgakushū 115
King James Bible 172
King Lear 54, 71, 73, 160, 172
Klein, Lucas, 36, 52, 78, 85, 161, 182–83
Knapp, Bettina L. 102–3
Kodama, Sanehide 63–64
Kokinshū 32–34, 38, 46, 126–27, 133–36, 149, 151–53
kokufū 135
Kripke, Saul 26
Kuki, Shūzō 125–53. *See also* Claudel, Paul; Paris
　Autumn and Spring, poetry on 148–51
　Buddhism and Bushidō, ideas on 145–46
　Claudel, meeting with 125
　criticisms of 127
　cyclical model of time 145–46
　idea of *iki* 144
　Japanese philosopher 125, 144
　Japanese poetry, ideas of 126
　modernity, approaches to 130–31
　in Paris, 129–31
　Parisian life 147
　philosophy of "pagan" 134

　poet in Paris 144–46
　Pontigny, speech at 132
　Shintoism, view on 134
　works, problems identified in 128
Kuki, Shūzō 1
Kuhn, Thomas 23–24, 29
Kultur 98
kunqu tune 69
kyakurai 93
Kyoto school of philosophy 125

l'Art Poétique 21
l'Ombre Double 108
La Muraille intérieure de Tokyo 141–42
Lachaud, Françoise 139
The Lady from the Sea 104
Lady Rokujo 103
Lai, Eric 71, 80
Lang, Chin-San 183, 185, 187–88
Laozi 156
Le Souffle 142
Lermontov, Mikhail 162–63
Li Bai 162, 187
"Li Sao" 16
Li, Yu 162, 187
Li, Dian 180–81
Li, Zehou 185, 188
Liao Chai Chih-I 176
Liar Paradox 34
Literary Chinese 168
literary works 6, 11–12, 14–15, 26–29, 32, 43, 68, 85, 110–11, 114, 116–17, 155, 191, 193, 195
literary worlds theory 6, 10–11, 22, 25, 32, 35, 45, 51
Little Theater Movement 104
Lloyd, G. E. R. 12, 23–24, 34, 43, 45, 48, 84, 120, 159, 194
Longing for Worldly Pleasures 69
Longobardi, Niccolò 159
Lopez, Donald 36
"lower-level kind of theorizing" 11, 84
Lu, Sheng 36–37
Lu, Xun 168

mūgen Nō 117
Mallarmé, Stéphane 105, 130, 149
Malraux, André 127, 130
Manabe, Akiko 64
Mandelstam, Osip 162–63
Manyōshū 136

Mao, Tse-tung 167–69, 180, 185
Maoism 168–69, 179–80, 187
mappō, concept of 91
Marra, Michael 129, 147–48
Marx, Karl 5
May Fourth Movement 167–68, 170
Mayeda, Graham 146, 148
Meiji era 143
Meinong, Alexius 25
Meister Eckhart 141
menglongshi. See also Misty poetry 169, 178
Metaphors (1960) 80
Millet Dream story 37–39
Millet-Gérard, Dominique 118, 139
Mishima, Yukio 12, 14, 37, 41, 83–91, 96–104, 111–21. See also *Kantan*; *Hanjo*
   adaptations of classical Nō 83, 89
   Buddhist themes 87, 96, 103–4
   classicism and romanticism 99
   familiarity with modernist experimentations 99
   fascinated with European literature 98
   first modern attempt 86
   fraught stance towards women 88, 90
   letter to Kawabata 100
   modern Nō 98
   "mystical" worldview 104
   opposition between night and sun 99
   source material 84, 101, 103
   transcending ancient and modern literature 101
   transhistorical valuation of literature 101
   treatment of psychoanalysis 103
Misty poetry. See also *menglongshi* 170, 178–79
Modern Poetry in Translation 170
modernism 1, 8, 11, 28, 45, 47, 58, 85, 98, 129–30
Moretti, Franco 5, 9, 14, 26–28, 32, 36
Mount Yōhi 37
mountain village (*yamazato*) 92
Murasaki, Shikibu 2, 28
Myers, Lucas 55
Myth and Religion of the North 160

nationalism 127
natural vagueness 11
"New Moon" 181
New Theater Movement 104
Nihonga movement 143
Nishida, Kitarō 125
Nishino, Ayako 84, 86–87, 93, 106–8, 118, 150

Nishino, Haruo 93–94
Nō play, 12, 37–38, 40, 46, 54, 63–65, 69–70, 73–74, 83–89, 91, 93–94, 100–109, 113, 115–21, 142–43, 150, 192–93
Norbu, Jamyang 35
Norman invasion 164
Numano, Mitsuyoshi 5, 43

Obama, Yoshinobu 146
Ōhashi, Ryōsuke 127, 144
O'Connor, Daniel 58
Odyssey 58
Oida, Katsuhiro 56
Okamura, Tsuneya 127
"On Difficulty" 3
ontological vagueness 2–3, 13, 15, 22, 34, 42–48, 51, 82, 98, 121, 188
open-mindedness 47
oratorio 53–54
Orghast 56
oriental theater 68
Osamu, Hashimoto 88–89
Owen, Stephen 179–81
The Oxford Companion to Music 53
Ozawa, Masao 135

P'u Sungling 176
Padmasambhava 35
Pantheism 175
pantheistic mysticism 132
Paris 129–136, 144–153
   historical conditions in 129–36
   interwar period 130
   Kuki Shūzō's time in, 144–53
Parī shō kyoku 150, 153
Parī shinkei 149
Parr, Audrey 141
Partage de Midi (1906) 140
Pasternak, Boris 162–63
Pavel, Thomas 9, 10, 12, 25–26, 106, 110
Peking opera 71
Péri, Noël 87
Peters, Anne Lande 104
Petit, Jacques 128
Phèdre 28
Pien (1966) 80
Pillow of Kantan 86
Pincus, Leslie 129, 145
Pinguet, Maurice 118
planetarity, concept of 16
Plath, Sylvia 51, 53

The Player Queen 172
Popa, Vasko 170
possible worlds 10
Pound, Ezra 8, 63, 130, 182, 187
Powell, Anthony 85
Priest, Graham 30–31, 34–35, 38, 46–48, 120–21, 126, 153
pseudo-Buddhist ontology 115
Pure Land Buddhism 92
Pushkin, Alexander 162–63

Qian, Zhaoming 8, 187
Qu, Yuan 16
Quine, W. V. O. 23–24, 34–35, 43

Racine, Jean 28
Ransom, John Crowe 55
"Rashōmon" 39
Regenerations 66
Reid, Christopher 57
Remains of Elmet 171
Renondeau, George 87
Révon, Michel 87
Rimbaud, Arthur 130
Rimer, J. Thomas 92
Roberts, Neil 165
The Romance of the Western Chamber 70
The Romantic School 100
romanticism 99, 165
Ross, Stephen 11
Russell, Bertrand 25
Russian literature 162

sabishisa 149, 152
Sagar, Keith 175
Saint-Amour, Paul 11, 51, 68
Saint Augustine 137, 156
Saint Geneviève 141–43
sakaki 140
Sakurai, Shōichiro 129
"Salt" 183, 186–89
Samuel Beckett's Library 68
Sartre, Jean-Paul 125
Sata, Kimiko 126
Saussy, Haun 2, 10, 12, 23–25, 28–29, 31–33, 35, 40–41, 43, 45, 75, 84–85
Sayeau, Michael, 57–58
Searle, John 25
The Selected Poems of Tu Fu 6–7
Shakespeare 73, 169
Shakespeare and the Goddess of Complete Being 161

shamanism 57, 66–67, 70, 77–79, 81, 169
Shen, Jiji 36–37, 39, 86
Sherlock Holmes: The Missing Years 35
Shih, Chung-wen 70
Shijing 135–36
Shikyō 135
shimenawa 140
Shingeki 104
Shingon sect 94
shinksakunō 12, 87, 100, 118
shinsaku 100
Shintō 134, 138, 140, 142–43, 152
Shintoism 3, 126, 134, 137–38, 143
Shite 107–9
Shu, Ting 178
Si fan (kunqu play) 69–70
Six Dynasties 135
Soliloquy of a Bhiksuni 69
Sōtō Zen 32, 93
Souffle des quatre souffles 142, 150
Soulier de satin 86, 96, 98, 106, 108, 110–12, 114, 116, 118–20
spiritus mundi 56
Spivak, Gayatri 4, 16–17
Starrs, Roy 145
Steiner, George 3
Strawson, P. F. 25
The Structure of Iki (Iki no kōzō) 144
The Structure of Scientific Revolutions 23
Sun and Steel 98
Susanō (Japanese deity) 140
"Sylvan's Box" 47

Takada, Yasunari 145–46
The Tale of Genji 101, 103
Tan, Chee Lay 178–80, 187
Tang 9, 15, 26, 36, 38–40, 44–47, 70, 135–36, 162
tanka 132, 147, 152
Tarskian theory of truth 34
Tatsumi, Takayuki 16
Tendai sect 94
tetralemma 30–31
Theater in the East 68
Thornber, Karen 4
Tibetan Buddhism 51, 63, 176–78
Tokugawa era 130
Tokyo 129–36
Towards Non-Being 126
Traditional Chinese Stories: Themes and Variations 176

"The Trance of Light" 171–75, 183
"translation style". See also *menglongshi* 169
triangulation 12–15, 83, 94
Trinacty, Christopher 169
Truffet, Michel 138, 142
Turville-Petre, E. O. G. 160

"Une Charogne" 84
une nouvelle logique 21, 48
urban poet 163–64

Vachon, André 105–6
vagueness 2–3, 11–13, 15, 17, 22, 34, 39–40, 42–46, 48, 51, 61, 78, 82, 98, 117, 121, 180, 188
"Vampire" 52–53
Varley, Paul, 39, 91–92
Venus and Adonis 66
Verlaine, Paul 1, 65, 149

Wagner, Richard 17, 105, 140
  Tristan and Isolde (1859) 140
waka 136
waki 86, 107–8
Waley, Arthur 45, 86–87, 101–3
Wallerstein, Immanuel 9
Wang, Shifu 70
The Wanderings of Oisin 54, 66–67, 71
Wang, Zhihe 156
Warwick Research Collective 5
Wasserman, Michel 128, 138
Watanabe, Moriaki 139–40, 142
weak theory 10–11, 14, 47–48, 51, 68, 84
weakness 11, 47
Weissbort, Daniel 52, 170
Western civilization 159
What Is World Literature? 1, 4

"The World Inside a Pillow" 36
world literature 1–2, 4–6, 9–15, 17, 22–24, 26–28, 34, 38, 40, 43–48, 51, 82, 84–85, 116, 121, 127, 158, 161, 180, 187–89
  dimensions 43
  ontological vagueness 48
  and weak theory 47–48
world philosophical system 157
worldliness 5, 10, 103
Wu, Yiching 168

Xu, Zhimo 84

Yagisawa, Takashi 30
yamato uta 136
Yang, Lian 178
Yasunari, Kawabata 98, 100–101
Yeats, W. B. 54–56, 59, 63–67, 69, 75, 84, 87, 98–100
  and Shakespeare 75
  Greece is half-Asiatic 64
  Nō theater 63
  shamanism 66–67
  source of inspiration for Hughes 54–55
Yeh, Michelle 187
Yorkshire 13, 58, 75, 164–65, 169
Yu, Dafu 168
Yuan, Zhen 70

Zeami Motokiyo 84, 91–96, 104, 108, 115, 117–19
  The Mirror and the Flower or *Kakyō* 93
Zen Buddhism 92, 107, 132
Zhang, Longxi 16
Zhenzhong ji 36–40, 86–87
Zhou, Zuoren 168
Zivilisation 99

www.ingramcontent.com/pod-product-compliance
Lightning Source LLC
Chambersburg PA
CBHW021826300426
44114CB00009BA/345